+HV5125 .A34 1991

Addictions

Addictions

Personal Influences and Scientific Movements

Edited by

Griffith Edwards

Transaction Publishers
New Brunswick (U.S.A.) and London (U.K.)

New material this edition copyright © 1991 by Transaction Publishers, New Brunswick, New Jersey 08903.
Originally published in 1979, 1981, 1983, 1984, 1985, 1986, 1987, 1988, 1989 by *British Journal of Addiction*.

All rights reserved under International and Pan-American Copyright Conventions. No part of this book may be reproduced or transmitted in any form or by any means, electronic or mechanical, including photocopy, recording, or any information storage and retrieval system, without prior permission in writing from the publisher. All inquiries should be addressed to Transaction Publishers, Rutgers–The State University, New Brunswick, New Jersey 08903.

Library of Congress Catalog Number: 90-11117
ISBN: 0-88738-343-2 (cloth)
Printed in the United States of America

Library of Congress Cataloging-in-Publication Data

Addictions : personal influences and scientific movements / edited by Griffith Edwards.
    p. cm.
  Includes index.
  ISBN: 0-88738-343-2
    1. Alcoholism—Study and teaching.   2. Drug abuse—Study and teaching.   3. Alcoholism—Prevention.   4. Drug abuse—Prevention.   5. Alcoholics—Rehabilitation.   6. Narcotic addicts—Rehabilitation.
    I. Edwards, Griffith.
  HV125.A34   1990
  362.29—dc20   90-11117
                                                                     CIP

Contents

Notes on the Contributors   ix

Acknowledgements   xi

Introduction: Interviews as Rich and Unusual Material   xiii
   Griffith Edwards

I ADDICTIONS AND INTERNATIONALISM   1

Interviews
1. JOY MOSER, WHO, interviewed by Griffith Edwards   3
2. AWNI ARIF, WHO, interviewed by Griffith Edwards   25
3. ARCHER TONGUE, ICAA, interviewed by
   Griffith Edwards   37

Discussion
4. Major Accomplishments, Subtle and
   Interactive Influences   49
   Irving Rootman

II INFLUENTIAL FIGURES FROM THE USA   55

5. MARK KELLER, interviewed by Sheila Blume   57
6. SELDEN BACON, interviewed by Mark Keller   67
7. ROBERT STRAUS, interviewed by John F. Wilson   81
8. DAVID J. PITTMAN, interviewed by Ruth M. Singleton   105
9. DONALD GOODWIN, interviewed by Demmie Mayfield   143
10. GENEVIEVE KNUPFER, interviewed by Robin Room   155

11. DON CAHALAN, interviewed by Robin Room   163

Discussion
12. Starting on the Fringe: Studying Alcohol in a
    Wet Generation   179
    Robin Room

III CONTRIBUTIONS FROM THE UK   187

Interviews
13. D. L. DAVIES, interviewed by Griffith Edwards
    and David Robinson   189
14. MAX GLATT, interviewed by Griffith Edwards   207
15. BING SPEAR, interviewed by Gerry Stimson   227
16. BENNO POLLAK, interviewed by Griffith Edwards   249
17. PHILIP CONNELL, interviewed by Griffith Edwards   267

Discussion
18. Two Separate Plays: The Evolution of Britain's
    Alcohol and Drug Policies   291
    Griffith Edwards

IV CANADA: THE ADDICTION RESEARCH FOUNDATION   297

Interviews
19. DAVID ARCHIBALD, interviewed by Alan Ogborne   299
20. HAROLD KALANT, interviewed by Robert Popham   315
21. WOLF SCHMIDT, interviewed by Reginald G. Smart   337

Discussion
22. What Made the ARF?   345
    Reginald G. Smart

V THE WIDE WORLD   353

Interviews
23. JAMES CH'IEN (Hong Kong), interviewed by
    David Robinson   355

24.	KETTIL BRUUN (Finland), interviewed by Robin Room	365
25.	MICHAEL BEAUBRUN (Trinidad), interviewed by Howard Rankin	377
26.	JORGE MARDONES (Chile), interviewed by Lucia Santa Cruz de Ossa	385
27.	JAROSLAV SKÁLA (Czechoslovakia), interviewed by T. Halik	395
28.	IGNACY WALD (Poland), interviewed by Robin Room	403
29.	PIERRE FOUQUET (France), interviewed by Jonathan Chick	411
30.	GEORGE PÉQUIGNOT (France), interviewed by Albert J. Tuyns	419
31.	MUSTAPHA SOUEIF (Egypt), interviewed by F. A. Yunis	427

Discussion

32.	Intolerance of Intellectual Frustration *Marcus Grant*	445

Index   449

Notes on the Contributors

The People Interviewed

A short bibliographic note is given on the person who is the subject of the interview at the start of each appropriate chapter. Given that much detail on the individual's career is likely to be contained in the text of the interview, these introductory notes have purposely been kept very brief.

Contributors to the Discussion Chapters

Griffith Edwards is Editor of the British Journal of Addiction, and Director of the Addiction Research Unit, Institute of Psychiatry, London, UK.

Marcus Grant is Senior Scientist in the Division of Mental Health, WHO, Geneva, Switzerland. He is in charge of the Division's alcohol and drug programme.

Robin Room is Director of the Alcohol Research Group of the Medical Research Institute of San Francisco at Pacific Presbyterian Medical Center, Berkeley, California, USA.

Irving Rootman is Director, Program Resources Division, Health Resources Division of the Health Promotion Directorate, Health and Welfare, Canada, Ottawa.

Reginald G. Smart is Director of Prevention Studies, Addiction Research Foundation, Toronto, Ontario, Canada.

The People Conducting the Interviews

The names of the people conducting the interviews are indicated in the contents list. To them are owed the editor's very warmest thanks.

Acknowledgements

The interviews published in this book originate from the *British Journal of Addiction,* and I am grateful to the BJA for copyright permission. A financial contribution to costs of the book's production has been made by the Society for the Study of Addiction. Secretarial support has been provided by Patricia Davis, the BJA's editorial secretary. Technical assistance was given by Daniel Edwards.

All royalties accruing from sales will be paid to the Society for the Study of Addiction, a registered charity.

Introduction:
Interviews as Rich and Unusual Material

Griffith Edwards

Through the medium of interview transcripts, this book offers contact with the experience, thinking and values of 27 men and women who, over the postwar decades, have taken varieties of highly important leadership roles in shaping national and international scientific and policy responses to alcohol and drug problems. Thus it is intentionally a different book than the more usual set of review chapters. Interviews offer an intimacy, a degree of unguardedness, a reaching after the half-formulated essence of things. They give us those hints at autobiography and the person behind the science which would never be found in a "Recent Advances" type of volume. And it is exactly in this kind of unusualness that the astonishing richness of the material which is published in the present book can be seen to reside.

What is taken from a reading of these interviews must be dependent on the perspective of the individual reader. At one level it is to be hoped that this is a book which will be read by many people for simple enjoyment and for the inspiration and refreshment of spirit which comes from contact with the courage and creativity to which these interviews bear witness. But at another level these transcripts constitute material of quite unusual scholarly interest to the student of dependence studies and related policy formation. In years to come these personal statements will be valuable to historians, but meanwhile there can be no doubt as to their ability to throw new light on many contemporary concerns.

Personal Influences

The title given to this book includes the phrase "Personal Influences" and the nature, diversity and extent of the influences exerted by the subjects of these interviews raises important questions. In general, the heroic view of history as something constructed by the deeds of great men and women is today not too fashionable. The historian will in this instance rightly insist that what has happened over these decades in the drug and alcohol field must be understood in terms of technical innovations, the larger background social processes and the great play of ideas. Reading these interviews, though, one's belief may be reinforced that history is indeed also made by the right person entering into an underdeveloped field at the right moment and then pushing at issues with a lifetime's commitment. We need to know more about who these people were and are, by what diverse routes they get into the field, how they were trained, what held their commitment in place. D. L. Davies claimed that he came into psychiatry because he was looking for a bed and rations; Mustapha Soueiff burnt his poetry and with that temptation resisted, set himself to the study of psychology; Max Glatt "always wanted the underdog to win". By and large this is a generation which was making rather than entering a formal specialism.

If one wanted to select a prime example of what analysis of these texts might tell us regarding influences *between* people, a tracing out of what is said about E. M. Jellinek might be revealing—his name comes up time and again and in relation to many countries:

> I suppose the first impression I had when I first met him . . . was, "What a funny little man . . ." I began to get a feeling that this man came very close to what I would call genius.
> *Seldon Bacon,* U.S.A.

> I was most impressed by Jellinek. . . . I visited Jellinek in his hotel room in Geneva which he had transformed into a library and in fact spent half a day with him talking and talking.
> *Kettil Bruun,* Finland

Introduction: Interviews as Rich and Unusual Material   xv

In the early fifties, we received a visit from Professor Jellinek. . . . This started my friendship with him, which lasted till he died.
Jorge Mardones, Chile

Jellinek was a memorable personality, a fascinating person, very strange, brilliant sometimes and childish at other times. He bought large areas of forest in Brazil, hoping that one day they would make a road through it and he would become a millionaire.
Joy Moser, WHO

Jellinek was a man of amazing intellectual depth and a man credited with much of the pioneer work in moving the field scientifically. I have mixed feelings about Jellinek. He was brilliant, but he loved to play intellectual games.
Robert Strauss, U. S. A.

I remember a discussion in Aubrey Lewis's office with Aubrey Lewis and Jellinek, this curious little tubby man who looked as if he'd stepped out of a cartoon.
D. L. Davies, U. K.

These few quotations by no means exhaust the listing of references made to Jellinek in this book. In their varied tones of fondness, adulation, and criticism they exemplify, however, what has been said about the special nature of interview material. Is it advantage or disadvantage that the drug as opposed to the alcohol world seems so far not to have produced any universally influential figure comparable to E. M. Jellinek?

Scientific Movements

So much for a brief consideration of the "personal influence" theme. There are many aspects of "scientific movement" which readers will be able to identify as cross-cutting a range of interviews. The significance of interdisciplinarity, the pervasive importance of internationalism, the birth and growth of research centres and the institutional basis of science, the role of government and the inner stories and processes of committees, reports and policy formation, are all issues which are debated and illuminated at many points in these interviews. Another matter which can be identified as linking the concerns of several different contributors is the relationship between action and research. To give a few examples, David Pittman, although himself a research worker and academic sociologist, has experienced no tension in stepping over the border into the action world and has taken a leading role in establishing detoxification facilities in the U.S.A. But one can then turn to Don Cahallan's view that "an alcohol research centre as such should not get involved in advocacy . . . you can make your findings available to outsiders who can serve as advocates". Harold Kalant tends to take Cahalan's side in this debate and says, "I feel that it's dangerous for the scientist to become an advocate when he purports to do it in his role as scientist. It risks making him adopt potentially non-scientific attitudes." And again these are only a few selected quotations bearing on an issue to which many of these experts find themselves drawn to speak, or to which they bear witness by their own work.

How These Interviews Came About

The interviews which are now published in this book have all appeared over the last ten years in the *British Journal of Addiction* (the journal of the Society for the Study of Addiction). The BJA recently celebrated its centenary: although British in name it is widely international in content and outlook. It is a monthly refereed scientific journal which publishes research reports and scientific reviews, but at the same time it aims rather specially to provide an international forum for debate and opinion. It is thus concerned with the stimulation, sharing, and formation of ideas as well as with the formal published end-products of science. Within that vision of its remit that interview series was conceived.

The selection of subjects for interview is inevitably arbitrary and there are many key actors who do not (as yet) feature in the list. We have aimed at an international spread and have in particular been concerned to get beyond the all too frequent Anglo Saxon limitation. In general we have sought to interview subjects who have been in the field long enough to be able to rise a little above the battle and take an elder stateman's view.

The instructions to the person conducting the interview have always been to aim for informality while at the same time preparing the interview carefully. Having dealt with the more obviously salient issues, the interviewer is then asked to reach for "the story

Introduction: Interviews as Rich and Unusual Material

beind the story", behind what *really* happened, the beliefs and motivations as well as the outward facts. Fees are never given either to interviewer or subject, but it is traditional that the Editor provides the price of a good meal for two. The transcripts then go through a careful and protracted process of editing, and nothing is published until the subject is content that the final version accurately reflects his or her views. So that the subject remains absolutely centre-stage, it has been customary that the interviewer is identified only as "BJA." For purposes of the present book the cover of anonymity is, however, now broken and the interviewers identified on the Contents page.

The Commentary Chapters

An important feature of this book is the specially written series of commentary chapters which open the discussion around particular groups of interviews. Certain issues raised in this introductory chapter will be taken further while many additional questions are also identified and discussed by these expert commentators. These essays are intended to stimulate rather than foreclose debate and it should again be emphasised that this book is not a didactic text or a moral primer seeking to point easy lessons to be learnt from history. Within the BJA's traditions, this is a book intended to stimulate an active, involved, and questioning debate and that is as much the aim of the link chapters as the interviews themselves.

I

ADDICTIONS AND INTERNATIONALISM

1

Interview with Joy Moser

JOY MOSER, b. 1921. Education: Teacher's Certificate followed by BA (English, French, Russian), University of London; in 1960 gained MPH, Columbia, NY. 1948–1950, Abstractor and Acting Director for Dairy Science Abstracts, UK. Worked for WHO Geneva 1950–1981, first as Editor, then as Scientific Assistant and finally as Senior Scientist, Mental Health. Continues with consultant work for WHO Regional Office for Europe.

BJA: *What led you to work with WHO?*

JM: I came to Geneva in 1950 in response to an advertisement in *The Times* for an editor at WHO. I had to edit books, articles, all kinds of things and found it fascinating work from which I learned a great deal. After a year I got into a newly formed Information section.

BJA: *What was your background before WHO?*

JM: A mixed background in nutrition, education, languages and then, just before coming to WHO, two years as an abstractor, preparing summaries of publications from all over the world for a dairy science abstracts journal.

BJA: *Why then Geneva?*

JM: Well, as with so many people who come to Geneva, to WHO, there was the great hope that one's work might be doing some good in the world, though certainly editing seemed rather a far cry from that ambition. I must say too that I was very keen on the

4 Addictions

international idea. Maybe historically patriotism was a useful concept in raising the level of concern for people's welfare beyond the confines of family and clan: but as communications were making the world smaller, more people were becoming interested in the welfare of other countries beyond their own. My love of languages probably pushed me in that direction too. I had tried earlier to get into the Food and Agriculture Organisation in Rome, but there were no posts available.

BJA: What happened next in your WHO career?

JM: After my second year it was discovered that the information post was actually being paid out of the funds of the Mental Health Unit, as it was then called, under Dr. Hargreaves. I was appointed as an assistant in that Unit which meant that instead of doing odd jobs for people in a number of sections I would be trying to help just one section with bibliographic research, writing a few articles, helping to prepare meetings. The Mental Health Unit at that time was Dr. Hargreaves, a secretary, and nobody else until I joined. WHO was housed in the Palais des Nations. I found working with Dr. Hargreaves personally very rewarding. He was in charge of Mental Health from 1948–1955. He had the habit of just letting people do what they wanted until he saw whether they were any good at anything, and I enjoyed that thoroughly. He was preparing a project on the hospitalization of mental patients for an Expert Committee meeting. He asked me to collect material on the relevant legislation, which was published: very dry stuff it seems now. Much more fascinating was to help with four meetings on the Psychobiological Development of the Child, with people like Piaget, Margaret Mead and Grey Walter, who met for the first time in Geneva but continued for years afterwards to work together.

BJA: It sounds as if you were even by then a natural taker-on of problems, be it dairy produce, mental health legislation or child development.

JM: I found it fun to be learning all the time I was working. Of course I made many mistakes but I get terribly bored if I have to work along just one line. I like to start off on new things.

BJA: Can you tell us something about Dr. Hargreaves's impact on the Mental Health Unit?

JM: He had a tremendous impact. When it came to an Expert Committee, he had a great capacity for picking brilliant people, very different in personality, who could nevertheless get on together, and then he would sit down, dictate for three hours to his secretary, and there would be the report. If you go back to the first report on Mental Health you will see in it an outline for almost everything we have ever done since.

BJA: When did your work first touch on alcoholism?

JM: Well, actually, it was with Dr. Hargreaves, who was very keen that some sensible things should be done about alcohol problems. He therefore employed Professor Jellinek and I was asked to work with him. Jellinek was a Consultant at WHO from 1950 to 1957 (Geneva, the Americas, and the European Office.)

BJA: Have you any idea why with all else that WHO had to deal with Dr. Hargreaves thought it was worthwhile to spend hard money on employing Jellinek?

JM: He believed that alcoholism was tremendously widespread, very much misunderstood, and that there were possibilities of diminishing the extent of the problem. Jellinek was a memorable personality, a fascinating person, very strange, brilliant sometimes and childish at other times.

He had travelled widely. Originally he came from Czechoslovakia, I believe, and was related to Mercedes Benz. He bought large areas of forest in Brazil, hoping that one day they would make a road through it and he would become a multi-millionaire. But he died too early for that. He wrote a lot of verse, which was often highly amusing. He never appeared to be working hard but he produced a great deal. Although we pretend nowadays that speaking of the public health aspect of alcohol problems is something very new, in fact if you go back to the old reports you will find that this perspective was discussed even during Jellinek's time at WHO.

BJA: *What was Jellinek's task at WHO?*

JM: His task was to develop international work on alcohol and alcoholism. He started by helping to organise several meetings which were reported in the Technical Report series. The first [1] dealt with general and theoretical questions, particularly the classification of alcoholism and excessive drinking. The second [2] was concerned more with the treatment and rehabilitation of alcoholics, and with statistics and epidemiological inquiries on alcoholism and alcohol consumption. Jellinek's famous summary of phases of alcoholism was reproduced here. He also ran several regional seminars which did much to raise the level of scientific interest in these topics. I helped him to search for material on the alcohol situation in many countries of the world and he prepared an inquiry that was sent to a number of experts. An unfinished book on the responses was later published by the Addiction Research Foundation. A further aspect of this work was provision of advice to governments—mostly in the European and American regions. I believe that while he was with us he was already writing his famous book 'The Disease Concept of Alcoholism.'

BJA: *What happened to the WHO programme when Jellinek left?*

JM: There was no continuation of his work for several years because the person who replaced Dr. Hargreaves was not keen on this line of development.

BJA: *I am trying to see the shape of the story up to the point you have taken us. It looks as if Hargreaves's vision had got alcohol problems on the agenda, WHO had then done the orthodox thing and called in a consultant, got some papers written and organised some meetings. But then they just let alcoholism slip from sight?*

JM: In a sense. But the budget in WHO is terribly limited and one of WHO's objectives is to interest governments in specific problems within health programmes. You can't keep banging governments over the head with the same problem and unless they themselves show that they wish to do something about a particular topic there is not too much point in WHO continually saying 'Now what are you doing about this?' So I can't think it was necessarily a bad thing that there was a break.

BJA: And after the hiatus, what next?

JM: Well, the next thing was the arrival of Dr. Pieter Baan as Chief of the Mental Health Unit. During his first days he said to me 'Well, I have been told I have to make an international mental health programme—what would you do if you were in my place?' Just off the cuff I said the first thing I would do would be to try to get somebody representing mental health in each of the regions. When I first came to WHO there was only one region represented by a separate office, and that was the European Office which was based in Geneva. But after some years there was a lot of talk about decentralisation. We gradually got our six regional offices and one of them had a psychiatrist. Baan then asked me what I was particularly interested in and what I would like to work on, and I said, well, alcohol and drug problems, about which I didn't know very much but would like to learn more, mental retardation and suicide prevention. They all seemed pretty important and hadn't been tackled too much, and I thought they should receive keener governmental attention. Baan came from Holland. He was trained as a psychiatrist and as a criminologist.

BJA: So under the Baan regime the alcohol initiatives were able to get going again?

JM: One of the first things we did was to meet some of the people who were active in the alcohol field. Since they were almost on our doorstep we first met Archer Tongue and people from his organisation (ICAA)—we hadn't met Eva Tongue by then. I had the great privilege of attending some of the ICAA meetings. This was an excellent way to get to know people in a number of countries and to learn something about their work. At the time it seemed to me that most of the work at this period was rather pathetic attempts at treatment of alcoholism. Just before Dr. Baan arrived I also had the marvellous opportunity of going to the United States for a year to take a Masters in Public Health at Columbia University. For part of the time I joined a small group of psychiatrists studying public health and administrative aspects of psychiatric services. This involved getting to know something of the New York 'underworld', including the alcohol and drug scene. During the course we had to write a thesis and I thought, well, with some knowledge of nutrition and some knowledge of psychology of education, there weren't many subjects I could tackle, but alcoholism might be an interesting field. Then I really began to read up on everything I could find on drinking problems.

BJA: *So your interests in alcoholism were very much developing?*

JM: Yes. Dr. Baan put me more or less in charge of the WHO mental health work on alcoholism and drugs under his guidance because at that time the WHO drug work was mainly to do with drugs and not with people. Baan was very keen to take into account the person who was using the drugs rather more than WHO had been doing up to then. And he agreed that I should go on with the work on suicide and mental retardation. But it was impossible at that time to concentrate too much attention on any one topic, because the mental health programme was rapidly expanding. I was involved for instance also in Dr. Lebedev's work on biological psychiatry and Dr. Lin's activities concerning the classification, diagnosis and epidemiology of mental disorders. I also had the exciting experience of taking part in our three travelling seminars on psychiatric services organised in the U.S.S.R. (1965, 67, and 70) where a good percentage of the participants were from the developing world. By the third seminar there was considerable exchange of experience and a start to planning improved national services.

BJA: *What was the alcoholism world like at that time?*

JM: It was a strange world with a peculiar population, tremendously varied, ranging from highly scientifically-minded people to others who seemed quite obviously cranks even to a person pretty ignorant about the subject. There were many who wanted to treat alcoholics but at that time very little consideration was being given to possibilities of preventing alcohol problems, and little thought to alleviating the impacts on the family.

BJA: Would it be right to say that in the '60s a WHO 'programme' essentially meant meetings and preparing reports, at least so far as something like drinking problems was concerned?

JM: Yes, but if you put it so baldly I think you miss the reason for having the meetings and preparing the reports. These activities were not just to inform people but also to get people together so that they could think more about what could be done in their own situation, using and adapting the experience from very many different countries. Moreover, an important meeting was considered not just as an isolated event, but as the culmination of a considerable amount of advice and preliminary activity by many people and preparations that would take more than a year to complete. An example would be the Expert Committee on Services for the Prevention and Treatment of Dependence on Alcohol and other Drugs [3]. It was fascinating to be closely involved in the planning of this meeting, held in 1965.

BJA: Had anyone at that time any vision of national policies, thinking at policy level?

JM: I am sure there were such people but I didn't know much about them in the early '60s. Perhaps in Scandinavia [4] and in Canada, more at a Provincial level. This vision must have been behind some of Jellinek's work too. But in the late '60s the first steps were taken in planning WHO work on national responses to alcohol and drug problems, and this was a basis for much of the late developments on national policies. By 1968, for activities concerning alcohol and drugs I was apportioned an annual budget equivalent to a month of consultant salary. On this frail foundation I recklessly decided to organise a new kind of seminar where the participants, selected by their governments, would be expected to present carefully prepared reviews of the national situation related to alcohol and drug problems. A week would be spent in each of three host countries willing to organise field visits and discussions on their attempts to deal with these problems. Finally, the participants would review the seminar and discuss how the experience could be adapted for use in their own countries. There would be no reading of long papers! Griffith Edwards enthusiastically joined in the planning and introduced many novel ways of sharing experiences. Thanks to the collaboration and hospitality of the host countries (Netherlands, Poland and U.K. England) and the tremendous input of the consultants and their colleagues, it was possible to hold the seminar in 1971. Dr. Cameron, Chief of the Drug Dependence Unit, joined in the organisation of the seminar. This experiment aroused such interest that a similar seminar was held in 1972 in Sweden, Yugoslavia and Switzerland. Altogether administrators and psychiatrists from 33 countries attended these meetings.

BJA: *Was the enthusiasm generated by these seminars just allowed to die down, or was there some continuity?*

JM: There was definitely some follow-up within the 33 countries that had participated. This was perhaps helped by preparing a publication [5] on the work and requesting the participants to suggest amendments to the early drafts. In the Regional Offices, too, there were important follow-up activities, especially in the Americas and in Europe, whose mental health staff had been involved in the seminars.

BJA: *When this decade of laying the groundwork had been achieved, in the '70s you moved into rather different activities?*

JM: Yes, I gradually began concentrating more and more on alcohol problems, though in the early '70s I had the privilege, thanks to Dr. Lambo's initiative, of being able to visit a number of countries to see something of mental health services in general, particularly in the developing world, and to discuss the planning of these services with governmental authorities. Maybe people were less afraid of me as a non-expert than they might have been of a highly-qualified psychiatrist who knew a lot about his own field and was convinced that the way psychiatric services were run in his own country was the best approach. My report on travel in nine African countries was discussed in draft with the Director of the Regional Office for Africa, Dr. Quenum, and used for developing the Region's mental health programmes. I suppose some of the ideas came from my public health training. The report contained suggestions on an alternative training for psychiatrists that might prepare them better to work with communities, to train less highly qualified health workers for more effective diagnosis and care of mental illness and to organise mental health services that were more dependent on community links. The use of psychiatrists to do more than care for the individual patient seemed essential in countries where in some cases there was only one trained psychiatrist for a million or more of the population. This experience helped me to organise an Expert Committee meeting on Mental Health Services in Developing Countries, held in 1974. The running of the meeting was most ably taken over by Dr. Harding, who had joined WHO a month previously. He made use of my paper 'Development of basic mental health services: an operational research proposal' to work out an excellent project on strategies for extending mental health care, carried out in several developing countries.

As I travelled around, I certainly tried to look at anything that I could discover to do with alcohol problems. I must say that in most of the developing world I didn't find too much interest in trying to deal with these issues, although some people would make sweeping statements about the enormous extent of the problem or the fact that there wasn't a problem in their country at all.

BJA: Did people at WHO in those days actually talk about an 'alcoholism programme'?

JM: Well, I would say that the first long-term plan on alcohol-related problems was prepared in 1975. By that time the Mental Health unit had grown into a Division under Dr. Norman Sartorius as Director. He suggested a restructuring without separate Units (such as the recently coalesced Drug Dependence and Alcoholism Unit) but where staff members would have main responsibility for specific projects and also collaborate in others. The plan for alcohol problems was found acceptable but practically no regular budget funds were forthcoming. It was therefore most timely that the Director of NIAAA (National Institute on Alcohol Abuse and Alcoholism, U.S.A.) came to see Dr. Lambo, now the Deputy Director General of WHO, and suggested that

NIAAA would be happy to provide some funds for WHO to work on alcohol problems in a bigger way, if only we could put forward some suggestions for suitable work. This approach by NIAAA followed WHO's invitation to that Institute to participate in the 1971 seminar.

BJA: The fact that NIAAA offered money precipitated WHO into a different style of programme?

JM: To some extent, yes. It precipitated the development of a few important projects which we hoped might serve not exactly as models, but as a useful basis for further development.

The first NIAAA-assisted project concerned disabilities related to alcohol use, and this was partly selected by NIAAA because they considered that the findings of such a study would be useful to them in the U.S.A. Luckily we had excellent consultants who felt that the funds available and the interest of the topic could enable us to produce something which would be of use for a much larger number of countries that just one—a more suitable task for WHO. Actually a WHO Expert Committee had already in 1950 [6] pointed to the need for a commonly accepted terminology concerning dependence on alcohol and other adverse effects of drinking. Attempts to achieve this aim were continued at several Expert Committee meetings and seminars. More recently though WHO had become increasingly interested in defining and measuring disability instead of concentrating on diseases. It was argued that such an approach would help to focus attention not only on possibilities of prevention or limitation of functional incapacity, but also on the need to reduce the consequences of the disability for the individual, the family and society in general. WHO therefore gladly accepted NIAAA's offer of financial and technical assistance for a WHO project that aimed at increasing international agreement on criteria for identifying and classifying disabilities related to alcohol consumption. Between 1973 and 1975 a steering group prepared and discussed extensive reviews of the state of knowledge on these matters. All this material was synthesised by Dr. Edwards and the complete documentation was submitted to a wider group of investigators from various parts of the world. This group's final report was published together with several of the working papers [7].

One result of this project was that the term 'alcohol dependence syndrome' described in the report, was accepted for the ninth revision of the ICD. Moreover this project seems to have promoted considerably increased recognition that it is not enough to focus on treatment of the person with this syndrome (the 'alcoholic'). Many other disabilities related to alcohol consumption are likely to be of greater public health significance because they are so prevalent and have such an impact on society. Actually the term 'alcohol-related disabilities' did not become very widely accepted, but the alternative term employed in the project—alcohol-related problems—soon came into very general use. At the same time, interest was growing in the need to develop more effective ways of preventing or limiting the impact of alcohol-related problems.

BJA: Was WHO able to do anything further about promoting this interest?

JM: Yes, indeed. Again, thanks to NIAAA, funds became available for two further projects, one on the prevention of alcohol-related problems and the other on community response to alcohol-related problems.

BJA: Were these projects carried out in the same way as the previous one?

JM: No, but they both relied very much on the findings of the disabilities project and they both involved the collaboration of governments and of a variety of experts in the alcohol field. The experience acquired in the two seminars was also valuable here.

BJA: Would you describe the two projects briefly?

JM: The projects were run simultaneously and were interrelated. For the prevention project, the first stage was to collect and review information from the literature and from responses to an inquiry. On this basis a preliminary document was drafted and sent to the Regional Offices and to experts, with a request for amendments and additions. This process was repeated in two succeeding drafts before publication [8] so that a considerable number of interested persons became involved. During a second stage, an abbreviated form of the inquiry used for the 1971–72 travelling seminars was circulated to countries, together with any information already available in WHO. Gradually a collection was made of summaries of the information for 29 countries [9]. Again the process of consultation, amendment and approval was used, in the hope that governments would make use of the data collected as their own material, rather than looking upon it as yet one more document compiled by an outsider. In fact the 1982 Technical Discussions showed that this had occurred. The drafts were also discussed at several meetings in the WHO Regions.

The project on Community Response to Alcohol-Related Problems was a much more ambitious endeavour. It was carried out as a research and action project, mainly in three countries where the governments welcomed the collaboration with WHO. It aimed to develop mechanisms for exploring how communities and nations as a whole respond to alcohol problems and how more appropriate responses might be developed. Firstly, how do you find out what these problems are and how extensive they are in a specific setting? What harm do they do to the individual and the community? And, what, if anything, is being done to prevent such problems or to limit their impact? An important objective of this project was to stimulate investigators to work with both a community and the national authorities while making use of the experience of other investigators working in settings where the situation was different.

BJA: Why were only three countries selected to participate in this project? And what were the criteria for selection?

JM: Partly because of the exploratory nature of the task and its complexity, it was felt that working with more than three countries in the beginning would make the project unwieldy, and there were time, funding and staffing limitations. Criteria for selection were worked out at a preliminary meeting of a 'steering group' of consultants. They agreed that, if the project findings were to be useful to a wide range of countries disturbed by alcohol problems, the selection should include one country in the developing world, one industrialised country and one undergoing very rapid social and economic changes. In all cases the government of the proposed country should be willing and eager to be involved because of an expressed need to deal more appropriately with alcohol problems. In the event, Zambia, U.K. (Scotland) and Mexico collaborated in the work and in this way three different WHO regions were also represented.

BJA: *In your opinion, was this a valuable project?*

JM: I think it was an extremely valuable project. Firstly, it showed that the complex research attempted can be carried out in very different situations. Of course a great deal was learnt about how some of the most sophisticated methods, for instance the epidemiological surveys and the data analysis, have to be modified. Then the idea of reporting back the research findings to the national authorities as a basis for discussion and further planning was well received and seemed to be particularly successful in Mexico. Involving the communities in the actual research and follow-up action was much more difficult, except in Scotland where something similar had been undertaken before this project started—it had been hoped that this might be a good model for the other countries. However, the attempt has perhaps underlined the fact that there is much still to be learnt about how to carry out research—*with* a community rather than merely *on* a community.

The fact that the governments of each of the three collaborating countries agreed to host a final meeting to discuss the results of the project and to invite representatives of neighbouring countries, did much, I feel, to extend the impact of the project. Investigation in additional countries have used some of the research instruments devised for the project to carry out parts of the work and others may be assisted by the publications prepared [10, 11, 12].

BJA: *So far as alcohol problems are concerned, does the world need WHO, could it get by if WHO pulled out from this area tomorrow?*

JM: Some countries might get on with these things if WHO pulled out. But I certainly have held very strong views that some kind of central agitation and central co-ordination of efforts, together with the establishment of a forum so that people can learn from each other, can have excellent results. It's difficult though—you can't set up a controlled experiment on that sort of issue.

16   Addictions

BJA: *Over these many years you have seen things develop. Do you have any feelings that governments are now really taking drinking problems any more seriously?*

JM: I think there has been a groundswell of change, and one of the reasons may have been that WHO did try to get people from many countries to collect information on what was happening in their own country and put it down in black and white and compare it with what other people were doing. I think this may have helped, but one can't be sure that any impetus will be carried through to action.

BJA: *Can you give any examples of nations which are taking drinking problems more seriously?*

JM: Just at random I would mention Papua New Guinea—it does seem that the efforts of WHO and other people who have gone there have aroused the concern of the government. I'm not sure how far the recent work in France has been pushed a little further forward by WHO's programme. In Australia and New Zealand it looks as though the WHO efforts may have strengthened the hand of those who felt that the governments should take alcohol problems more seriously. In Mexico and in Zambia the results of the community response project were certainly taken very seriously by the governments. But I have been disappointed by the efforts in Africa in a way: I had hoped that what we had been trying to do there would have greater repercussions, though I suppose that in Africa the whole sweep of health problems is so huge that while you are dying of malnutrition you can't think too much about alcohol problems—even though they may be linked. However, the WHO efforts there are continuing, partly in connection with a long-term project on the development of mental health programmes.

BJA: *How does one turn nations towards more serious interest? What are the strategems?*

JM: As I've said, I think one of the first things that has to be done is to get the government and its representatives involved with finding out what exactly is happening in the country itself. It is so easy for a country to say it has no alcohol problems or that it has vast alcohol problems. For instance, when I was in several West African countries I tried, in a naive way, to find people who would go with me to the Customs or to other relevant places and often they discovered for themselves something about the problem. I remember in Dakar someone phoning a colleague of his in Customs and to his astonishment he discovered how much alcohol was being imported and exported, and he realised that trade in alcohol was very much a part of the problem. And he said 'I can phone up somebody else who knows a lot about another aspect of the alcohol situation—the influence of growing Islamic faith in our country.' And this informant went on to say that there are certain tribes that never drink and other tribes, also Moslem, which still drink and sometimes drink very heavily. He said 'I have noticed the big change in young people—they are going to drink whatever happens, and they are drinking more and more, and I wonder how much this is to do with the increasing amount of alcohol available.' A little probing opens up these questions, these self-awarenesses, and that's perhaps a basic strategem for change.

BJA: *Is it legitimate to try to persuade a nation which is wondering whether it can achieve economic solvency to tackle drinking problems, or is one just going to be laughed at if one says that somewhere early in the foundation of your State and your new economy you should take alcohol problems seriously?*

JM: If a country has got to the stage where it has developed a Health Ministry or Ministry of Economics or whatever these Departments may be called, then they must have some mechanism for developing health programmes and economic programmes, and I think it is within these programmes that alcohol and alcohol problems should be taken on board. When funds became available in WHO to organise an Expert Committee Meeting on Problems Relating to Alcohol Consumption [13] I ensured that these questions came on the agenda. Under the chairmanship of Professor Kendell, the Committee made strong recommendations that governments should develop a national alcohol policy and should implement programmes for preventing and managing alcohol problems within a framework of general health and national development. During the meeting Committee members emphasised that in some areas undergoing rapid social and economic changes there is a particular danger of great increases in the availability of alcohol and consequently in the extent of alcohol problems. It was felt that these matters should receive urgent consideration by the national authorities concerned. Certainly when we had the Technical Discussions at the 1982 World Health Assembly there appeared to be tremendous interest in ensuring that alcohol problems were included for consideration in international health and development programmes.

BJA: Do you think that within the developing world, at a political level, there is any real likelihood of drinking problems being taken seriously?

JM: Judging by the kinds of things that representatives of developing countries said during the Technical Discussions I believe that there are great possibilities of the topic being taken very seriously. But whether that concern will remain at a theoretical level or will be put into action is difficult to predict. One doesn't have to go to developing countries to see the conflict between the need to take action and the fact that by the sale of alcohol governments have a tremendous source of revenue. Here I wouldn't distinguish very much between developing and developed countries.

BJA: You have mentioned the Technical Discussions several times. Could you explain what these are?

JM: Yes, these discussions have become part of the annual World Health Assembly, which brings together representatives of all the WHO Member States to advise on the WHO programme and budget. Each year a specific technical topic is selected by these representatives for concentrated discussion two or more years later at a special session lasting 1-1/2 days. The topic 'Alcohol Consumption and Alcohol Problems' was selected in 1979 and the discussions were held in May, 1982. In order to sharpen the focus on action, it was decided to concentrate on the development of national alcohol policies and programmes.

I was asked to prepare for and organise these discussions and was able to use the occasion to draw together many of the threads of experience accumulated over the years. The Member States were approached officially about a year beforehand and requested to comment on a brief background statement and inquiry and preliminary discussions were held in several of the Regional Offices, in some cases using information collected in previous WHO projects. Delegates from more than 100 countries, together with representatives of international organisations, participated in the Technical Discussions. The participants divided into six groups for very lively debate on why national alcohol policies are needed and what strategies might be adapted for use in different socio-cultural and economic situations. These alternatives were looked at in a context of national strategies for health. A review [14] based on these discussions has been prepared. It contains summaries of the responses from 57 countries on their situation concerning alcohol problems and policies for dealing with them.

BJA: *What is your sense of balance as to how driving and messianic one should be in dealing with a social problem like excessive drinking, as opposed to going slowly?*

JM: The messianic approach might do more harm than good, but trying to get people to look at what the problems really are and decide themselves whether they need to do anything about it is urgent. I don't think any nation is going to learn too much from guidelines based on knowledge of one particular country, but if the guidelines include some practical suggestions on how you start looking at your own national problem I would think that is where WHO might press.

BJA: *Do you think that within WHO the proper place for an alcohol problems programme is Mental Health, or would you put alcohol elsewhere?*

JM: No, I don't think it should necessarily be within Mental Health. Maybe it would be wiser for it to have a separate identity and many more links with many other parts of WHO. But the complication there again is partly budgetary, because there would have to be a personnel structure which would enable such a programme to be pushed through the various channels, and you can't have such a top heavy complicated structure for every topic with which WHO is dealing. Personally, I always thought that drinking problems should come into Family Health, but then again it depends very much on the staff and structure of the particular Division.

BJA: *Have you any strong views as to the extent to which drug and alcohol programmes should be combined within WHO?*

JM: My views have vacillated. Again, it's partly a question of the people who are running the programmes. What I have learnt from our experts has certainly persuaded me that there are many matters in common between alcohol and drug problems. There should at the least be a very close link between the two programmes. But there is already a vast store of experience in the alcohol field that is not necessarily all directly relevant to other drug problems. Unless WHO has at least one person knowledgable about the alcohol literature, about ongoing programmes, and about the wide variety of specialists in the field, the impetus of the international efforts so far is likely to die away, at a time when many of the problems are increasing.

BJA: *If you were today telling a young person with a bibliographic background who had just arrived in Geneva regarding the distillate of those things you had learnt about international work and which don't go into reports, what would you say?*

JM: I think my experience has taught me that one has to be exceedingly open to learn all the time. One has to listen to people. It is also very necessary to try to see the particular topic one is working on within the perspective of a wide range of other problems. I have learnt too that the more one travels the more one sees differences in people's backgrounds, ways of speaking, hospitality, but also more and more the similiarities. You don't have to go to meet the highly placed people in far off countries with any fear but rather with humour and humility. I must admit that I myself have not always shown too much humility in headquarters but this was partly because I was very much concerned that programmes I was dealing with should find a place on the agenda of WHO. But in travelling around the world I have felt immediately at home whatever the scenery or whatever kind of people I have met. I was fascinated to realise that it was rather easy to talk to people. It's difficult for a young person who is travelling for the first time on WHO business to get this feeling that people everywhere are similar to oneself, that we are all going to make our mistakes, that we are not going to put all our eggs in one basket, that we are not just going to follow the dictates of a group of experts, but that on the other hand, interest in what people are trying to do can often lead them to do something a little more successfully.

BJA: *What makes for success or for failure in international work? Are there any general principles as to why some ideas become dusty reports while other efforts in small ways become effective?*

JM: Unless you are really going to involve people from the very beginning in any project, they are not going to take much interest in the outcome. All the time it's a matter of working with people, trial and error, and then you may get some success. Moreover, I don't know where you put the dividing line between success and failure. I think it's often a matter of a pendulum.

BJA: *Was it unusual when you started at WHO to find a woman on this sort of international stage?*

JM: I don't think I have really noticed that as a problem. I have never been a feminist. I just consider that women have a lot to offer and men have a lot to offer. Certainly I remember several outstanding women in WHO in those early days and the Organisation has constantly tried to increase the percentage of women in senior posts.

BJA: *Looking back on all these years of experience in Geneva, did you take the right job? Are you glad that you answered that advertisement in The Times?*

22   Addictions

JM: I personally feel it has been a tremendous privilege to have worked in WHO. The experience has been fascinating, exciting, demanding and most rewarding. But I think the question ought to be put differently: Did WHO take the right person? Of course, I was not recruited initially by WHO to deal with alcoholism, but by the time I left there was pressure from many quarters for WHO to establish a long-term post specifically concerned with alcohol problems. I was happy to see that at least a first step had been taken and a two-year position created, with a competent person to run what has gradually become a programme on alcohol-related problems.

References

1. World Health Organisation (1951). Technical Report Series No. 42. WHO, Geneva.
2. World Health Organisation (1956). Technical Report Series No. 48. WHO. Geneva.
3. World Health Organisation (1967). Technical Report Series No. 363. WHO, Geneva.
4. Bruun, K., Edwards, G. and Lumio, M. *et al.* (1975). *Alcohol Control Policies in Public Health Perspective,* Finnish Foundation for Alcohol Studies, Vol. 25, Helsinki.
5. Moser, J. (1974). *Problems and programmes related to alcohol and drug dependence in 33 countries.* WHO Offset Publication No. 6, Geneva.
6. World Health Organisation (1951). Technical report Series No. 42. WHO, Geneva.
7. Edwards, G., Gross, M. M., Keller, M., Moser J. and Room, R. (1977). *Alcohol-Related Disabilities.* WHO Offset Publication No. 32, Geneva.
8. Moser, J. (1980). *Prevention of alcohol-related problems: an international review of preventative measures, policies and programmes.* Addiction Research Foundation (compiled with the help of contributors from more than 80 countries in the six WHO Regions and published on behalf of the World Health Organisation), Toronto.
9. Moser, J. (ed) (1980). *Prevention of alcohol-related problems. National and subnational profiles of alcohol use, alcohol-related problems and preventative measures, policies and programmes.* WHO document MNH/80.18 (compiled with the help of the six WHO Regions and contributors from 29 countries), Geneva.
10. Rootman, I. and Moser, J. (eds) (1983). *Community response to alcohol-related problems. Report on Phase I of a WHO project.*

WHO document MNH/83.17 (compiled and edited on behalf of an international group of project collaborators), Geneva.
11. Rootman, J. (ed.) (1983). *Community response to alcohol-related problems. Report on Phase II of a WHO project.* WHO document MNH/83.18, Geneva. (These two documents (10 and 11) have been amalgamated and will be published by NIAAA.)
12. Rootman, I. and Moser, J. (1984). *Guidelines for investigating alcohol problems and developing appropriate responses.* WHO Offset Publication No. 8, Geneva.
13. World Health Organisation (1980). Technical Report series No. 650. WHO, Geneva.
14. Moser, J. (ed.) (1984). *Alcohol policies in national health and development planning: including a summary of the Technical Discussions held during the Thirty Fifth World Health Assembly.* WHO Offset Publication, Geneva.

2

Interview with Awni Arif

AWNI ARIF, b. 1926. Graduated MD, University of Baghdad; Doctorate in Public Health from Columbia, NY. After working in Iraq was at WHO (Geneva) 1960–66 as a medical doctor in the drug dependence unit. From 1966–69, Director General of Health and Preventive Medicine, Ministry of Health, Baghdad. From 1969–86, worked firstly for WHO in Tripoli, Libya and Pakistan and then (from 1976), as Head of Drug Dependence Program, WHO Geneva. Continues with international consultancies.

BJA: *Would you mind saying something first of all about your professional background and what led you to work on drugs?*

AA: I qualified in medicine at the University of Baghdad and then stayed on to read public health administration in the School of Medicine. In 1957 I went to the United States of America where I gained my Master's degree and doctorate in the field of health administration and preventive medicine. I then stayed on to teach in the School of Public Health in Columbia University, New York. While at Columbia I did some field work on drug abuse in New York. As you know, in the 1960s there was a big outbreak of heroin-taking in the States. I undertook some surveys on heroin which I presented as part of my postgraduate work, and a report was published.

BJA: *So there you were, in 1957, a young man who had done his training in Baghdad. In America you were suddenly launched into a very different culture, a totally different scene from the traditional Arab society; in which you had grown up. How did it feel?*

AA: Well, I had a big shock when I arrived. University life, the campus, people from many other countries. At that time more than 50% of the students were 'foreigners' and the other 50% American. I started doing research with them, working with them, attending lectures, and learning a lot about other cultures.

BJA: *At that time had you any thoughts about joining WHO?*

AA: I was not intending to work for the World Health Organization at all. However, quite unexpectedly, I received a formal letter from the Organization asking me if I would apply for a post as Medical Officer responsible for the 'Drug Addiction Unit' within WHO in Geneva. At that time it was called the 'Drug Addiction Unit'.

BJA: *So the letter came out of the blue and set the whole direction of your career?*

AA: Yes, a letter from WHO, from the Director of the Division, arrived saying there was a vacant post. I postponed my answer until I had spoken to the Dean of the School of Public Health. He said "Well, there is nothing to lose, so why not complete the form and send it."

BJA: *So that's what you did?*

AA: Yes. I discussed the situation with my wife and we agreed that it would be nice to have a year or two in Geneva. So I posted the form and forgot about it. And 2 months later I received a letter from the Chief of Personnel of WHO congratulating me on being appointed to the post and asking me to report for duty. So off I went to Geneva, and on 1 February 1960 took up responsibilities in the Drug Addiction Unit. At that time I would say that the Organization was dealing only with the evaluation of drugs for their dependence liability. Nothing had been done in the areas of epidemiology, prevention, treatment, or related research. The only research being undertaken was on monkeys, to identify the dependence liability of new drugs. But from that time onwards more emphasis was given to those neglected areas.

BJA: With whom else were you working?

AA: With Professor Halbach, who is of course a very well known pharmacologist, working on drugs. I worked in that position for 6-1/2 years.

BJA: Looking back, what did you achieve during that time?

AA: Professor Halbach continued to work very effectively in the field of pharmacology and dependence liability and that sector of responsibility clearly had to continue. I was dealing with the epidemiology, prevention, treatment, training, and starting to collect relevant information and data. I think it is fair to say that for the first time we started shifting the balance a little—in this area in the past there were a hundred people talking about pharmacology and no one talking about any other dimensions.

BJA: And then Dale Cameron took over?

AA: Yes, I went back to Baghdad at the request of the President of Iraq. They wanted me to serve as Director-General of the Health Services and I stayed in that post for 3 years. I told them that during that time I would organize the services on a public health model. At that time, in 1966, the services of the Iraqi Ministry of Health were merely curative and little had been done in the field of public health. So we instigated a new public health law and established various departments, particularly a large directory of preventive medicine and public health services which covered epidemiology, city health, communicable diseases, malaria control and so on.

BJA: And after you had completed the 3-year assignment in Iraq?

AA: Well, during those 3 years I knew I was going back to Geneva. I had not cut my ties with WHO. I used to visit Geneva as a member or as head of the Iraqi delegation to the World Health Assembly every year. I was also head of the Iraqi delegation to the

Regional Committee for the Eastern Mediterranean which met once a year. I also continued to learn how WHO operates during this time. When I had completed my 3 years in Iraq I was requested by the Organization to return to WHO headquarters in Geneva and take up my old post. I told them I already had experience at headquarters level, experience in University teaching and national administration and that I would like to see something of WHO field work. So I accepted the post of WHO Representative in Tripoli, Libya, for 4 years. At that time we had more than 35 WHO experts working in Libya on malaria, tuberculosis and other communicable diseases, sanitary engineering, water supplies, training, establishing a dental school, and so on. That work was a great experience. From there I moved on to the post of WHO Representative in Pakistan—a very large country with many health problems and a need for collaboration with the World Organization. While I was working in Pakistan the post in Geneva fell vacant because Dale Cameron retired. Dr. Ling took over but soon left to join the UN system and I received a letter asking me to apply for the position of Senior Medical Officer in charge of the Drug Dependence Programme. So I returned to Geneva and took up this post from 1976 to the end of 1985. That was 9-1/2 years.

BJA: *A remarkably rich and varied background. Is WHO the same sort of organization as it was when you first knew it, or has it changed in any radical way?*

AA: The officials of the Organization were small in number. We used to have regular staff conferences every fortnight in one small conference room and everyone knew each other by their first names. Communication was excellent because of the small number of staff and also, of course, the programme was small. This was followed by the period during which many countries became independent, particularly African countries, the decolonization process increased rapidly and, consequently, the demand on WHO in all health fields also increased. So this new building had to be built. During this period the staff have increased considerably in number to meet the needs of WHO Member States.

Interview with Awni Arif   29

BJA: *Has the vision in any way changed? Does WHO stand for the same things as when you first joined the Organization, or has it had to rethink its definition?*

AA: In the past 10 years most countries, particularly developing countries, have acquired a new generation of physicians and other health professionals. Many of them have been trained on WHO fellowships abroad returning to their countries to join the new generation of professionals. WHO is changing from a policy of having a large number of WHO staff working at country level for 2 year postings and who were engaged on all manner of projects. That old formula has now changed completely. We now have very few WHO staff at the country level other than WHO representatives who are now called WHO Programme Coordinators. In fact, very few countries have any WHO staff there at all. It is better to send a consultant for 1 or 2 weeks or even longer, to assess the situation, work with national colleagues and go back again briefly the following year. That way you give more incentive to the countries themselves to do the work rather than the countries depending on experts from outside. That is really the big shift in the World Health Organization's programme. We have also moved forward in our ideas on the levels and complexity of health programme planning. The grass roots level of planning is very important from the country level, up to the regional and global levels. Even in Geneva when we talk about a programme at the global level, it is actually initiated and conducted at country level. Of course, the major shift is WHO's goal of Health for All by the Year 2000 through strategies of primary health care.

BJA: *If you look back on the work you have done on drugs with WHO, what have been the achievements?*

AA: We have very limited resources. The global drug dependence programme and activities related to WHO responsibilities under the international drug control treaties are part of the Mental Health Programme of WHO. There are two staff members working in the Division of Mental Health dealing with this problem: my colleague handles the work concerning the international drug control treaties and I was responsible for the part of the programme dealing with the assessment, epidemiology, prevention, treatment, training programmes and development of technology and research. The Regional Advisers in Mental Health at the WHO Regional Offices collaborate with us in these fields. The other two major areas of the WHO Mental Health Programme are dealing with prevention and treatment of mental and neurological disorders and psychosocial factors for promotion of health. Without the generosity of temporary advisers and world-wide collaborators we would not have got very far. What did we achieve? As I've said before, the most important success has perhaps been this shift in emphasis—the problem of drug abuse, drug dependence, is no longer only a drug problem. We have learned to look more at the problem of human beings, environment, society, with the drugs as just one element. We have the agent (the drug) and we have the host (the human being), and the interaction with the environment. Symbolic of this shift in perspective was the WHO study on drug problems in the sociocultural context, which resulted in important WHO publications *Drug Problems in the Socio-cultural Context* and *Drug Use and Misuse: cultural perspectives*.

BJA: *Any other achievement?*

AA: For the first time we have started to collaborate with countries in developing programmes for treatment. A programme would start with a pilot project—a small project integrated into the total health service, undertaking some training at country level, some operational research, in order to see what works best in that sociocultural situation. We also provide laboratory services assistance, in a small way, mostly financed by UNFDAC, the United Nations Fund for Drug Abuse Control. We are able to see programmes develop where the addict is treated as a human being worthy of help and not as a criminal.

BJA: *Can you give an example of such a country programme?*

AA: In 1976 I was in Rangoon, Burma, and I asked "where are your addicts?". They took me to a mental hospital which had attached to it a separate closed building. There was a cell with a metal door and metal windows and an inside toilet. They said

"Those are the addicts". Today the same centre is a beautiful, open, clean hospital, like any other hospital. This reflects a very fundamental shift of opinion by the national authorities, the decision makers. There are many other examples where a country has changed from a system of imprisonment to open treatment, either on a community basis or an institutional basis as an interim measure. Looking back one can see this change in the attitude of health authorities towards the drug problem as one of WHO's most important achievements in this area.

BJA: *Has the WHO drug programme had any other sort of important impacts?*

AA: The training programmes have been an important innovation. In developing countries one of the prime shortages is trained manpower, so we have devised a model which involves intensive training for 3 weeks. These workshops have been held each year for 7 years, three in Hong Kong and four in Thailand. They have mainly served physicians nominated by developing countries from Africa, the Eastern Mediterranean, South East Asia and the Western Pacific Regions. So far a total of 181 physicians have graduated. Today the graduates are leaders in this field and are responsible for work on drug dependence in their own countries. Some of the physicians trained are in planning positions and some of them are organizing their own local training courses. I can give you an interesting example. In 1984 I was requested by the Government of Afghanistan to visit that country to look at the problem of drug abuse. I had discussions with the Ministry of Health and the Ministry of Home Affairs. I asked to see the psychiatric hospital where they had a few drug-dependent patients. I went there and was surprised that three of the doctors recognized me and said "Dr Arif, we were on the first WHO training course held in Hong Kong on the management of drug dependence. We told you at that time, when we were doing our evaluation of the course that we didn't have any heroin problems in Afghanistan and that probably we were wasting our time spending 2 days talking about heroin dependent persons. Our problem was only cannabis and opium smoking. But when we came back from that course we found that in Kabul we had a heroin problem. Now you see this ward is full of young heroin-dependent persons".

BJA: *Any major gaps in achievements so far?*

AA: One of the major gaps for developing countries is that physicians and other professionals have not been trained how to carry out research or to design research protocols. Any future training course must deal with this issue.

BJA: *What do you see as the blocks on further progress? Despite everyone's efforts drug problems in many parts of the world get worse. Why have we not succeeded further?*

AA: Well, the nature of the problem is very different from any familiar problem, such as a communicable disease, and the complexity is greater. Drug dependence beings misery to the person and the family. Forget about all the health consequences for a moment and look at the disruption to the community. People get caught up in bribery, theft, criminal ways. We are looking at more than a 'disease'.

BJA: *Do you think that in 10 to 20 years time the tide of the drug problem is going to be turned back, or is your message that we propose small and sensible remedies, but that we are largely at the mercy of an uncontrollable tide?*

AA: I would say that in the next 10 to 15 years many national authorities will have major communicable diseases under control. I would even guess that in the foreseeable future cancer may be under greater control. I think that the major problems would then be accidents, drugs, alcohol and smoking, and cardiovascular disease. I think that substance abuse will thus be recognized on a level with the great, classical public health issues, and we may get more resources. But we cannot sit back and wait until we have all the answers. For the time being we need to do what we can, even for small gains. You cannot wait because the data tells you that we have only a 20% success rate in treatment—that does not mean that you stop treatment. We don't stop prevention just because we don't have evidence that a given programme produces brilliant success rates. I believe that we have to live with the problem: I don't believe in the possibility of eradication. Contain the problem to a limit which is acceptable. And the reason for saying that is that we are not dealing with a microorganism for which we can develop a vaccine: we are dealing with human behaviour, human beings. We are dealing with society and drugs. If you control one drug or eradicate one drug, there is always a new drug appearing. So I believe that we have to live with this problem and I think politicians, decision makers, have to acknowledge in their policies that we are not going to wipe out drug problems in the next 5 to 10 years. That sort of ambition would be a big mistake.

BJA: Do you think that in many countries at a leadership level there is an accurate understanding of the nature of drug problems and an adequate commitment to action?

AA: Well, I would divide country response into two types. Countries which are under international pressure—big power pressure for political reasons—have to respond, do something. They don't want their image to be that of a drug exporter. Many other countries only respond on an *ad hoc* and token basis, for example when there is something glamorous to say on television or reporting on the death of a famous actor from an overdose of heroin. Newspapers take the matter up and the government then responds in the simplest way—usually that means radio and television anti-drug campaigns—a response which is probably inappropriate and sometimes counter-effective. However, that is the cheapest token response to the problem. Such countries are sometimes forced into taking action with the motivation coming, not because politicians want to act, but because public opinion develops at a community level, putting pressure on the politicians to do something. So far very few countries have really developed comprehensive policies for drug abuse control, looking at the overall problem in a way that embraces both control of supply and demand reduction.

BJA: Turning to another question, what can you say about the problem of cocaine production in certain parts of Latin America?

AA: We are not learning from history. History tells us that when we suddenly stopped cultivation where people had been growing the poppy for centuries and using opium as part of the socio-cultural setting, opiate use (such as the use of heroin) completely burst its boundaries and we were then too late to drive it back. Heroin appeared and spilled out into India, Pakistan and Sri Lanka, and it has now reached the West. We are not looking at coca and cocaine. The economic and social causes of the dyke giving way may be different, but otherwise the story threatens to be the same. Cocaine itself is the most reinforcing of existing drugs. Five years ago powdered cocaine was virtually limited to North America. Now you can find it in Africa, South East Asia, Australia, Japan, some countries in the Middle East and of course Europe. It's the heroin story all over again—a drug breaking its traditional geographical boundaries and socio-cultural embeddedness, and 'new technologies' of use, followed by the rapid world-wide spread. Actually we are too late to take action, and that, I fear, is the harsh lesson of history.

BJA: As someone who has seen its use in many different cultures, what is your current opinion on the health implications of cannabis?

JM: I would say that the consensus of opinion has changed over the last 6 years. Before that one saw a movement for liberalization coming from the young; campaigns in newspapers and on television, that cannabis should be legalized, that it should be sold like cigarettes. That movement has receded. In 1981 we published the results of a collaborative study on this topic which was conducted by WHO and the Addiction Research Foundation of Toronto. We selected 15 scientists and asked them each to review a sector of the field. We examined their papers at a meeting and produced a small document, not more than 40 pages, on the behavioral consequences of cannabis use. The conclusion was that to a certain extent, not in every area, cannabis is harmful. I have seen many young people on cannabis drop out of school, losing 3 or 5 years of education because of this drug. In the past marijuana, or cannabis, particularly in the United States and Europe, had a low THC content—perhaps 0.1 to 3% During the past 6 years we have seen plant material containing up to 24% THC from several countries.

That carries more harmful consequences. There are many reports of psychoses associated with cannabis use and further scientific testing of that question is important.

BJA: Someone walks into your office, tries the desperate task of taking over where you left off. What sort of person should that be?

AA: Well, I would like to see a person like an adventurer here, a discoverer. A person who likes a challenge.

BJA: That's yourself!

3

Interview with Archer Tongue

ARCHER TONGUE, b. 1919. BA, University of London. Executive Director of the International Council on Alcoholism and Addictions since 1952. Has represented ICAA on WHO committees and on the UN Narcotic Commission. Extensive international experience as consultant, lecturer, and meetings organiser.

BJA: *Mr. Tongue, what is the 'I.C.A.A.'?*

AT: The International Council on Alcohol and Addiction (up to 1968 we were the International Council on Alcohol and Alcoholism). There's quite a bit of history behind those letters. I.C.A.A. is one of the older international organizations. It was founded in 1907 at an international congress on alcoholism in Stockholm. The reason for its founding was basically that the series of congresses on alcoholism, which had started in 1885 in Antwerp (the centennial meeting will be held in 1985 in Calgary), had no permanent organizational committee. It was felt that instead of having an *ad hoc* arrangement set up each time, some kind of permanent office which could also serve as an information centre should be brought into existence. Then, as now, funding was difficult. In fact, if you read our first annual report and then every 10 years up to the present time, from the financial angle you might be reading the same report. Nevertheless, one or two governments were behind us. Norway was the first government to support what was initially called the International Bureau Against Alcoholism. Not perhaps a happy title in English, but a direct translation from the French. Until 1921 the organization had its home in the Swiss Secretariat Against Alcoholism, which is now the Swiss Institute for the Prevention of Alcoholism in Lausanne. That was our parent body. The same gentleman, Dr. Robert E. Hercod founded both organizations.

BJA: What sort of organization was this 'Bureau'?

AT: The Bureau was influenced by the then current state of activity in the alcoholism world and was therefore very much dominated by the Temperance movement. It was not, though, a prohibition body. It is not always recognized in Anglo-Saxon circles that the Temperance organizations, particularly on the Continent, have been active in the field of treatment and rehabilitation of alcoholics from very early days—and are indeed up to the present. They were some of the pioneers. One of the main examples is the Blue Cross, not to be confused with the Blue Cross Insurance in the U.S.A. or the protections of animals in the UK. So, while the Bureau was heavily influenced by the temperance thinking, there was always a co-operative relationship with the medical profession, with health administrators, and with scientists in the research field.

BJA: Who were the Bureau's real Founding Fathers?

AT: They came from Italy, Sweden, U.S.A., Serbia, Netherlands, Germany, Finland, New Zealand, Switzerland, France, UK, Denmark, Norway, Canada, Austro-Hungarian Monarchy. They included at least three directors of psychiatric hospitals, a clergyman, a lawyer, a magistrate, a university professor, two doctors, two Temperance representatives and a man of letters.

BJA: So the Bureau started out as a sort of holding body for running international meetings?

AT: That was one of its activities but it was also intended as a documentation centre. It aimed under that heading to assemble relevant information, translate it into English, French, and German and circulate it to interested people.

BJA: *Presumably the Bureau and its activities provide just one example of the general trend toward 'internationalization' of certain problems that was getting underway at that time?*

AT: Yes but there are differences, for instance, the drug control system had a very different history. From the Shanghai Conference in 1909 the drug problem was seen as an international concern. Although the first international scientific conference on alcoholism was held in Paris in 1878, alcoholism continued to be seen largely as an issue to be dealt with at national level. There were though agreements on the supply of spirits to the African nations—Brussels (1890–1912) and St. Germain-en-Laye (1919).

There were also some incidents, as for example the tension between Spain and Iceland in 1922 over the fish-wine issue. Spain wouldn't take Iceland's fish unless Iceland took Spanish wine. But although one could mention instances such as this, (despite the work of the Bureau) alcoholism remained basically a national problem.

BJA: *Tell us now something about how you came into this field. When did you arrive at I.C.A.A.?*

AT: I arrived in 1952. It was still really the immediate post-war period. I found six rooms, a rather out of date library, a lack of finance, and certainly an organization. The Bureau was serving as the secretariat to the International Union Against Alcoholism, a federation of what were mainly temperance societies. There were two secretaries—one a French lady and the other Australian. They had somehow kept things going although those war years had been very difficult for the Bureau. When the Germans visited Lausanne during the war, on the afternoons they came across the lake, the Australian lady stayed at home. The Bureau's first Director, Dr Robert Hercod had just retired.

BJA: *He'd been there since 1907?*

AT: He'd been there since 1901! You see, he'd actually founded the Swiss Secretariat in 1901, and the Bureau shared its offices. Just after the war there had been an interim director, Dr. Henri Gachot, who is still living at a great age in Strasbourg.

40   Addictions

BJA: *What were your first problems?*

AT: Sandwich problems. I was sandwiched in this way: Jellinek had come to Geneva as the WHO consultant on alcoholism and had begun to set up an international scientific organization with a journal, while on the other side a rather forceful temperance group had started an international organization which had considerable backing. I began to wonder whether my organization would be squeezed out of existence. So I saw that we had to find a particularly distinctive international contribution if we were to survive. The scope and philosophy of the organization had to be widened to take in new developments, particularly those which were to be observed in the U.S.A. after Prohibition ended. Those developments included Alcoholics Anonymous, and the idea of 'National Councils on Alcoholism'. Both those movements were based on the concept of alcoholism as an illness: the alcoholic and not alcohol was the problem. We had in those terms to make people understand alcoholism as an illness; the alcoholic was someone who would get alcohol whatever the regulations on alcohol. This movement stood in contrast to the position of those who based their work on abstinence for the individual, or at least on drinking in moderation.

BJA: *How did you go about things?*

AT: I began to open negotiations with these new groups and interests. The first State programmes were starting to develop in the U.S.A.—the North American Association of Alcoholism Programmes (later to become Alcohol and Drug Programmes of America) came into being, and I began to develop relations with such bodies. The only international meetings going on at that time, apart from three important but small symposia that Jellinek arranged in connection with World Health Organisations were Copenhagen, Denmark (1951); Buenos Aires, Argentina (1953) and Noordwijk, Netherlands (1954)—the traditional international congresses which the Bureau had organized every few years. In this setting it seemed to be very clear that the growing body of professionals who were interested in alcoholism treatment needed to get together annually in a forum where they could share ideas and experiences. So that was how the idea of the annual Institute was born. The first meeting was held in 1955 and they continue to this day.

BJA: *What accident or intent led you personally to Lausanne and to this job?*

AT: Well, that's a complicated question. A conjunction of circumstances. Initially I had no idea of going into this field. I had studied history and had thoughts of becoming a teacher and then I went into business. However, in a curious way childhood had exposed me to a certain interest in the problem. My father only drank a sherry at Christmas, and my mother didn't drink at all—in the house there was only a bottle of brandy for medicinal purposes. But I'd heard my father say sometimes, 'Oh, yes, he's got problems, he's too fond of the bottle'. That was the phrase—'too fond of the bottle'. There was a relative of ours who was I suspect rather too fond of the bottle, and he would come to us when he was down and out and needed some help. Then in my short period in business I came across drinking problems which influenced absenteeism and performance on the job, and this also interested me. But an important influence came from being a Quaker; I went to work for the Society of Friends in various administrative capacities. One of my jobs there was connected with the temperance issue.

BJA: *Were the Quakers total abstainers?*

AT: Well, that's a subject in itself! The early Quakers, in the eighteenth century, were not all abstainers; some brewing firms originated from Quaker families—I believe Barclays, for example. But the Evangelical Movement of the nineteenth century had an effect on Quakerism, so much so that there was a general move toward acceptance of abstinence as the best approach, reflected in the Books of discipline of the Society.

BJA: But how did your Quaker work touch on temperance?

AT: I became the Secretary of the Friends Temperance Union from 1946 and for about 6 years I worked at Friends' House, in Euston Road. The Union later changed its name to, I think, Friends' Temperance and Moral Welfare; I think it's now changed again. The interesting situation was that there was an enthusiastic group who believed in total abstinence, while there were also a large number of people who were abstainers, but who didn't.

I also worked for other departments of the Friends, and my first experience of congress organization was preparing the World Congress of Friends in Oxford in 1952.

BJA: You ran the conference?

AT: I was the executive organizer. About 1300 people participated living in a number of Oxford colleges. I went straight from there to Paris, where the 24th International Congress on Alcoholism was taking place, and then took up my duties in Lausanne. For a few years I still worked also for the Friends' European section.

BJA: Had you previously gone out to Lausanne to have a look, or was it a blind date?

AT: No, I went out to meet the Committee. The finances seemed rather grim, but I guess I was young at that time and thought . . . I'd see what I could do.

BJA: How many languages did you speak?

AT: What I had learnt at school—French, German and Spanish, with an English accent. Now I've learnt to read a few more languages which has been essential to the job. In the sixties my wife Eva, a Hungarian lawyer, began to work actively in the organization being the Deputy Director. Her input and energy facilitated the development of I.C.A.A. activities particularly in the expanding field of drug dependence.

BJA: And what happened over the following 30 years? Looking back what have you seen?

AT: Undoubtedly the taking of alcohol problems into the programme of WHO was one of the major events and influences which I was to witness. One must credit Jellinek with pioneering that move. Then if one stands back and tries to analyse the flow of history, it's very evident that in several respects the U.S.A. was a potent influence on alcoholism thinking. This American influence may have been held back by the second World War but you can certainly pick up signs of the impact of American alcoholism on Europe by the late 1940s. The WHO and American themes are intertwined, with Jellinek perhaps the linkman. The subject began to be recognized as legitimately within the health field, and the recommendations of WHO to governments contributed to this acceptance of alcoholism as a public health problem. In 1954 countries like France and the Soviet Union, for example, started governmental programmes in Alcoholism prevention and treatment. These influences brought about a change of attitude in many countries—you could see throughout the Fifties country after country setting up alcoholism programmes. I remember Jellinek saying to me 'Of course, your country (Britain) will be the last one to do so'. In 1960, Max Glatt came to the congress in Stockholm and I guess he was one of the first to try to develop the new type of programme in the UK. So I think that one might say that the very fact that alcoholism was put into WHO's programme and that governments were thus confronted with recommendations, had a considerable impact on those developments.

BJA: *And the more specific American influences?*

AT: Gradually there was more and more contact between European workers and their North American colleagues, so that many of the concepts which had come into play in the U.S.A. after the ending of Prohibition began to be known in Europe—predominantly the 'disease concept'. To an extent of course things went on in Europe the European way: there was not the abrupt transition from Temperance or prohibition thinking on alcohol, to 'alcoholism as an illness', which was what one saw in the U.S.A. And sometimes of course there was a lack of awareness in North America of the European contribution. I remember going to a centre for women alcoholics in Salt Lake City, where the staff very proudly told me that this was the first womens' alcoholic centre in the world. I said 'Well, I didn't want to be impolite as a guest, but you know, I live in a city where we've had a home for women alcoholics since the end of the nineteenth century'. The challenge was to bring North America and Europe into mutual and fruitful contact.

BJA: *In the event, do you believe that the new American 'disease concept' won hands down, like the American grey squirrel chasing out our poor red squirrel?*

AT: Europeans are notably reluctant to give up their own habits of thought. In any case, the disease concept was a re-discovery not an idea arising *de novo*. It had been a familiar idea in nineteenth century Europe. In Germany, the first treatment centres had opened in the mid-nineteenth century, and there were a large number of them. In Lausanne in the I.C.A.A. Library we have a Russian book surveying with photographs the various alcoholism treatment centres in Britain, and that dates from 1901. Different European countries responded, of course, in their own ways to post-war American influence. Over many issues there is a kind of innate affinity between the Scandinavian, Dutch and German ways of handling problems and Anglo-Saxon approaches—ideas from North America were likely to strike a sympathetic cord. You can see that to a certain extent in the way A.A. developed in Europe although even in that instance there are variations which are very interesting—why was A.A. so strong in Norway and Finland, but not in Denmark or Sweden? But I would say that the Latin countries were more resistant to North American ideas, and still are. Eastern European countries are very cautious about ideas emanating from North America, for example looking upon Alcoholics Anonymous almost as a secret society which cannot be accepted because if you bring alcoholics together you must have the doctors and the social workers present. In terms if it's a medical problem and an illness, then the specialists in illness must be dominant.

BJA: *Were the WHO Expert Committees important?*

AT: If we look at the 1950s when Jellinek was at WHO, we saw in the earliest WHO report on this subject an emphasis on 'alcoholism as an illness', a health problem. In the 1960s it was the combined approach to alcohol and other drugs and the concept of dependence, but what is significant is the great change of emphasis which is evident when you come to the Expert Committee of 1978—'Problems related to alcohol consumption'. This shift clearly follows the work of Ledermann in France and Schmidt and de Lindt in Canada, so you now have WHO concerned to encourage national authorities to develop *alcohol* policies—which will reduce the consumption of alcohol. The wheel has come full circle. It was at an I.C.A.A. meeting in Frankfurt in 1964 that Wolfe Schmidt heard Ledermann present a paper and they were able to spend an afternoon together. Ledermann was an important influence in focussing our attention again on alcohol as opposed to just the disease, and on this issue, there generally evolved a very strong input from the European side—the influence of Nordic thinking and research, for instance.

BJA: *Would it be too simple to see the 'disease concept' in its post-war form as an example of the extraordinary power of American ideas, with the later re-discovery of the actual importance of alcohol constituting something of a European led (or Europe and Canada) counter-revolution?*

AT: There could be some truth in this but I would like to believe that we were getting to an *international* formulation of our ideas about the problem.

BJA: *What about the idea that price should be used as an instrument of health policy? In your historical judgement, is that going to be politically feasible?*

AT: I think it should be taken into account in planning but I am a little worried if it is seen as the main, or only thrust in this area of prevention. I think it's obvious that the impact issues of pricing on availability is of extreme importance, but the danger at the present time is of putting too much faith in these measures. Historically speaking, the various programmes of education on alcohol and alcoholism have had only limited success. It would be wrong to put all one's eggs in one basket, there must be an integrated approach in which the public are brought into support of the policies which are introduced. You have got to work on a change in public understanding. I think that the disease concept brought people in many countries to an understanding that there was indeed a problem, and this is why I am a little worried by the erosion of faith in that idea.

BJA: *You sketch out these many and great changes over 30 years. What part has the I.C.A.A. played?*

AT: In the Fifties we began to see our role as complementary to WHO—WHO was having Expert Committees and symposia, to which came a small number of experts or government designated people. As I mentioned, we thought that there was a need to have something for the broad professional public so that there could be an international and interdisciplinary interaction. We were accused at one point of being too pro-American by some of our friends on the Continent. Our great problems were, of course, the heterogeneity of the public that we sought to serve and the fact that finance often prevented us having as high a standard of presentation at these meetings as we would have wished. We were faced in the late Sixties, with the question as to whether to take in drug dependence. This opened up the scope of our work tremendously. We had an entree into a lot of countries which previously looked very askance at any suggestion that alcohol was of importance. We managed, I think, to establish a kind of forum which went all the way from the alcohol industry and the pharmaceutical industry to the Temperance movement. I think that was healthy. We also started certain on-going international groups on specific subjects such as education, business and industry, alcohol policy and epidemiology.

BJA: *Is I.C.A.A. unusual in that it generously and modestly brings people together, but it doesn't really campaign or try to move the world? It seems to be so different from the great international campaigning movements on say slavery, or drugs. I.C.A.A. appears to have been a sounding board rather than a voice. After all these years, what is I.C.A.A.?*

AT: That's the real issue, you see. People have at different times brought up this question—the need for an organization with teeth—which could make pronouncements, but our membership is such that members don't always share the same views on any subject. Indeed, it's amazing to me sometimes that we've been able to keep people in the same room. So that explains why we are not ready to campaign, say, on issues such as methadone treatment or on marijuana legislation, or even on a definite policy with regard to limitations on alcohol supply or in the 'controlled drinking' questions. We have been able to do things in a quiet way, very much by means of contacts. Our influence had often been a hidden one. For example, the spread of detoxification centres from Eastern Europe to North America in the sixties. Another example from Brazil: in Sao Paulo we brought into contact people in the health and criminological fields, who were both concerned about drugs and alcohol, who worked in the same city but who hadn't ever met. The first time they came together was in an international symposium which we had put on. It's very simple— to get people to know one another. Of course, when we look at the United Nations and the specialized institutions, we sometimes get the impression of dinosaurs moving slowly along, and we can be more flexible. We can get things together on an informal basis and we don't have to go through much red tape. I.C.A.A. as an N.G.O. (Non-Governmental Organization) has been able to bring issues to the attention of the relevant U.N. Agencies. In the U.N. system the role of the N.G.O. is not simply that of Yes Man to one establishment.

BJA: *We have talked about the past and the present. Have you any sense of the future directions in which we are now moving?*

AT: Well, concerning alcohol problems, internationalisation is at a point of no return. Even in terms of the sheer physical mobility of people (be it migrant workers, tourists, or even travelling recovered alcoholics and drug dependent persons), the whole scene is one in which we can never go back again to the position that each country is an island unto itself. Although in the past we had all these international conferences, basically they were relaying national experiences, but they didn't really approach the real international questions. Perhaps it's all bound up with the deeper issue as to how far the United Nations system is workable, or the best way to develop international co-operation. There are anachronisms around: the control system for drugs is one of them. Its effects on actual drug taking and the amount of time spent on 'control' are not proportionate. Drug control as we today know it does not to my mind provide us with a model for the future. Pronouncements and decisions can evolve from the international apparatus which do not relate to human problems or the needs of human beings. Whether there's any better way or whether an evolution will take place, I don't know. If you ask about the future of alcohol and the drug question, I believe they have to be seen in the context of how we organise international dealing with human problems as a whole, whether it's refugees or food problems, or the safety of ships at sea, or individual lifestyles.

4

Discussion. Major Accomplishments, Subtle and Interactive Influences

Irving Rootman

From 1979 to 1981 I was in the Division of Mental Health at the World Health Organization WHO in Geneva where I managed the WHO project on Community Response to Alcohol-Related Problems. In that capacity, I worked very closely with Joy Moser and to some degree at least with Awni Arif and Archer Tongue. Yet, until I read the interviews in this section, I did not fully appreciate their accomplishments or the factors which influenced them. What then were their major accomplishments and what were some of the factors which acted on them to both facilitate these accomplishments or to make them more difficult?

In terms of accomplishments, in my view at least, Joy Moser's major accomplishment during her career at WHO was to legitimize and give prominence to alcohol as an international issue. This was not easy to do in the context of an organization which was preoccupied with the control of infectious and communicable diseases such as malaria and smallpox and which at the same time was chronically short of resources. Yet in part, through persistence, commitment, and sheer force of will, she was in fact able to put and keep alcohol on the agenda of WHO as evidenced by the 1979 Expert Committee on Problems Related to Alcohol Consumption and the 1982 Technical Discussions on Alcohol Consumption and Alcohol Problems, both of which she stimulated and organized.

Another of her accomplishments was that she began to build a network of people throughout the world sharing a common interest in alcohol-related problems. She did this through visits to countries, organization of meetings and projects such as the Community Response Project which involved participants from several countries, and facilitated exchanges of information between them.

With regard to Awni Arif, one of his main accomplishments was raising the consciousness and helping to improve the skills of physicians and other health professionals throughout the developing world in relation to drug problems. He did this mainly through the training programs which he spearheaded but also through his many trips where he met with physicians and public health officials.

A second major accomplishment was to help develop country programs in relation to drug problems. That is, much of his work was directed at supporting initiatives at the country level, working at least in part through WHO Regional Offices. He was also instrumental in introducing a cultural dimension to the analysis of drug-related problems through meetings and publications on the topic.

As for Archer Tongue, it is clear that his major accomplishment in the alcohol and drug fields was to provide a neutral international forum through which professionals and others interested in alcohol and drug issues could get together to share their ideas and experiences. An example of the value of such a forum is the reference that he made in his interview to the propitious meeting between Ledermann and Schmidt at an I.C.A.A. meeting in 1964. Another example is the spread of the idea of detoxification centres from Eastern Europe to North America in the sixties for which he deservedly takes some credit.

Archer Tongue also made a significant contribution to the field by placing issues on the agendas of international agencies. As he points out in his interview, because of their independence from governments, the I.C.A.A. can present a view that is different from those of governments and other official bodies, and in fact I heard him do so effectively during my brief tenure at WHO.

To sum up to this point, it is clear that the three people whose interviews appear in this section were able to exercise some influence on the course of international events and developments

Major Accomplishments, Subtle, and Interactive Influences 51

in the alcohol and drug fields. This is not to suggest that the accomplishments cited are exhaustive—they clearly are not. It is also not to suggest that they single handedly achieved them—they certainly worked with others. It is rather to suggest that in a complex milieu with many competing forces, they in their own way made significant contributions to the development of the alcohol and drug fields at the international level. This leads to the question of what influences acted on them to permit them to make these contributions and perhaps to impede their making even larger contributions?

Without doubt, one of the major influences on all three was their own *personal life experiences*. For example, Joy Moser's early experience as an abstractor influenced some of her subsequent activities such as the prevention project in which profiles of alcohol problems in countries were prepared and which resulted in a publication based on input from contributors in more than 80 countries. Similarly, one of the approaches used in the Community Response Project (synthesis of background information) derived largely from her abstracting experience. It is also plausible that Awni Arif's experience as an immigrant in the United States contributed to his interest in the sociocultural aspects of drug abuse and his experiences at the Regional level of WHO contributed to his subsequent emphasis on country approaches. Archer Tongue's Quaker background may have had some impact on the "honest broker" approach that he employed throughout his career at I.C.A.A. It is also clear that the academic training of the three played a role in their subsequent activities, with Archer Tongue taking the more casual long-term approach of the historian and both Joy Moser and Awni Arif taking the more impatient action-oriented stance of the public health professional.

A second major influence, which is perhaps more apparent in the case of Joy Moser than the other, was the impact on them of *strong personalities*. As mentioned in the interview, she was exposed to people like Margaret Mead, Piaget, and Jellinek during her career at WHO and it is very apparent that the approaches of these memorable people found their way into her work. Jellinek in particular had a significant influence on her thinking. As she notes, many of the ideas about the public health aspects of alcohol problems which she promoted were discussed in

Jellinek's time at WHO. In addition, she often spoke of Jellinek and the influence that he had on her commitment to the field of alcohol problems during my association with her. Although it is not clear from the interviews with the other two that they were as influenced by strong personalities, it is not unlikely.

A third major influence on the contributions of the interviewees was the *organizational context* in which they worked. Working in an international organization like WHO or I.C.A.A. imposes certain constraints on employees. There are constraints having to do with protocol, organizational mechanisms, history, and resources. Such constraints sometimes make it difficult to innovate. On the other hand, they can sometimes be used effectively by employees to achieve programmatic goals. An example would be the way in which Awni Arif was able to use the Regional Structure of WHO to establish country programs in drug abuse. Another example is Joy Moser's effective use of Expert Committees and Technical Discussions and Archer Tongue's use of Congresses to bring people together. At the same time, it should not be denied that without the organizational constraints, especially in resources, the interviewees might have accomplished more than they were able to.

One important aspect of organizational context that deserves special mention is the influence of immediate superiors. In the case of Joy Moser in particular, it was clear that the fate of the alcohol programme at WHO at any time hinged significantly on the attitudes of the Division Directors. If the Director was interested in the issue, it received some attention. If not, it received little. One factor in determining the attitudes of WHO management was the perceived availability of funds. Thus, when the United States indicated a willingness to support projects in the alcohol field a number of initiatives supported by the management occurred. Without such external support, it is difficult to sustain interest.

Finally, we come to the influence of *ideas* or *scientific movements*. It is clear as we look at the experiences of the three interviewees throughout their careers that they were indeed influenced by the ideas of their times including those ideas derived from science. One idea for example which had a major influence on all three was that of "internationalism" which was reborn after the Second World War. It is hard to imagine how they would have been able to sustain their efforts on the international stage without a strong belief in the efficacy of this idea which at least in part has some basis in a rationalistic or scientific view of the world. Another idea which influenced at least Joy Moser and Awni Arif is the notion of the epidemiologic triangle of host, agent, and environment which underpins much of public health. Although they appeared to give particular emphasis to one or the other of the three elements during their careers (e.g. Joy Moser seemed to give particular weight to the agent alcohol and Awni Arif to the host and environment), they never lost sight of the triangle itself.

A third set of ideas which influenced all three were changing ideas about alcohol and drugs based in part on scientific developments. For example, the idea of alcoholism as a disease promulgated by Jellinek was an important influence on Joy Moser and Archer Tongue in the 1950's and 1960's and perhaps longer in the case of the latter. This idea was eventually relegated to a less important spot in Joy Moser's mind by the work of Schmidt and de Lint who promulgated the single distribution theory of alcohol use, which in turn was also applied to drug abuse and began to exercise some influence in that field as well. In both fields, this theory led to an increased emphasis on policies by WHO and other bodies. Similarly, the notion of alcohol-related problems which Robin Room promoted in the 1970's came to play an extremely important role in Joy Moser's thinking and work and I suspect also in Awni Arif's work in the drug field. Finally, the idea of "public participation"which was revived in the United States and to some degree in the United Kingdom in the 1960's and 1970's, played a role in Joy Moser's thinking as reflected in her emphasis on participatory research in the Community Response Project.

Thus, it would be fair to say that ideas or scientific movements did play an important role in the work of the interviewees. At the same time, it would also be fair to say that these ideas or movements were not the only factors that influenced their accomplishments. As suggested earlier, personal experiences, exposure to strong personalities and organizational context also played important roles and no doubt there were other factors as well. Unfortunately, it is impossible to determine the relative influence of each of these factors on the basis of the evidence at hand. However, it is certainly true that the unique combination of these factors with the personalities of Joe Moser, Awni Arif, and Archer Tongue produced their unique accomplishments. It is unlikely that these combinations of circumstances with identical personalities will ever occur again, but perhaps we can learn enough from their experiences that we can replicate their successes and avoid their failures. I hope this discussion has made a contribution to that end.

II

INFLUENTIAL FIGURES FROM THE USA

5

Interview with Mark Keller

MARK KELLER, *b. 1907, Austria. Editor, bibliographer and scholar. From 1941–62 was lecturer in applied physiology, Yale University Center of Alcohol Studies, and then moved to Rutgers (1962–77) as Research Specialist when that center relocated. From 1943–77 edited* Journal of Studies on Alcohol; *Editor Emeritus and from 1981–84, Acting Editor. Professor Emeritus Rutgers from 1977; Adjunct Professor Brandeis from 1980. Developed the Classified Archives of the Alcohol Literature.*

BJA: *You are on record as saying that you were present at the moment of the re-birth of scientific interest in alcoholism. Can you tell us something about that happy event.*

MK: Yes. My boss Dr. Norman Jolliffe, of New York University Medical School, had been studying nutritional diseases at Bellevue Hospital, in the Psychiatric Division, and most of these diseases were found in alcoholics. That Hospital was admitting something like 10,000 alcoholics a year. That was in 1933–35, just after the end of Prohibition, so we had lots of 'clinical material' and Jolliffe was curing those patients with something which was then fairly new—vitamins. But at the end of one day, when we were discussing some cases we had just reviewed, all of whom were re-admissions, Jolliffe said, 'You know, Mark, I must be doing the wrong thing. I keep curing these guys, and they keep coming back. Why are they drinking that way? That's what we should be studying!' I think that was one of the most dramatic moments in my life, because I almost jumped out of my skin when I heard him speak those words—they were so true. And I hadn't realised it, I hadn't observed it, I didn't know we would have to think that way, at that time. But he did. The very next day we started to design a research on alcoholism. We thought it was going to take a couple of weeks or so but it just got bigger and bigger. We began to see more and more involvements. We could see that we had to turn not just to psychiatrists and biochemists, but that we were going to need sociologists and social workers. Jolliffe said, 'If we are going to find out about the drinking of these patients, we are going to have to go into their neighbourhoods and into their homes, we can't do this only in our laboratories'.

BJA: What happened next?

MK: It took some months to design a study, which ended up as a proposal for a 7-year project. Jolliffe didn't immediately succeed in getting support. He took the proposal to Dr. John Wyckoff, Dean of the Medical School, who thought it was the most wonderful thing that had ever been proposed. But he said, this is going to take a lot of money. The only place where you can get that kind of money is the Rockefeller Foundation. So, in order to do that, he went to Chancellor Chase, Chancellor of New York University, and they went to the Rockefeller Foundation. Dr. Alan Gregg was the Rockefeller man for medicine in those days. He came around and looked us over and he liked what he saw. But the Rockefeller people decided that if they were going to put all that money in this direction (I think it was half-a-million dollars, which doesn't sound very big today) it was important that they should help Jolliffe to build up his scientific reputation. He was quite a young man, as assistant professor. So they thought he should become an international expert, and gave him 20,000 dollars to take a trip to Europe and visit all the people there who knew about alcohol research. And Jolliffe did that.

BJA: What happened when he came home?

MK: Unfortunately, while Jolliffe was still in Europe, Dean Wyckoff died suddenly, and the Rockefellers used that as an excuse for withdrawing from supporting this research. I have always suspected that there was some other reason and that this was just an excuse—we always have had difficulties in getting the big foundations to fund alcoholism research. But in the meantime Dean Wyckoff and Chancellor Chase had decided that this project needed a wide basis of sponsorship and they had formed a national committee to support it. This national committee included practically all the great names in science at that time. And this group was disappointed that the research was not going to be funded after all by the Rockefellers, and they didn't want just to go out of business. So they formed themselves into a scientific committee and created a Research Council on Problems of Alcohol with its main purpose to seek money to aid such work. Actually, this Research Council never succeeded in raising a lot of money—I don't understand the whole story and I was not personally involved. But the most important funding that they got was a grant of 25,000 dollars from the Carnegie Corporation for a review of the biological literature on the effects of alcohol on man. This grant was to my boss, to Jolliffe, and I credit myself a little bit that we got that help because without quite knowing what I was doing I had begun to gather and systematise the literature about alcohol. So we had this grant to review the literature, and we needed somebody to run the review. It was for this purpose that Jolliffe went to Worcester, Massachusetts, and persuaded E. M. Jellinek, who was the biometrician in the schizophrenia research project there, under Roy Hoskins, to come to New York to manage this alcohol review.

BJA: What year was that?

MK: This was now 1939. While the grant was probably made in '38, we started the review in 1939. We took a small suite, two offices, at the New York Academy of Medicine, next to their library which was, at the time, and perhaps still is, the second best medical library in this country. Only what is now the National Medical Library is greater. (It was then the Library of the Surgeon General.) We made this review over a period of about 18 months and reports were beginning to come out and needed publication. One of the scientists on the scientific committee of the Research

Council was Dr. Howard W. Haggard, Director of the Laboratory of Applied Physiology at Yale University, famous for a number of reasons. His research on alcohol, which was done very soon after Prohibition, created a great deal of public interest, and resulted in the Laboratory at Yale receiving many questions about alcohol which Haggard realised that his staff, who were physiologists and biochemists, were not able to answer. So Haggard was interested in a broader perspective on alcohol problems and in 1940, when the review was almost finished, he founded the *Quarterly Journal of Studies on Alcohol.*

BJA: *Initially as a medium for publishing your reports?*

MK: Initially to help with that task, but he was a man with a lot of vision, and he immediately saw it as a journal which would publish many other research reports on alcohol. When the review was finished Haggard invited Jellinek to come to Yale to complete writing up the reports from the review, and also to take on some other work. Jolliffe remained in New York. And Haggard also invited Jellinek's staff to come with him. Martin Gross, a psychiatrist, Anne Roe, a psychologist, Vera Efron, a linguist and mathematician, and myself. Another person who came along with Jellinek to Yale was Dr. Giorgio Lolli. He was originally a physiologist who had been trained at Serianni's Laboratory in Italy, and who eventually became a psychiatrist, interested in treating alcoholism primarily and later other things.

BJA: *What were you—have you given yourself a professional title?*

MK: Nobody was ever able to figure out what I was, but Selden Bacom, when once asked that question, decided that I am a semanticist.

BJA: *What was the general response to the research which then came out of Yale—to Jellinek's project?*

MK: The general response was one of great interest and appreciation. Nobody at that time was doing anything along those lines and a lot of people realised that such work was needed. Society had had a great deal of trouble with alcohol and the great experiment with Prohibition hadn't succeeded. People were worried over what was going to happen next. The various States of the U.S.A. were adopting masses of laws about alcohol, really the same things as had been tried for thousands of years, as the records will show, beginning with Hammurabi, King of Babylon 4,000 years or so ago.

BJA: Already existing academic institutions were not interested?

MK: The Universities were not interested. I think it had to do with the stigma on alcohol. The academic world shied away from it. So that we were, in the 1940s, really alone in trying to do something in this line at Yale. We started with a small staff, but we kept acquiring more people. We acquired a sociologist—Seldon Bacon. He came around to the laboratory one day because he had a project in the jails, where he did some research for the Connecticut Prison Association at their request, and had discovered that most of the people were in jail because they had been drunk. We acquired a legal scholar, a former Dean of a law school, Edward G. Baird. We acquired an educationist, Raymond G. McCarthy. We acquired another sociologist, Robert Straus, an experimental psychologist, John Flynn, a librarian, Rhoda Jackson, an industry specialist, Ralph Henderson, and for brief periods an anthropologist, an economist, and others. My documentation staff grew steadily as with Vera Efron, Hulda Rees Flynn and Sarah Spock Jordy in the lead we undertook the total abstracting and indexing of the world scientific literature on alcohol and many documentation and publication tasks besides the Journal, among them the classified *Abstract Archive,* the *International Bibliography,* and a series of popular pamphlets and a series of scholarly monographs. So now we had a lot of characters around in the Laboratory who had nothing to do with physiology or biochemistry. They were studying alcohol from all kinds of perspectives, and this 'social' representation was bigger than the Laboratory staff of 'hard' scientists. We founded, in about 1943, the Yale Plan Clinics, which were the first public clinics to treat alcoholism, and founded a Summer School of Alcohol Studies, directed by Jellinek with a very broad perspective and with an inter-disciplinary faculty, about the same time. Eventually we became the Center of Alcohol Studies.

62   Addictions

BJA: Haggard's influence? How could he effect all this at Yale?

MK: He was one of the two most popular professors in the University. And also a very good money raiser. So the University let Haggard be.

BJA: What was behind the move from Yale to Rutgers?

MK: We are 20 years later. It sounds like a title of a Dumas book. Twenty years after. A new President was appointed at Yale in 1950. He did not like the Center of Alcohol Studies at all. Worse still, it was located practically across the street from the President's residence. He didn't even like the Laboratory of Applied Physiology. He had an image of Yale in which such activities did not belong, really. He wanted to get rid of the Center, in fact he let us know it in a not very subtle way very soon after he became President. It happened that at the same time, within the next year or two, Haggard retired, first informally, then formally. I think his formal retirement came in the mid-50s. It fell to Selden Bacon to fight the President on this issue. The reason it fell to him was that when Jellinek left Yale to go to the World Health Organization, Bacon succeeded him as Director of the Center of Alcohol Studies. And Bacon is a Bacon of the Bacons. He fought the President and fought him off for 10 years. But finally, in 1960, the Yale Corporation voted that the administration should help the Center of Alcohol Studies to find a more appropriate home.

BJA: Like the Bowery.

MK: Yes—that's what the President hoped.

BJA: So you had your walking papers in 1960.

MK: Well, Bacon did a very shrewd thing. He sent the news that the Center was going to move to the newspapers. It made nationwide headlines. It made the front page of the *New York Times*. There had been jokes, probably originating at Harvard, such as, 'What does Yale have? Yale has Levi Jackson, and the Center of Alcohol Studies'. Levi Jackson was the captain of the football team. And more than the President at Yale didn't enjoy that kind of humor. The result of the newspaper release was that many universities, all over the country, enquired, and we began to negotiate with universities. Now Selden had to be in on all these negotiations, so he took himself a partner to each one. We really had serious negotiations with only three universities, Brown, Columbia and Rutgers. I was the partner in the negotiations with Rutgers. And I liked Mason Gross, the President of Rutgers, very much. And I wanted us to go to Rutgers. We ended up going to Rutgers.

BJA: *The timing?*

MK: We completed these negotiations in 1961 and went to Rutgers in 1962. I moved the documentation division in February 1962 and the rest came two or three months later. Soon after, we were helped by Mr. R. Brinkley Smithers and the Christopher D. Smithers Foundation, as well as the Federal Government money, to erect our own building on the Rutgers science campus.

BJA: *Now, 20 years after, in 1962, had the social climate toward alcohol research changed very much?*

MK: I think it had. For one thing, we were by then able to get considerable support from the Federal Government, from the National Institute of Mental Health. They helped us to make the move to Rutgers and supported us with grants, especially supporting the documentation division with grants, from the beginning in 1962. We had earlier, about in 1945, founded what was to become the National Council on Alcoholism. We called it the National Committee for Education on Alcoholism and we housed it for its first few years. Marty Mann's office was in our building. It could be believable to people that the committee was not another temperance organisation—if it was at Yale, and connected with the Center, if it had this scientific connection. We had also founded the first organisation of educators on alcohol and narcotics. So that there had been a broadening out of interest. A lot of people came to the Summer School each year and went out with a broader conception of alcohol problems and began doing something about them. We—Bacon—

also had a very strong hand in creating the Connecticut Commission on Alcoholism, the first such State commission. A lot of things we did became models for people to do in other places. Other State commissions were created, other Summer Schools were created, other alcoholism clinics were opened, other study centres started to come into existence. And even other alcohol journals began to be published, to the dismay of my staff—for we had had a corner on the market, except for the *British Journal of Addiction*. But I told them, the more other journals that are published, the bigger our circulation will be. And that's how it turned out.

BJA: So there was a growth and groundswell of interest by 1962, very different from the earlier days.

MK: Yes.

BJA: Looking back, do you see any turnings that were missed or wrong steps taken?

MK: I would say, from my viewpoint, that the separation of the National Committee, which was to become the National Council on Alcoholism, from Yale, that divorce, which occurred around 1949 approximately, that was very bad. I was terribly disappointed that it occurred. What happened apparently was that the Committee concentrated totally on alcoholism and helping the suffering alcoholics. It was very natural, because the people who worked in the Committee were mostly members of Alcoholics Anonymous—Marty Mann and Yev Gardner and others. They had started to be interested in alcohol problems, and our staff thought that the National Committee, or the National Council, was going to be a public health organisation like the cancer organisation, or the poliomyelitis or heart organizations, which would, for instance, raise money to support research. The National council didn't do that. Research was the most important thing to the Center, and we were specially interested in the possibility of prevention. The National Council, influenced by its A.A. membership, was not interested in prevention, even though they gave it lip service, or in research. They were interested in helping the alcoholic.

Our staff, and especially Haggard and Bacon, and I guess Jellinek, went along with the split, and actually promoted the divorce. I think I was the only one who didn't want it to take place.

BJA: A different question—with your interest in archives, do you think there may be great sources of important information lying around untapped?

MK: Yes. For example, in Bellevue Hospital I once dug up from the basement all the old records of alcoholic admissions, going back I think to the middle of the last century. At the beginning, the age of admission for alcohol intoxication began at something like 12 years. I then noticed a very interesting fact, that the lowest age of admission rose steadily over time. It got so that 16 became rare, 17, 18. At the beginning of that period very young boys used to go to work, 11 or 12 years old. And getting a paycheck was an entitlement to 'drink like a man.' But later on, youngsters went to school to a later age, and this caused the age of alcoholic admission to rise. Now that's an interesting social phenomenon which might be worth exploring. It makes one wonder what's going on today, when apparently the age of boys and girls getting drunk is dropping. Something has had to have happened in our society to effect such a strange reversal.

BJA: What have been the real underlying changes in society's attitudes to drinking and drinking problems?

MK: There are fashions in the way of looking at things. We had a time when alcohol was blamed for everything. It was blamed for poverty, it was blamed for crime, it was blamed for disease, and this led to doing something extreme and eventually to Prohibition. That produced such problems that you had to get rid of Prohibition. And there followed a reversal of viewpoint. There followed a period when alcohol was unblamed by everyone—it's not alcohol which is causing these diseases, it's the lack of vitamins. It's not alcohol which is causing the poverty, it's that the poverty is causing people to drink, and so on. I think that actually we are now beginning to see the next reversal, so alcohol is again beginning to be blamed for everything. Therefore I think I can predict that after a period of time we will have another shift to unblaming.

BJA: *The future of research?*

MK: I think that not enough has been done by the people who are most strongly concerned about alcoholism to emphasise the need for research and support of research. It's almost as if people who are interested in alcoholism don't really believe that we are ever going to learn to understand what there is behind alcoholism, why it's a disease and how it could be prevented, as has happened with other diseases. I think there is a lack of faith in that kind of outcome which is behind the lack of widespread general public concern for research in this field, such as there is, for example, for research on heart disease and on other diseases, some of which have been essentially conquered as the result of research. There's a different kind of feeling apparently about alcoholism. People who are working in this field should, though, do more to gain public confidence in the possibility—personally, I believe it's probability—that if we keep on researching, we will find out enough about alcoholism not only to be able to treat it successfully in those who already have the disease, but to prevent it through understanding what it is. I would not advocate any one line of research. In such a complex of problems—and benefits—as alcohol use entails, in a disease as complex as alcoholism, we surely need multidisciplinary, multifaceted, multidirectional researches. Someone will eventually integrate them—I think of another Jellinek.

6

Interview with Selden Bacon

SELDEN D. BACON, b. 1909. *Undergraduate and postgraduate training in sociology at Yale: PhD. First research on alcohol problems in 1943. Became Director of Yale Center for Alcohol Studies in 1952, continuing to direct this center on its move to Rutgers and until retirement in 1979. Co-founder of National Committee for Education on Alcoholism, which later became the NCA. Service on many national and international committees.*

BJA: Selden, how did you come to get involved in alcohol studies?

SB: I became involved chiefly because of a request from the State Government of Connecticut, particularly from Chief Justice Maltbie, for a study of people going to jail in that state. There was concern about the growing need for workers in the great rush of war orders that were coming in during 1943; the fact of large numbers of employable people going to prison was not felt to be 'good business'. Originally this study was to be undertaken by professors, deans and the like, but after 3 or 4 months nothing was being done, and finally, I (at the low level of instructor) was asked if I would undertake the survey. I had just made a study of police for my Masters degree, and with a grant from the U.S. Social Science Research Council, I had studied police departments all over the country. For this research on arrest and jails I was to have questionaires which we would apply through volunteer helpers to every person arrested in each of the five largest Connecticut cities and in five of what we called bedrooms towns, adjacent to those cities.

BJA: *And this work was to lead to contact with other Yale researchers?*

SB: As we got into this project I heard of a group at Yale under Howard Haggard, whose name I certainly knew well, who had become primarily concerned with studies in the general field of alcohol physiology. So I went over to 4 Hillhouse Avenue and there I met Dr E. M. Jellinek who was quite interested in what we were proposing to do. He was then coming out with two books, *Alcohol Explored* [by Haggard and Jellinek] and also a brilliant history of psychiatric and medical studies dealing with alcoholism. I became concerned not only with what I could learn from the Laboratory of Applied Physiology (as the Yale Center of Alcohol Studies was then called) but also in learning about the fellowship of Alcoholics Anonymous. In looking for volunteers, to help do the questioning, we had gone to IBM, and one of their staff was a member of AA.

BJA: *How long did it take to complete that study?*

SB: We completed that study in about a year. With more than half of the cases (excluding minor traffic violations) being related to alcohol, the report was finally brought but as a pamphlet called 'Drunkenness in Wartime Connecticut'. It was strongly sociological in perspective, showing the differences in social and demographic background between those arrested for 'alcohol problems', and all other arrested persons. This work also led to proposals for setting up special public facilities to work with alcoholics in an outpatient clinic setting. The Connecticut Prison Association, which had been very important in influencing Judge Maltbie and others to get the original survey conducted, agreed to give two-years' support for the establishment of clinics to be run by the Laboratory of Applied Physiology in both Hartford and New Haven. This led to legislation being passed so that a State Commission could set up its own alcoholism clinics. I was appointed to that first Commission, and at its first meeting was voted as its Chairman. From then on, I had this mixture of policy and administrative concerns with alcoholism and alcohol problems, population sets, and also a sociological interest in defining and describing the type of phenomena we were talking about. And these interests led to my joining the staff of the Laboratory of Applied Physiology on a half-time basis, remaining the rest of the time with the Department of Sociology. I would judge that three important reasons for my getting involved in alcohol studies were, first, my sociological background in the sphere of crime and criminal justice; second, the widely perceived loss of manpower through arrest and jailing (which turned out to be caused in longest part by drunkenness); and, third, the presence of physiologic and psychologic research groups headed by Haggard and Jellinek.

BJA: *Howard W. Haggard, E. M. Jellinek and yourself, were the three most important people in the development of alcohol knowledge during the generation beginning in the 1940s. What was your earliest impression of Jellinek?*

SB: I suppose the first impression I had when I first met him in the old Hill House Street Laboratory, was, 'What a funny little man'. He had extraordinary scope. He clearly knew a great deal about medicine and about psychiatry and much about physiology. He was almost by definition a biometrician and statistician. And I think that his competence in many languages was important: I began to find out that not only could he speak five or six modern languages, but also one or two Central American Indian dialects and one or two African dialects, and he really found it amusing to read texts in eleventh century Latin as a pastime. I began to get a feeling that this man came very close to being what I would call a genius, in that he had many literate or vocal languages and also numerical languages within his grasp, while he could apply this learning to substantive questions and illuminate any analyses by his acquaintance with a variety of philosophies. Sometimes, I must say, I think he would play with questions in order to postpone coming to the real answer. He was an extraordinary academic character. His many abilities, especially in the field of statistics, left me with a feeling I had a great deal to learn from this man. As regards to statistics, I myself was close to zero or subzero competence, having certain ideas that at times would make Jellinek and Vera Efron burst out in laughter.

BJA: So what directions did your work then take?

SB: When I had been there for 3 or 4 months and had finished my more academic study of the arrested people in Connecticut, I asked Jellinek what I should do, pointing out that I was not a psychiatrist and not a physiologist, 'so what do you think, Dr Jellinek?' He finally came up with seven or eight suggestions of what I might do. From my point of view, Jellinek was a statistician, a biologist, a humanist and an historian, but social science was, I thought, really quite remote from his understanding. As a result of his suggestions, I started to write a long letter to 'Bunky', as I was soon calling him, about what I thought a social science approach in this field would be; this formulation did not make any use of the eight or ten suggested studies which he had proposed to me, nor did he ever bring those up again. My long letter, after striking out the 'Dear Bunky', was published as the first memoir of the 'Section of Alcohol Studies' with the title of 'Sociology and the problems of Alcohol'. I can only say that I think that Jellinek was the most all-round intellectual, and almost a paragon, for his scope and his incisive questioning. I don't in any way mean to denigrate some of the other people who were my teachers and later confreres in the field, but Bunky was in some ways a unique personality.

BJA: The big boss, the Director at the Laboratory of Applied Physiology at Yale, was Dr Howard W. Haggard. It was he who brought Jellinek to Yale. He founded the Journal of Studies on Alcohol, he gave Jellinek the means to develop the Center of Alcohol Studies, and he later appointed you to succeed Jellinek as Director of the Center of Alcohol Studies. How do you see Haggard and the perhaps currently underestimated role which he played? How did you and Haggard relate to each other?

SB: There wasn't any question about Howard W. Haggard being the boss, ever. Howard Haggard was one of the ablest public speakers that I ever encountered, whether in dealing with undergraduates at Yale or with professional audiences of physicians or public health personnel, or with the general public. I once noted that I thought he broke every given rule about public speaking He spoke too fast, he seemed to speak miles above the heads of his audience, he made sophisticated jokes and sarcastic remarks, and yet he was a brilliant speaker. His book *Devils, Drugs and Doctors* was a classic. I think Howard Haggard had an historical perception of questions in the fields of health, education and communication, that was almost basic to what I was to perceive as the main thrust of the Center of Alcohol Studies. I'm incompetent to make any judgement about Haggard as a physiologist, but I think he had a broad, positive and intuitively always correct perception of the role of medicine and science and education and knowledge in relation to the whole world of ills and diseases. He was a very impressive person and an enormously successful money-raiser, but he was in some ways rather impersonal. For instance, I do not ever remember having gone to Howard Haggard's house. We often went out to lunch together—Haggard, Jellinek and myself, Greenberg, Keller and McCarthy, and others of the staff, but one never had the feeling of being an 'intimate pal' of Howard Haggard. On the other hand, his relationships with people like Billy Phelps and Clement Fry and even members of the Elizabethan Club were really quite impressive, and, in my own department, both Keller and Davie had the highest regard for Howard Haggard. He was an extreme individualist and was often at odds with The University Administration, but he was a powerful character in this field and, as you commented, it was through Haggard that Jellinek came into alcoholism studies and was enabled to make his enormous contribution.

BJA: *And how did Jellinek and Haggard get on together?*

SB: It is amusing that in many ways Jellinek was ill at ease with Haggard. I can remember Jellinek lecturing to the school one summer, say in '45 or '46, and he was getting along beautifully. For Jellinek could give a very bad lecture or he could give a very good lecture. But there he was up on the platform and going along elegantly, when Howard Haggard walked in and sat down in the back row; all of a sudden Jellinek's presentation dropped to his worst. Haggard was an executive in every sense of the word; he knew how to deal with people, he certainly knew how to deal with me. He and I, I think, got along very well. I was the only—what can I call it?—almost the only typical 'Yalie' on the whole staff, and this amused Haggard and he knew just how to use it. This was, perhaps, one of the reasons why he decided that I would be the better person to be in charge after Jellinek left, because I might be able to get along with the bureaucrats in charge of the University. I think he felt that I would stand up for the Laboratory more effectively than some of the others on the staff.

BJA: Selden, you were involved in creating at Yale the world's first interdisciplinary centre of alcohol studies, and later you succeeded Jellinek as its Director. What do you think is the value of such a specialized study center? What's it for? What should it be?

SB: Well, that is a question which has bothered a good many people and I think the answer, to date, despite my belief to the contrary, has been that there probably should not be a fully rounded centre, involving half-a-dozen different, quite different, disciplines. I feel that it has enormous value. One of the major thrusts, as I saw it, persisting from at least 1943 or '44, right up until today, has been an appeal to recognise the complexity of what we are studying, that it is not simple. It is 'the issue', not the substance alcohol, which has brought this field into being. It could be that scientists would, for instance, have been very interested in alcohol because of its various properties. But that has not been the basis of any major continuing interest in the field. Rather, it has been matters of trade, matters of behaviour, matters of crime, of disease, or immorality, which have always stimulated and allowed support for continuing study in this field. It was our experience through the time we were at Yale, and also at Rutgers, that we could bring in a person who was an expert in, say, experimental psychology, economics, or something like that, and it would take them up to two years to acquaint themselves with the larger field of alcohol phenomena so that they did not burrow down into tiny little specialized holes. In order for the biologist or the sociologist or the anthropologist or the psychologist or the criminologist or the tax expert to really make a contribution to this field, I think they have to know what the larger aspects of human and group use of alcohol may be, and, what people over the past 150 years have written about or tried out. There are no simple answers; no sociological answer, no physical answer, no theological or other type of answer, which will alone solve our alcohol problems. If researchers and scholars are to make a contribution, their contribution must fit that larger field. Jellinek was an awfully good example of someone meeting this challenge.

BJA: A personal question. You've been described as a Bacon of the Bacons; in fine, an aristocrat. How came you to leave the comfortable castle of the Professorship in Sociology at Yale, to tangle with the problems of the lowly drunkards on Skid Row? To engage yourself in studying a subject so stigmatised in the early 1940s that the Yale administration became unhappy over its presence on that hallowed campus?

SB: Well, I'm not sure about the aristocracy. I do take some pride, perhaps, in a fairly well authenticated claim that about 15 generations back I can consider a relationship to Francis Bacon, for whom I have a great admiration. Perhaps the New Haven Bacons consider themselves aristocracy. But I don't know that I shared that view. If so, I was the most unconscious aristocrat, which may have allowed a more perfect form of snobbery than otherwise would be possible. I found the intellectual challenge of the work very great; namely, I was able to translate what I had somehow picked up from studies of social science into this alcohol field and, so far as I was aware, no one else had done this. So it was new, I was there first, and this must have been exceedingly gratifying to the young ego. Secondly, I had a background, academically, in school and college, that was mostly what you would term humanistic. But I think I knew enough even in 1944 and '45, to sense that alcoholism was not limited to what were called Skid Row drunks. My early experience with AA made this very clear. There weren't too many Skid Row bums in any AA groups that I met with. I don't want anybody to think that I was a member of AA. I wasn't. I never paid the price of admission. And then, the people I associated with academically in the alcohol field were anything but social scientists. Rather, they were biochemists, physiologists, psychologists, biometricians, lawyers, public health experts. I was bringing in something new and, at the same time, learning something from other people. So it was mutually very rewarding.

BJA: Which of your studies would you consider the most important?

SB: Well, I don't think I would have much question on that. I don't like the title, but it is 'Sociology and the Problems of Alcohol'. It had a sub-title: 'Foundations for a Sociological Study,' which is much better than the next phrase—'Of Drinking Behavior'. It was a very general statement of a social science approach to drinking phenomena. I borrowed heavily from almost everybody who was important to me as a graduate student, particularly the Sumner-Keller background (Albert Galloway Keller), Bronislaw Malinowski, and a mixture which I got at second-hand from stimulus-response and Freudian psychologies. In this nexus I could see the data gathering, and analysis could become an organised and meaningful whole. Incidentally, that monograph started out as a letter to Bunky Jellinek. And somehow it made sense not only to some other sociologists, but also to others in the alcohol field. A rather strange combination. A Mr Piel, who was one of the better known brewers in America, wrote me a letter telling me how important he thought this publication to be. I got letters not only from sociologists, but from some members of AA and from several clergymen of different denominations, with whom, apparently, I had been able to communicate. Later on I was able to translate some of these ideas into Jellinek's portrayal of the progressive phases in alcoholism. I remember, in 1949, bursting into a seminar Bunky was conducting in Texas and saying, 'I think I have something to add to that progression'. I took over for 25 minutes and, using the format I had in 'Sociology and the Problems of Alcohol', I translated his steps into social science terminology. And Bunky said, 'Do you know, I think that's a very clever idea'. And that was one of the most flattering remarks I ever got in my life. I think that, in a basic sense, this was my most fundamental contribution and, even when I look back at it, I think it was pretty good. I can't say that for all the things I've written.

BJA: From the viewpoint of your conception of what a study centre about drinking and alcohol problems would be, do you feel that the move from Yale to Rutgers was successful?

SB: Well, that's very difficult because of the word 'successful'. Successful for what? The move kept the centre, which had been at

Yale, alive, and allowed the Classified Abstract Archive, the Journal of Studies on Alcohol, and the Summer School of Alcohol Studies, and a core of interdisciplinary research people, to continue for at least the next 15–20 years. Yes, in that sense you could say it was successful. Whether the over-all field was helped by that move, is very hard to say. It is true that the antagonism felt by the then president of Yale to the Center and the Laboratory was very strong and a continuing burden. There were at least four different occasions over ten years on which I received word that the Laboratory was to close up within one month. Once, this was to happen within six days, and three days later over 200 students and 10 additional faculty were arriving for the Summer school. And that sort of harassment, which was abetted by a certain group in the Yale Medical School, did not help in any way. On the other hand, if perhaps I had been a more able diplomat, the Center could have stayed at Yale. That a State University was in many ways a more appropriate place, and that Rutgers, especially under the guidance of Mason Gross, its president, was extraordinarily helpful, could hardly be denied. We were able to keep the Center going because the field was just about moving into high gear in terms of mass acceptance, organisation and the like. And, yes, we had invitations from several institutions. I think the Rutgers administration and the Rutgers locale and the Rutgers community, were extraordinarily favourable and proved to be very helpful.

BJA: Well now, what do you today think are the most important directions for research in the alcohol field? Social or Biological studies?

SB: If you are going to force that choice, I'll go right out on a limb and say that I think that social science studies, at this time, are without any question the more important. The reason being that the biologists are, up to the present, far, far ahead in terms of methods, measurements, knowledge. But the concern, which allows and makes possible the fruition of scientific research, stems from what the public of a given society thinks to be the problems. I think the difficulties facing us today have to do with, not the liver, or the kidney, or the genes, but have to do with 'what is a problem?' 'How do you know?' 'How do you describe it?' 'How do you measure it? 'How do you define it?' It is not sufficient to pick up a word, such as alcoholism or drunkenness, and blandly go on and say, 'well, that's the problem,' when it turns out that many of the people who are directly involved differ violently on what they consider those words to refer to. I think the social scientists have to be able to give working definitions (I don't say final definitions), of problems and categories of problems, and relate those problematic phenomena to drinking phenomena (most of which in most societies are not problems) as well as to other aspects of living. Then we will be able to make use of more specialised sciences and use the knowledge they give us to greater effect.

BJA: *Some sociologists have recently denigrated what they call 'the medical model of alcoholism', as well as the disease conception of alcoholism. How do you as a sociologist see the disease conception, alcoholism as a disease? Is that formulation in conflict with the sociological view?*

SB: Well, I suppose I would be almost pigeon-holed as a sociological perceiver of these data, although I think it must be agreed that I did a great deal between 1945 and, say, 1960, to communicate widely the notion of alcoholism as a disease, so that clinics and other therapeutic developments and research could occur. I don't think too much of the disease concept of alcoholism as a final or complete description of alcoholism. That there is a disease aspect of alcoholism I would say is undeniable. Until we get a working definition of alcoholism, however, I don't believe that it will do very much good to promote a disease label. There are going to be many problems related to the lives of people who drink in such a fashion that they agree drinking creates problems for them and all those around them. Under what labels are we going to put that behaviour, and what part of it is to be called alcoholism? If disease is seen from a sociological or anthropological perspective, I think it would be defined as those conditions and behaviors which are responded to by what is called the medical profession, doctor, shaman or whatever. But the problems they deal with may change. It may be that people who swear a great deal will come to be regarded as sick people and we will have cases of swearingitis.

It may be that people who are lazy will come to be viewed as people who should be attended by a physician and his associated aides and so forth, and so laziness will now become lazyitis. We can go on through all sorts of behaviours and conditions which at one time in a given society were apparently a crime or a sin (or something perfectly wonderful) and which, at various times, have or have not been dealt with by those called doctors. If the medical group, whatever it is, becomes enormously psychological in its orientation, then psychological labels are going to be attached. If the responses to such problems, such frightening matters, come from, let's call them, social engineers, then I suppose the terminology will become sociological or of a social work category. But whatever the terminology which is used by the people who everybody agrees should be in charge this does not mean that their terminology provides an adequate basis for describing that condition. The medical description is by itself though important, quite inadequate, but, by the same token, it seems to me that there is little question that if you give a certain type of sociologist complete command, so that he only studies the customs and the sanctions and fails to study psychological traits and the physiology, you will again have a very poor picture of alcoholism. I think the same is true in respect to many great areas of human problems, whether or not they deal with alcohol—in every instance we are going to have to produce a more broadly oriented picture that one art or one research discipline can provide.

BJA: Some leading sociologists, in Finland, Canada and some in the U.S.A., have recently advocated that to reduce alcohol problems, there should be government policy to reduce the availability of alcohol. Do you agree that such measures would be effective?

SB: By and large I do not think they would be too effective by themselves. This is one of the better examples of oversimplification, of failure to gain data which would be relevant to what the advocates of such measures have in mind. Many of the people who have made the studies which allegedly underpin this approach have used extraordinarily refined, careful and sophisticated measurements. But many of these investigators have, in fact, never observed drinking problems, let alone drinking. They work entirely on theoretical assumptions, for example that 'if there is so much alcohol available then it must be consumed', and 'the more that is consumed the more problems there will be.' This is a very nice theory, especially for people who want a quick, simple answer which can be put into operation by somebody else. That there is a direct relationship between amounts consumed and what are called problems, is a figment of the imagination *unless one can define what is meant by 'problem'*. To my knowledge the key item in measurements of this sort has been the relationship between recorded cirrhosis, and amounts of alcohol legally sold and recorded in given jurisdiction, divided by the number of people, perhaps only those of 'drinking age', in the area. The reports frequently obtained a high correlation between larger amounts of alcohol and higher cirrhosis rates. It is interesting to note that in this country, the U.S.A., of all the problems of alcohol which have attracted attention, cirrhosis is only a very, very small part. In clinics, whether there would appear to be more than 10 or 12 per cent of cirrhosis among alcoholism patients is doubtful. In other problems, such as youthful drinking misbehaviour, automobile accidents influenced by alcohol, and so on, it is doubtful whether even 1 or 2 per cent of those involved would be recognised as cirrhotic. There are also all the complexities related to distribution of drinking levels within the population. On this basis it is stated that problems will rise or fall with alcohol consumption. I find this quite unbelievable. It becomes an imaginary, very simple and beautiful system in a closed mathematical sense. There is a good deal of theory (and even a little data) to indicate that mass reductions of availability will principally affect users who are not the target of the programmes. This is a good example of taking a single aspect of a very complex set of phenomena and then putting into effect a simple answer.

BJA: Do you, as philosopher in both sociology and alcohology, do you see it as appropriate for sociologists to go beyond research and become advocates of specific types of legal measures?

SB: Social scientists have a great contribution to make by gathering, analysing and presenting definitions and pictures and explanations of what it is that is happening. But for them to join policy groups is a very dangerous matter. Dangerous from the point of view of effective information being gathered and analysed and communicated. I know that I was accused, and perhaps in quite justifiable fashion, for having an almost schizophrenic career, in that at times I seemed to be the sociologist trying to study group behaviours and group processes in relation to this matter, while on the other hand I was active in helping to develop a movement. But it is also true that at the beginning of any movement, somebody is going to have to help in developing policy. Many of the earlier directors and board members and leaders in this 1945–1970 alcoholism treatment movement were directly or indirectly from social science. I think their activism affected their gathering of information, influenced the questions they were asking, and gave a particular policy slant to their publications which probably diminished the usefulness of their scientific contributions. I remember Dr. Haggard used to say that research starts with the public, then, in some instances, gets taken over by the scientific researchers, and finally when they are through, gets turned back to the public to accept or reject or compromise in some form of application. The scientists are somewhere in the middle of this process and they often cannot divorce themselves from policies and applications. This is a very difficult problem. At the moment, however, the need in social science is for more scientific study and far less involvement with policy and administrative operations. That researchers can contribute to policy and consequent action by gathering disciplined data, providing analysis, indicating areas of question, testing applications and proposing options for action is clear enough, but this is a far cry from encouraging, backing, or carrying out programmes.

7

Interview with Robert Straus

ROBERT STRAUS, b. 1923. Undergraduate and postgraduate training in sociology, Yale University. From 1947–1956 various academic and research positions in Yale and Connecticut before in 1956 becoming associated with University of Kentucky: Professor and Chairman, Department of Behavioral Science, Kentucky 1956–87, and now Professor Emeritus. Chairman, Cooperative Commission on the Study of Alcoholism 1966–69 and work on many national committees. Member, Institute of Medicine of National Academy of Sciences, Phi Beta Kappa, Sigma XI.

BJA: *I know that you have been studying alcohol abuse and alcohol-related issues for more than 40 years. One thing I'd like to ask is how did this all get started?*

RS: Well, it was pretty much by chance. It began in 1945 when I was a graduate student at Yale. I had recently been married and was looking for a job to augment our income. Selden Bacon, with whom I had taken a course in Criminology, offered me a job at twenty dollars a week for 20 hours a week. The assignment was to go to the skid row area of New Haven and interview men who were working at a Salvation Army Men's Service Center to see what could be learned about alcohol use among homeless men. I interviewed 203 men who were admitted to the Center over a period of a year. And that's how it started.

BJA: *And prior to that you really hadn't been interested or involved in the alcohol field?*

RS: No, actually my major interest as a sociologist was in health care. That was before medical sociology had been recognized as an area of study. In fact, sociologists were ignoring medicine and health. It was hardly ever mentioned in sociological texts. But I was interested, primarily, because of my family background. I had a great uncle and an uncle who had been physicians and a grandfather who was a pharmacist. My mother, throughout my entire memory of her, was a volunteer at the Yale-New Haven Hospital where she developed programs for diversional therapy for children. This actually became a model for a national trend. She wrote a book called *Keep Busy*,[1] about things to do to amuse sick children in bed, which was the first thing of its kind that was ever published. That's where my primary interests lay. In fact, my dissertation at Yale started off having nothing to do with alcohol. I was looking at the history of public medical care and trying to identify conditions that were associated with the assumption by governments of responsibility for the health care of particular groups. As it turned out the early history of public medical care was primarily a history of medical care for seamen. That was the title of my dissertation when it was published, *Medical Care for Seamen*.[2] But when you get into the whole subject of seamen and their life style and health care needs, alcohol has played a prominent role. So in a way the interests of my dissertation and my alcohol research were not unrelated but certainly the relationship was accidental.

BJA: *So you were working on alcohol and the homeless and your doctoral dissertation at the same time?*

RS: Yes, I received my Ph.D. degree in 1947 and my dissertation was published as a book in 1950. The report on 'Alcohol and the Homeless Man' was my first publication and it was a 45-page article that appeared in the *Quarterly Journal of Studies on Alcohol* in 1946.[3]

BJA: *So what were the major findings when you interviewed this large number of homeless men?*

RS: One was that although a significant number of these men used alcohol heavily, it wasn't nearly as universal as was then generally believed. As I recall, it was just under 90%. But a good many of those who used alcohol did not drink in the way most alcoholics do. They didn't appear to be addicted. They had pretty good control of their drinking and they could go for several days without drinking if they had a job and a place to eat and sleep. Their drinking seemed to be an adaptation to a life style which was very much dominated by dependency. We learned that a high percentage of these men came from broken families, many at least by their adolescent years had only one parent, and many had experienced some kind of institutional living quite early in their lives. This was either a child-rearing institution or in the military as soon as they were of age. Their subsequent life patterns were characterized by moving from one kind of situation to another in which the basic necessities of life were provided and dependency was reinforced. They might have been inmates in an institution. They might have had live-in jobs in an institution, or in other kinds of work that provided a place to live, food and a regimented routine. Examples included railroad labor camps, lumber camps and the merchant marine. In general, we characterized these men as undersocialized. They hadn't learned the skills for getting along in normal society, making their own decisions, providing for themselves. And so they had drifted from one highly dependent way of living to another, and alcohol use seemed to become part and parcel of this. Particularly, they seemed to feel a need to drink when their other dependency needs weren't being met. Many of these men, once they were being taken care of, didn't express the same need for alcohol that we tend to think of in a truly addicted person. This was a finding that was of some interest at that time because it was different from prevailing assumptions. We first saw this pattern in the New Haven Study and then, a few years later, Raymond McCarthy and I did a study of about 450 skid row men on the bowery in New York City. Essentially, we found pretty much the same patterns there. In fact, we called the report based on the New York Study, 'Nonaddictive Pathological Drinking Patterns of Homeless Men'.[4] We stressed the nonaddiction aspect of it.

Another thing that came out of the New Haven Study which had a profound effect on my career was my meeting a man, whom I've called Frank Moore. He was an unusually intelligent and articulate person. After I had talked with him a number of times, he agreed to provide a life history. In 1948 we published a paper on the first 40 years of this man's life.[5] He had had an unusual childhood which led to institutional living, dependency on the military, prison and a number of live-in job settings, and the development of alcoholism. He and I then decided that we would continue to record the events of his life. I was thus able to follow prospectively the life of this man, who was essentially a homeless alcoholic through some 350 unusually well-written letters that he wrote to me, through occasional personal meetings, through contacts with his mother who was living for part of this time, and through contacts with people whom he encountered in various institutions. Shortly after his death in 1972, we published a book called *Escape from Custody*[6] which included a summary of his early life as he had reported it retrospectively, and then a 27-year prospective record of his life from ages 41 to 68 which was largely based on his letters and our meetings. It was a very unusual opportunity for a behavioral scientist to be able to study a human life in this way.

BJA: It was a fascinating book. One question I wondered about in reading it was what triggered this interest for you when Frank Moore walked in? What insight made Frank Moore the choice for this?

RS: It was a mutual kind of interest. He was an unusually intelligent man. He told a 'truth is stranger than fiction story' of his early life which I probably never would have published if it hadn't been corroborated by his mother. He had intellectual insights that absolutely set him aside from every other person I contacted in this homeless man study. On the other side, he was a man who was enormously lonely, in part because his intelligence set him aside from people who were the natural peers of his lifestyle. I provided someone who was interested in him, who treated him as an intelligent human being and respected what he had to offer over the years. I also supported him in a number of ways; primarily through showing interest in him, but also, for example, by sending him books and providing clothing and chocolate fudge which he loved. I also sent him some money almost every time I wrote to him which was approximately 350 times in response to each of his letters to me. I made efforts to keep in contact with him and was probably the only friend he had on a sustained basis.

BJA: Now I wonder if you can describe what the study of alcohol was like in the historical context of the immediate post World War II era. Was alcohol an accepted area of study or was Bob Straus sort of on the fringe in terms of sociology?

RS: Everyone who was studying alcohol in almost any discipline in those days was on the fringe. The people in biochemistry, physiology and medicine who were studying alcohol were on the fringe. The people in psychology were on the fringe and, yes, the people in sociology were on the fringe. I think part of that had to do with the uneasiness of the society over alcohol, coming out of the prohibition experience. With the field still dominated by the extremes of wet and dry, drinking was either good or evil. The scientists who were involved tried to walk a neutral path, but there were constant attempts to paint them as being for or against alcohol. Another factor was that alcoholism was highly stigmatized. It was considered a sign of moral degradation. It was hidden. It wasn't discussed. In fact, when I first went into the field, most of the existing descriptions of the characteristics of alcoholics were based on captive populations, such as homeless men, jailed inebriates or inmates of mental hospitals. These provided a very distorted impression of the nature of alcoholism. Scientists who became involved in alcohol studies tended to derive some of this stigma associated with alcoholism. Many of their peers felt that it was not an appropriate field to be involved in. The group at Yale who worked on alcohol research were quite courageous because their activities were an obvious embarrassment to many of their professional colleagues. There was a movement at Yale, which succeeded eventually, to get rid of the Center of Alcohol Studies. The professors of English, the professors of Classical Literature, the professors of History weren't comfortable to have the Yale name associated with the publicity that their colleagues in Alcohol Studies were getting.

86 Addictions

BJA: So it was essentially a taboo topic in a lot of ways.

RS: I think taboo topic is a good term.

BJA: It's hard to imagine, given the scope of both the problem and the study today.

RS: We've come a long way.

BJA: Could you talk about some of the people who were important in the field at that time and in your life and the forming of your long-term career?

RS: Selden Bacon has to be the most significant person. Selden is the one who offered me an opportunity to work in the field. Selden supported my career in an extraordinarily unselfish way. For example, the alcohol and the homeless man study was Selden's idea. He made the arrangements. He hired me to collect the data and then he just assumed that I would write and publish the report in my own name. He provided a great deal of help, but there was never any question of even co-authorship. When one thinks of many academic practices, this was an unusually generous move on his part. He was also very supportive when my dissertation was defended at Yale, even though it was not in the alcohol field. Later on, in our two major collaborative studies which were co-authored, it was at Selden's initiative that I received credit as the first-named author. Selden was a very brilliant, imaginative person. I often wonder what might have happened for the field if Selden hadn't been drafted into heavy administrative responsibilities at the peak of his productivity as a scholar. His personal contributions to the field are still thought provoking and significant.

There are many other major people at Yale to be mentioned. Howard Haggard really launched the alcohol research program at Yale and was Director of the laboratory and Chairman of the Department of Applied Physiology. He actually started doing research on alcohol in the 30's before the war. I didn't know Haggard very well because at about the time I came into the field, he was drafted by the University to head a major fund raising development program and after that he moved into a gradual retirement. Another significant person was E. M. 'Bunky' Jellinek, a biometrician, who was brought to Yale by Haggard in the late 30's. Jellinek was a man of amazing intellectual depth and a man credited with much of the pioneer work in moving the field scientifically. I have mixed feelings about Jellinek. He was brilliant, but he loved to play intellectual games and I have long felt that his report on phases in the development of alcoholism,[7] which had a very significant impact on the field, was taken far more seriously and was popularized much more than it deserved or than Jellinek intended. The phases became so well known, that for a long time, when other investigators asked alcoholics to describe their drinking histories, they tended to get a recitation of the phases. I believe that the impact of that report was to create and reinforce a false impression of homogeneity and to delay the important recognition of heterogeneity in alcoholic experiences.

Ray McCarthy, an educator and a very close personal friend, was my colleague on the second homeless man study. Still living and currently very active in alcohol research related to the elderly and to women, Edith S. Gomberg, is a psychologist who was also at Yale at the time. And by all means, I should mention Mark Keller. Mark, another man of great intellectual depth, was brought to Yale to edit the *Quarterly Journal of Studies in Alcohol* which was started in New Haven in 1940. Although Mark had a limited formal education, he is a true scholar of amazing knowledge. Over the years, Mark probably developed as great a breadth of understanding of work that was being done on alcohol in many different disciplines as anyone else I know. He is a man who has the capacity intellectually to understand biological research and social and behavioral research with equal clarity and he has never been inhibited by discipline boundaries because he never studied any of the disciplines in a formal way. There are many others who might well be mentioned, but these are some of the giants with whom I have had the privilege of working closely.

BJA: *Just how long were you involved in alcohol studies at Yale?*

RS: After 2 years of working part-time while I was a graduate student, the best job I was offered was a full-time appointment in Applied Physiology at Yale. I then served for 6 years as a member of that faculty, primarily doing the research on alcohol studies. The Applied Physiology Department was the home of what became the Yale Center of Alcohol Studies. I was there part-time from 1945 to 1947 and full-time from 1947 to 1953.

BJA: *What do you think were your most significant products out of that period?*

RS: We've mentioned the homeless man studies and the life history. In 1947, Selden Bacon and I began a study of drinking attitudes and practices of college students in the United States. We included 27 colleges of various types throughout the United States and about 17,000 students. I think this was probably the first truly national survey of the drinking patterns of any group. It provided an opportunity to address a number of stereotypes about college drinking that turned out to be terribly inaccurate. One of the major assumptions at the time was that there was something specific to a college experience that influenced the drinking of students. We found actually that the drinking patterns of students were correlated more with their parents practices and attitudes than with anything that was specific to the college setting. This study provided an opportunity to learn a good deal about survey research. This was before the days of the computer and we had to analyse our data on an IBM counter-sorter machine. This took cards on which coded answers to various questions were punched, and counted and sorted them into particular pockets according to the coded information. We ran that machine for about twelve hours a day for more than a year in order to analyse only part of the data. It was an interesting experience. We would run our data through the machine all day and then go over our findings in the evening and decide what we wanted to run the next morning. Today our entire analysis could be made on a computer in a few hours. *Drinking in College*[8] was an attempt to look at the practices and attitudes and values of college students in the context of major differences in drinking patterns in the United States; geographically, according to different religious backgrounds, and according to many other socio-economic criteria. The study is still being cited when people look at drinking by college students today.

The second study that I would mention was one that Selden Bacon and I did of the characteristics of alcoholism clinic patients. In the early 40's, there weren't any special treatment programs for alcoholics. Alcoholics Anonymous had started in the late 30's and was still in its infancy. One part of the Yale Center program was the development of two experimental clinics. There were called 'Yale Plan Clinics' because the Yale establishment didn't want the word alcoholism associated with them. They were designed to see how effectively alcoholics could be treated on an outpatient basis. Ironically, they were started with the idea that they might help relieve the pressure on jails, but the typical population of arrested inebriates wasn't able to use these outpatient clinics because they had no community roots. Instead, once these clinics received a little publicity, there was an outpouring of people seeking treatment who had jobs and families. It was the previously hidden alcoholics who came around and began to seek clinical services. Well, after a couple of years, this pattern was emulated throughout the State of Connecticut. The Yale Plan Clinics were taken over by a newly established state-supported Connecticut Commission on Alcoholism and a number of state-supported programs, largely based on the Yale Plan, were established in other parts of the country. We were able to get records from the first nine outpatient clinics in the United States and look at the characteristics of their first 2023 male patients. We called the study *Alcoholism and Social Stability*[9] because, in contrast with the then prevailing stereotypes of alcoholics as primarily disturbed or impoverished skid row type individuals, we found the majority of the alcoholics who were being treated in these clinics were still married and living with their spouses; they held relatively steady jobs; they had lived in the same communities and often the same homes for a significant period of time. So, although there was some instability compared with the general population, when compared with prevailing assumptions about alcoholism, there was a good deal of stability. This was a very important finding in terms of dealing with the stigma of alcoholism. Because as we were able to describe alcoholism as something associated with people who were not totally disreputable, I think more and more people were willing to come out of the closet and seek help.

One other study that has a warm place in my heart, although it wasn't all that significant in terms of the field, was one I did with Phyllis Williams based on diaries maintained by a group of Italian-Americans in which they recorded notes on their drinking and related events.[10]

BJA: That's one of my favourite studies.

RS: It was certainly one of my favourites because of the depth and variety of information we received when we simply asked people to write down everyday what they had had to drink, along with notes on such matters as the circumstances of their drinking, what was going through their minds, the association between their drinking and other things they were doing, the people they were with, the meals they were eating and the meaning of alcohol to them. Methodologically, it was a study that demonstrated the kind of richness and meaning of data that one can obtain from human beings who are reasonably motivated. That study also helped dispel the myth that there is something distinct and homogeneous that we can call Italian drinking (or French drinking or German drinking or Spanish drinking) because there was considerable variety in the drinking experiences and patterns of these people. One striking finding was that the drinking patterns of individuals were correlated with the nature and extent of their assimilation into American society. There were Italians who had been in this country for 30 and 40 years who were living in relative isolation in Italian neighborhoods whose drinking was still like that of Italians in Italy. At the other extreme were people who had been here only 3 or 4 years but who were living in primarily American neighborhoods and had become rapidly assimilated to American patterns of living, eating and drinking. This is a relatively unknown study today, but I think if it as one of the more significant pieces of my work during that period.

BJA: I think of that study because along with alcohol studies in general, the hallmark for me of your work has been the emphasis on the meaning, dimensions and the importance of qualitative analysis. I guess it was 1953 when you decided to leave Yale.

RS: Well, I left in 1953 but I actually made the decision a year or two earlier.

BJA: Could you tell us about what motivated that. I imagine that was not an easy decision.

RS: No, it really wasn't. Because I don't know of anyone who's had a better opportunity to concentrate on meaningful research early in a career than I was given by Selden Bacon and the others at Yale. In explaining the move, there were three things that need to be considered. One was that I was born and grew up in New Haven. I had taken three degrees at Yale. The only time I had been away was for a stint in the Army during World War II. I'd given a lot of thought to the importance of changing communities and universities in terms of my personal growth. A second consideration was my major interest in health, medicine and patient care. This had been sustained during the period that I was working at Yale, through summer and weekend opportunities to do some staff studies for the Connecticut Governor's Commission on Health Resources which was headed by William R. Willard, then an Assistant Dean in the Yale Medical School. I developed a close working association with Bill Willard. In 1951, he went to Syracuse to become Dean of the State University of New York's Upstate Medical Center there. Shortly after that, I was facing the question of whether I wanted to devote my entire career to alcohol research. I felt that I either had to make a break then or that I would be cutting myself out of alternatives. Having grown up in New Haven, having had this long experience at Yale, and having the broader medical interest, I decided to make the break. So I wrote a few letters, one of them to Bill Willard. I had an immediate response, saying that he had decided to expand the base of medical education at Syracuse to include the social and behavioral sciences and he had thought of me as someone with whom he'd like to talk. So we made a trip up to Syracuse and in the spring of 1952, he offered me a job and I accepted for a year later. The reason for the delay was that I was committed to finishing *Drinking in College* and two or three of the other studies that I was involved in at the time. It was a hard decision to make but it was a decision for which there were a number of fairly compelling reasons. It was a decision based on the attraction of another opportunity, but made difficult by the wonderful opportunity I had had at Yale.

BJA: My guess would be that at that time behavioral science and medical education was probably also a taboo topic to some extent.

RS: It certainly was among most medical educators. The job that Bill Willard created at Syracuse was the first position for a social scientist on a medical school faculty that was supported by the basic budget of the school. There were a few other social scientists that the Russell Sage Foundation was supporting on a 1- or 2-year residency basis in various hospitals and medical schools. But Dr Willard made a commitment that carried the message of his conviction that the social and behavioral sciences should be basic to the education of physicians. Although I thought I was going there primarily to do research, when I arrived in Syracuse, Dean Willard had allotted 3 hours a week in the curriculum of first-year medical students for a course in social science. The 3 hours a week had been taken from Anatomy. I remember particularly during that first year, whenever any student had a problem in Anatomy, they were told by the faculty in Anatomy that "If it wasn't for that 3 hours that our misguided Dean took and gave to this ridiculous social science course, you wouldn't be having any trouble with anatomy". This made for quite a challenge.

BJA: *How do you think the switchover affected your perspectives on alcohol studies and research?*

RS: Strange as it may seem, after I left Yale where there was a concentration of expertise on alcohol, I found that I was in greater demand. People who were looking for someone to give a talk or provide consultation about alcohol and alcohol problems didn't have many places they could turn to other than Yale. So when they found that there was someone at the State University of New York, this may have seemed like a little variety. I don't think I lost any credibility in making the move. I think, perhaps for curious reasons, I gained it. Also, *Drinking in College* was published just after I arrived in Syracuse and it received a fair bit of publicity on a national level as well as locally. I was quickly involved on committees, giving lectures and consulting in the Syracuse community, in New York State and with a number of national organizations having to do with alcohol. I also started some research at the Veterans Administration Hospital in Syracuse, studying institutional dependency in a select group of men whose records showed at least ten admissions to a VA Hospital. I wanted people who were institutionally dependent. Of course, it turned out that almost everyone of these individuals had a drinking problem.

BJA: *During this time you continued the life history with Frank Moore.*

RS: Oh, yes. That was interesting. While I was in New Haven, we saw each other fairly frequently. He was an itinerant and he was following a route through southern New England. He would be in New Haven for a while and then he might go to New London, Providence, Boston, Wooster, Springfield, maybe down to Hartford, over to Troy-Albany, down to Mount Vernon, Bridgeport and back to New Haven. That was his geographic territory and when he would get restless or get drunk, he would move from one place to another. When he came to New Haven, I usually heard from him in the middle of the night. He often called from a bar and was usually drunk. I'd go down, get him a room in a cheap hotel, and we would sit somewhere where he was comfortable, drinking coffee and talking. I tried a number of times to get him out to my house, but he wasn't comfortable doing that. Then, when we moved to Syracuse, Frank moved. His new circuit was Troy-Albany, Utica, Syracuse, Rochester, Buffalo and down to Binghamton, across the southern tier of New York, back east to Mount Vernon or Poughkeepsie and up to Albany to Troy again. It was a very similar arrangement. Unpredictably I'd get a call from Frank, almost always at night. I always tried to see him if there was any way. That went on throughout the 3-1/2-year period that we were in Syracuse. When we left Syracuse and came to Lexington, Kentucky, Frank started down this way, but he broke his leg jumping from a freight car in Pittsburgh. While he was in Pittsburgh, he was advised against coming further south. He was told, I think quite correctly, that the jails didn't have the amenities that they had in New England. So he went back to New England. We continued the life story through correspondence for about 10 years until eventually I was able to re-establish personal contacts with him during the last few years of his life.

BJA: *You had a fairly quick geographic shift to Lexington, Kentucky.*

RS: Things were going well in Syracuse. We had built a house and had been in it only about 9 months when one night Dr. Willard came around and told of being invited to visit Lexington where the

State was planning to build a new medical center and had asked him to come as the Vice-President of the University and founding Dean of the Medical School. He said that if he decided to go, he hoped I'd come with him. I looked around this nice house we had built and thought, "Oh my, we're not going to be here very long". My wife, Ruth, as she has always been was supportive of the move because it was an exciting professional opportunity. It did not take long to make the decision. We came to Lexington in 1956 and had the opportunity of starting absolutely from scratch in planning the facilities and program, and recruiting people for a new medical school and medical center. We asked colleagues in other medical schools, "If you had the chance to start over, what would you do differently?", and we collected all their suggestions and tried to do many of these things.

BJA: *You seemed not have wanted for another enormous challenge. That's quite a shift from an established medical center to building your own.*

RS: It was a great experience.

BJA: *Did the move to Kentucky shift your focus any in terms of your participation in the alcohol field?*

RS: I was able to continue involvement in alcohol issues. I had done a couple of community studies in Syracuse, in addition to the VA dependence study, and I was continuing to do some publishing in the alcohol field. Shortly after we moved to Kentucky, my interest in the field became known. It was like moving into a desert as far as thirst was concerned because I was immediately asked to serve on a State Commission on Alcoholism and I had numerous heart-breaking phone calls from people who had family problems and were looking for help or suggestions. Also, at about the time that we moved to Lexington, the federal government was finally beginning to become involved in alcohol concerns. In 1958, I was invited to participate in a special group put together by the National Institute of Mental Health to consider ways in which NIMH could support the development of national policy recommendations. There was an organization of officers from State and Provincial programs on Alcohol that played a key role. This group included some prominent Canadians associated with the Addiction Research Foundation in Toronto which was an outstanding program. A series of meetings in Washington led to a grant from NIMH for the support of what became known as the Co-operative Commission on the Study of Alcoholism, co-operative meaning U.S. and Canada. I was asked to be a member of the Commission and was one of four members of a Steering Committee that was responsible for getting things started. David Archibald, Head of the Addiction Research Foundation, chaired that group. It took us a couple of years to develop the scientific staff which was eventually located at Stanford University and get the Commission off the ground. Then I chaired the Commission for about 3 years and was succeeded by Jack Philp. The Commission's activities continued until 1966 and resulted in a book, *Alcohol Problems: A Report to the Nation,* which contained a number of recommendations for federal policy and federal action.[11] It was written by Tom Plaut, a sociologist who deserves credit for helping the Commission pull things together and submit a significant report. It was not a smooth operating Commission. There was much dissension between the Commission and the staff that had been assembled at Stanford. Also, E. M. Jellinek, who had been brought in by the Commission and was being very helpful as a Consultant to the staff, died at his desk at Stanford in 1963.

The Co-operative Commission activity led to another significant experience. In 1966, Lyndon Johnson became the first President of the United States to mention alcohol problems publicly. He directed John Gardner, the Secretary of Health, Education and Welfare, to set up a National Advisory Committee on Alcoholism. I was asked to chair that Committee. Work in Washington in the 1966—68 years was very rewarding because there was finally national momentum. It was the period of the 'great society'. The National Advisory Committee was a good group. It represented lots of expertise and worked together very effectively. We prepared an Interim Report at the end of 1968.[12] This contained many recommendations that eventually were included in the national legislation that under Senator Harold Hughes' leadership created the National Institute on Alcohol Abuse and Alcoholism (NIAAA).

BJA: Since you mentioned the NIAAA, I have a question about the federal government's growing role in the alcohol question.

RS: The establishment of NIAAA gave both increased financial support and special focus to an activity that had been initiated by the National Institute of Mental Health in the early 1960's. It was in the early 60's that some grants for research on alcohol problems began. In the mid-60's a center for intramural alcohol research within NIMH, and a specifically designated alcohol grant program were started. NIAAA has been a very important organization. I happen to feel that the opportunities that NIAAA offered were really not fully realized in the first 5 or 6 years. I had a basic point of disagreement with the initial policy that was based on the position that the major thrust should be in treatment and on an assumption that we really didn't need more research because we had the knowledge we needed. I've never felt that way. During those early years, only a small percentage of the funds appropriated for the NIAAA were used for research. I had very little to do with NIAAA during those first few years. When they were looking for a new Director, after about 5 years, I was invited over to Washington to see if I'd be interested, but at that time I wasn't interested in any move. I was also invited over the next time they were looking for a new Director, but by then, they were looking for someone with a strong administrative background and I didn't feel I was qualified. I did continue my interest in the field. I continued my involvement through a number of their conferences and recently I served for 3 years as a member of the National Advisory Council on Alcohol Abuse and Alcoholism. I feel that the shift of primary emphasis within NIAAA from treatment to research has been a appropriate move. Treatment hasn't suffered because it's been supported in other ways. But the research advances in alcohol in the last 10 years have been just amazing. We've moved from very simplistic notions about the actions of alcohol in the human body to a point where we're able to identify some very important and basic questions fairly clearly. That's real progress in any field. The most gratifying trend for me is that the alcohol field is moving to a point where the leading scientists are beginning to recognize the need to integrate theory and research from the biological and the behavioral sciences. We're moving toward some truly integrative biobehavioral thinking.

BJA: You've used that concept for a long time. How do you see that concept has changed over the years in the alcohol field, this biobehavioral notion that you've espoused ever since your appointment in Applied Physiology at Yale?

RS: Back at Yale, Haggard had the notion that you should study alcohol problems by involving people from all the relevant disciplines and he, Jellinek and Bacon put together an organization that included people from the biological and medical sciences, and also anthropology, sociology, psychology, history, law, religion, education. These were all represented in the group at Yale. It was multidiscipline. There was recognition of important relationships between the actions of alcohol on the human body and the fact that drinking was a form of social behavior governed by customs, attitudes, and beliefs and a form of psychological behavior responsive to the impact of alcohol on the central nervous system. This was well recognized in the 1940's, but, still if you read the literature in the 40's, with rare exceptions, that literature was essentially reporting what was known within the various separate disciplines. This tradition has continued and there would be many who would argue that not a lot has changed. What I believe has changed is this. The biological research on alcohol today has resulted in a shift from a focus on commonalities of response to a recognition of and respect for biological heterogeneity and the uniqueness of individual responses to alcohol associated in some cases with as yet unidentified genetic markers. Basically, the concept that we have to emphasize is that the biological responses of the individual are meaningful only if people drink and the nature of these responses depends upon the cumulative exposure of the individual to alcohol. Cumulative exposure depends upon drinking experience and experience takes place in a social setting in which behavior is influenced by cultural beliefs and patterns, economic and regulatory forces, peer behavior and beliefs and by individual psychological responses. The meaning of alcohol's effect on mood depends a lot on individual psychological characteristics. The action of alcohol as a tranquilizing, sedating drug is much more meaningful for an individual who is characteristically uptight and anxious than for an individual who is secure, relaxed and has a good self-image. So we must put all these things together; the variable meaning of alcohol induced mood modification as it relates to personality and psychological characteristics, and the variable meaning of sensitivity to alcohol at the biological level as it relates to exposure to alcohol at the social and behavioral level. We're beginning at least to give lip service in our scientific writings to the importance of putting these things together. What we don't have is a cadre of individuals with enough understanding of each other's disciplines to communicate very effectively in terms of research design. We don't have support within the disciplines so that people feel secure in working across some of these disciplinary lines. We don't have institutional support in many places for working across interdisciplinary lines. Academic rewards are more apt to come to people whose work is perceived by their disciplinary peers as major contributions to the discipline rather than to problems which are, from a discipline perspective, more diffuse.

BJA: *Do you think your work with the Institute of Medicine may have helped to some extent in promulgating a broader biobehavioral perspective?*

RS: I'd like to think so. I've had two experiences with the Institute of Medicine. In 1979, they appointed a committee to do a study for NIAAA called *Alcoholism, Alcohol Abuse and Related Problems: Opportunities for Research*.[13] This committee, on which I served, was a relatively small multidisciplinary group. The report that came out of the Institute of Medicine in 1980 was essentially six separate reports on the status of alcohol knowledge and research in biochemistry and genetics, neuropharmacology, clinical and epidemical issues, psychosocial issues, prevention and treatment. Although numerous potential opportunities for integration across disciplines were implicit, they weren't explicitly stated. Then in 1987, another report came out of the Institute of Medicine called *Causes and Consequences of Alcohol Problems: An Agenda for Research*.[14] This was prepared by a Committee that I had the privilege of chairing. In the second report, the importance of and some specific suggestions for the integration of conceptualization and the integration of research are made explicit. Now we are waiting for action. That's where we are.

BJA: *This whole period was a very interesting one. Escape from Custody was published in the mid-70's and three different times you have had sabbatical leaves that were basically alcohol-related and provided rather significant opportunities for you to get away and focus on a first love, perhaps.*

RS: It's interesting you mentioned that. Of course, here in Kentucky my first love after participating in the planning process has been the Department of Behavioral Sciences which we established as a basic science department in the medical school and which has been extremely gratifying in terms of the colleagues and students we've had and the participation in developing medical behavioral science and behavioral medicine as very basic to medical education and research. But I maintained my interest in alcohol and throughout my years in Lexington, there have been opportunities to share ideas with several leaders in various aspects of addiction research, including Harris Isbell, Abe Wikler, Bill Martin, Arnold Ludwig, John O'Donnell, and Richard Clayton. Finally, in 1968, after 13 years in Kentucky, I was able to take a sabbatical leave in which I actually went back to Yale. The Yale Center of Alcohol Studies was no longer there. It had moved to Rutgers, but I had friends in Sociology who were very hospitable and I went primarily to work on alcohol research. I drafted much of the preliminary manuscript for *Escape from Custody*. Frank Moore was still living. I saw him quite a few times while I was there. I proposed that we go ahead and publish it and it was actually his decision that it would be published posthumously. He had a lot of ego involvement in the study. He'd read most of the manuscript as it evolved, but he wanted it to be complete. I also worked on what became a monograph called 'Alcohol and Society' that was published in 1973 as an entire issue of a journal called *Psychiatric Annals*.[15] Ten years later I was able to take a 6-month sabbatical in 1978 which was spent in Berkeley, California with the Alcohol Research Group. Don Cahalan provided hospitality and another wonderful opportunity to think and write. It was an ideal kind of academic situation where if you had an idea you wanted to share, you could almost always find two or three other people to sit around a table and talk about it. I found the group that Don

Cahalan had assembled, Robin Room and others, to be a very stimulating and fertile group of thinkers. It was such a valuable experience that when we had a chance 8 years later to take another sabbatical for 6 months, we went back to Berkeley. While at Berkeley the second time, I worked on a number of things including a fair bit of writing with Robin Room that became integrated into the second IOM Report.

BJA: *I guess one of the natural questions that might follow at this point is what are your current feelings about how alcohol research ought to be going to today. Do you see gaps in the field that really need to be addressed?*

RS: I think we've gained a gratifying amount of knowledge and we have much more to learn in all of the relevant disciplines, but the biggest need, I think is to learn how to put our knowledge together, how to integrate it. We haven't talked much about prevention and treatment. One of my main concerns today is that there is a large gap between the knowledge we have and the knowledge we are applying to prevention and treatment. I think our prevention programs still tend to send out messages that emphasize commonality of response and do not adequately emphasize what we know about the considerable variability in individual responses to alcohol. I think our treatment strategies really haven't changed nearly enough to reflect what we know about the impact of alcohol and what we're learning about processes of addiction. Rather than take the position that we know what to do, we need to increase our research of and our knowledge about the treatment process and the prevention process. So in addition to pursuing basic biological research and basic behavioral research on the relationship between alcohol and human beings, I think we need more research on the processes of prevention and treatment.

BJA: *I know that, at least technically, you retired last year, but you don't sound very retired at the moment. Could you tell us something about your plans for alcohol-related research and your own plans for your 'retirement'?*

RS: Well, I'm trying to catch up on a number of research projects, not all alcohol-related. There's a study of Kentucky centenarians; a study of blood pressure control among the rural poor; and a study of families of patients with Alzheimer's Disease. I'm also associated with a National Institute on Drug Abuse supported Center for Research on Drug Abuse Prevention here at the University of Kentucky. I'm working on a manuscript that will be part of a book dedicated to Selden Bacon that is being edited by Paul Roman. Then, when I get all these loose ends put together, I hope to find the capacity to look at current knowledge in the alcohol field and suggest specific ways for the geneticists, the biochemists, the neuroscientists, the psychologists and the sociologists to move from generalities to specifics with respect to the integration of their theories and their research. That's what I'd like to be able to do. This is a theme that I have touched on in two recent papers.[16,17]

BJA: *It sounds less like a retirement and more like a sabbatical.*

RS: I hope to continue to urge other people to do truly interdisciplinary thinking and research because when you come right down to it, when you talk about interdisciplinary research, the need is not unique to alcohol. It's something that today is true in all of science. The problems we're dealing with no longer lend themselves to the traditional disciplinary lines. In fact, in many respects, the disciplines have become anachronistic. They really exist primarily in the structure and power base of university departments. They don't exist in the nature of research that's going on within these departments. When we talk about interdisciplinary research, I've always thought of alcohol as an ideal model for breaking down some of the barriers between the disciplines because the whole nature of the relationship between alcohol and the human being is one that involves, if you come down to it, all of the disciplines of science and, indeed, the humanities, as well. I've often said that alcohol, as a substance is capable of permeating all the tissues of the human body and that alcohol problems permeate virtually all the issues of human society.

References

1. Straus, Alma F. (1937) *Keep Busy* (New York, G. P. Putnam's).
2. Straus, R. (1950) *Medical Care for Seamen: the origin of public medical services in the United States* (New Haven, Yale University Press).
3. Straus, R. (1946) Alcohol and the homeless man, *Quarterly Journal of Studies on Alcohol*, 7, pp. 360–404.
4. Straus, R. & McCarthy, R. G. (1951) Nonaddictive pathological drinking patterns of homeless men, *Quarterly Journal of Studies on Alcohol*, 12, pp. 601–611.
5. Straus, R. (1948) Some sociological concomitants of excessive drinking as revealed in the life history of an itinerant inebriate, *Quarterly Journal of Studies on Alcohol*, 9, pp. 1–52.
6. Straus, R. (1974) *Escape from Custody: a study of alcoholism and institutional dependency as reflected on the life record of a homeless man* (New York, Harper & Row).
7. Jellinek, E. M. (1946) Phases in the drinking history of alcoholics. Analysis of a survey conducted by the official organization of Alcoholics Anonymous, *Quarterly Journal of Studies on Alcohol*, 7, pp. 1–88.
8. Straus, R. & Bacon, S. D. (1953) *Drinking in College* (New Haven, Yale University Press). [Reprinted 1979, Westport, Ct, Greenward Press.]
9. Straus, R. & Bacon, S. D. (1951) Alcoholism and social stability, *Quarterly Journal of Studies on Alcohol*, 12, pp. 231–260.
10. Williams, P. & Straus, R. (1950) Drinking patterns of Italians in New Haven: utilization of the personal diary as a research technique, *Quarterly Journal of Studies on Alcohol*, 11, pp. 51–91, 250–308, 452–483, 586–629.
11. Plaut, T. F. A. (1967) *Alcohol Problems: a report to the nation* (New York, Oxford University Press).
12. National Advisory Committee on Alcoholism (1969) *Interim Report to the Secretary of the Department of Health, Education, and Welfare,* December (1968) (Washington, D.C., U.S. Government Printing Office).
13. Institute of Medicine (1980) *Alcoholism, Alcohol Abuse, and Related Problems: opportunities for research* (Washington, D.C., National Academy Press).
14. Institute of Medicine (1987) *Causes and Consequences of Alcohol Problems: an agenda for research* (Washington, D.C., National Academy Press).
15. Straus, R. (1973) Alcohol and society, *Psychiatric Annals*, 3, No. 10, pp. 8–107 [entire issue].

16. Straus, R. (1986) Alcohol and alcohol problems research 10. The United States, *British Journal of Addiction,* 81, pp. 315–325.
17. Straus, R. (1988) Interdisciplinary biobehavioral research on alcohol problems: a concept whose time has come, *Drugs and Society,* 2 (in press).

8

Interview with David J. Pittman

DAVID J. PITTMAN. *Received BA and MA from University of North Carolina and PhD from Chicago. From 1963–76 Director of George Washington University's Social Science Institute and from 1976–85 Chairman of Sociology; currently Professor of Sociology at George Washington. Formerly President of the North American Association of Alcohol Programs and Member of Board of Directors of NCA. Publications on alcohol and drug problems, criminology, mass media and health care.*

BJA: *You were born and reared in North Carolina, where you obtained your undergraduate and part of your graduate education at the University of North Carolina, Chapel Hill. Your education was interrupted by your service in the Army Air Force. You completed your education at the University of Chicago, where you earned your Ph.D in Human Development. How did your early years and educational experiences influence your choice of career?*

DJP: First you have to understand that I grew up in a southern area of the United States marked by racial discrimination, which was institutionalized by law. I remember, as a child, not understanding the rationality of this segregated system, and probably this experience led me to be an early activist in my orientation. In one sense, you might say that I thought I could solve the problems of the world—as do many adolescents. This feeling was probably intensified by my entering university at the age of 16, which made me younger than most of my peers. I developed a more activist orientation towards social problems at the University of North Carolina, which has always been on the frontier of the development of innovative ideas. At that time Blacks were not admitted to the University; I remember joining organizations which had as their goal the admission of Blacks to the University. My horizons were further extended by travel in this country while at the University and in the Armed Forces.

BJA: *Was there a particular professor who influenced your choice of career?*

DJP: It's very difficult to single out the professor who had the greatest influence on my career—but it would have to be Nicholas J. Demerath, who introduced me to the exciting field of sociology, and particularly urban sociology. I was very impressed by the studies which we read that were done by the University of Chicago researchers, such as Nels Anderson's pioneer study entitled *The Hobo,* and from these I developed a romantic fascination with urban problems in particular and social problems in general. Nick Demerath was very much an activist himself. I had experimented with the idea of going to law school, to medical school, and considered various other endeavors, but sociology seemed to be what I was interested in, and I chose this as my career. Subsequently I attended Columbia University in New York City for a short period of time and came under the influence of a very noted social researcher, Allison Davis, who was a visiting professor there. He advised me to go to the University of Chicago to complete the doctorate degree in Human Development, which is an interdisciplinary field of study that encompasses the fields of anthropology, sociology, physiology, and clinical psychology. It is from this training that I developed my strong orientation to interdisciplinary studies and action. Davis also served as the chairman of my dissertation committee at Chicago.

BJA: *The social problem, then, that you addressed in your dissertation was jailed public drunkenness offenders and alcoholism in general, which then became the focus of your career. Would you discuss the kinds of influences or motivations in your early background which dictated this particular social problem to you?*

DJP: The role of the family always plays a strong factor in one's interest, although it may not be apparent at the time. Probably in the back of my mind was an experience that happened to my father when I was a child, which I didn't understand at the time. I should say parenthetically that my father was an alcoholic—a binge drinker. As a child of an alcoholic, I have no drinking problem myself. But I remember the time that my father left his own community to visit another one, and he had drunk too much. He was arrested and jailed overnight for public intoxication. My mother always had taught me that he suffered from an illness and not from an immoral condition. It struck me as being the height of folly to jail an individual who had an illness.

The problem of public drunkenness offenders was more extensive than I had ever conceived it, in the sense that, being from a law-abiding family, I thought it would be only people who committed serious crimes who went to the county jail. Much to my surprise I found, when doing the study in Rochester, that two-thirds of the individuals who were incarcerated in this county jail for periods of time up to one year were there for the simple charge of public drunkenness and for no other charge whatsoever. This came as quite a shock to this individual, then in his 20's. It was something for which the textbooks had not prepared me.

BJA: Were there actors in the field of alcoholism, colleagues, or academic literature perhaps, which also influenced your decision to research alcoholism?

DJP: In terms of pioneers in the sociological field, I must re-emphasize the influence that the research which was done by Nels Anderson in the 1920's, when he actively became a field participant with the men of skid row, had on my thinking. Unfortunately, this lack of field and/or clinical experience in some contemporary alcoholism researchers means that they do not have 'a feeling' for the context in which various groups drink, such as the skid row denizens, people who are beset with problems of unemployment, etc.

The social context for alcoholism research in America and internationally in the 1950's is important. The major group of researchers and scholars were at the Yale Center of Studies on Alcohol. I had the good fortune to meet and have numerous discussions with the late Raymond McCarthy, who is best known today for his educational programs to reduce the incidence of alcoholism, and who was connected with the Yale group. Also influential was that eminent scholar with the encyclopedic mind who was connected with the Yale group, Mark Keller, who edited the first co-authored monograph that I did. Also I became very conversant with the works of Selden Bacon, who was viewed by many as the 'Father' of sociological studies in alcoholism.

Also an important influence in retrospect was Robert Straus, who had completed the study with Selden Bacon of *Drinking in College;* he was a faculty member at Syracuse when I was at the University of Rochester. His encouragement to a graduate student struggling with his first major research project was helpful, as well as was his willingness, always, to discuss various ideas.

Another decisive influence in choosing this field was that great, brilliant individual who encouraged me in my career, 'Bunky' Jellinek. His words of wisdom to me in this country and abroad, when I was in Amsterdam in 1961 to pursue this field, and his kindness to me will never be forgotten. Probably his book *The Disease Concept of Alcoholism,* had more influence on my later career in alcohol studies than the work of any other individual. I think the whole field of alcoholism owes a tremendous debt to him. He was truly an interdisciplinary scholar.

BJA: *The book,* Revolving Door,[1] *which became a classic, evolved from your Ph.D. dissertation at the University of Chicago. Would you give a description of the milieu which brought forth such an outstanding study.*

DJP: Literally I almost walked into the research project on the chronic drunkenness offender. After obtaining a master's degree in Sociology at the University of North Carolina, Chapel Hill, I decided that instead of going directly for a doctorate degree, since I wasn't sure I wanted to make a life commitment to the academic profession, I would teach a few years to see if I would really like it. The pressures from my family were extremely strong, that is, that one would never become financially successful if one had an academic career. I secured a position as a sociology faculty member at the University of Rochester. There was a very active organization, The Health Association of Rochester and Monroe County, which had an alcoholism committee. They were concerned with the jailed population at the Monroe County Penitentiary, really a regional jail. The individuals most concerned with this group were the late Jack Norris, who was the medical director of Eastman Kodak, and also was later a non-alcoholic trustee of Alcoholics Anonymous, and the Reverend Thomas Richards, who ran a mission for skid row denizens. Ray McCarthy, who was the Director of Alcoholism researcher of the New York State Commission on Mental Health, believed that a study should be done on this population and helped to secure the funds. Much to the credit of the Health Association, and especially to Jack Norris, they decided to ask for sociological directions of this study, and I was assigned by the Chairman of Sociology, Earl Koos, along with a colleague of mine, Wayne Gordon, to participate in this study. Therefore I got in on the ground floor of this study, which also matched my needs and simultaneously gave me an anchor for a dissertation topic for the University of Chicago degree.

Rochester in the early 1950's was a place where innovative ideas in alcoholism were widely accepted, although one might say that the attitude towards jailed inebriates was one of *noblesse oblige* when looked at from the 1980's perspective. However there was a concern for the physical and social welfare of these individuals. To better understand the situation, I decided to spend time on skid row, although the men there always told me I should be home and not there. Their questions were: What was a young man such as I doing down there? Why did I want to ruin my life by becoming a 'drunk'? Or, it was an inappropriate place for a young person to be—a bad influence. The community was very cooperative. The study was done for less than $10,000, but the amount of volunteer time and private resources contributed by the community was impressive.

BJA: *Why do you think this study had such an influential impact on the field of alcohol studies?*

DJP: It's because of the study's findings that repeated jailing of public drunkenness offenders who were alcoholic had been a failure in deterring these men from drinking inappropriately. The study advocated the concepts of treatment and rehabilitation of this population instead of punishment and custodial care, which had failed. We found that these men had never received any treatment for their problems and that they were involved in what Mark Keller and we called a 'Revolving Door'; that is, periods of sobriety while incarcerated (but frequently they were able to make home brew in the institutional context) and periods of drunkenness in the community before being re-arrested. Our study indicated that the jailed men were basically lower-income, under-privileged, or from stigmatized groups; 'respectable' public drunks were only fined. All that a 'revolving door' alcoholic was doing was serving life imprisonment on the installment plan. Furthermore, in the final chapter of the book, *Revolving Door,* we outlined an agenda of social action. We recommended that a new system for chronic inebriates, built on the concepts of treatment and rehabilitation, should be instituted through the vehicle of treatment centers, for which I later coined the term detoxification centers, in which these men, rarely women, would receive systematic medical, psychological, and social treatment, as well as planning for their aftercare in the community. In short, in the first draft report in 1955, over 30 years ago, we advocated decriminalization of the public drunkenness offense because it was a victimless crime. It is a tragedy that today some states and localities still use jail to punish chronic drunkenness offenders, despite the futility of this system.

BJA: *Then really the 'Revolving Door' brought out the fact that prison reinforced alcoholism rather than helping the alcoholic in any way.*

DJP: Yes, clearly it indicated that it was a waste of money, and still is a waste of money, in that only the rare alcoholic would be deterred from drinking because of being incarcerated. The

'Revolving Door' study has implications for the current crackdown on individuals who drive while intoxicated. In my opinion, there are two broad groupings who are drunk drivers—those who are chronic, addictive alcoholics who need treatment, and they are not going to stop their drinking just because they are placed in a jail cell, and a second group of social drinkers who will respond to the therapy of incarceration. Thus mandatory jailing of all drunk drivers for their first offense without any screening as to the severity of their problem is an unenlightened social policy.

BJA: *You did this study in Rochester. Were there tangible, positive results which ensued from this study?*

DJP: Unfortunately I was not able to participate in the establishment of the halfway house for a limited number of jailed inebriates as a consequence of this study. The jailed inebriates were given the option of serving a jail term or securing treatment at this halfway house. My non-participation was due to my leaving for another university. I was offered a position as assistant professor of sociology and psychiatry at Washington University in 1958, with the support of my former mentor, Nick Demerath, who was the chairman of their sociology department and the director of their interdisciplinary studies, the Social Science Institute. So I went west to further my professional career.

BJA: *At this point then you were, to quote, 'a man with a vision'. Was Washington University the kind of university in which you felt you could accomplish your goals?*

DJP: In 1958, when I came to Washington University, it was an institution on the move in the behavioral sciences, and my appointment in this university was an ideal one for a young sociologist. A supportive gentleman was the chairman of the psychiatry department, Dr. Edwin Gildea. He and Nick Demerath were open to innovative ideas and creative activities; they asked only that I develop a research career of my own choosing. Ed Gildea knew that I was interested in the field of alcoholism, and he told me there was a young psychiatrist at the public mental health hospital, George Ulett, who had an old, unused hydrotherapy ward which he had been trying to convert into an alcoholism ward. So Ed Gildea suggested to me that I should go to the Malcolm Bliss Mental Health Center and see if I could work with Dr. Ulett. I replied that it sounded like an excellent idea. Fortunately, that semester I had only one sociology course to instruct, leaving much time for research. Washington University at that time was a place that was not beset by rigid bureaucratic rules, and a scholar did not feel the immense tenure pressures that young academics do today.

BJA: *Was St. Louis, as you perceived it, the kind of city in which you felt you could achieve the kinds of social changes you hoped for, although it is viewed by many as a very conservative city?*

DJP: St. Louis at that time was, and still is, a city which has always been open to change in many areas. There was an active group of people already interested in alcoholism, and perhaps the major figure who played such a significant role in future community events was a newspaper reporter, Marguerite Shepard, at the *St. Louis Globe-Democrat*. Marguerite was an individual who would seize an idea, and not let it die. She knew about the many abortive attempts to found an alcoholism treatment facility and a council on alcoholism. She, in fact, brought to my attention a dedicated physician, one of the most humane and compassionate individuals I have ever known, Joseph Kendis, who was the first physician in Missouri to treat alcoholics as patients. In fact, at that time he was known as the 'drunk doctor'. This was long before private and public health insurance plans covered alcoholism as a primary diagnosis. Dr. Kendis knew more about the clinical treatment of alcoholics than anyone that I had ever come in contact with in the past or would in the future.

Marguerite kept advising those of us who wanted to create an alcoholism facility in this old, unused hydrotherapy ward, that we would have to wait for an event that would seize the public's attention in order to obtain the community's interest. Such an event did occur. It was unfortunate, but it did give the impetus for the development of the alcoholism facility. A decorated World War II veteran, who had been previously hospitalized for his drinking problem in the mental hospital, committed suicide; he had told his wife many times that he would kill himself before returning to a mental hospital that had no treatment for his alcoholism. This event, covered extensively in the press by Marguerite Shepard, more than any other dramatically illustrated to the community that a separate and unique community facility was needed for the treatment of alcoholics.

In 1960 along with my colleagues, George Ulett, and a social worker Dorothy Stauffer, we were awarded a Hill-Burton grant from the United States government to help renovate the hydrotherapy ward into an alcoholism unit. The thing we lacked, however, was approximately $50,000 to match this grant. Everywhere we went we found moral support but no money; the city did not have money for this, the state did not have any money, and the federal government had only this hospital construction matching grant, so we had to raise it ourselves. This has been described in my article, 'The Open Door: Sociology in an Alcoholism Treatment Facility'.[2] But to make a long story short, the community, through the efforts of many private citizens and individuals, some of whom were members of AA, and members of the community power structure, did contribute the matching $50,000, which in 1986 dollars would be approximately $300,000, to build this alcoholism facility. This was a tremendous vote of confidence from hundreds of individuals who contributed their own money to this bold venture.

BJA: This alcoholism center formally opened in February 1961, and was the first treatment center for indigent alcoholics in the state of Missouri. What would you say were the major influences in the design of this treatment facility which you derived from your studies in Europe?

DJP: In 1960, I attended the Fifth European Institute on the Prevention and Treatment of Alcoholism in Paris under the auspices of what was then named the International Bureau Against Alcoholism, which was directed by Archer Tongue and headquartered in Lausanne, Switzerland. I was invited to give a paper on my research from the 'Revolving Door' study; and also later that summer I attended the 26th International Congress on Alcohol and Alcoholism in Stockholm. I spent about 3 months in Europe in 1960, and visited a number of major alcoholism research and treatment centers. Furthermore, I traveled extensively to Europe every year, sometimes as many as half a dozen times yearly in the 1960's, and have continued to do so in the 1970's and 1980's, so it is very difficult to pinpoint particular years when I absorbed international ideas. But the St. Louis Alcoholism Treatment and Research Center was a composite of the therapeutic community that Maxwell Jones had developed in Great Britain for the treatment of the mentally ill, the Amsterdam Consultation-Bureau for Alcoholism directed by Henk Krauweel, and the treatment center which Dr. Hans Rotter ran in Vienna, Austria, all of which impressed me. Also I was strongly influenced by the work of the Poles in terms of their sobering-up station in Warsaw. Their center, located in former army barracks on the Vistula River, showed me what a very diligent group of individuals could do with a small amount of money.

BJA: Did sociological principles play any role in the design of this unit?

DJP: The St. Louis Center incorporated the physical design and therapeutic principles derived from sociology; these ideas are found in my article[3] in the *British Journal of Addiction*. It is very rare that a sociologist is given the opportunity to design a medical facility for alcoholics for any group of patients. One of the things I felt indispensable was that the patients should not physically be separated from the care-taking professions. That included the physicians, the psychiatrists, the medical residents, the social workers, and the nursing staff—everybody should be housed in the same therapeutic community and be a part of the milieu that would help the patients to recover. From this, we developed a treatment team that maintained its continuity throughout the 1960's and early 1970's; this was the triumvirate of Joe Kendis, the internist, Laura Esther Marie Root, the social worker, and myself, the sociologist. Laura was a former student of mine at the University of Rochester, and I recruited her from the public welfare agency in Rochester to be our chief social worker on the unit. There were other individuals involved, but the ability of the three of us to work together was the benchmark for developing further activities in the treatment and research field. One of the major things that I felt essential was that the door to the unit should be unlocked, that the patients had to live in an environment in which alcohol was ubiquitous, and therefore to lock them up in a unit would do nothing but enforce the idea that they were still being incarcerated for their alcoholism problem.

BJA: *As I recall, not too many patients left the ward even though it was unlocked.*

DJP: Many of the psychiatrists felt that all of our patients would be leaving against medical advice, and I remember one psychiatrist saying, "Could we start the ward as a locked one and see how it works?" We refused. But we did a study on the 'elopement' rates from the unlocked and locked wards in this hospital, and more patients, we found, eloped' from the locked wards than from the unlocked ward.

BJA: *In the early 1960's when the stigma attached to alcoholism was so great, you published* Carousel,[4] *which dealt with the chronicity of the disease and the many difficulties which had to be overcome, not only with lay persons but with professionals also. Would you discuss the difficulties encountered in obtaining the cooperation of the various health agencies and the professionals.*

DJP: Prior to establishing the Center at Malcolm Bliss, we felt it would be an excellent idea to do a study of all of the health and welfare agencies in St. Louis, as well as a sample of physicians and social workers who were supposed to provide the care for alcoholics, to determine what their sentiments or attitudes were to the treatability of the alcoholic and how the alcoholic would perform in a treatment setting. We knew that it was rare to find any not-for-profit hospital accepting alcoholics with a primary diagnosis of alcoholism and that there was considerable negative sentiment; however, the results of this study, which were subsequently published by the United States Department of Health, Education and Welfare in 1965,[5] indicated that we were not fully aware of the degree of difficulty we would confront. There was a pervasive feeling that alcoholism basically derived from a moral weakness and was not a treatable illness. Also, alcoholic patients were viewed as being undesirable patients because they lacked motivation and did not pay their bills. A major finding of this study empirically demonstrated that the alleged lack of motivation by alcoholics to change was partially derived from the care-taking professionals themselves, the physicians, the social workers, the nurses, etc. who defined the prognosis for alcoholic patients as poor, and therefore they did do poorly. For example, one illustration will suffice. One intake social worker at a major medical center said to an alcoholic patient who came for help, "What are you doing here? You know we don't have any success with alcoholic patients." Now, if that's not a turnoff for somebody who is trying to receive help for his problem, then nothing is. The lack of motivation on the part of many people in the care-taking professions came from the facts that they recognized the community was not making an adequate effort to treat alcoholics, that they were unable to accept the chronic features of alcoholism as a disease, and that they were perplexed as to what the treatment of the alcoholic should be. Furthermore, it was extremely difficult to secure accurate and up-to-date information on the treatment of alcoholics.

BJA: *Since there was so much concern in the early 1960's about whether treating alcoholic patients was worth the money which was being expended, I understand that you conducted a follow-up study[6] on the first patients treated at the Malcolm Bliss Alcoholism Treatment and Research Center. I believe this study yielded highly positive results. What were these results?*

DJP: The study showed that whether the individual was in an experimental or control group, even the minimal amount of treatment, namely a 7-10-day detoxification stay in the hospital, could produce positive results. Furthermore, most of these patients had never had any treatment for their alcoholism. This reminds me of the study conducted by Griffith Edwards in Great Britain, in which it was reported that even the giving of systematic advice to individuals about their drinking problems brought about positive changes in their drinking patterns at follow-up. Our follow-up study did prove, however, to the satisfaction of skeptics in the medical and social welfare community, that even indigent and lower-income alcoholics could be helped if treatment were provided. At the same time we did not find any individual who had returned to normal drinking in our sample. Therefore, this follow-up study was the major reason for the skepticism that I developed in reference to the idea that alcoholics could return to normal drinking.

BJA: You mean they did not return to normal drinking successfully?

DJP: Yes, that's correct. I think part of the problem is what we mean by normal drinking. A number of the individuals in this sample had been able to drink for a short period of time, or even a number of months, without getting into difficulty, but eventually their drinking led to problems.

BJA: Do you feel in retrospect that this study was a true picture of the kinds of success evidenced as time went on?

DJP: No. These were extraordinarily successful results. There is a sociological lesson to be learned here whenever a new facility is being created in which great rapport has been established among staff members and they are starting on a new venture about which they are excited, enthusiastic, and feel they are blazing new trails, then every effort is made to provide excellent services to the patient, and the patients themselves feel that they are unique and are a part of something important. Also, the patients were proving to themselves that they were worthy of treatment. Furthermore, no bureaucratic treatment procedures had been institutionalized, and we did not abide by the hospital manual of rules and regulations. It became a sort of 'we' against 'they' philosophy in terms of this mental hospital. The patients, as well as the clinical and research staff, were desirous of making this unit a success. I felt then that it would be very difficult in my lifetime to recapture the kind of excitement I experienced working in this experimental alcoholism treatment center, but later almost the same enthusiasm developed on my part with the establishment of the St. Louis Detoxification Center.

BJA: *You must have witnessed the rise of the idea 'return to normal drinking', and I know that you were very critical of D. L. Davies' position. With hindsight, what do you make of this whole business? What was the significance of D. L. Davies' paper. What is the meaning of this controversy? Do you see it simply as factual error or as a movement which reflects some more ancient and deeper alignments? What do you think of the Rand study?*

DJP: Yes, I know that I was extremely critical of the D. L. Davies' paper, which was entitled 'Normal Drinking in Recovered Alcohol Addicts', which appeared in 1962. My quarrel with Davies was always the title of the paper, 'Normal Drinking . . .' By normal drinking, I made the assumption that the individuals could drink spirits, wine, or beer, and would not have to be concerned whether they would get intoxicated or not. The cases that Davies reported I would refer to as 'nibblers'; and I know my friend, Max Glatt, the former editor of this journal, also referred to them as such. They drank only on very special occasions and drank little sips of wine and beer. That wasn't normal drinking to me. I think Davies' study did serve a valuable purpose; that is, that an alcoholic is, in terms of AA philosophy, only one drink away from a drunk, should not be interpreted literally, although certain scholars have interpreted it that way. I know clinically that a number of individuals treated in alcoholism facilities are able to drink normally for periods of time before having problems. There is probably always the possibility of spontaneous remission, and some individuals may be diagnosed as alcoholic who are not truly alcoholic, and a false diagnosis has been made. As a physician uncle of mine used to say, there were times when a patient was cured, however he had been incorrectly diagnosed in the first place. Thus this possibility is open. I think there is more danger of that today, where there is promiscuous diagnosing of individuals as being chronic alcoholics (at least in the United States) when they are basically problem drinkers or irresponsible individuals who use their drinking as an excuse for their behavior.

BJA: *Since you were saying that for a short time some patients would drink normally and then relapse, I would surmise that you would favor more longitudinal studies being done.*

DJP: Yes, that's correct. I think that is the 'proof of the pudding.' There was a longer follow-up of the Davies' patients conducted by Griffith Edwards that was published in 1985 in the *Journal of Studies on Alcohol,* which stated that the majority of these individuals did not continue their 'normal' drinking. Edwards' study is the type of longitudinal one that is so needed in the research field because he has followed these patients for around 30 years. His results have more validity to me that short follow-up studies of 6 months to a year. Short follow-up periods are a major deficiency of the Rand study and those of the Sobells. Ideally one would like to follow these individuals as Edwards did with Davies' patients, not for a period of 1 year or 2 years, but for 5, 10, 15, 20, 30 or more years, or until they die.

BJA: Do you feel that studies on this 'return to normal drinking' should be funded?

DJP: Absolutely. No organization, whether it is Alcoholics Anonymous, the World Health Organization, or the Federal government, should say that certain topics are 'off limits' for research.

BJA: In other words, individual behavior patterns are not static.

DJP: Right. And there is no super-empirical truth that no addictive alcoholic can return to normal drinking. Maybe a minute fraction of alcoholics can return to normal drinking if there is a radical alteration of their whole life circumstances, situations, and so forth. For example, there is no question that some men in the Armed Services in Vietnam, who displayed alcoholic behavior there, found this problem disappeared upon their return to the United States. Therefore this is not something that is etched in granite.

BJA: It appears that you are something of a 'workaholic'. In 1963, you were appointed the Director of the Social Science Institute at Washington University, where together with two of your colleagues, Professors Alvin Gouldner and Lee Rainwater, you obtained another grant of approximately $1 million to study a public housing project. With the many social problems rampant in this milieu, your focus was to be on the alcoholism problem as it existed in lower *project. With the many social problems rampant in this milieu, your focus was to be on the alcoholism problem as it existed in lower economic levels. Would you discuss this project and some of the more important findings?*

DJP: Yes, you are quite correct in terms of my being a workaholic, and I am also a 'travelholic'. I always recharged my batteries by boarding an aircraft and going to Europe, to Amsterdam, London, or Paris for a while or to Athens and Rome. But I always visited people in the drug dependency field or attended meetings. These were working vacations as well as a way to get away from everything. But in a more serious vein, the late Professor Alvin Gouldner, a noted sociologist, and Lee Rainwater, now at Harvard, and I did receive a large grant to study a low income public housing project in St. Louis, the infamous Pruitt-Igoe Project. My research task, with the aid of a superlative researcher and frequent collaborator, Muriel Sterne, was to study the drinking patterns of the residents. Since the residents were mostly Black Americans, Muriel Sterne did a review of the literature on Black drinking behavior and problems. She found it an under-researched area. Also we conducted one of the first ethnographic research studies of the Black drinking patterns in an urban center, and the results of this were published in the monograph, *Drinking Patterns in the Ghetto.*[7] What we found, and this theme has been very much in the forefront of my later writings, is that the problems of economic deprivation derived from under-employment or unemployment, together with discrimination and prejudice, played a significant role in the creation and maintenance of drinking problems in this lower income Black community.

BJA: *The Alcoholism Treatment and Research Center became a member of the North American Association of Alcoholism Programs (NAAAP). It is currently known as the Alcohol and Drug Problems Association (ADPA). I understand you were very active in this organization in the 1960's.*

DJP: The years that I spent as a board member and president of the NAAAP were among the most interesting ones in my life. In 1963, I became a board member of the NAAAP, which was composed of the directors of alcoholism programs and treatment units in the United States and Canada as well as individual members. In 1965, I became the president of the organization and was able to use this position as the platform for certain social policy ideas which I had. At that time the federal government's alcoholism effort was almost nil. In charge of these federal activities was Dr. Carl Anderson, who played a significant role in my own career in terms of giving me advice and counsel on how to get through the bureaucratic maze to obtain funding from the federal government. Furthermore, he had only one secretarial assistant; they were the total personnel assigned to monitor the alcoholism problem, which was composed of an estimated 6 million alcoholics. Federal appropriations expended on treatment and research were meager. It is to the credit of Carl Anderson, one of the early pioneers in the American alcoholism movement, that in his quiet, gentle way he was able to bring attention to this problem. Carl Anderson was probably the most important federal figure in the American alcoholism movement in the late 1950's and the 1960's, and it would be a tragedy if his accomplishments were ignored or forgotten.

The decision of the board of directors of the NAAAP and the executive secretary, Augustus Hewlett, was that we would make an effort to influence the course of events by supporting a federal alcoholism bill which would provide not only research funds for individual researchers but also block grants to the states for alcoholism programs. The major elected federal officials who were instrumental in the early effort for a national alcoholism program were the late Representative Elliott Hagan of Georgia, who introduced the first alcoholism bill in the United States Congress in 1962, and former Senators Frank Moss of Utah and Jacob Javits of New York, who were strong advocates of increased federal activity and convinced many of their skeptical colleagues that national action was appropriate. The major non-elected officials who were involved in this effort were George Dimas, who was the director of the Oregon Program on Alcoholism and who served as president of the NAAAP prior to and after my term of office, Gus Hewlett, Peter Barton Hutt, a Washington lawyer with Covington and

Burling, who led the effort to challenge the legality of jailing public drunkenness offenders, and myself as the president of the NAAAP. This group, plus a large number of other very helpful individuals at the state and local levels, played the major role in creating the climate which eventuated in the first alcoholism legislation passed by the United States Congress in 1970.

BJA: *As I recall, you became very enthusiastic about a development in the United States Congress. What was this development? The time I am speaking of took place during the NAAAP annual meeting in Atlantic City in 1965.*

DJP: Oh yes, I remember that. The goal that all of us had worked for, that there would be Congressional Hearings in the House of Representatives before the Committee on Interstate and Foreign Commerce on a proposed bill to establish a federal commission on alcoholism, was a dream that came true. I remember staying up all night long at the hotel in a strategy session, smoking packs of cigarettes (subsequently I've quit), and planning the testimony with the various state and municipal delegations about who would appear before the congressional committee to plead the case for increased federal recognition and funding for alcoholism. There was no divisiveness in the alcoholism field at that time, for involved in the planning sessions were Marty Mann, the Director of the National Council on Alcoholism (NCA), and perhaps the most influential person in mobilizing communities to accept alcoholism as a treatable illness, and Selden Bacon, the Director of the Yale and later the Rutgers Center on Alcohol Studies, then the preeminent alcoholism research organization in the United States. Testifying before the Congressional Committee were all of us, Marty Mann, Selden Bacon, Gus Hewlett, Phyllis Snyder, Director of the first municipal program for alcoholics in Chicago, which was started by Mayor Richard Daley, and Don Dancy, the Director of the West Virginia State Alcoholism Program, and myself. The point is that in 1965, the American alcoholism movement spoke with one voice, whether it was a private or public group, or whether it was a research or an action oriented group.

BJA: **Why was this?**

DJP: In the mid-1960's, there were few individuals who were interested in this area. The Prohibition experience was still fresh in the minds of the major political figures and the general population. Most civic leaders were skeptical of our motivation, in that they wondered whether this was a return to Prohibition with all of its attendant problems, whereas others accepted the legacy of the attitudes prevalent in American society, prior to and reinforced by Prohibition, that alcoholics were morally weak individuals who could solve their problems if they really used their willpower. The fact that all groups were trying to obtain treatment services for alcoholics and research funding for studies to understand this problem kept personality conflicts and ideological differences beneath the surface.

BJA: **Were there other American developments in the mid-1960's that created a climate for changing attitudes toward alcoholics and alcoholism?**

DJP: Definitely. The 1960's of President Kennedy's 'New Frontier' and especially President Johnson's 'Great Society' and 'War on Poverty' programs were in an era in which the orientation was that the federal government could aid in solving all of America's problems, including alcoholism. By 1964, a high level committee on alcoholism had been established in the Department of Health, Education and Welfare by Secretary Celebrezze to study the effects of alcoholism on the nation's well-being. This committee sponsored several national conferences on the chronic drunkenness offender and accidental injury in Washington in which I participated.

One of the most important developments was President Johnson's appointment of the President's Commission on Law Enforcement and Administration of Justice and the President's Commission on Crime in the District of Columbia in 1965. Both of these commissions had as one of their specific foci the public drunkenness offender. Their interest was based on the fact that in the mid-1960's one-third of all arrests in the United States were for public intoxication, or about 2 million of the 6 million annually. Furthermore, the Commission members were aware that public intoxication statutes were under legal attack, not only in the District of Columbia but in many other jurisdictions including North Carolina. Peter Hutt was the prime legal strategist in the efforts to overturn these laws when they were applied to chronic alcoholics. I felt fortunate to be chosen as one of the alcoholism consultants to both of these commissions, and subsequently I prepared a position paper on the Public Drunkenness Offense[8] for the President's Commission on Law Enforcement and the Administration of Justice.

BJA: *Did the Commission accept any of your recommendations?*

DJP: Yes, their final report in 1967, made significant recommendations on the drunkenness offense, many of which were based on my advice. This was one of the major highlights of my career, for the recommendations that a young academician had made in Rochester in 1955 were now being suggested by this august body as national policy. The Commission recommended the following: that drunkenness should not in itself be a criminal offense, that the community should establish detoxification units as part of a comprehensive treatment program, that communities should coordinate after-care resources, including residential housing and research by private and governmental agencies in alcoholism, and methods of treatment should be expanded. These were forward-looking recommendations for the late 1960's, some of which were to be achieved in the 1970's and 1980's, but it would be less than candid to say that these recommendations have been fully implemented today. Some communities have never adopted these enlightened goals of the Crime Commission. In fact, in certain areas there has been regression.

BJA: *Would you trace the history from the opening of the Alcoholism Center at Malcolm Bliss to the subsequent development of the Detoxification Center in St. Louis?*

DJP: The pioneer work done at the Alcoholism Treatment and Research Center was instrumental in one sense for the development of the first detoxification center to open in North America for persons detained by the police for public intoxication. This

Center was known as the St. Louis Detoxification and Diagnostic Evaluation Center.

Much credit should go to a group of Catholic nuns, the Sisters of St Mary's, who were in charge of an older hospital in the inner city, St. Mary's, which had always cared for the poor and the stigmatized. As a consequence of the recommendations of the President's Crime Commission, the Law Enforcement Assistance Administration made available a grant to the St. Louis Police Department for the establishment of the St. Louis Detoxification and Diagnostic Evaluation Center. Thus the Center, a 30-bed unit with 24-hour medical and nursing coverage was opened in November 1966, with an annual budget of approximately $200,000. This was a collaborative endeavour of the St. Louis Police Department, the Sisters of St. Mary, and the Social Science Institute of Washington University, which I directed.

In retrospect these events give me a great sense of pride. The recommendations that I had made earlier in the book, *Revolving Door,* I was able to see placed into operation in my lifetime.

BJA: Was there any research conducted to evaluate the Detox Center's effectiveness?

DJP: Yes. An evaluation study of the effectiveness of the St. Louis Detoxification Center was conducted under the auspices of the Social Science Institute by a young police officer, Jim Weber, who also was a sociology graduate student at Washington University. The goals of his study[9] were to measure the effect of the new process for handling public inebriates in time-savings for the police and indirectly for the courts and penal institutions, as well as the impact of the short-term treatment in the Detox Center on the subsequent behavior, including drinking, of the inebriates. In short, Weber's goal was to determine whether the revolving-door cycle for public drunkenness offenders could be changed. Jim Weber interviewed a random sample of the male patients, around 150, as I remember, approximately 4 months after their discharge from the Center. His results were encouraging in that they demonstrated that the police used less time to handle drunkenness cases, and that at follow-up approximately one-half of the patients showed improvement in their life situation. The most positive aspect about the study was that many of these individuals could be helped and rehabilitated. However, the success rate, as it has commonly been termed, was not as high as it would have been with upper and middle income patients who have more resources at their disposal.

BJA: How do you compare the social climate of the 1960's with that of today towards public drunkenness offenders?

DJP: This period of time, the late 1960's in America, was one of great innovation and social change. Thus the St. Louis alcoholism, research and treatment group, including myself, became known throughout the world as being synonymous with detoxification centers and a concern about public drunkenness offenders. However, treatment innovations in processing public drunkenness cases had already taken place in Czechoslovakia, as early as 1948, in Poland, where it was routine to treat public drunkenness offenders in a medical setting, and in Sweden, which had created a governmental commission to study decriminalization of drunkenness as early as 1963. I do remember that I was asked to testify in Great Britain before the Working Party on Habitual Drunkenness Offenders in 1969, which recommended that public intoxication offenders be removed from the criminal justice process.

Our optimistic belief in the late 1960's and early 1970's that all public drunkenness offenders would be removed from jail cells and receive adequate treatment never fully materialized. There were a number of reasons for this not occurring—one of which is that low income public drunkenness offenders do not have a high priority in the public legislative agenda. No detoxification center had full access to the kinds of transitional resources that were necessary for the adequate treatment of these individuals, such as the provision of halfway houses, domiciliary care, or even custodial care. Society has never been willing to invest the kinds of resources needed to cope with this problem. Further, we were accused of moving the 'revolving door' from the jail to the hospital, because we constantly accepted persons who relapsed. In medical science the worst cases frequently are studied in special clinical wards for that disease. If we accept the idea that alcoholism is a chronic illness characterized by relapse, then we should be as concerned about the worst cases of alcoholism as we are about the ones that have the best prognosis.

There also has been a conservative drift in certain states that have the wherewithal to decriminalize. California, the largest state, has never decriminalized the public drunkenness offense, which the majority of states, including Missouri, have done. Missouri has a full array of social and medical detoxification services today. The British also have fallen by the wayside; it is my understanding that the detoxification centers that were established are being phased out. Certain individuals now are saying that maybe it is a good idea to jail public low-income alcoholics, since then they would receive custodial care at least. To paraphrase a quotation, those who do not learn from the mistakes of the past are doomed to repeat them in the future. And that is basically where we stand on decriminalization today. The future of this movement over the next few decades is bleak.

BJA: *Given the fact that the jails are so overcrowded and hospitals are looking for patients to fill empty beds, it doesn't seem feasible to move the care of the alcoholic to the jail cell, does it?*

DJP: I think that is a very germane point. In a number of American states, they are under a court order to improve the conditions in correctional institutions. They are overcrowded, and a breeding ground for evil deeds that lurk in the hearts and minds of men, from murder to homosexual rape. You probably are less safe in a jail than on the outside. Under the cost containment programs of the current administration, there are massive vacancies in the hospital facilities. Using these vacant beds would be an efficient way to expand care for lower-income alcoholics, but it would cost money.

We also have again the problem of the homeless in America which strikes me as being ironical. This is where I came in, in 1955, 30 years ago. We were talking then about homeless alcoholics, and now all the country's popular magazines are running articles on the homeless—especially 'bag ladies'—who are composed of individuals who are largely either chronic alcoholics or former mental patients who have been released to the community. If American society is willing to commit the necessary resources, then more humane treatment can be obtained, not only for homeless alcoholics but also for mental patients as well. It is a sad commentary on Western civilization, and particularly the United States, that individuals are still being incarcerated for the consequences of a disease, and that we cannot afford to provide treatment for those from the lower-income groups. Certain individuals do not realistically wish to face the fact that there are homeless alcoholics and that skid rows still exist in American society. The emphasis too frequently has been on upper and middle class alcoholics to the exclusion of lower income ones. I don't think that I will ever stop being an activist on the issue that it is inappropriate to be jailing, in any jurisdiction or in any country, people who are addicted to alcohol without providing them the option of treatment.

BJA: *By the mid-1970's a more conservative trend emerged in the United States. Was this reflected in the alcoholism field and in the organizations in which you participated?*

DJP: I think the conservative trend in the United States accelerated after America reduced its involvement in Vietnam, and was reflected in many areas including alcohol and drug policies. After the initial enthusiasm generated by the passage of the Hughes-Javits Act in 1970, which was renewed in 1974, the interest in the public drunkenness offender and the skid row alcoholic began to fade. The rush to enact state decriminalization laws in the early 1970's and the tendency to reduce the legal purchase age for alcoholic beverages began to wither away by the late 1970's.

In retrospect, too much money was appropriated for alcoholism activities in the 1970's and the early 1980's, and a number of ill-conceived research, treatment, and educational projects were funded. Literally millions of dollars were thrown at alcohol problems in the community, and when a 'quick-fix' solution was not obtained, new approaches were explored. This has always been a problem in American society in that we expect rapid solutions to problems.

BJA: How do you view the present more conservative climate and the movement toward 'alcohol control policies' and the enthusiasm for Ledermann? Your monograph, Primary Prevention of Alcohol Abuse and Alcoholism,[10] *addressed this issue.*

DJP: I believe the major problem with the Ledermann model is that his disciples have continued to maintain as dogma the basic proposition that knowledge of the mean consumption of alcoholic beverages in any population, which is only one parameter of the distribution of consumption, is adequate to determine the other parameter, namely, the dispersion of consumption as measured by the standard deviation. Thus the Ledermann model of the lognormal distribution of alcohol consumption and the attempt by control theorists empirically to justify it still requires the two parameters to be known to construct the distribution, namely the mean and the variance of the consumption. Attempts by his disciples, of whom there are many, to assume an invariant property in the dispersion still has not been scientifically proven. Furthermore, the Ledermann hypothesis is not empirically verified on a cross-cultural basis and is built upon Western European and North American populations.

BJA: Would you elaborate on the meaning and direction that this fascination with Ledermann has for alcohol policies.

DJP: Ledermann's hypothesis, as it has been adopted by his disciples in Canada, the United States, the parts of Europe, has implications for the future direction of alcohol control policies in all Western countries. My remarks are directed specifically at the United States. This theory, that a reduction in the per capita consumption of alcohol beverages will result in a decreasing number of cases of alcoholism and alcohol related-problems, has brought forth a number of proposed measures to reduce per capita consumption. These basically have been to restrict or ban the advertising of alcohol beverages on the electronic media in the United States. The idea behind this is that advertisements motivate people to behave the way they do vis-à-vis a particular product. I think this is a rather naive assumption when it comes to drinking behavior. The most important factors in terms of governing how much individuals consume are built upon familial influences, peer group influences or informal group pressures, and also individual belief systems which derive from the subculture in which the individual is reared.

BJA: *Are these the results of your study on advertizing?*

DJP: Yes. There was a major study, conducted under my direction on 'The Effects of Alcohol Beverage Advertizing Practices and Messages on Alcohol Problems and Alcoholism in the United States',[11] in which it was found by my colleague, Donald Strickland, and myself that only a minute fraction of alcohol consumption in our youth sample could be related to electronic advertisements, and that none of this studied populations's alcohol problems could be statistically related to advertizing exposure.

Other restrictions which have been advanced are that the containers of alcoholic beverages should carry health warning messages; increasing the legal purchase age for alcoholic beverages, under the threat of the loss of highway traffic safety funds, to the age of 21 years; and restricting the availability of alcoholic beverages to certain locations, days of the week, and times of the day.

BJA: *There seems to be a polarization of the actors in the field of alcoholism on how extensive alcohol control measures should be. How does this affect the alcoholism field, the future, and the actors themselves?*

DJP: I think one of the tragic developments of the 1980's is the kind of schism that has developed in the alcoholism field. Many organizations, founded to help the alcoholic and his or her family, were organized on the assumption that they would take no position, either positive or negative, towards the sale or restriction of the sale of alcohol products. This type of alcohol policy neutrality from the 1940's through the 1970's set the stage for progressive developments in research, treatment, and education. This consensus has become unraveled in terms of the new 'public health' model towards alcohol control.

BJA: *Do you think there is any solution to the current friction in the alcoholism field in the United States?*

DJP: Absolutely no. I don't see any solution for the cleavage that exists in the alcoholism policy field in the United States; for example there are now two nationwide councils on alcoholism. One is the National Council on Alcoholism and the other is the American Council on Alcoholism, each of which have different agendas and approaches to alcohol policy issues. There is the specter, as President Eisenhower mentioned in his farewell address to the nation in 1961, that the federal government as the major provider of research funds may dictate the agenda for the research, despite the safeguards that are built into the system by peer review, by indicating what problems are important and what are not relevant. There are very difficult days ahead for the alcoholism movement in the United States, for the alcohol beverage industry will be fighting to preserve its right to market a legal product, in face of very active groups who wish alcohol control policies to be stricter than they are currently.

BJA: *Does your experience as a member and board member of the NCA and your experience with Marty Mann, with whom you worked during your affiliation with the NCA, provide any insight into the current divisiveness in the alcoholism field?*

DJP: The National Council on Alcoholism was a very vibrant organization when I served on its Board in 1966, until I was not re-elected in 1982 because they had adopted a partyline of tolerating no dissent. I think that when any organization reaches the point it cannot tolerate dissent, then it has lost its *modus operandi* and its effectiveness. There always have to be 'gadflies' in an organization. I do cherish the years that I served as a member of the Board of Directors of the national Council on Alcoholism and received its prestigious Silver Key Award in 1978, but the death of Marty Mann in 1980 played havoc with the voluntary field of alcoholism. As long as the charismatic Marty Mann was alive, she was able to keep under control the tensions which existed among recovered alcoholics, professional scholars, clinicans, and interested lay persons, and also the alcohol beverage industry. Marty, being a recovering alcoholic herself, knew the difficulty of getting people interested in this area. Probably no other public figure in the mid-20th century had a greater impact on the communities' response to alcoholism than she did.

BJA: In order to effect social change, how important do you believe it is to be involved with political and community action and participation in political dealings? Or, do you agree, as Selden Bacon seemed to be saying in his recent BJA interview, that scientists should stick to their roles as scientists?

DJP: I don't take Selden's comment as being literally the case, for Selden in his own career was involved in social change. For example, he served as a board member of the NAAAP, and the Yale Center was very much involved in developing Yale-Plan Alcoholism Clinics; furthermore, his early work on the drunkenness offender in Connecticut had an applied basis to it.

Actually it is very difficult to be apolitical in this field, for alcohol policies are very much public policies. They have not been assigned to the area of scientific decision, and it is rather naive to think that any problem would not have a political aspect to it. The question of the level of private or public funding that will be provided is a political question. The location of the field of study of alcohol and alcohol problems is a political one. Will it be a multidisciplinary research center, such as the former Yale and now Rutgers Center on Alcohol Studies, or will it be specialized, that is, having only a few major foci for its concentration? The latter is currently the federal government's policy of having nine or ten alcohol research centers, which they support, devoted to specific problems. I think this is a major error in the sense that alcohol problems and issues are interdisciplinary in nature, and there is a great deal that can be gained from having a variety of disciplines and having interaction with the researchers, whether the field be sociology, psychology, psychiatry, or the natural and biological sciences.

BJA: *Were you not very active in the political arena yourself?*

DJP: Yes, I have had a long-term active involvement in alcohol issues, not only in the state of Missouri but nationally and internationally. Dating from my appointment to the first Governor's Commission on Alcoholism in Missouri in 1962, I served for approximately 10 or 12 years in all capacities ranging from member to chairman of the Commission from 1972 to 1975. I resigned from the Governor's Commission when I was appointed by Governor Bond to the Missouri Mental Health Commission (MHC) to represent alcoholism and drug abuse interests, and I served on the MHC until 1978. While I served in these capacities, Missouri enacted all of the major innovations which I, along with many others, had fought very hard for, namely, the decriminalization of the public drunkenness offense, the establishment of detoxification centers, the provision of mandatory health insurance coverage for alcoholics in all firms that employed four or more workers, and the creation of employee assistance programs for all state employees with alcohol and drug problems. I have a sense of pride that in the mid-1980's none of this legislation has been repealed.

I think the 'proof of the pudding' is to disseminate one's research findings to the elected political figures who are making the decisions and to interact with them on a face-to-face basis. The problem with a number of alcohol researchers today is that they have never had clinical experience with live alcoholics or individuals who have alcohol problems, and have not had to deal with elected political officials. When you talk with these elected officials, you find that alcoholism and alcohol problems do not occupy a high priority for them. There is one major exception, and this is drunk drivers, because these individuals may kill an innocent person. This gets the attention of the legislators more than any other issue on today's political agenda. Other alcohol issues, such as increased taxes or advertizing restrictions are too controversial for most politicians.

BJA: *Do you feel that there is still an opportunity for young researchers in the field of alcoholism?*

DJP: Definitely. Given the increase in the number of individuals in the field, the major thing that concerns me is their having a career that is anchored in an institution that is not solely dependent upon the vagaries of governmental funding.

BJA: *Your book,* Society, Culture, and Drinking Patterns,[12] *co-edited with Charles R. Snyder, showed for the time an unusual sweep of transcultural awareness. Was there ever tension between individual nationalisms and a larger worldview?*

DJP: I really don't think so. The co-editor of this book, Charles Snyder, who had already published the classic monograph, *Alcohol and the Jews,* and myself, because of my extensive travels throughout the United States and the European countries, had already developed an awareness of the importance of going beyond cultural barriers or nationalistic concerns. Partially this came from the training which we received in anthropology to view all societies that have existed historically and cross-culturally as experiments in civilization. Both of us were teenagers during the Second World War, from 1939 to 1945, and this experience had a profound influence on our thinking. Western civilization as we knew it was under attack both in Europe and the Pacific, and whether it would survive was problematic for a time. In my first journeys to Europe, all the places were familiar from the news, and I realized the interconnection to the United States. There was not the chauvinism that seems to mark nations so much today. We were still idealistic in that we thought there could be world peace through world health in the 1950's and 1960's.

Of all my publications, I think this is the best one, for most of the articles were written especially for this collection, and the extensive introductory notes written by Chuck Snyder and myself were meticulously done and made the book into a coherent whole.

Although *Society, Culture, and Drinking Patterns* has now become a classic that is out of print, all I can emphasize is that it required a tremendous amount of hard work and dedication on the part of all the contributors, including the editors, who received no honoraria. The commitment of all the authors to this endeavor would be hard for any editors to obtain in the current milieu of the 1980's. Furthermore, the number of individuals doing behavioral science research in alcohol studies was so small at that time, probably not more than 40 to 50, and we were a very well integrated group of individuals. In one sense we were also stigmatized by studying individuals who were 'unworthy' of study. It's hard to communicate to the younger generation the stigma which was attached to this field. There is a saying in this country that research goes where the federal funds are, but at that time when these scholars, such as Ed Lemert, Earl Rubington, Joan Jackson, Chuck Snyder, Selden Bacon, Joe Gusfield, and others contributed to this volume, they had no massive federal research grants; their contributions came from their dedication to scholarship. All the royalties from this book went to the professional organization, the Society for the Study of Social Problems.

BJA: *Also, about this time, in the early 1960's you published, together with Archer Tongue, the Director of the International Bureau Against Alcoholism, a* Handbook of Organizations for Research on Alcohol and Alcoholism Problems.[13] *What was the underlying motivation or purpose of this publication?*

DJP: I have always been a great advocate for furthering international communication in the field of alcoholism research and treatment, since the findings that are obtained from one country are to a certain extent culture bound and there is a need to have a worldwide view. The problem of increased international cooperation was the focus of informal meetings in which I participated at the 26th International Congress in Stockholm in 1960, and the European Institute for the Prevention and Treatment of Alcoholism in Amsterdam in 1961. At that time, the late Henrietti Casier, a Belgium researcher in Biochemistry and a warm and supportive friend of mine, and Archer Tongue, an extremely diligent and hard worker in the field of furthering international communications, and I decided that it was essential in terms of facilitating international communication to provide researchers with a handbook of organizations involved in alcoholism research and problems. As far as I know this was the first systematic collation of international organizations involved in alcoholism research; you can use this publication as a benchmark to measure the rapid research expansion which has occurred in the last 20 plus years. We were deeply indebted to the philanthropist, Brinkley Smithers, for the financial aid that made this project possible.

BJA: *In the 1960's there was much activity and great strides in the United States in gaining recognition of alcoholism as an illness and providing services for the then estimated 6 million alcoholics in the country. In 1968, the 28th International Congress on Alcoholism was held in Washington, D.C., and you, as the Chairman, headed this Congress. What was the significance of this international meeting?*

DJP: I think that the real significance of the 28th International Congress was that in retrospect it showed that the scientific study of alcohol issues had come of age. It was, up to that time and to the present, the largest gathering of research scientists in the field of alcoholism. Also noteworthy is that it attracted the largest number of participants since the congresses began in 1885. There were around 1600 delegates present. Some comments about its orientation would place it in perspective. Most of the previous international congresses had an abstinence orientation. In fact, scientific orientation to alcohol studies began to rear its head in the congresses that were held in the 1950's, with the scientific approach becoming ascendant in the International Congress held in Stockholm in 1960, and in Frankfurt in 1964.

BJA: *Was this the first Congress held in the United States?*

DJP: This was the first Congress held in North America since the 1920 International Congress, which was held in Washington, D.C. also; that one was really a celebration of the ratification of the 20th Amendment to the constitution, which instituted Prohibition—that noble experiment which failed. I think that one of the major accomplishments of the 28th International

Congress was that it brought together research scholars from all of the continents and was scientific in nature. The program committee's goal was to have presentations from an international point of view and to present the many facets of alcohol problems from different countries. This International Congress set the stage for the passage by the U.S. Congress of the Hughes-Javits Alcoholism Act in 1970.

Furthermore, these Congress Proceedings[14] were published under the editorship of Mark Keller (with Timothy Coffey). Anyone who wants to get a perspective on the state of knowledge on alcoholism in the world in 1968, could profit from the reading of these proceedings.

BJA: The International Congress on Alcoholism brought together individual researchers from many nations. Did this bring into focus any kinds of tensions which may have existed between the countries?

DJP: Not really. I don't think international tensions or nationalistic feelings were exacerbated by this Congress. One of the major purposes which it served was to allow persons with like interests to become acquainted.

BJA: You also did a study of the drug scene in Great Britain.

DJP: I actually was only one of four people who did the study, *The Drug Scene in Great Britain: Journey Into Loneliness.*[15] The major collaborators in this work were the noted British psychiatrist, Max Glatt, and myself. When I first visited Dr. Glatt's treatment facility at St. Bernard's Hospital, I was surprized to find that he had teenage drug addicts whom he was treating in the unit. I had been reared in the American sociological tradition—that there was not a significant number of drug addicts in Great Britain and that they had the ideal system. I discussed my observations of the youthful addicts with Max on one of my frequent visits to his home in North London. Almost ritualistically, I always set Saturday aside to spend with him, his charming wife, Gisele, and his son Julian, exchanging ideas. His wife, while providing excellent hospitality, participated vigorously in our discussions. Max was always full of new ideas derived from his clinical practice, and he is one of the major figures in the modern alcoholism movement.

We thought a new study of the British drug scene would make an excellent research project. He was able to recruit for the study a young Englishman, Donald Hills, and I obtained a young Washington University graduate student who was studying under me, Duff Gillespie, who was the same age as the young drug addicts in Great Britain. Our book was very critical of the system of handling drug addiction at that time. We indicated that perhaps the drug problem was exacerbated by over-prescribing of drugs by a limited number of psychiatrists. Later that situation was corrected; however the popular press now again indicates that there is a youth heroin addiction problem in London in the mid-1980's.

BJA: There was much debate on the research and treatment 'marriage' between the dry drugs and the wet drug alcohol, which was discussed in your article 'The Rush to Combine'.[16] Do you feel they should be grouped together as one? Will each receive the kind of attention needed if they are combined in the sense of treatment, research funding, etc?

DJP: Part of my initial negative reaction to the combination of 'dry' and 'wet' drugs came from the experience in Great Britain where an attempt was made at St. Bernard's Hospital to treat both alcohol addicts who were in their late 30's, 40's and 50's with dry drug addicts in the teens and 20's in the same unit. These age dissimilarities made a harmonious unit impossible. Neither group understood the other. There was just too much age and cultural dissimilarity between these groups. Of course alcohol is a legal drug, and this has social ramifications for it, whereas the dry drugs, marijuana, hashish, cocaine, heroin, are illegal drugs. This means that there are social and legal differences between the two. Since this article was published, it is rare to find young persons today who are not abusers of a multiplicity of drugs.

In the American government, the National Institute on Alcohol Abuse and Alcoholism and the National Institute on Drug Abuse are two separate organizations. Of course, there is still much more attention being paid to the dry drugs, especially cocaine, than to the wet drug alcohol. The mere fact that one is legal and the others illegal is a social fact that cannot be overlooked.

BJA: *What about the progress in the last three decades on the international scene?*

DJP: When I first entered this field there was very little contact between the few alcoholism researchers in the United States and those in Europe. I remember Marty Mann, who attended as an official American delegate the first post-war International Congress on Alcoholism in Switzerland in 1948, relating to me that it was no more than a gathering of 'drys' (prohibitionists). She felt that her attendance had not been productive in that so few individuals could comprehend the idea of a recovered alcoholic such as herself, or that there could be a scientific study of alcohol issues. Subsequent international congresses were held under the auspices of the International Bureau Against Alcoholism (Archer Tongue joined as its director in 1952), which was perceived in America as a 'dry' organization at that time.

In the summer of 1960, I visited the International Bureau in Switzerland. It was located on the second or third floor of an older building in Lausanne. Archer was an extremely dedicated individual who worked for a pittance and was trying to move the Bureau from a 'dry' orientation to a scientific one. His struggles to obtain adequate funding for the International Bureau at his own personal sacrifice is one of the unwritten chapters of the international alcoholism movement. In order to aid the International Bureau in the early 1960's, my university purchased a number of copies of proceedings of international congresses in order to help him meet the bills. Through his quiet but diplomatic manner, he was able to bring the International Bureau into the mainstream of the scientific approach to alcoholism and alcoholism problems. In this task he was aided by his dedicated spouse, Eva Tongue, a lawyer, who was a native of Hungary.

The Tongues, through the International Council, did more to foster international cooperation through the annual Summer Institutes and periodic International Congresses than have any other organization in the post-war period. Therefore their efforts to get other international bodies, such as the World Health Organization, to become re-interested in the issues of alcoholism and alcohol problems reached fruition in the late 1960's, and continue today. Both of these individuals are the unsung heroes of making international cooperation possible long before there were American federal funds available for this activity.

Although the international co-operation is well established today, one must be aware that there are strong international tensions that are involved when it comes to the question of alcohol control policies. Given the fact that a significant proportion of individuals in certain countries derive their livelihood from the production, distribution, and sales of alcoholic beverages, these countries will be resistant to any extreme alcohol control measures, which would mean that their products would not be competitive on the world market.

References

1. Pittman, D. J. & Gordon, C. W. (1958) *Revolving Door: A Study of the Chronic Police Case Inebriate* (Glencoe, Ill, The Free Press; New Brunswick, N.J.: Rutgers Center of Alcoholic Studies). [Out of print.]
2. Pittman, D. J. (1966) The Open Door: Sociology in an Alcoholism Treatment Facility, in: Arthur B. Shostak (Ed.) *Sociology in Action* (Homewood, Ill, Dorsey Press).
3. Pittman, D. J. (1963) The role of sociology in the planning and operation of alcoholism treatment programmes, *British Journal of Addiction*, 59, pp. 35–39.
4. Pittman, D. J. & Sterne, M. W. (1962) *The Carousel: Hospitals, Social Agencies, and the Alcoholic*, Report presented to the Missouri Division of Health.
5. Sterne, M. W. & Pittman, D. J. (1965) The concept of motivation: a source of institutional and professional blockage in the treatment of alcoholics, *Quarterly Journal of Studies on Alcohol*, 26, pp. 41–57.
6. Pittman, D. J. & Tate, R. L. (1969) A comparison of two treatment programs for alcoholics, *Quarterly Journal of Studies on Alcohol*, 30, pp. 888–889.
7. Sterne, M. W. & Pittman, D. J. (1973) *Drinking Patterns in the Ghetto*, Vols I and II (Washington University, Social Science Institute).

8. Pittman, D. J. (1967) Public intoxication and the alcoholic offender in American society, in : *Task Force Report: Drunkenness*, pp. 7–28, President's Commission on Law Enforcement and Administration of Justice (Washington, D.C., U.S. Government Printing Office).
9. St. Louis Detoxification & Diagnostic Evaluation Center (1970) *Final Report*, Law Enforcement Assistance Administration (LEAA), United States Department of Justice #0–373–790 (Washington, D.C., Superintendent of Documents, U.S. Government Printing Office).
10. Pittman, D. J. (1980) *Primary Prevention of Alcohol Abuse and Alcoholism: An Evaluation of the Control of Consumption Policy* (St Louis, Mo, Social Science Institute,Washington University).
11. Pittman, D. J. & Strickland, D. E. (Co-Principal Investigators) (1981) The Effects of Alcohol Beverage Advertising Practices and Messages on Alcohol Problems and Alcoholism in the United States, Grantor: U.S. Brewers Association, 1979–1984, *The Effects of Alcohol Beverage Advertising Practices and Messages on Alcohol Problems and Alcoholism in the United States*, Preliminary Report (St Louis, Mo, Social Science Institute, Washington University).
12. Pittman, D. J. & Snyder, C. R. (Eds) (1962) *Society, Culture, and Drinking Patterns* (New York, John Wiley) [out of print].
13. Pittman, D. J. & Tongue, A. (1964) *Handbook of Organizations for Research on Alcohol and Alcoholism Problems* (Lausanne, Switzerland, International Council on Alcohol and Alcoholism).
14. Pittman, D. J. (1969) The 28th International Congress on Alcohol and Alcoholism: background scope and purpose, in: M. Keller & T. G. Coffey (Eds) *Proceedings of the 28th International Congress on Alcohol and Alcoholism: Vol. 2: Lectures in Plenary Sessions*, pp. ix–xii, Washington, D.C., September 1968 (Highland Park, NJ, Hillhouse Press).
15. Glatt, M. M., Pittman, D. J., Gillespie, D. G. & Hills, D. R. (1967) *The Drug Scene in Great Britain: Journey Into Loneliness* (London, Edward Arnold Ltd; Baltimore, Md, Williams & Wilkins).
16. Pittman, D. J. (1967) The Rush to Combine: Sociological Dissimilarities of Alcoholism and Drug Abuse, *British Journal of Addiction*, 62, pp. 337–343.

9

Interview with Donald Goodwin

DONALD W. GOODWIN, MD, b. 1931. Entered medicine after a career in journalism and a first degree in English. His earlier research on alcoholism was conducted at Washington University (St. Louis) where he was director of the Center for Addictions. From 1976 he has been Professor and Chairman of the Department of Psychiatry, University of Kansas. Contributions to the study of drinking problems have included work on genetics, alcoholic "blackouts," and influence of alcohol on creativity. Recipient of Jellinek Prize.

BJA: *You are primarily known as a psychiatrist and for your research in alcoholism. I think it would be of interest to hear how you chose a career in medicine. I understand that, in fact, medicine was something of a second career for you.*

DG: Medicine *was* a second career. Between college and medical school, 7 years passed, 2 of them in the U.S. Army and 4 in New York working as an editor and columnist for a newspaper syndicate belonging to the New York Times. Then I returned to undergraduate school for a year of premedical training to qualify for medical school. I was admitted to medical school at the age of 29. So I had a 2-year career in the Army, if one would call that a career, and a 4-year career in newspaper work before going into medicine.

BJA: *What was it that appealed to you about medicine?*

DG: My interest came by accident. I was in the Army and somebody made a mistake and gave me a job as a psychiatric social worker. I had no background in social work but liked it. I was surrounded by psychiatrists and psychologists and thought this was a great field. There was a good library where I was stationed and I read the works of Freud and others. I became enamored of psychiatry and an ardent Freudian and wanted to go to medical school. I was an English major. I didn't think I had a chance of getting it, so I went to New York and got a job. Then a friend talked me into at least applying for medical school, which I did.

It happened to be a period when it was rather easy to get into medical school. I was admitted in my home state, at the University of Kansas. They were interested at the time in music majors and English majors and I had worked as a newspaper writer and that appealed to them. Today I think it probably wouldn't help at all to have a background like that, probably a hindrance, but I just happened to be lucky and apply at a time when that's the kind of people they were looking for.

BJA: You started out in medical school with a career in psychiatry in mind?

DG: Yes, definitely. I was a psychiatric social worker in the Army and liked psychiatry and, as I say, I became an ardent Freudian. Karl Menninger was from my home state and a boyhood hero of mine. I had read his books and am very proud that Dr. Menninger is a member of our faculty. We are just a few miles apart from Topeka and our two Departments interact regularly.

Dr. Menninger was probably as responsible as anybody for my interest in psychiatry, dating back before I went in the Army. English majors, I might add, in the United States, are particularly susceptible to Freudianism. There are no more staunch Freudians than the New York literati. Then I was an English major, most of the writers, publishers and the center of culture seemed to be New York City, which is the reason, when I got out of the Army, I headed for New York City where all my heroes lived. I lived there for 4 years. Except for taking courses from Lionel Trilling and W. H. Auden, I never ran into one of these heroes, but being with them, breathing the same air, was a heady experience for me. Those were wonderful years in New York City in the late 1950's.

BJA: *I suppose it's no secret that you are not one of the pillars of the psychoanalytic community now. Apparently your English majorship and Karl Menninger lost their clout.*

DG: I became disillusioned in medical school. I found that psychiatry was not particularly respected by other medical specialists. I became interested in internal medicine, in fact, and almost went into that specialty. At that time I still thought psychoanalysis was the only psychiatry that existed. I was concerned about the analysts' lack of concern for evidence. Later, as a resident at Washington University in ST. Louis, I found that there were other versions of psychiatry, and ones I could respect.

BJA: *How did your interest in alcoholism come about?*

DG: I trained at Washington University in the last part of the 60's when Washington University was undergoing sort of a golden age. It taught a kind of psychiatry that was congenial to me at that time in my life. Having just come out of medical school, I liked the way physicians acted like physicians and not like swami and they had a practical approach to psychiatry I felt was also scientific. The approach had the further attraction of being generally unpopular in the United States, so that it was a bit like living in Israel surrounded by Arabs. That's a good feeling and brings people together. Over time it stopped being a minority in-group and more 'mainstream,' at least in the sense of producing a volume called DSM-III, which is largely a product of Washington University. The psychodynamic movement continues to exist. Indeed, perhaps a majority of U.S. psychiatrists are trained in psychodynamic ideas, but nevertheless the respect for data and a return to a more medical approach to psychiatry seems to be occurring. Of people who are taking over leadership positions in the field in America, fewer and fewer are analysts and more are non-analysts so I think psychiatry in the United States, after 40 years of analytic dominance, has returned to its good senses and is now approaching, in a pragmatic way, with a relatively open mind, how people become the way they are.

Now, with regard to my interest in alcoholism. I really enjoyed my experience at Washington University with Eli Robins and Sam Guze and a whole group of people I felt very much at home with, and I decided I wanted to stay in academic medicine and do research. Everybody at Washington University had a specialty. There was Murphy in suicide, Winokur in depression, Guze in hysteria . . . all the faculty had subspecialized in some aspect of psychiatry and it seemed to me that the way to get a name in academic medicine was to become identified with one area, devote most of your efforts to that area and not spread yourself around.

So I more or less deliberately sought out an area that hadn't already been taken over by somebody else in the department. I chose alcoholism on the grounds that (a) the government was starting to spend money for alcoholism research for the first time and indeed we just got a large alcoholism grant at Washington University, which I could share in spending, and (b) alcoholism is a big field. It has social aspects, medical aspects, crosses a lot of disciplines and also permits a physician to use the information that he learned in the course of becoming a physician. As once was said of syphilis, to know alcoholism is to know medicine. I liked that very much because one thing that I didn't like about psychiatry was that it seemed the medical training was largely irrelevant.

Psychiatry in the 1960's was almost synonymous with psychotherapy and psychotherapy didn't seem particularly related to muscles, bones and glands and could probably be done just as well by people who had never gone to medical school. Therefore, alcoholism had the advantage of forcing one to keep up with the liver and brain and practically everything else that one is exposed to in medical school, including the immune system, etc, so I liked that part about it. I also liked the fact they were spending money on what was a big problem. There was no shortage of people who had the illness but there *was* a shortage of people who were interested in it.

In medicine alcoholism had been a pariah, either ignored or actively scorned by a large majority of physicians who considered alcoholism a hopeless condition, largely restricted to people with weak characters. Therefore, I wasn't going into an overcrowded field. I could rapidly achieve a reputation as being a specialist without necessarily knowing very much. It was easy to get a reputation rapidly in a field that nobody else knew much about.

BJA: *'Rapidly' certainly does describe it. What would you consider your most important research?*

DG: The Danish adoption studies. We were the first group to find that children of alcoholics had a high risk of becoming alcoholic even when they are raised by adoptive parents and not exposed to their alcoholic biological families. This suggested there was a biological vulnerability. We are now engaged in studies, some still in Denmark, trying to home in on the nature of the vulnerability.

The Danish findings were replicated by two other groups, one in Sweden and one in Iowa, so consensus was reached that whatever factors operate (and there obviously are many factors that lead to alcoholism), biology is one of them. Some people seem more biologically susceptible to acquiring the 'bad habit' of excessive drinking than others. Awareness of this became a handle for further work.

BJA: *Your particular research that you cite and this whole line of thought that resulted from it depended heavily on the opportunity you have had to utilize the Danish adoption apparatus. How did you get access?*

DG: That was a real windfall. Toward the end of my residency, I learned that a group headed by Seymour Kety with Paul Winder and David Rosenthal were conducting studies in Copenhagen with Fini Schulsinger and Sarnoff Mednick, utilizing adoptees. It was relatively easy to use adoptees as subjects in Denmark compared to other countries. Among other things, Denmark had centralized records that one could get access to through Schulsinger. I mentioned the matter to Sam Guze and George Winokur, mentors of mine at that time, and we went to Washington and visited with the people who were doing the studies. They were interested in schizophrenia. They weren't interested in alcoholism. They generously allowed us to use their adoption material. Meanwhile, I had an opportunity to go to Copenhagen and visit with Dr Schulsinger. I submitted a grant and, one year out of residency, received funds to conduct an adoption study in alcoholism in Denmark. More grants followed and we are still studying Danish children of alcoholics.

BJA: *Do you have any other thoughts about vulnerable groups?*

DG: I am intrigued by several studies published in the past few years reporting that a sizeable minority of alcoholics, upon being carefully asked, give a history of an anxiety disorder that seemed to have preceded their heavy drinking. The disorders tend to be different in men and women with women reporting more agoraphobia and men reporting more social phobias. Both the agoraphobic women and social phobic men seem to have used alcohol early in their lives as a means of coping with their phobias and then it appears that the coping got out of hand and that alcoholism resulted. There is sort of a taboo about treating anxiety pharmacologically in alcoholics or treating alcoholics with any kind of medicinal agents. However, it may be that there is a subgroup for whom pharmacological treatment might be helpful. It should be pursued in any case.

BJA: *I understand you and your colleagues in Kansas City have done some work on the so-called Oriental flushing phenomena.*

DG: Yes. When I was just getting into alcoholism research, a young psychiatrist in Boston reported that a fairly high percentage of Orientals developed a skin flush that looked rather like measles after consuming a small amount of alcohol. This appeared to be genetically based because even Oriental babies flushed when they were given alcohol. This, to my knowledge, had never been reported previously, although presumably Orientals have flushed ever since there have been Orientals. The flush was accompanied by dysphoria, sleepiness and sometimes nausea, so this reaction to a small amount of alcohol is a powerful deterrent to heavy drinking, perhaps explaining the rather low alcoholism rate in the Orient.

In any case, a number of us in this country were fascinated by this heretofore never described condition that affected so many people and we started recruiting Orientals and gave them alcohol, usually graduate students at universities. We would give them alcohol and watch them flush. Some groups reported that the flush was associated with an increase of acetaldehyde and then enzymologists went to work and reported that Japanese flushers had atypical forms of both alcohol dehydrogenase and aldehyde dehydrogenase. The combination of these atypical forms resulted in an accumulation of acetaldehyde that presumably was responsible for the Oriental flush. In just a few years the chemical pathways involved in this rather remarkable phenomenon were pretty well worked out and now people ask, "What good is it to know these things?" I am not sure exactly what good it is but one hopes that if one knows how millions and millions of people are protected from excessive drinking by a physiological intolerance for alcohol, such intolerance conceivably could be grafted, so to speak, on those who are not physiologically intolerant. I don't know whether that is a practical idea or not but at any rate, on the grounds that the more you know about something the more likely you are to find something useful, I have always encouraged people to pursue this type of study. As a result, we at Kansas University were amongst the first to discover that you could prevent the Oriental flush by giving a combination of antihistamines to the subject before the subject drank. Now, if the Oriental flush is the world's number 1 alcohol problem (many people would not call it a problem but nevertheless it is a problem for people who would like to drink), we have apparently produced a 'cure' for the Oriental flush. This has received little attention.

BJA: *I understand that you have been also interested in the problem of alcoholism among writers.*

DG: Yes. One of the first things I learned when I got into the field was that the group with undoubtedly the highest prevalence of alcoholism among any group in the world consisted of famous American writers. At that time we had six Nobel Laureates in literature and four were alcoholic. One was a very heavy drinker and the sixth was Pearl Buck who may not have deserved the prize. This is a prevalence rate of alcoholism even higher than among the Irish of Boston.

This interest led me to write a book which is now in the hands of a publisher. In the course of writing the book I became convinced that there was in America in the 20's through the 50's a literal epidemic of alcoholism among American writers so that it was indeed difficult to draw up a list on *non*-alcoholic American writers for that period. Why should this happen in America in this century? We had never had so many drinking writers in the past.

No other country, although many had their share of drinking writers, had a great majority who were alcoholic. It seemed to be a curiously American phenomenon in this century and I was interested in speculating about the causes. My speculations, I trust, will soon be available in bookstores.

BJA: What changes have you seen in the field of alcoholism in your career?

DG: There certainly is more research going on. Our government is spending more money. It didn't used to spend *any* money, so any money is more money. Alcoholism has become somewhat more socially acceptable—destigmatized—so that now famous people check into the Betty Ford clinic and then have a press conference. Rather than conceal their problem, they almost exalt in it and make it a badge of honor and we now have in America many celebrities who have become sober and have become celebrities almost because of sobriety as much as anything else. We had a politician in Kansas City recently running for office who was accused by his opponent of being absent from his post in Washington a good deal of the time and the politician responded indignantly, saying that his opponent obviously knew the reason that he had been absent so much was that he was being treated for alcoholism. Here was a man who would rather be considered alcoholic than lazy.

BJA: Any comments about current styles or fashions in alcoholism treatment?

DG: Yes, I think that Antabuse or disulfiram, the only drinking deterrent drug available in the United States, is terribly underused. I think a lot of people with alcohol problems would benefit from Antabuse who aren't offered it. Many learn to take it on their own schedule without benefit of professional advice. They take it when they feel they need it. This sounds like heresy. However, alcoholism comes in many forms and shapes and it is all not the same. I have a patient who uses Antabuse for travel. In years past, afraid of airplanes, he went to the airport bar early before the flight and consumed some anxiolytic substances and then continued this on the plane. By the time he got where he was going he was just beginning, so by the next day, after closing down the piano bar that night, he was not in very good shape for a meeting. He wasn't much of a drinker at home. Now he just takes an Antabuse before he travels. His career has boomed. I know of other examples of people who use Antabuse if they know when an occasion is coming up where they are going to be tempted to drink and they just make up their mind they are not going to. I know other people deliberately plan a time in the future, maybe months ahead, when they are going to stop taking Antabuse for a few days, so that it leaves the body. Then they get drunk for a day or two and start taking it again. This gives the individual a degree of control. Obviously, there are many this will not work for. Still, there is an antagonism toward Antabuse which is unfortunate. Antabuse, after all, can be prescribed by any physician. Despite all the talk about side effects I think that in the amounts we prescribe these days these side effects are rare. Certainly Antabuse is not nearly as dangerous as the act of drinking large amounts of alcohol.

I want to say a word about inpatient versus outpatient treatment of alcoholism. Griffith Edwards, editor of this journal, as well as some investigators in the U.S., have compared inpatient and outpatient treatment. Outpatient seems to do as well. In the U.S. we have something called the Minnesota Model referring to hospitalization for fixed periods. The person spends 28 days in a treatment unit and is treated by alcoholism counsellors, nurses and rarely sees a physician. This has come to be considered the gold standard for treatment, and this is unfortunate. The evidence suggests other, less expensive treatments do just as well.

About the AA (which is always risky to talk about unless you are going to be 100% totally committed to it), the problem is that of those who attend a few meetings only 12 to 15% continue attending. This leaves 85% for whom the AA does not seem to be helpful—at least they don't give it a chance to be helpful. What happens to these people? You get the impression from some AA members that they are doomed. This is simply not true. Those of us in the field know lots of people who have not become AA members but recover.

BJA: What do you think about the disease concept?

DG: Diseases, to begin with, are something people see doctors for. Diseases are to doctors what groceries are to grocers: their specialty and their livelihood. What constitutes a disease has changed over historical time but usually indicates the presence of a known or suspected physical or psychological vulnerability that compromises the organism's ability to survive and function effectively in a particular environment.

Physicians are consulted about the problem of alcoholism and therefore alcoholism becomes, by this definition, a disease. It also fulfills a narrow definition of disease that requires the presence of a biological abnormality that leads to maladaptation. The evidence that alcoholism involves a biological vulnerability is just as strong, or perhaps stronger, than the evidence that hypertension or adult-onset diabetes involves a biological vulnerability. Hypertension and adult-onset diabetes both run in families. This is not conclusive evidence for 'genetic' or 'constitutional' factors, inasmuch as families often share the same dietary habits and lifestyles. However, it is widely assumed that both involve a biological susceptibility that often seems to require precipitating factors, such as overweight or excessive salt intake, to produce clinical disease.

The evidence that alcoholism is influenced by biological vulnerability comes mainly from adoption studies in which children of alcoholics, raised by non-alcoholic adoptive parents, still become alcoholic at a high rate: a rate three to five times higher than occurs in the families of non-alcoholics. 'Biological susceptibility' is not necessarily synonymous with genetic. It is conceivable that perhaps the mother was drinking during pregnancy and this in some fashion created the vulnerability. However, it seems more probable to most of us that genetic factors are involved. Also, like salt in hypertension and obesity in diabetes, habits, conditioning, learning and availability of alcohol obviously are involved in the development of alcoholism in susceptible individuals.

To summarize, I think the evidence that alcoholism can properly be called a disease is just as strong for alcoholism as it is for many medical conditions universally regarded as diseases.

Interview with Donald Goodwin 153

BJA: Is alcohol ever good for you?

DG: Maybe one in ten or twelve who drink find it's very bad for them. They become alcoholic. Of the other eleven out of twelve who drink, some drink too much, and I doubt that that's good for them. For what appears to be the majority of people, it's hard to really say that alcohol is harmful for them, assuming they don't get into an automobile and drive over the legal limit or perhaps other circumstances where even smallish amounts of alcohol might be harmful.

There is now a fairly large literature indicating that alcohol produces an increase in high density lipoproteins, called the 'good cholesterol,' which is associated with a decreased risk of coronary artery disease. According to some studies, a bottle of beer has about the same effect on high density lipoproteins as a 20 min jog. There are also studies reporting that people who drink moderately live longer than people who drink excessively or people who don't drink at all. This may not have anything to do with alcohol. Moderate drinkers are perhaps moderate in other ways that contribute to longevity. Nevertheless, moderate drinking and longevity are correlated, if not causally.

As far as alcohol being good for you otherwise, I think anything that provides pleasure and increases sociability, that makes the introverts a little less introvertish, shouldn't be knocked all the time. Also, it brings in a lot of taxes.

BJA: Having very effectively finessed that question, can you comment on current drinking patterns in this country.

DG: We are drinking less. Consumption of alcohol has fallen in the past few years in the U.S. from around 2.8 gallons per capita in absolute alcohol to around 2.4. What is the basis for the change? People are smoking marihuana and that may be a partial explanation. The obsession we have in this country with thinness and with health—particularly thinness—makes the calories in alcohol undesirable.

Also, attitudes have changed. One used to go to a party and a glass of potent alcohol beverage was thrust immediately into your hand. Now you often have people asking what you would like to drink and if you opt for coffee or soft drink you don't become ostracized. Maybe among the kids there is still some ostracism towards the person who doesn't drink but I think people are lightening up on this and becoming more tolerant of people having choices.

Also, I think the heavy emphasis on the penalties attached to a drunk-driving arrest in this country is having a definite effect on drinking patterns, at least in bars. I don't know whether the bar business is in decline but I would be surprized if it wasn't because now we have laws where the bartender is legally accountable if something bad happens.

BJA: *What books have you written recently?*

DG: I just published a book called *Anxiety* Oxford University Press. It has now been picked up by Ballentine and is being released as a paperback. They plan to put out this book with a rather garish cover that says ANXIETY in frightening looking type in airports to see how many people would buy one before boarding an airplane. I am a little skeptical, but there are also going to be paperback in grocery stores and it will be the first time I have had a really mass distributed book. In working with Ballantine on *Anxiety* we went back to a book wrote some ten years ago called *Is Alcoholism Hereditary?* published by Oxford. It is now out of print and Ballantine has asked me to revise the book and they will try to sell it. Other than that, Sam Guze and I are working on the fourth edition of a psychiatric textbook called *Psychiatric Diagnosis.* That is pretty much where I stand with books.

10

Interview with Genevieve Knupfer

GENEVIEVE KNUPFER, b. 1914. Professional training in sociology (Brussels; Wellesley Mass., Columbia, NY); and in Medicine (Rochester, NY): MA, PhD, MD. Assistant Director (1959–62) and Project Director (1962–68), Drinking Practices Survey, California. Consultant to Social Research Group, Berkeley from 1979, together with many other research consultancies. Work for WHO's alcoholism program. Private practice in psychiatry 1956–85, and clinical work in various mental health agencies.

BJA: *Where did you grow up?*
GK: My parents were born in New York, and I was born in Düsseldorf, a few months before the outbreak of the first World War. So we came back to the U.S.A. and after the armistice we went to Brussels. My parents selected Brussels because Germany didn't seem a very good place to be in after the war. The family stayed in Belgium until 1936. I went to school there until it was time for college. Then I went to Wellesley, Massachusetts, which meant travelling back and forth to Europe each summer—which was wonderful fun in those days because of the transatlantic steamers.

BJA: *You have unusual credentials in having both a doctorate in sociology and a qualification as a psychiatrist. Which came first?*
GK: I was in sociology first. In college I figured out that although I really wanted to be a writer of literature, if you are a writer and you are not any good, you've got nothing. Whereas if you are a

scientist you can add a little brick into the wall being built by a group of people, so I thought that was safer. Then I thought physical sciences have gone too far already so let's do the social sciences, and that how I got involved.

BJA: *And you were at Columbia, which in those days was the center of survey sociology, or quantitative sociology, in the U.S.A.?*

GK: As a matter of fact, I was unaware of that emphasis when I started my graduate work at Columbia. My idea for a dissertation was to address the question whether revolution was necessary in this country. The argument had been raised that it was not necessary, because of the much greater social mobility in the U.S. compared to other countries. So I did a survey, asking people about their occupations and the occupations of their fathers. However, it so happened that my adviser, Paul Lazarsfeld, was interested mainly in methodology—so the dissertation was about 'Indices of Socio-economic Status',[1] not about revolution, and the results of my survey ended up as one sentence in one footnote. However, Paul insisted that we had to have one chapter on more cultural, theoretical issues because this would be necessary to satisfy one member of the committee, Robert Lynd, one of the authors of *Middletown*. The resulting 'Portrait of the Underdog'[2] is the only part of my dissertation that was ever published.

BJA: *How did you make the decision to go to medical school?*

GK: Oh, well I got involved in psychoanalysis, first because of intellectual interest, then as a patient. Also I had become discouraged with social science research because the results were always so inconclusive. So I thought I would feel more useful if I was helping people. At the time I was enthusiastic about the ideas of Wilhelm Reich, but I was told "It's very unorthodox, so you'd better have a medical degree before you practice this therapy." So I went to medical school. Probably I went to medical school partly because I found it safer to be in school than out in the world. Anyway shortly afterwards I found the Reichian system far too cultist for my taste and I ended up instead being much more of an eclectic therapist.

BJA: So you went to medical school with the intention of moving into psychotherapy?

GK: My intention was to be a psychiatrist and forget all about research. However, in my residency I get involved in listening to Gregory Bateson and Don Jackson, and their enthusiasm for the theory that schizophrenia was due to the schizophrenogenic mother giving contradictory messages to the child and thus fouling him up. I had a great urge to do some work on that problem, to test the theory because I thought it very poorly documented. So I wrote a research proposal, having by then abandoned my determination not to do research. But the Stanford Department of Psychiatry wasn't interested and somehow in the course of this whole business I ran into Wendell Lipscomb who was interested in getting somebody to do alcohol research. He'd got a grant and was looking for a director. But I was in private practice and didn't have the time to be director. I was on the Peninsula and it was too far away. So we agreed to find a director and that's how I met Ira Cisin, and he took on that job. Ira moved to George Washington University a couple of years later and then I took on the directorship. That work started out as simply a descriptive study of drinking patterns. But it's so difficult in sociology to stick to simple description and one always has some idea of solving the problem or of what kinds of people have the most trouble with their drinking, and why. We were also interested in what made people abstainers, and to what extent this choice was based on profound religious conviction, or just a custom. As for the study of people with major drinking problems, it emerged immediately that there was a difficulty here with which I am still struggling: the researcher is up against the fact that there are too few people in any general population survey who fall into this category to allow a large enought group for analysis.

BJA: Around 1962 you became interested in longitudinal research?

GK: Yes, that seemed important, because everybody knows that really serious problems with alcohol develop over time, and we wondered how you could predict that kind of eventuality. Some people in any sample drink heavily and get into trouble and then decide to stop drinking or drink less, while others continue and progress. There are some very interesting questions here, and not much has been found out.

BJA: *The original study was limited to drinking patterns and although it asked about heavy drinking, it wasn't trying to measure 'alcoholism'. Is that right?*

GK: Yes. What we learned was that we had been excessively cautious as regards the types of questions people would agree to be interviewed on. We were just inching up on them in a delicate way, edging toward asking them what degree of problems they had experienced. We put the top amount of drinking to begin with at only 4 or 5 drinks, and that left us without any knowledge of the higher levels. Later we realized that people were quite willing to admit to 12 drinks in an evening and that that type of person would think you were slightly silly if you asked 'Do you ever have as much as 5 drinks?'

BJA: *When you wrote up that first drinking problems survey in 1967 it was called 'the epidemiology of problem drinking',[3] it wasn't called 'the epidemiology of alcoholism'. Why did you make that choice? In terms of what the field expected, the natural thing to do would have been to write something that was talking about the epidemiology of alcoholism.*

GK: I've always been obsessed with the notion of being clear, of making explicit definitions for what you are saying. An example of this preoccupation of mine with 'what do we really know?' occurred when I was in about 10th grade. The teacher announced that we were going to study Descartes and described his approach to 'truth' as beginning with a *tabula rasa,* which I took to mean that there would be no unproven assumptions. What was my disillusion when, the next week, I found that quite a few basic propositions had somehow crept into the argument! I felt cheated! I continue to be keen on that issue. For instance when the disease concept is being discussed we are hardly ever treated by either side to a definition of what they are talking about. Anyway, I already felt at that time that the concept of alcoholism was a bit too vague to pin down. All you could say was that there seemed to be some trouble here. At the time the 'movement' to solve the 'alcoholism' problem was not all that powerful politically, so nobody really cared very much when I said 'problem drinkers' instead of 'alcoholics'.

BJA: *You also started, I think, to be particularly interested in women's drinking patterns.*

GK: Yes, I was for instance interested in the strong interactive influence of the husband's and wife's drinking. The effect we found was really substantial, so that you could be pretty sure that a woman who drank a certain amount would have a husband who would drink more. What is especially interesting to me is the connection with gender roles in general—a very large topic, I'm afraid—but strikingly illustrated by the very large differences between men and women in drinking patterns and drinking problems.

BJA: *What about the kind of clinical practice you have been doing and the relation between that and your research work?*

GK: There was very little relationship between the two, actually. In private practice on the San Francisco Penninsula, you are usually dealing with people who are relatively well educated and who have neurotic rather than psychotic or behavioral problems. I found treating neurosis very interesting and this work also strengthened by obsession about trying to recognize very clearly what you know and what you don't know. The contrast was this. I had one friend who did psychotherapy, and she once told me, "I always know exactly what is going on." I had another friend who said, "I really don't know what's going on but I hope that every now and then I think of a good thing to say that will be helpful." Needless to say I tend toward the latter stance. Practice seemed to keep me in touch with reality, as opposed to what happens to many people in research, who forget that the world out there is still as complicated and difficult as it ever was, while research goes on another plane.

BJA: *What are your major research interests at present?*

GK: Because of the difficulty which results from such a small proportion of subjects in any sample being really heavy drinkers, what I'm doing now is putting together several different surveys; all those that had enough questions in common, so as to make a larger sample and then see what can be found out about *really* heavy drinking. I am finding that the patterns are very different in different social groups. You couldn't do that type of analysis without a sample of at least 10,000 people.

BJA: *Do you think that growing up in two cultures gave you any special perspective on drinking in America, or did that come only with research work?*

GK: The former very probably. There was very little feeling for a temperance movement in western Europe as I knew it, and all kinds of people drank varying amounts. I remember my mother was a bit surprised to learn that the little boy next door got beer with his lunch. Of course since I was not in the States at the time of Prohibition I never knew anything about that first hand.

BJA: *Do you have any general principles which have guided your approach to research?*

GK: Oh sure. I have always been fascinated by the intolerance of ambiguity discussed in the book *The Authoritarian Personality*.[4] People often believe in science as if it were a dogma, just like the word of God, because they don't like to think that nobody really knows the answer. Too often the conclusions of a research publication, no matter how tentative; are what is remembered. Too seldom are the basic data really spelled out. To my mind, that is what we need to look at, not at the lot of arithmetical means, multiple regressions and correlation coefficients. I suspect, for example, theat the term 'statistically significant' means to many people 'significant' in the more general sense. My recent paper on 'Drinking for Health'[5] was an attempt to expose some of these fallacies. Another area in which I would like to see improvement is the *definition* of the problem that is being studied. For instance in psychological research, aside from alcoholism, there is a tendency to believe that you have solved the problem of definition if you have a scale made up of 50 to 100 items, the belief that the arithmetic can make it *different*. Such researchers always forget that the criterion for the validity of any scale is clinical judgment and the only reason you employ the scale is because you cannot afford clinical judgment. It's not that the scale is superior.

BJA: *What is your opinion on the disease concept of alcoholism?*

GK: The belief that alcoholism is a disease is very important to lots of people. I have many objections to it. Unfortunately, there is so little clear thinking in the many discussions of it. What is a disease? What is alcoholism? There is little agreement on those questions. Some people think alcoholism is any drinking that is more than they approve of. Now there are all kinds of human behavior that seem silly, unwise, destructive, unhealthy, anti-social—are they all diseases, just as in the past they were often labelled 'possession by devils'? It is true that some of these types of destructive behavior do strike one as 'sick'. There is a difference, for example, between those who get drunk rather frequently but have no serious regrets and regard the episodes as well worth the fun, and, on the other hand, those who really wish desperately to stop and can't seem to do it. Then, of course, questions of obsessions and compulsions involve large obscure topics such as free will. Questions of inherited tendencies involve the important question of how differently different people handle these inherited tendencies. It all seems to me to need a lot of clarification before much scientific progress can be made.

References

1. Knupfer, G. (1946) Indices of socio-economic status: a study of some problems of measurement, *submitted in partial fulfillment of the requirements for the degree of Doctor of Philosophy* in the Faculty of Political Science (New York, Columbia University).
2. Knupfer, G. (1947) Portrait of the underdog, *Public Opinion Quarterly*, 11, pp. 103–114.
3. Knupfer, G. (1967) The epidemiology of problem drinking, *American Journal of Public Health*, 57, pp. 973–986.
4. Adorno, T. W., Frenkel-Brunswick, E., Levinson, D. J. & Nevitt Sandford, R. (1950) *The Authoritarian Personality*, pp. 461 ff, 480 ff (New York, Harper & Row).
5. Knupfer, G. (1987) Drinking for health: the daily light drinker fiction, *British Journal of Addiction*, 82, pp. 547–555.

11

Interview with Don Cahalan

DON CAHALAN, b. 1912. BA and MA from State University of Iowa; PhD Washington University. Director of Opinion Research Center, University of Denver, 1946–49; attitude assessment research U.S. Army 1949–52; research consultancies and market research 1952–64; Program Director of Social Research Group, George Washington University, 1964–70 and at University of California (Berkeley) from 1970–78, with professorship in Behavioural Science. Professor of Public Health Emeritus from 1978.

BJA: *How did you get your start as a social psychologist?*

DC: Before I got into alcohol research, my career reflected the vast changes of the last 50 years, especially the depression and World War II, which affected lots of careers and had profound effects on work experiences and aspirations. Another factor was the beginning of survey research in the U.S. and the fact that before about 1955 there was really no government funding for behavioural science research. It was all a hand-to-mouth business. Starting in 1938, when I got out of college after training in social psychology and journalism at the University of Iowa (working with Norman C. Meier, a former professor of George Gallup's), among other things I was a researcher for the Gallup Poll in Princeton, a field worker for the Department of Agriculture, then worked at the Boston *Herald-Traveler* as research director, then at the Civic Researcher Institute in Kansas City conducting surveys on civic problems. Later I was a Naval officer for 4 years, first as a naval air operations officer and then in the Navy Department in Washington conducting research among civilian personnel and other items of interest to the Navy. After the war I was an associate professor at the University of Denver and the director there of an affiliate of the National Opinion Research Center, now at the University of Chicago. I then spent 2 years in Germany as director of attitude research for the Army and Air Force and for several years conducted military surveys in the States, including measuring troop reactions to atomic bomb maneuvers out in Frenchman's Flat in the Nevada deserts. And then I was head of a small market research company in New York just before I got into alcohol research in 1962.

BJA: *And your upbringing?*

DC: Montana and Iowa, during the depression. In a family of eight, and my father was one of 17 children of my grandfather from Tipperary. It was rather primitive subsistence farming, but we didn't know we were poor until we grew up and went away to school and saw how other people lived. That kind of background can make one feel optimistic about the future, because it couldn't get anything *but* better. We had a spirit to get out and get an education and get away from the damn farm; and all eight of us managed to go to the University of Iowa.

BJA: *And when you went to the university, you got involved in public opinion research, and really got in on the ground floor of a new enterprise?*

DC: Oh, yes; I did my master's thesis on the failure of the *Literary Digest* poll in 1936. Which predicted that Alf Landon would get elected over Roosevelt.

BJA: *At that point public opinion research was a kind of a scout movement?*

DC: Yes. It was something like the Holy Grail mentality. We felt that it was a means of bringing about greater democracy, and replacing the pundits' opinions with actual facts about the state of the world's public opinion. We were rather evangelical about the whole business. That was a legitimate point of view at the time, although more recently we've gotten to consider surveys as mere data.

BJA: *After quite a long time, then, as both an academic and a commercial worker in the public opinion research field, you came into alcohol studies?*

DC: Yes. I got into that in 1962, through a colleague, Ira Cisin, professor of sociology at George Washington University and director of the Social Research Group there. He offered to have me come there to run the first national probability sample of the U.S., under his grant from the National Institute of Mental Health. It was a chance to get my doctorate and return to academic life. Also it was an opportunity to work on complex research problems—alcohol is a tough nut to crack. But the origins of the national surveys, which still are continuing, actually were right out here in California in the State Department of Public Health, in the late 1950's, and were headed up by Wendell Lipscomb; Genevieve Knupfer and Ira were there at the time, and Walter Clark; and Robin Room, who is now director of the Alcohol Research Group, started there with that Berkeley group. The concept was to do an inductive study of drinking behaviour and drinking problems and thus get away from the dependence at that time on clinical studies based only on alcoholics. The California studies were done before I got involved in alcohol research and those deserve great credit in terms of testing various hypotheses as to the nature of drinking behaviour and drinking problems, including pilot tests in which they actually went back to police records to check up on whether subjects had been arrested for drunkenness and the like. These checkups were all very painstakingly done, and the national surveys were built on this base. The first national survey was conducted in 1964–65.

BJA: *Before the national survey went into the field, you directed surveys in Hartford (Connecticut) didn't you; and that actually was your doctoral dissertation?*

DC: Yes. And that was a pilot test for the drinking-problems part of the national surveys, which we conducted after we had finished the first survey, which was on drinking behaviour and heavy drinking; the first survey didn't go into drinking problems particularly. Incidentally, the main contribution of the first national survey was that we found for the first time that the heaviest drinkers were really those aged 18 to 23 or 25 years. This was very different from the concept that heavier drinking developed later than that, which was based on the fact that the median clinical alcoholics are in their 40's. It changed the picture of heavy drinking, really, as a precursor of alcoholism. We had new findings also by ethnic origin, sex, socio-economic status and so on, which provided the baseline for studies of change. These findings were written up in *American Drinking Practices* (1969). Now about the surveys of drinking *problems:* using the California pilot studies of San Francisco as a base, with some modifications, at GWU we conducted a followup in 1967 of some 1,300 adults and asked them about their drinking problems, especially during the last 3 years. This led to the publication of my *Problem Drinkers* (1970) and to the Cahalan-Room book, *Problem Drinking among American Men* in 1974.

BJA: *I'd like you to think back to when you first came into alcohol studies. Did it strike you that there was anything special about the field of alcohol studies at the time? Was it just another study, like studying margarine?*

DC: One thing: it was a highly sensitive issue. And in relation to that, much denial is claimed for drinking. For example, the California validation studies I referred to earlier indicated that people would report the types of problems they had had, but would minimize the number of times that they had been arrested. We were fortunate in having those pilot studies to enrich the responses we would get on the national surveys. Before the alcohol surveys, I had done a number of surveys about social issues such as race relations, and measured attitudes of medical personnel; but nothing on alcohol, except that I do recall that in 1962, Ira Cisin and Jim Fox of the National Institute on Mental Health (who engineered the NIMH grant for our first national alcohol study) got me involved in attending a conference and writing a chapter in a book on *Alcohol and Traffic Safety* (1963). Through that experience I got acquainted with a lot of the people in the alcohol field. This probably led to Ira's offer to have me join him at George Washington.

BJA: *You came there when the team for the national studies was just being assembled?*

DC: That's correct.

BJA: *And had you had experience with national surveys before?*

DC: Oh, a great deal, at the National Opinion Research Center and the Gallup Poll; and then too, in my military research, I picked up experience in self-administered questionnaires and attitude scales. However, again, our drinking studies were very much of a team effort. The California people made a very major contribution.

BJA: *You worked along with Ira at George Washington University from 1962 until 1968. Then the studies moved with you to Berkeley?*

DC: Yes. Ira was very generous. He gave me the chance to take the national surveys operation to Berkeley as a branch office of GWU's Social Research Group, and to combine it with the ongoing research operation there which was headed by Genevieve Knupfer, who had moved to England temporarily. When I got to Berkeley the staff consisted of Robin Room as the only professional and a librarian and a couple of clerks. We went after new funding the next year and took steps to move the research unit administratively into the University of California School of Public Health in 1970. This was at the height of student unrest and attention to youthful use of drugs; so there was a great deal of interest in the courses we taught in the School on alcohol and drugs and shortly thereafter we got a training grant from the new National Institute on Alcohol Abuse and Alcoholism, which included graduate postdoctoral fellowships which continue to this day under the direction of Robin Room. In the 1970's, the staff grew to about 25, in addition to field workers.

BJA: *Can we concentrate on the training program for a minute or two. This started in 1971. Would you say that it changed in any way the nature of the work in the Social Research Group?*

DC: Yes; it vastly enriched it. Starting back in my University of Denver days, I was struck with the importance of a university base for research centers in enriching everybody's lives. You should think of a systems basis, where you get feedback to the researchers from faculty and from students (particularly graduate students and postdocs) and library facilities, and a chance to influence the contents and the tenor of university courses—and especially to provide an interdisciplinary emphasis to the research—not just sociology, but anthropology, social psychology, social welfare, public policy, law, and sociomedical fields such as epidemiology and health administration and planning and health education. Over the years, we have directed or provided the data for about 30 doctoral dissertations and have trained more than a dozen who are now serving in academic posts in the States and abroad. In recognition of our work, our Alcohol Research Group became one of nine federally-supported Alcohol Research Centers in 1978.

BJA:
Now, after you came to California, in fact, you became involved with what was then the State Office of Alcohol Program Management, in advising Loran Archer, who was then the head of it? And became involved in what became the large California Prevention Demonstration Project?

DC: Yes. I got Loran Archer interested in this and we got funded for it. Robin Room also became involved. It led to a series of before-and-after studies to try to affect tendencies toward drinking or limiting drinking. These studies, which were taken up under my direction by Larry Wallack, found pretty much what we suspected: it's easy to change attitudes, and it's possible to change values slightly; but changing behaviour is not that easy. Very expensive projects have yielded not too many conclusive findings, but we suspect bigger and better studies probably will be funded over time. But it helped dispel the naive notion of many administrators that all you need to do is change opinions and put out a lot of information through cutesy commercials of one kind or another. In fact, the commercials which were designed purposely to inculcate the idea that two drinks would be enough, were taken by many of the people who saw them as actually being ads for beer or wine. So, people in this culture are set by the media to expect that when they see something about alcohol on the tube, it must be selling the alcohol.

BJA: In your retirement, for a while you did a number of other things that had nothing to do with alcohol. But recently you have written a new book, Understanding America's Drinking Problem *(1987).*

BJA: How did you come to do this?

DC: After I retired in 1979 and turned the Alcohol Research Center over to Robin Room, I did other things, including some history and a how-to genealogy book, and some fancy loafing; but in 1986 the publishers of my *Problem Drinkers* wanted me to write a sequel to it. Thinking about it, I felt that drinking behaviour had not changed that greatly in the last two decades; and that instead of writing about details of moderate changes in drinking, I ought to tell the story of the politics of alcohol and alcoholism in the U.S., and what might be done to remedy a situation of grossly mounting costs with little improvement. In the book I've described the alcohol scene as a gigantic shell game, where the alcohol industry, the treatment industry, and the insurance industry are all comfortable with treating alcoholism as an expensive disease, but nobody is interested in primary prevention—because nobody can make any *money* out of primary prevention. This incidentally, was the central theme of my 1979 article in the BJA, 'Why Does the Alcoholism Field Act Like a Ship of Fools?' All of these folks are comfortable in treating the alcoholic after he's gotten there; it's a very expensive exercise. And the alcohol industry claims to be earnestly interested in supporting alcohol research and treating the dread disease of alcoholism; but never for a moment would they want labels on bottles or anything that draws attention to the fact that alcohol is, as Ernie Noble has said, "The dirtiest drug of all" and is causing far more deaths and costing a great deal more money both here and abroad, than is true for any other drug. Now one thing I must confess, I've long been an advocate of objective research on alcohol problems; and that's why I had very seldom ventured opinions on what might be done about injurious drinking. But I was retired now and wouldn't be conducting new drinking surveys; and over the years I had worked up considerable affect about the chicanery and deceptiveness of the alcohol industry; and the fact that our own studies of drinking problems (in which we found that many people moved into and out of heavy drinking over short periods of time) were bitterly attacked by many people in national lobby groups, such as some officials in the National Council on Alcoholism (which has changed much since that time) who said that our research lent support to the disease-theorists' arch enemies, those who advocated that some presumed alcoholics could resume normal drinking. So, we were tagged with the onus of being responsible for the Rand Report, whereas I didn't even know those good people. And I was also ticked off about the almost universal tendency of the print media to soften the damage being done by alcoholic beverages—one of the chief sources of advertising revenues.

BJA: So what does this book say?

DC: In the book, I have told how American emphasis on individualism and short-term rewards is related to our Constitution and to the fertile field for buck-passing in alcohol controls which prevails. We've got Congress; we've got the administration; we've got a popular vote; and we have the effects of the media. That makes it very easy for buck-passing and no real controls on alcohol. I made a case for putting most aspects of alcohol control into one agency, such as the Food and Drug Administration—which would include the present NIAAA—with power to control not only research but also production, taxing, marketing, and advertising of alcohol. This would be much on the Scandinavian model. But the liquor industry has too much at stake in the present divide-and-conquer scheme to let this happen—at least very soon. As a matter of fact, the NIAAA at the present time is being threatened with being relegated to becoming a unit in the National Institute of Health, just doing research and staying out of policy matters altogether.

BJA: *Reflecting back, when you came into the field in the 1960's, what would you say were the attitudes of survey research people in the alcohol field about alcohol policy issues—was this something that people paid much attention to?*

DC: Oh, no. We were then concerned almost exclusively with measuring drinking behaviour rather than with policy issues. Our research, in addition to the central purpose of measuring how much people drank under various circumstances, was also designed to test the concepts of Jellinek of the Center for Alcohol Studies at Rutgers. That perspective was that alcoholism is a progressive disease, a one-way street. (The people at Rutgers at that time were very closely tied in with the founding of the National Council on Alcoholism, which was taken up with promoting the disease concept because it helped get alcoholics better treatment.) The same influences also operated on the quite good studies of Hal Mulford of Iowa, who used quota samples in a national survey which covered many of the same points that we dealt with in our national probability samples soon afterward. Ours was not based upon his, except that it had somewhat the same common heritage of testing Jellinekian concepts.

BJA: *When it came to alcohol policy or prevention what were Ira Cisin's views?*

DC: He was very antagonistic to the whole business of taxing or controls on alcohol. This, he said, was none of our business as researchers. His was a libertarian point of view. He very much disliked the excesses of prohibition, as many people do, and all of the alcohologists did. They didn't want to have any part of a return to prohibition. And moralism applied in much of prohibition. Things have changed because a new breed of public health workers has drawn attention to the health problems of alcohol in much the same way as they have the health problems of smoking. And so there is now more of a public health and good-health-habits emphasis. Another thing that happened is that some of the leading alcohologists had been heavily subsidized by the alcohol industry themselves and were not about to be critical. Specifically, the National Council on Alcoholism had been receiving a heavy subsidy from the alcohol industry. When Ernie Noble took over as executive vice president of the NCA, one of his first acts was to get rid of the four members of the executive board of nine members who represented the alcohol industry. He said there was no place for them, we don't want to accept any future money from the industry. So that divorcement has helped to turn the NCA around almost completely to its being a broad-based, eclectic organization which is very much concerned with prevention as well as with treatment. They are now pushing for various kinds of legislation and constraints such as more equitable taxes, labels on containers, better control on marketing and advertising, and the like.

BJA: You talked about a generational change, the new public health people. Have your own views changed over the last 25 years, since you came into the field?

DC: Yes, I was first preoccupied with problems of measurement and running a research organization, and didn't pay much attention to policies or prevention. Being associated with the School of Public Health and public health researchers both here and elsewhere as more public health people around the world got engaged in surveys of various kinds, made me more aware and concerned with the mechanisms of alcohol production and distribution and alcohol education and control.

BJA: If someone who today headed an alcohol research unit came to you for advice, what advice would you given them on how to build up a research program?

DC: For one thing, there should be representation of the various disciplines. And I still think an alcohol research center as such should not get too involved in advocacy. Let somebody else do the advocating. In the past I've been critical of researchers—not in my own organization—who have done research and also got involved in advocacy and polemics on what should be done about the findings. But you can make your findings available to outsiders who can serve as advocates. Also, I think a university connection is terribly important to a research service. The Alcohol Research Group still has that through its training grant, which is still supported by the NIAAA; and I'm happy to see that under

Robin's direction, it has gone more and more in the direction of supporting postdoctoral fellowships, because that gives us the selfish opportunity to learn from more mature scholars and it's been a healthy thing. Also, the encouraging of foreign and U.S. visiting scholars of one sort or another on a short-term basis. And I think that our type of operation, and the one at the Addiction Research Foundation in Canada, should grow more alike in what they do. In short, we would probably do more in the way of publishing our own findings. However, one has to be careful lest the publishing tail wag the research dog.

BJA: What do you hope for the future of alcohol research?

DC: For one thing, the NIAAA is being pushed around by a lot of politics in the present administration in Washington. They are setting up an OSAP, the Office of Substance Abuse whatever; and the Alcohol, Drug, and Mental Health Administration has tried to usurp the functions of the NIAAA. There is a power play to relegate the NIAAA to being a research adjunct in the National Institutes of Health. I am sure this would be welcomed by the alcohol industry, too, because it would tend to weaken influences toward more control over alcohol. I would like to see an overall agency with a lot of clout. I would also like to see a blue-ribbon commission set up to assess the *real* needs of biomedical and behavioural research, instead of the present process whereby the review committees (which NIAAA certainly has tried to run fairly) are vulnerable to logrolling whereby people will say, "Well, if you vote for my buddies or my colleagues' program, I'll vote for yours." There is that implicit old-buddy network; and I am in no way implying dishonesty as such. We in the behavioural sciences think that this is especially a risk among the biomedical fraternity, because you will notice that the biomedical people tend to give high ratings to just about any medical project, whereas when it is a behavioural research project, even the behavioural researchers on the committee will tend to be divided on giving a high or low rating. I think there is too much emphasis upon deterministic biological (including genetic) research altogether, because you can't do that much about these things from an action standpoint. Genetics as a root cause of alcoholism is being much talked about these days, but nobody has said anything about the proportion of total variance that could be accounted for by genetics. And there's not enough research at all on environmental factors, especially cultural ones—the things that *can* be changed. Now this emphasis on biological and medical research sounds very scientific, but it also means postponing coming to grips with the legal and ethical questions in the field, because you could always study these things forever, because of the mystique, prestige and status of the medical profession. There's a great deal of artful dodging going on in the whole process, in my opinion. I do think, too, that there are very big scientific payoffs to be had in comparative international studies. We have learned a great deal from the British and European experiences, and particularly from the Scandinavian countries.

BJA: *If someone asked you to justify doing national surveys on drinking patterns and problems, what would you see as being their main significance: what can they tell us?*

DC: There hasn't been much of a real change in the last 20 years. There have been some subtle things, particularly in women's drinking, and of course there had been quite a rise in youthful drinking. And incidentally, our national surveys to begin with did not cover those under 18 years, because of our naive fear it would be too sensitive a topic, that we would get into trouble about parental consent. Nowadays we do cover drinking among those under 18 years. And these national surveys should be done over the years; not too often.

BJA: *How often, in your opinion?*

DC: Every 5 years, unless there are some big events happening, such as changes in the laws, marketing practices and so on. Without such studies we obviously don't know whether campaigns are being effective or not. One change that has taken place is that whereas people are drinking just about as much as before, they seem to be enjoying it less. They are more anxious about their drinking; there's more of a trend toward its being uncool to get roaring drunk. Some of these subtleties you can chart as you go along. Sometimes it's not necessary to have national studies; you can do experimental studies in limited areas, and you can vary the mix between before-after experimental studies and the large, massive national surveys. One thing I think that ought to be done is to broaden the scope of the alcohol questions in the studies that are being conducted by the National Center for Health Statistics. They are doing not only massive surveys every year covering quite a bunch of questions on health and health-related behaviour; but they are also doing this in conjunction with medical health examinations and thereby being able to pin down the relationship between the attitudes, expectations, and behaviour as reported by individuals, and the measurement of changes in health status over time. Only through those kinds of measurements, on a continuing basis, can we get a lever on what changes are happening and how these might be influenced.

BJA: You also spent some time in your research career on longitudinal studies, on studies of people's changes over time. Do you have anything to say about what we can learn from them?

DC: Because of budgetary constraints, we have tended to do our studies too closely together. At intervals of 2 years or 4 years, we have reinterviewed people to find out what changes there have been in their behaviour. (That's the subject of *Problem Drinkers* (1970) and *Problem Drinking among American Men* (1974) and many articles by members of our group.) What we got out of our short-term change studies is that people vary a great deal over a short time; they go into and out of heavy drinking and drinking problems. So it's a much more fluid situation; and one can no longer think of alcoholism as a progressive disease that can only operate in one direction. But there ought to be more followups to measure changes over longer periods. Kaye Fillmore is the principal investigator on a very interesting series of Berkeley-based international trend studies of drinking entitled the 'Collaborative Alcohol-Related Longitudinal Project', which is funded by the NIAAA and affiliated with the World Health Organization. In it, behavioural scientists from many industrialized countries are co-operating and pooling their data to search for events and demographic factors which are associated with cross-cultural similarities and differences in changes in the levels of drinking and drinking problems over time.

BJA: *You've spent years looking at patterns of behaviour and how things change in the American population. Do you have any predictions for the future on what's going to happen with drinking patterns and drinking problems?*

DC: I don't think it's likely that there is going to be much of a reduction in drinking problems real soon. Not if the present congeries of interests prevail—the alcohol industry, the treatment industry, and the insurance industry. There's no money, as I said earlier, in primary prevention, although there's plenty of money to be made in creating the problems, treating them, and insuring them. It will take the combined efforts of federal and state administrations, Congress, the general public through organized lobbying, and co-operation of the media to effect any changes in the light of all these special interests. Looking back, it seems to me that changes in American drinking behaviour have occurred primarily as a result of very vast lobbying political activity by such groups as the Anti-Saloon League at one time and the prohibition repeal efforts by Franklin D. Roosevelt, John Raskob, and politicians like Al Smith, during the depression when they saw repeal as a means of placating the working man by giving him a beer, and raising money for taxes—rather naive in view of the fact that alcohol costs more to repair people than it does in terms of the taxes raised. And we've seen the significant effect on such sharp lobbying with Congress on the part of the Mothers Against Drunk Driving. They have used emotional appeals by mothers who have lost their children through somebody else's drunken driving. Largely as the result of this there were passed uniform state 21-year-old drinking laws and much harsher laws about drunken driving. So in a pluralistic society such as we have, it takes all of these four 'estates', as Lord Bryce (George Gallup's best press agent) called them, to effect any real change. I just hope there are going to be some real changes in the present high level of alcohol problems by concerted lobbying and possibly (as I suggest rather cynically in my book) by buying out the alcohol industry by giving them tax advantages for reducing production, in the same way as we subsidize farming, or as in the European Common Market. Carrot and stick combined, to buy them off. If you can't fight them, buy them. I just hope that with astute lobbying and better legislation, something can be done to bring down the high level of alcohol problems and the high costs of treatment. However, I am not holding my breath about this. I only hope, as Comrade Khruschev once said, that this happens before the shrimp learns to whistle.

References

1. Cahalan, D. (1983) Motivational and educational aspects of drinking-driving, in: B. Fox & J. Fox (Eds) *Alcohol and Traffic Safety*, National Institutes of Health, Public Health Service Publication No. 1043, pp. 189–219 (Bethesda, MD, NIH).
2. Cahalan, D. (1970) *Problem Drinkers: A National Survey* (San Francisco, Jossey-Bass)
3. Cahalan, D. (1979) Why does the alcoholism field act like a ship of fools? *British Journal of Addiction*, 74, pp. 235–238.
4. Cahalan, D. (1987) *Understanding Americs's Drinking Problem* (San Francisco, Jossey-Bass).
5. Cahalan, D., Cisin, I. & Crossley, H. (1969) *American Drinking Practices* (New Brunswick, Center of Alcohol Studies, Rutgers University).
6. Cahalan, D. & Room, R. (1974) *Problem Drinking Among American Men* (New Brunswick, Center of Alcohol Studies, Rutgers University).

12

Discussion. Starting on the Fringe: Studying Alcohol in a Wet Generation

Robin Room

Like others interviewed in this book, the U.S. scholars included above come from a particular generation: those who were alive but at least 60 years of age in the mid- to late 1980s. This gives them a number of things in common. They entered professional life at the time of a rather "wet" generation in American society—a generation that as college students in the 1930s and 1940s tended to regard any problematization of alcohol as reactionary, small-minded, and atavistic. By and large, they are not from the vanguard wet generation for whom drinking, and indeed heavy drinking, was a symbol of liberation from "Victorian morality", but from a younger generation who "inherited . . . the innovations of their predecessors without much of their self-consciousness".[1] But still, the idea of focusing on alcohol issues as a research topic—and all those interviewed have worked more consistently on alcohol than on other psychoactive drugs—was not something any of them fixed on at an early age; indeed, in each account, there is an accidental quality about their steps into the alcohol field. To focus on alcohol problems, Straus reminds us, was to choose to be "on the fringe", often of a relatively low-status subspecialty—of psychiatry in medicine, of social problems in sociology. To make the choice, one had to be a bit of a maverick, one whose choices were not ruled by considerations of the pecking-order in one's discipline or profession.

The limitation of the collection of interviews to those active in the last few years means that many of the founding figures of the modern alcoholism movement and of modern alcohol research—such figures as E. M. Jellinek, Marty Mann, Howard Haggard, and Raymond McCarthy—are represented only through the reflections of others. The reminiscences of some members of this earlier generation have found expression in other forms, notably in a dissertation based on extensive interviews.[2] An implicit criterion for selection for interviewing in the present volume is that the subject's primary work was in the addiction field, which filters out figures, some happily still among us, who served as mentors for those interviewed but whose work reaches across several fields—such figures as Samuel Guze in St. Louis, Ira Cisin in Berkeley and Washington, John Seeley in Toronto, and Howard Haggard in New Haven.

We thus have a set of perspectives from what is more or less a single generation in alcohol studies. We can notice a couple of characteristics of those included. As a whole, it is not a generation with many female researchers; the relatively few women alcohol researchers of the generation—for instance, Joan Jackson and Edith Lisansky Gomberg, as well as Genevieve Knupfer—found themselves bringing feminist perspectives into alcohol studies well before the rise of the modern women's movement. Nor are alcohol researchers of this generation drawn from the full range of American ethnic diversity. Hints of the prejudices encountered by those who, like Jellinek, did not fit the mold of the "typical 'Yalie' " can be found in Bacon's interview and Johnson's dissertation.[2] The disciplinary distribution of those interviewed is remarkable: four sociologists (Bacon, Straus, Pittman, Knupfer), a social psychologist (Cahalan), two psychiatrists (Goodwin, Knupfer), and a documentation specialist (or perhaps "semanticist"—Keller). Where are the biological researchers who presently predominate in, for instance, the officers and membership of the Research Society on Alcoholism? The answer seems to be that the biologization of American alcohol research starts with a slightly younger generation, with those who now direct several of the national alcohol research centers and the NIAAA intramural research program. There certainly had been biological alcohol research in the 1930s and 1940s—the names Bowman, Jolliffe,

Starting on the Fringe: Studying Alcohol in a Wet Generation 181

Carlson, Greenberg, and Williams come to mind—but biological research played far less of a leading role in the 1950s and 1960s than it does today. The beginnings of the building of modern North American biological alcohol research can be glimpsed north of the border and later in this volume, with David Archibald's hiring of Harold Kalant in 1959 to set up a biological research program to explore what in Kalant's view was an "almost virgin territory".

In all alcohol research, and not only in biological studies, one of the most dramatic changes of the last 25 years has been in the size of the alcohol research field. Although in their early literature review work Jellinek and Keller had to master the thick residue of research from the temperance era, the world of active alcohol researchers entered by the interviewees was much smaller than today's. At least through the early 1960s, most American alcohol researchers must have known each other personally, and centers with more than a couple of researchers were very few: in the mid-1960s, besides Yale/Rutgers, one might think of Seattle, St. Louis, Berkeley—and, of course, Toronto. Now there are a dozen national alcohol research centers, several state- and privately-funded centers, and many other significant groups of researchers.

In the beginning was Yale, one has to conclude, whether one is talking about modern alcohol research or about the modern alcoholism movement. Keller reminds us that there was a prehistory in the 1930s, but by the early 1940s New Haven had become the Rome of American alcohol research and of a budding alcoholism movement. The Yale Center's attraction was international—elsewhere in this volume, we read that a pilgrimage to Yale was one of the first steps in the field for David Archibald in 1948 and for Kettil Bruun in the late 1950s. Several U.S. figures interviewed above played some role in the alcoholism movement—in the push to get policy recognition of and treatment provision for alcoholism as a public health problem. Bacon, Pittman, and Straus, we learn, each at some time served on a commission on alcoholism in the state in which they worked. Pittman played an active role in the push to decriminalize public drunkenness. For a time in the late 1940s and early 1950s, Bacon played a leading role in the public relations and political lobbying of the nascent movement.[2,3] Straus chaired the National Advisory Committee on

Alcoholism, the 1968 report of which served as the staff work behind the formation of the National Institute on Alcohol Abuse and Alcoholism (NIAAA).[4]

Nevertheless, by and large, social researchers, including most of those we hear from here, had an uneasy relationship with the alcoholism movement. In particular, by the end of the 1950s, sociologists and some of the administrators of the new state and provincial alcoholism agencies were uncomfortable with the single-minded focus on alcoholism[2,5] which had occluded the kind of broader focus exemplified by Bacon's earlier manifesto.[6] In 1960 Straus, noting approvingly the emergence of a "second generation of alcohol researchers", remarked that earlier researchers had often been the "victims of popularization" by "the ever-present militant proponents of an alcoholism movement".[7] As we learn from Straus' interview, both he and Archibald were involved in the late 1950s in efforts to open up the field to new influences, as the National Institute of Mental Health (NIMH) started to provide the first important federal funding for research in the field. In the next few years, these efforts bore fruit. By the early 1960s, the first publications on alcohol from the St. Louis Psychiatry Department, by Lee Robins, Guze and others, were appearing, opening up the terrain Goodwin moved into later in the 1960s. One of the most significant of these reports appeared in a book, coedited by Pittman, which remains unequalled as an example of the broad base of sociological alcohol studies.[8] The first probability-sample general population study of drinking patterns was funded by NIMH in 1959, initiating a series of studies directed in due course by Genevieve Knupfer and then by Don Cahalan, which eventually developed into today's Alcohol Research Group in Berkeley.

As the field developed in the 1960s, the touchstone for this new and broader approach became the shift from talking about "alcoholism" to talking about "alcohol problems" or "problem drinking".[9] Knupfer's adoption of the latter term[10] was followed and expanded on by Cahalan.[11] When the report of the Cooperative Commission which Straus had initially chaired (see his interview) finally appeared in 1967, it was entitled *Alcohol Problems,* rather than the "Alcoholism" which was part of the Commission's name.[12] A few years later, Straus provided his own detailed exposition of a broader "problems of alcohol" perspective.[13]

The shift in perspective opened the way for a new "public health" approach to the prevention of alcohol problems to enter the U.S. scene, an approach largely pioneered elsewhere—among others, by Archibald, Schmidt and Bruun.[14] But it was younger generations of researchers and eventually of public health activists who were in the forefront of this further step in the U.S. Although Cahalan, as he discusses, has recently adopted such a "public health" approach[15], a more general response of his generation of researchers is closer to that he describes for Cisin: certainly Bacon expresses a skepticism and Pittman an antagonism to alcohol control approaches, and Keller has recently also expressed his qualms about alcohol policy advocacy.[16]

In this perspective, those interviewed form a transitional generation in the longer sweep of the history of responses to alcohol in America. In Blocker's recent interpretation of this history,[17] in terms of cycles of reform moving from moral suasion to coercion, their stories belong largely to the earlier stages of an unfolding fifth cycle. A common theme in the interviews is the shift in cultural perspective between their youth and the present. Thus Keller contrasts the period of what has been called "problem deflation" concerning alcohol in his youth with the "problem amplification" of the temperance era and of recent years. Goodwin notes the recent fall in consumption levels, and speculates on its causes. Straus remarks that "we've come a long way" from the marginalization and stigmatization of alcohol research in the late 1940s.

As members of the first modern generation of scholars to start their careers in alcohol studies, each of those interviewed set a standard and an agenda in their first few years of work in alcohol studies for a whole tradition of later work. I have already mentioned Bacon's "Foundations for a Sociologic Study of Drinking Behavior", still looked to as a guidepost for research directions.[18] Present-day reviews of empirical studies of alcohol and homeless men frequently begin with Straus' pioneer study. Pittman's work on samples of public drunkenness arrestees set a standard in its field which has not been surpassed. Goodwin's work remains a major reference point for the burgeoning field of studies of alcohol problems heritability. Not only college studies, but also all general-population studies of drinking, bear traces of the influence of Straus and Bacon's landmark study of *Drinking in College*. Epidemiological studies of alcohol dependence and drinking problems still reflect Knupfer's detailed measurement of aspects of problem drinking in general populations. Cahalan's analyses of national surveys on drinking patterns and then of drinking problems provide the initial anchor-points for analyses of changes in American drinking practices and problems. And Keller's meticulous architecture of the documentation of the field provided a cumulative information base for later generations of alcohol researchers that, even today, has no equivalent in studies of other drugs.

Preparation of this discussion was supported by a National Alcohol Research Center grant (AA 05595) from the U.S. National Institute on Alcohol Abuse and Alcoholism to the Alcohol Research Group, Medical Research Institute of San Francisco. Ron Roizen, Bob Straus, and Gretchen Thomas provided helpful comments, but are not, of course, responsible for the results.

References

1. Fass, P. S. (1977) *The Damned and the Beautiful: American Youth in the 1920s* (New York, Oxford), p. 270.
2. Johnson, B. H. (1973) *The Alcoholism Movement in America: A Study in Cultural Innovation*, Ph.D. Dissertation, Sociology, University of Illinois at Urbana/Champaign; University Microfilms 74-5603.
3. Room, R. (1978) *Governing Images of Alcohol and Drug Problems: The Structure, Sources and Sequels of Conceptualizations of Intractable Problems*, Ph.D. dissertation, Sociology, University of California, Berkeley; University Microfilms No. 79-14745.
4. Straus, R. (1988) Origins and development of federal support for alcohol research, *Alcohol Health and Research World* 12, pp. 272–274.
5. Room, R. (1983) Sociological aspects of the disease concept of alcoholism, pp. 47–91 in *Research Advances in Alcohol and Drug Problems*, vol. 7 (New York and London, Plenum).
6. Bacon, S. D. (1943) Sociology and the problems of alcohol: foundations for a sociologic study of drinking behavior, *Quarterly Journal of Studies on Alcohol* 4, pp. 402–445.

7. Straus, R. (1960) Research in the problems of alcohol: a twenty-year perspective, pp. 28–31 in *Multidisciplinary Programming in Alcoholism Investigation: Proceedings of a Conference* (Berkeley, California State Department of Public Health).
8. Pittman, D. S. and C. R. Snyder, eds. (1962) *Society, Culture, and Drinking Patterns* (New York, Wiley).
9. Room, R. (1987) Bring back inebriety? *British Journal of Addiction* 82, pp. 1064–1068.
10. Knupfer, G. (1967) The epidemiology of problem drinking, *American Journal of Public Health* 57, pp. 973–986.
11. Cahalan, D. (1970) *Problem Drinkers: A National Survey*, San Francisco, Jossey-Bass.
12. Plaut, T. (1967) *Alcohol Problems: A Report to the Nation* (New York, Oxford).
13. Straus, R. (1973), Alcohol and society, *Psychiatric Annals* 3, pp. 8–107.
14. Room, R. (1984) Alcohol control and public health, *Annual Review of Public Health* 5, pp. 293–317.
15. Cahalan, D. (1987) *Understanding America's Drinking Problem* (San Francisco, Jossey-Bass).
16. Keller, M. (1988) On NIAAA: background and perspective, *Alcohol Health and Research World* 12, pp. 269–271.
17. Blocker, J. (1989) *American Temperance Movements: Cycles of Reform* (Boston, Twayne Publishers).
18. Levine, H. G. (1981) Manifesto for a new alcohol social science, *Drinking and Drug Practices Surveyor* 17, pp. 20–29.

III

CONTRIBUTIONS FROM THE UK

13

Interview with D. L. Davies

DAVID LEWIS DAVIES, b. 1911, d. 1983. MA (Physiology) and DM, Oxford: FRCP, FRCPsych. War service as Major, RAMC. Physician, Bethlem Royal Hospital and the Maudsley Hospital 1948–76, and subsequently Emeritus Physician. Dean, Institute of Psychiatry 1950–66. Medical Director, Alcohol Education Center 1973–80. President, Society for the Study of Addiction. Work for WHO. Jellinek Prize 1979. Awarded CBE 1982.

BJA: *In 1962 you published your paper on 'Return to Normal Drinking'[1]. There is always a story behind the story. How did that paper come to be written—whatever put the idea into your head?*

DLD: The idea really owed its origin to Edgar Myers, who was my social worker for many years on the Professorial Unit. I always had four or five beds for alcoholics on those wards. Mr. Myers was responsible for the follow-up of our alcoholic patients. We had some years earlier published a two-year follow-up[2], and Myers pointed out to me that there was a group of people who were drinking but who were socially competent. He said to me 'You realize these people shouldn't happen': and I said 'Well they have happened'.

So then I mounted the further investigation and decided that on the analogy of the conventional five-year period for 'cure' of cancer, we would take people who had been discharged at least five years as basis for the study, so as to give a useful minimal period of observation. I then looked through the records and we followed-up some 93 men.

BJA: *Could you tell us something about your Record system?*

DLD: The Record system was part of the Professorial Unit record system, and every patient who came in was, within a week of admission, dealt with at an intake conference. And there a whole lot of information was filed on special forms. When he was discharged, his notes were again brought up to a discharge conference and a great deal more information was then on file. The Professorial Unit had a secretary who ran a follow-up office and this was a continuous exercise which went on for at least 10 years, and for all I know still goes on. On the documents it was stated how the patient was to be followed-up. He might be coming to out-patients, he might be seen by a social worker, he might have a follow-up letter, the letter might go to him or to a relative or to his doctor—all this was set out at the point of discharge so that it was perfectly clear to all concerned how the tracing was to be done. This was a standard system not just for the alcoholics. It was a very efficient system and the girls who ran it were very competent; there was little staff change over the 10 years. Every 6 or 12 months an enquiry letter would go out, and the answers were brought to me. If there were any difficulties I could ask for the patient to come and see me, or I could get my social worker to call on the patient. The 1956 paper was based on a follow-up where Mr. Myers personally investigated every patient once a month over the two years.

BJA: *When did Edgar Myers point out the fact that some people were drinking in a controlled way?*

DLD: It must have been quite some time after the 1956 paper was published.

BJA: *So really there was almost a 10-year gap between the original field work and your conversation with Mr. Myers?*

DLD: Yes.

BJA: *Which is interesting isn't it—that a whole 10 years could elapse before an important point could come out of the material?*

DLD: Yes. There was another follow-up. The first two year follow-up was published by Shepherd, Myers and myself,[2] but then John Wing, as an exercise for his DPM dissertation, did a subsequent follow-up of the third and fourth years.[3] That helped in a way because we could begin with a four year follow-up of the first 50.

BJA: *But for the 'Return to normal drinking' paper, how did you get your data on the people who were allegedly now drinking in a controlled fashion?*

DLD: Every one of them was personally seen. Certainly Edgar Myers saw them and I think I saw them all myself, in fact I'm sure I saw them all myself.

BJA: *That's all the seven or all the 93?*

DLD: All the seven.

BJA: *Could I raise an issue with you there, because you were then down to a relatively small number of people, a small series of individual case studies. Your paper gave in fact a lot of clinical detail and you certainly did not deal us short—we can form our own judgements, and my impression is that on most of these seven cases even the strictest critic would agree that there is masses of information to suggest these people had severe alcohol problems by any standards, or that in latterday terms they suffered from the alcohol dependence syndrome. It would be circular to say in retrospect, that they can't be 'real' alcoholics just because they regained control over their drinking. But a crucial question here is the validity of the follow-up information. Now I saw one of these 'returned to normal drinking' patients years later when he came into the Maudsley and he confessed that he'd been drinking like a fish the whole time, and even during the month when the QJSA published the account of his return to normal drinking, he was sitting in the back kitchen drinking in a very alcoholic way. He told me that when your research follow-up worker came to do an independent interview with his wife he let her know in advance that he'd bash the living daylights out of her if she told the truth, and she gave an account which was entirely false to substantiate his own false account. You made the best possible endeavours in dealing with a small number of people who might be motivated to be less than truthful, but do you think that the validity of your information is open to question, especially when no biological measures were done? There was no liver function testing, no physical examination, no blood alcohol levels.*

DLD: Yes, I think it's a valid criticism but what we are looking at is a piece of human behaviour, and it really comes down to how in fact do you record validly human behaviour. You can only do as best you can. You can watch it as far as you are able to watch it, you can ask the person, you can ask the people around him, you can make independent enquiries, you can still be wrong—if a man goes to these lengths to deceive you I would accept that. I would think that there are damaging criticisms that can be put up against conventional checks—you could always get a specimen back from the laboratory that's got the wrong name on it. I wouldn't say that just because you're using a piece of apparatus you are then 100 per cent certain that your information is valid. There is still a man to do it, there's still a girl to type the letter to you, there's still somebody to make a telephone call.

BJA: *There was other information about the social adjustment of these patients. Did you have to rely on what the patient or his wife said or were there other independent informants?*

DLD: Yes. The whole point of the histogram in the 1956 paper was that we didn't think we could record our results simply in terms of drinking, and the histogram took into account what we called social competence.

BJA: *Were you surprised by the evidence you uncovered on 'normal drinking' or were you setting out to substantiate a conjecture?*

DLD: I wasn't surprised. Quite honestly I'd never really given much thought to the outcome of alcoholism. I had never believed that a man could not return to normal drinking. I couldn't see why. I never shared this view. I wasn't very much in the alcohol field in a way, I was dabbling in it. I had the benefit perhaps of coming with a rather fresh mind to this question, and the outcome didn't seem to me odd at all. It was

Edgar Myers who thought it was very odd but I didn't really think it was odd.

BJA: *So although you came in from the outside, you landed yourself absolutely in the middle of an important debate after the publication of that paper. Even if you didn't go to find them they all came to find you. What were your feelings when the comments on the paper were published, and you saw the general reaction?*

DLD: I was surprised and the reaction was American reaction, really. I hadn't been to the States at that time and I certainly knew nothing about AA and the alcohol field in the States, and it was only when a friend of mine in the U.S.A. started to write me letters telling me of the outcry that I realized what had happened. I had one letter saying I could never now come to America—the writer said that AA would pelt me with bottles on the airstrip as I arrived. But subsequently this writer invited me to visit his unit and he asked along a lot of people from New York to meet me, and they were very nice and very pleasant. In fact I was all right.

BJA: *Some people know that they are likely to stir up trouble, it's one of their agreeable personal characteristics. Did you reckon on your previous track record that you were inconoclast?*

DLD: No, I don't think so. I didn't expect anything very special from that paper. I took it to Aubrey Lewis and he said well, I think it's worth publishing. He didn't seem surprised by it and I asked him where he thought it should be published, and he said try the *Lancet*. I sent it to the *Lancet* who returned it to me. I think they said it wasn't of sufficient general interest. So this assessment of the paper's excitement wasn't only my view. The editor of the *Lancet* didn't think it was of any great interest.

BJA: *Let's now leave that tremendously important piece of work and go on to something else which I think the readers of the journal will be interested in. As you know we have a very international readership, they know of your work, many of them now will have met you at meetings but still a lot of people would I think like to know more about what you have done, your general career, your general interests. Not everyone for instance knows that you were for many years Dean of the Institute of Psychiatry. Could you tell us something about your scientific background, because I think this is terribly relevant. You have already said that the reason why you were able to do very original work on alcoholism was that you were not enclosed in an alcohol world.*

DLD: Originally, I wanted to be a physiologist. I read physiology at Oxford as part of the medical training. I wanted to be a medical doctor too, but I didn't know what I wanted to do in the medical field. When I finished medicine I decided that I wanted to go back to physiology, and I did so for a short time. I became a demonstrator in physiology in Leeds but then I then found that physiology had changed enormously. I took my degree in 1933 in physiology and I went to Leeds in 1937, and I suppose that meanwhile there'd been a revolution. It had become biochemistry and before that it had been real physiology. After that it was applied biochemistry and I wasn't particularly interested in biochemistry. So I then thought I'd become a general practitioner and I pottered around doing locums in general practice for about 18 months, quite enjoyed it, but there was a war in the offing. I didn't want to settle down because I would be uprooted. One day I was doing a locum in Derby. About six inches of snow in February. An old farmhouse with water coming through the roof and dripping onto my bed. I developed a quinsey and that was before the days of antibiotics, and I was subject to quinsies which would lay me low for weeks. I went home to recover and I'd lost about 10 pounds in weight. I was very miserable. I came back to this place and a friend rang me up from a mental hospital and said would you do a locum? And I said, is it warm? And he said, it's marvellous. And I said, is the food good? He said, it's superb. I said well, that's the job for me. So I went off to do a locum to convalesce from my quinsey. And I liked it there, it was very pleasant, the food was excellent, the company was very good. It was one of the smallest mental hospitals in England I suppose. I had a very agreeable colleague with whom I shared a flat, and I suppose out of boredom I read textbooks on psychiatry and found that everything in the textbook was in fact in my ward, and it was a delightful experience since I'd read a chapter of the book and then find two or three cases. Or I'd see some cases and find a chapter in the book which described them. I became very interested and stayed in psychiatry. And then when I went into the Army, which was about three years later. I was medical officer in a field ambulance for two years though I had taken by DPM. And one day something happened, and I was posted into Army psychiatry. I finished up in charge of a 300-bed psychiatric unit in India. And then when I came back my job was open for me at this Derby Mental Hospital, but I'd got married in the meantime and I thought perhaps I didn't want to go back and work in a mental hospital, and I'd heard about the Maudsley. I never heard about the Maudsley in fact until I'd been doing psychiatry for, I suppose, a couple of years. It wasn't well known outside London in those days. Anyway I wrote to Aubrey Lewis, he interviewed me and I came here as what was the equivalent of a class three medical registrar, something like that. It was a post made available to people coming out of the Army whose training had been interrupted, and coming here I then started to learn real psychiatry. Although I'd been in charge of a psychiatric unit with a qualification and everything else, it was only after I had been at the Maudsley a few months I realized I'd been doing this with no real knowledge of psychiatry at all. It was just, I say 'just' in inverted commas, it was just experience.

BJA: *What rank did you hold in the Army?*

DLD: I finished up as a Major in the RAMC. I wasn't a very military figure I suspect.

BJA: *When you came to the Maudsley just after the war years, what was the intellectual climate like?*

DLD: It was a curious atmosphere in a way. One's colleagues were all people who had come back from the Army or the Navy or the Air Force. Various shapes and sizes. They'd all been selected by Aubrey Lewis. Aubrey was working to a plan in that he foresaw the development of a full blown Institute of Psychiatry. He wanted young people that he could train for different niches which he had already created in his mind. He wanted somebody for forensic psychiatry to take a very good example. Trevor Gibbens had come back from a prisoner-of-war camp and he'd got a lot of material he had collected on prisoner-of-war psychoses. So Trevor Gibbens was duly ordered to write an M.D. thesis on this, and then he was to be piloted into the forensic niche. I think Wilfred Warren had come back from the Navy, and he was showing an interest in child psychiatry so he was piloted in that direction. People did more or less mark themselves out in various ways or they were just *told* if they hadn't got any special bent—they were encouraged to take up some line of work, write a thesis on it or publish papers. At his right hand Aubrey had Eric Guttmann who was a marvellous man, and most people knew him, because he did the day-to-day work. He did a ward round pretty well every morning, right round the adult wards, so that all the registrars were chivvied by him and put through their paces. If a case cropped up which a registrar presented and he wasn't aware of the full interest, the next day Eric Guttmann would give him a list of references and he was expected to go off and read all about it. That was the sort of atmosphere. At the top it was very curious because although we weren't privy to what was going on in the Medical Committee, we knew that there were fierce rows going on because the reverberations echoed down the corridors. There were battles partly of an ideological kind. There was a group who were battling for what you might call a physical method of treatment in psychiatry, and there was a small group who wanted something we vaguely called psychodynamic psychiatry. Then there was Aubrey Lewis who really knew what kind of psychiatry he wanted, a psychiatry which had a place in it for all these things but didn't allow any of them to dominate the picture. And these battles were being fought out.

BJA: *How did you find your way through and develop your own particular interests, or were you piloted like the rest?*

DLD: Well I wanted to fill in the gaps in my training. I'd never done child psychiatry and I'd never done forensic psychiatry. I'd never done anything resembling psychotherapy, though I'd spent a lot of time talking to patients. So it was fascinating to me. I enjoyed it all but I never saw myself as being other than a general psychiatrist. I never saw myself staying on at the Maudsley because Aubrey Lewis was keen that anybody who was promoted to the senior staff should have a higher qualification, not just a DPM. I didn't do the MRCP because it was so many years since I'd done general medicine. So Eric Guttmann told me I must do a thesis at Oxford for the doctorate there; I had had a very interesting case of Friedreich's ataxia and I think it was Guttmann who drew my attention to the fact there had been some early work on psychiatric aspects, and eventually I did a D.M. thesis on this topic. My interest in general psychiatry was in physical methods of treatment. During the war there was a tremendous fillip for physical methods, with these hundreds and thousands of exhaustion cases all of whom were recommended for such help. We had huge wards in Army hospitals, with as many as 20 to 30 people in continuous narcosis for a week. Looking back it was a dreadful thing, but we thought we were the pioneers of a great treatment. And then after the war there was all this interest in leucotomy and people of my age believed that the golden era of psychiatry had dawned, and it would be drugs or surgery that would cure mental illness. It was as simple as that. And when I saw an article by Jacobson in 1950 on a new drug, Antabuse, as a physical method of treatment for alcoholism, it wasn't the alcoholism I was interested in, it was the new physical method of treatment. I went to Aubrey Lewis and said here's a new physical method of treatment and I'd like to try it, and he said, all right, try it.

BJA: *That's how you got interested in alcoholism?*

DLD: That's how I got interested in alcoholism.

BJA: *But you always remained a general psychiatrist? You never ran only an alcoholism unit?*

DLD: No, but I started a sort of alcoholism unit in I believe 1950. My beds were all male beds because in those days you worked in the male or female side of the professorial unit. I had I think 22 beds, and to these beds I began to admit four or five alcoholics at any one time. It was a 'special' unit in the sense that I had one social worker. There were only two changes in social workers over a period of about 16 years. And I myself gave continuity. The follow-up system was of course the PU follow-up system so there was continuity there too. We offered a comprehensive treatment approach and I don't know what there is in the present units that wasn't there in those early days, and yet the patients were deliberately not segregated from the others. It was my policy to keep them along with other psychiatric patients and give them the same facilities as all other psychiatric patients. Now alcoholics themselves often expected something different. They said they didn't belong, but I thought myself it was good for them. When they would say to me I'm not like other patients in the ward, I would say to them well you're not like them in one sense, in that the majority will go out fully recovered in the next few weeks and you won't.

BJA: *And while this was going on at the Maudsley what was the state of British 'alcohology'?*

DLD: Well, when I started it there was no *movement*, and I regarded this new unit as a special exercise. The first named alcohol treatment unit was Max Glatt's. I remember going to see him at Warlington Park in about 1952. For the first time I saw what is now known as an alcoholic treatment unit. It was very different from ours. In a variety of ways. They I think made virtue out of a necessity in that they didn't have social workers. So T. P. Rees who was then in charge, used nurses in a way as social workers, and I think this idea of the community nurse began probably there in Warlington Park, making virtue out of necessity.

BJA: *I am surprised at you saying there was no movement. What about the Society for the Study of Addiction, Yerbury Dent, and Lincoln Williams or what indeed about Mapother's interest, the debates that had gone on in the nineteenth and early twentieth century? Had all this really faded by then?*

DLD: There was some interest. Aubrey Lewis had always been interested in alcoholism, and it was he who started off Lincoln

Williams. Lincoln Williams had come to see him and said that he was looking for some niche for himself in the private sector of psychiatry and Aubrey Lewis suggested to him that there was a need for alcohol treatment facilities. He suggested to Lincoln Williams that he went to the States and looked at some of these places and spend some time there. Aubrey Lewis was interested in alcoholism very much and Mapother was; he wrote papers in the 1920s which can't be bettered. Many of the conclusions de Lint and Schmidt arrived at in the last 10 years, are clearly stated by Mapother in precise language in these paper of his in the 1920s. So there was an interest, but alcoholism was not regarded as a big problem. Everybody said that other countries had their alcohol problems but not Britain. Jellinek came here, I think in 1950 or 1951, and I remember a discussion in Aubrey Lewis's office with Aubrey Lewis and Jellinek, this curious little tubby man who looked as if he'd stepped out of a cartoon. He came along and said to Aubrey Lewis that he thought that we did have a problem and he wanted to get statistics, and Aubrey Lewis put him in touch with people at the Ministry of Health. I remember C. P. Blacker who was adviser to the Ministry in some aspects of epidemiology, saying to me that alcoholism wasn't a problem here and he thought that Jellinek was wasting his time, but they gave him what statistics they had. It was after that that Jellinek produced his prevalence figure of 350,000. The interest came after Jellinek's publications and after the WHO publications. People began to look round and say well, perhaps there is a problem and the statistics began to mean something. There was in this country the Standing Sub-Committee on Mental Health of the Central Health Services Council, some enormous title. I was on that and the Ministry brought up the question of alcoholism round about 1960, and I was on that sub-committee. We made the first recommendations and brought out the first circular. I have distinct recollections of saying at the time that I wasn't in favour of the ATUs, but that was the circular that set up the Alcoholism Treatment Units (ATUs). I had seen the Warlingham Park ATU, but I still thought that one did better by treating alcoholics in a general psychiatric unit. It didn't require any special expertise I thought. I'd never used group therapy but one of the arguments had been that they need group therapy, so you've got to have a group. I wasn't against group therapy but we only had four or five patients at a time, and there seemed no reason for it. So my comment when that first circular came out was that the Ministry was going about things in the way that political people deal with medical problems. If there is a drive towards doing something they set up a special unit, they can point to it in the House of Commons and say we spent so much money, there's a special unit, this is what we're doing. Otherwise they can't say what they're doing. There's always a political drive to do something special. I don't think that always coincides with the best clinical approach, which may not be to do something special but just to do something rather more within your general arrangements. My comment at the time was that the value of the ATUs will be proved when they disappear. This somewhat enigmatic remark meant that when there has been enough interest generated and there was a nucleus of people who felt sufficiently specialized to go out and teach other people, then everybody in general psychiatry will be able to do what needs to be done—because I've never thought that there is anything very special to be done. It didn't seem to me to be any different from any other problem in psychiatry and I still don't think it is.

BJA: So what is your feeling as to the way alcoholism has gone since those early days? Has it stumbled roughly in the right direction or is the gist of your argument that it really took a very bad wrong turning by becoming too specialized in its thinking, too divorced from what was very much your background which you brought to this area and which you insisted on still—that of the general psychiatrist?

DLD: Historically perhaps it could only have gone that way. The Maudsley was feeding teachers into the psychiatric system. The only real centre for teaching and research which was galvanizing British psychiatry in those days was the Maudsley and it had to fill chairs at the under-graduate teaching hospitals, it had to provide all kinds of other experts. Yet it was in a sense only a tiny organization to do that. It could not possibly have done anything about alcoholism, and have diverted itself from its main endeavour and taken on what was a relatively unimportant aspect of the whole subject. What was not very good about the special units was that when you set up a unit all that happened was that the man who happened to be looking after alcoholics in that place was designated the consultant, and he often was self taught. He had no special access to libraries or he wasn't in touch with any research that was going on, he wasn't aware of ideas that were floating around. Similarly the nurses. So I think the special unit movement began inevitably in an old fashioned way. It was dragged down by preconceived ideas, and there was little chance for a long time of any new ideas getting to work. We still see it. When we first started teaching in the summer schools 10 years ago our chief difficulty was entrenched ideas. It was an uphill struggle to break down these ideas and these attitudes and try and feed in something new. There is very much less of that around now.

BJA: *The summer schools began in the late 1960s. And yet by the late 1950s when the discussions about the setting up of Alcohol Treatment Units were beginning in which you took part, you were unhappy about the setting up of those units. You might have thought that tactically it might be OK but really on clinical grounds it wasn't the best thing. An educational campaign was what was needed, and yet again there was this 10 year gap between having available the material and the ideas, and the action. Was it just that the opportunity wasn't there then or that you were deeply imbedded in the administration which is another theme which has run through your career?*

DLD: No, I wasn't tempted to do anything particular about alcohol education at that time. I was of course immersed in post-graduate psychiatric education. I was Dean of the Institute, and the Post Graduate Medical Federation was very active then. We were filling chairs from the Maudsley in provincial universities, and some of the people going to these chairs knew a great deal about alcoholism because they'd worked on the unit here. Professor Kessel is a very good example. Professor Kendell at a much later date is another. Without thinking particularly about alcoholism, the leaven was leveaning the psychiatric lump, and in passing it was also leveaning the alcoholic lump.

BJA: *But obviously 10 years later that was not felt to be enough.*

DLD: Well then the impetus came quite differently. The impetus for the summer schools wasn't mine at all. The Camberwell Council on Alcoholism had been set up. One of the patients on my unit when he left decided that something should be done on community involvement and that's how the Camberwell Council came into being. It was a couple of years later that Peter Waters came along to one of the meetings and said he was off to the states to go to the summer school at Rutgers with the idea of starting a summer school here, and that was the first suggestion that I heard about anything of this sort. Peter came back and said that he had got some money from the Rowntree Social Services Trust. They then asked me to be associated. I'd no idea where it would lead, and so we held the first summer school in Birmingham.

BJA: *Could I catch up on something else you said. You told us the story of your original interest in alcoholism, that you were seduced in that direction by the idea of the time which was that when there was a drug treatment there was a breakthrough? Why are you now interested in alcoholism?*

DLD: Because it's a paradigm not only of a great deal of psychiatric illness but of the community 'illness', and I use the word 'illness' in quotes because I've a lot of views on whether it's an illness, a disease, or not. What fascinates me about this condition is that a man can die of cirrhosis of the liver due to alcoholism in Camberwell largely because he was born in Killarny. An extraordinary connection with a thread that runs all the way through from birth to death. It is what tuberculosis used to be: where you were born and the group you came from and your up-bringing and your antecedents and your nutrition and your job and your housing and your ventilation and your friends and everything else would determine the expectation of your dying of tuberculosis. Tuberculosis has largely gone but alcoholism in a sense has taken its place. It is the paradigm of the social malaise. It's the perfect subject for the borderland of social and medical interaction. It's in keeping with the concerns of the times because the drug treatment era is largely exploited, there is not going to be very much more advance in heroic surgery, there is not going to be very much more advance in anaesthetics. As regards infectious illnesses you don't need doctors, you need good sanitary engineers. We're now in the era of the disease of life style, over eating, smoking, drinking. All these conditions of life are the ones which are now causing the biggest suffering. It's now time for the approach of true social medicine as I see it.

BJA: What advice would you give to a young man or young woman coming towards their final qualifications who said—"I would like to devote my career to something as eminently worthwhile and as challenging as the field in which you and others have been working, how shall I shape my career. I want to take my career as seriously as Aubrey Lewis would have taken it. How do I now equip myself for this venture?"

DLD: Well I think I'd ask him firstly whether he wanted to specialize exclusively in what we'll call ethanology or whether he wanted to have it as a special but limited interest. In Great Britain there can never be more perhaps than 10 or 15 people who are wholly devoted to research in this field. There will never be the money to support more and we'll have to rely on people who are generalists with a special interest. If he wanted to be a generalist with a special interest I would ask him to do the training of a general psychiatrist and then I'd suggest that he attach himself one way or another to one of the specialized research centres.

BJA: Would you wish this aspiring specialist to study in the U.S.A.?

DLD: Well, Aubrey Lewis never liked anyone to go off and have an analysis until he's had a full Maudsley training on the grounds that after that person had a full Maudsley training and become a senior registrar he'd know what was good and what was bad, and if he then decided to have an analysis that was fine. What he abhorred was a man who had an analysis before he started general psychiatry because he thought that it warped his mind. I would say the same about ethanology. The man must not go to the States until he's really learnt about the subject in a good school here, then he should go and draw his own conclusions.

BJA: *Let's take up one further issue. There was quite a long gap when you didn't publish a great deal.*

DLD: I never regarded myself, and never have done, as a research worker. I never had any training in research. I've always regarded myself as a clinician and what I've done is what one would call clinical enquiry, rather than research. I did some other researches though, again of a clinical kind—one study I did on the breakdown of people engaged to be married,[4] something which intrigued me and on which I spent quite a lot of time. I've never regarded myself as a man who went round looking for things to research into as I suppose a research worker does. I've only researched into things that hit me, or that I noted and thought were odd and followed up. It's a different sort of approach.

BJA: *I think if I'd written that 1962 paper and I'd had that response to it, either I would have decided to become a lorry driver, or I would have repeated the work or would have returned to it fairly quickly.*

DLD: I did a few things. For example, because people said those seven patients who regained control over drinking weren't 'real alcoholics', I encouraged Dr. Donald Scott to look into alcoholic hallucinosis. We looked for people who had resumed normal drinking and who had indubitably been alcoholics in the sense that they had experienced alcoholic hallucinosis or delirium tremens. We published a paper on that work[5], and when I was in Finland on some other business, I spent a couple of days at Chris Bruun's request examining the members of his Polar Bear group[6]. So I did do bits to carry the theme further but at long intervals because I've always been thoroughly overworked and never had time. If that paper had passed without any comment I'm not sure that I would have published anything more on alcoholism or become as interested in it as I am now. I was more or less dragged into this battle from the touchline.

References

1. Davies, D. L. (1962). Normal Drinking in Recovered Alcohol Addicts. *Quarterly Journal of Studies on Alcohol*, 23, 94–104.
2. Davies, D. L., Shepherd, M. and Myers, E. (1956). The Two-Years Prognosis of 50 Alcohol Addicts after Treatment in Hospital. *Quarterly Journal of Studies on Alcohol*, 17, 485–502.
3. Wing, J. (1956). The 4 year prognosis of 50 alcohol addicts after treatment in hospital. Unpublished dissertation for DPM, London University.
4. Davies, D. L. (1956). Psychiatric Illness in those Engaged to be Married. *British Journal of Prev. Soc. Med.*, 10, 123–127.
5. Scott, D. F. (1967). Alcoholic Hallucinosis—an aetiological study. *British Journal of Addiction*, 62, 113–125.
6. Davies, D. L. (1969). Stabilized Addiction and Normal Drinking in Recovered Alcohol Addicts. In Scientific Basis of Drug Dependence. Edited by Hannah Steinberg. J. and A. Churchill Limited, London.

14

Interview with Max Glatt

MAX M. GLATT, b. 1912, Berlin. Studied medicine in Universities of Berlin and Leipzig (MD 1937); British qualifications include DSc, FRCP and FRCPsych (Hon). After coming to England various consultant appointments: Warlingham Park (1951–58) where he established first NHS alcoholism treatment unit; later directed similar unit for alcohol and drug problems at St. Bernards (1958–77). Editor, British Journal of Addiction 1962–77. Consultant to WHO. Has received German and U.S. awards.

BJA: *You first became known in the alcoholism field through your work at Warlingham. What can you tell us about the foundation of the Warlingham Park Alcoholism Unit—the prototype Alcoholism Unit in the U.K.?*

MG: It came into being not by a plan, but just by muddling along. I had come to Warlingham in 1951 after having got the D.P.M. I became interested in group therapy, and the groups in which I took part dealt mainly with various neurotic conditions but also with a few alcoholics. I didn't know anything about alcoholism, but the alcoholics struck me as interesting people with wide experience, and they were good talkers. But somehow they didn't fit in with what was happening. I remember in particular one chap who was a stock-broker. He had been a very successful man. But he had now been put into Warlingham by his family-firm on the condition that he would do something about his drinking but that if he didn't come out cured after 6 months he would be sacked. So this highly intelligent man went along to the various doctors in the hospital and asked each one of us what we did about alcoholism, and none of us knew what to answer—'there is nothing we can do'. When he was talking to me, I remembered a dentist who also had been at Warlingham a number of times and again he cut a lonely figure—a very nice, very intelligent man, who just walked around all day long with his books, hardly talking to anybody. He came back again and again. I also remembered a man who was, I think, admitted 11 times, usually in D.Ts. They all enjoyed Warlingham, which under T. P. Rees was a liberal, pulsating, active community—but they relapsed again and again.

Finally, it occurred to me that we had nothing much to lose if we took some of the drinkers we had at Warlingham and put them into their own group. It was about June 1952 that I found three other patients to join that stock-broker. We sat around talking about various things for an hour or so, and at the end of that session I asked them whether they wanted to meet again. They all said well, they didn't really think what was offered by me was other than a waste of time, but compared to the even more boring occupational therapy (better and bigger elephants), there was no harm in wasting another hour. And so we had a second meeting and it was clear that something was happening. I didn't know what was happening, and I had no clue about alcoholism. Yet within a fairly short period we got in touch with A.A., and those four people became the nucleus of the first A.A. group in the Croydon area.

BJA: Could you tell us a bit about what sort of place Warlingham was at that time, and something about its superintendent, Dr. T.P. Rees?

MG: Dr. T.P. Rees was one of the first superintendents to open all the doors of a psychiatric hospital, and he certainly was a personality. He allowed and encouraged any one of the junior doctors to do their own thing. His style of management was completely decentralized with lots of experiments going on. For example, Dr. Dennis Martin started the Pinel House Neurosis Unit, and quite a few others who later did pioneering work elsewhere, were very active at W.P.H. at the time, such as R. A. Sanderson, Dennis Scott, Ken Weeks, Stuart Whiteley, Arthur Sanker, and others. It was a very stimulating place where we were all allowed to do within limits what we wanted—as long as we did something. There was not much systematic training but through regular staff meetings and discussions we all felt we were learning a great deal. It was a free and easy therapeutic community and patients also were given a lot of freedom, a lot of responsibility and encouraged to take initiatives.

BJA: *Had you before 1952 in any sense charted the direction of your career?*

MG: I arrived at that point in my career really because of an utter muddle. I got out of Germany in 1937 just after getting the M.D. with a dissertation on a psychiatric theme (G.P.I.). In Germany at that time in order to get a doctorate you had to be given a topic by a University Professor. I had been thrown out from Berlin University in 1934 because of the tide of anti-semitism: one didn't know from one month to another what was going to happen, and every few months there was a new discriminatory law. But somehow I was allowed to finish medical studies at Leipzig University and I then tried to find somebody who would give me a topic for a thesis but at that time (1937) no German professor dared to help—till I finally arrived at the psychiatric clinic at the Berlin Charité Hospital. Here Professor Bonhoeffer (whose son, Dietrich, the famous theologian and an active anti-Nazi was murdered by the Nazis in 1945), gave me as a theme 'The Treatment of Syphilis and the Causation of G.P.I.' When I came to England in 1939 I had hoped that there was a Unit here treating G.P.I. with malaria. In England, a year after the outbreak of the war, because I had a German passport, I was interned and sent to Australia, coming back to the U.K. in 1942. I was then given a job in the Emergency Medical Service: at that time the general hospitals were evacuated to mental hospitals in the suburbs and I was working at Cane Hill, a large mental hospital in Surrey. I was a resident M.O. in charge of four general wards with mainly medical and surgical patients.

BJA: *And who introduced you to British psychiatry?*

MG: Well, after three or four weeks I felt I didn't have enough work to do, and I asked whether I could do any surgical and medical work on the psychiatric side of the hospital. The Superintendent must have thought me an idiot who hadn't learnt the first rule that one never volunteers. My interests were really in general medicine, especially neurology and cardiology, but I hadn't got any English degrees, and had no useful connections. Psychiatry? By 1947–8 when I was naturalized, I had been in psychiatric hospitals for several years, so I thought I would try the D.P.M. first but perhaps later try to get back into medicine. Having then got the D.P.M., I thought well, perhaps I should find out a bit more about psychiatry from a progressive mental hospital and that's why in 1951 I went to Warlingham. From group therapy, I think, I got into alcoholism.

BJA: *What strikes me on checking through the dates is that in 1952 you tried to get this group of four alcoholics together and three years later in 1955 you were publishing papers which are highly thought out, and which present the whole vision of what an alcoholism unit could be. It looks as though within a mere three years of starting you have had some surge of ideas and have got a vision that you can present to the world.*

MG: Oh, I don't know—I am very impressed with what *you* are saying but it wasn't like that at all. I got into alcoholism not knowing a thing about it; and I can say with good conscience that may have been a great advantage because I had no fixed ideas and no axe to grind. Afterwards, having met these few alcoholics and on listening to them finding that the few notions I may have had about alcoholism were utterly wrong, I felt quite guilty. Here were intelligent, pleasant people obviously suffering acutely and here I was without having a clue what to do next. So I continued listening to them and whatever they said to me made sense. I also began to read about the problem but there was nothing much written about alcoholism treatment in this country. The way you now describe it suggests I had this wonderful idea but I had no ideas whatsoever, I was just sitting there listening to a group of patients. But it very soon turned out to be a field in which hardly anyone in this country had taken any interest. Patients' own experiences surely have to be taken into consideration. There is said at the present moment to be an alleged controversy between the 'craftsmen' and the 'scientists', and even though it is quite clear that the so-called craftsmen should learn from research and not just go off with their own 'wild' ideas, so it seems to me to that so-called scientists also should listen to what the patient says. Anyhow at the time (1952) I just took notice of what went on in our discussions—it wasn't really my ideas but rather I was a blank sheet and I just recorded what came out of the discussions. At any rate, as soon as Rees allowed this Unit to be set up we had requests for admission from all over the country.

BJA: *So how long was it before you opened Pinel House and were fully in operation?*

MG: We started our first discussion in some dilapidated huts which later were to become Pinel House but when we began to have more patients, we were moved into one of the more modern villas. For some administrative reason, a few months later Dr. Rees took us out of the Villa again and put us into the middle of the old hospital which the alcoholics didn't like. After quite a bit of grumbling from me Rees said 'Listen, if you shut up and agree that we give you 12 patients in that ward and you and the alcoholics accept the demotion from the Villa, you can choose whoever you consider the two best male nurses in the whole hospital. That's how we got two excellent helpers, Mr. George Thomas (who 20 years later was given the M.B.E. for his work on the Unit), and Mr. Gray who unfortunately died a few years later from a coronary. We had a number of wonderful nurses throughout the years, and there we were with 12 male beds as part of a ward in the middle of the old building, though the few female alcoholics from the female side of the hospital attended the meetings as did social workers, psychologists, clergymen, etc. Pinel House only became the location of the alcoholic group much later, long after I had left.

BJA: *Where did the idea of each patient telling his life story come from, and how did your treatment evolve?*

MG: At the same time as the Alcoholic Unit started, we also did the life story in the Neurosis Unit which Denis Martin ran. Our treatment methods seemed to develop very easily and logically —group sessions, the formation of the A.A. group in the Hospital, the ex-patients reunions which started in 1954 at St. Martin-in-the-Fields, and the magazine written by the Warlingham ex-patients and the present patients.

BJA: *Were you yourself at that time very much engaged in the therapeutic work?*

MG: Yes, very much so. I had an intense clinical involvement and my interests has always been mainly clinical, although I have also always liked teaching and clinical research. At that time in Warlingham the alcoholics were only a relatively small part of my duties. Nevertheless, I wasn't married, I lived in the Hospital and I don't think I took many weekends off. I still remember most of the names of the old Warlingham Park alcoholic patients at that time, and I am still friendly with quite a few of them. From the beginning the chaplain had a group, the social worker had a group, the nurses had a group and all these allegedly new great ideas about interdisciplinary team work were obvious already at that time to anyone taking the trouble to listen to what patients had to say. I had an O.P. group in 1952, and saw alcoholics as out-patients from the beginning.

BJA: *How much was A.A. shaping your ideas in this early stage?*

MG: We worked closely with the A.A. although I always tried to make it clear to patients that the uncovering, dynamic hospital group therapy meetings were not A.A.—a lot of overlap but also certain differences—yet complementing each other. Obviously, we learnt a great deal from this warm-hearted, outstanding fellowship. In turn, I think ex-patients of the Units have greatly influenced the work of A.A. in this country; for example, in addition to the ordinary A.A. group meetings, many A.A. groups now function mainly as discussion meetings rather than a main speaker telling his story at very great length.

BJA: *Accepting your modest insistence that you learnt from your patients, nonetheless by 1955 you clearly had learnt, and your writings gave by then an extraordinarily coherent view of the possibilities of NHS treatment for alcoholism centred on specialised units. You were offering a new model of alcoholism treatment although it may have borrowed from the neurosis unit, and from A.A. Was there any sense of joy, of discovery, of something in which you could believe?*

MG: Of course. I had met these alcoholics, realized I didn't know anything, but soon found that the 'great men' in British psychiatry did not have a clue either about alcoholics. I realized how much these people were suffering, and had seen too how much their families were suffering, and then there didn't seem to be anybody to help. Not only did no one have an answer, but hardly anyone seemed to care (apart from A.A. and the members of the Society for the Study of Addiction). And I got the feeling that one ought to do something. I did not feel we were doing very much, but at least one was able to say that there was one place in the country which was *trying* to do something.

BJA: *Did you feel yourself consciously drawn into campaigning to make this not only a local model but something which could influence national thinking? I note that by 1961 the B.M.A. and Magistrates' Association produced a report which was very much inspired by your experience.*

MG: Because of the interest shown by patients, their families, A.A., probation officers, Churches, magistrates, etc. one began to feel that there was an obvious need for this type of experimental work and that it ought to spread further afield. We had lots of visitors to the alcoholic groups coming from abroad and they too were getting very interested. As for the B.M.A./Magistrates' Committee I did not instigate the setting up of their special sub-committee, and incidentally it was rather characteristically called the Alcoholics and Vagrants Committee. I was invited to one of their last meetings and gave evidence—the far from flattering outcome was a pessimistic feeling among the Committee members that nothing more could be done. But one of the Committee Members, Dr. Boardman, a paediatrician from Bristol, said he didn't agree with the pessimistic view. It was really his persuasive intervention which then led to a suggestion that I should write a paper and make some suggestions, and that paper was then accepted as the basis of the B.M.A. and Magistrates' Committee's report (1961). We also discussed at that time what should be done with alcoholic vagrants, and with alcoholics who were obviously killing themselves. Rather than just standing by and waiting till alcoholics kill themselves we ought to give them a chance at least to sober up and if when cold-bloodedly sober they still decide to drink themselves to death, then perhaps one can't do more. However the Committee felt that sufficient provision was already made for compulsory admission of those drinkers who required it.

BJA: *The Ministry of Health's memorandum on "The hospital treatment of alcoholism', published in 1962, substantially accepted the B.M.A. recommendations. Did you or others actively campaign for the ear of the Ministry of Health?*

MG: I certainly didn't campaign at all, although I knew Brigadier Phillipson who at that time had a position at the Ministry. Perhaps through the influence of Phillipson to a certain extent, the Ministry accepted what the B.M.A. memorandum had suggested.

BJA: *Did you give evidence to the Ministry?*

MG: Not at all, no, although I couldn't see what was holding them up, why nothing was done for alcoholics when we had plenty of alcoholics in the country in need of help. One often got visitors from abroad who came to Warlingham after they had already been to the Ministry and they had always asked the officials 'What do you do in England about alcoholics?', and they always got two answers. First, we have not got any alcoholics and secondly, all our mental hospitals are adequately equipped to deal with them. I'm afraid my contributions were limited to writing letters to the medical press on this issue, and giving lots of talks.

BJA: *In retrospect, do you feel that the people who then took up the ball and ran with it to the point where we now have 30 alcoholism units in the U.K. achieved what you had in mind?*

MG: On the whole, yes. We have all learnt, but one only learns gradually about alcoholism and its ramifications. The idea was never that every alcoholic should be treated in the same way; but quite a number of advanced alcoholics required hospitalization (and aftercare), and the haphazard admission of alcoholics into various hospitals over the whole country, with nurses and doctors who took not the slightest interest in them, was a waste of time. I was always sure that the majority of alcoholics could be treated as out-patients. I don't really think that the in-patient Unit was ever seen as a universal formula for treating all alcoholics, but if so that was certainly a misunderstanding. And from the beginning we were aware of the great influence of social problems on the causation and development of alcoholism. Again, as to the length of in-patient treatment, I believe we started off with one month and later it became a bit longer. Personally, I don't think I ever said we should always say three months—anyhow in the earlier years there were few A.A. groups and few G.Ps or other organizations to help in the necessary follow-up treatment, so that in those years such patients really did require relatively longer in-patient therapy than nowadays where there is much more community backing.

BJA: Do you have any impression that the special units, which had very purposely taken alcoholics away from scattered general psychiatry wards, as a side effect may actually have persuaded the professions that alcoholism is not a job for the generalist?

MG: I think there is something in your question, but we did try to point out from the beginning that alcoholism was the business of all doctors and every profession, but as you know many doctors and other professionals are only too keen to avoid involvement with alcoholic patients. The question may come down to the functions of the unit—I don't agree with them being called just Alcoholism *Treatment* Units—it was clear from the word go that these units were also excellent education and training facilities and a good base for research. Moreover as T. P. Rees said many years ago, not about alcoholism but about psychiatry in general, that the time surely would come when the hospital would only be one part of a community network, and in the same way we saw the in-patient unit only as one part of the total network with O.P. clinics, domiciliaries, collaboration with other specialists and G.Ps, etc.

BJA: When you first became interested in alcohol problems early in the 1950s, who else was on the scene in this country?

MG: Apart from the people in A.A. whom I really felt understood more about the whole thing than anyone else, there were the members of the Society for the Study of Addiction (the S.S.A.). The strong man was John Yerbury Dent, a charismatic personality. He believed in apomorphine, not as an aversion treatment but because of his theory that it had some effect on the hindbrain. He dominated the meetings of the S.S.A. The people who ran the S.S.A. were at that time mainly private doctors, some were G.Ps, and some psychiatrists, but it was mainly a physically oriented approach. There was once a debate between Dr. Carver and Dr. Dent. Carver's view was that neurosis led to alcoholism, whereas Dent's view was that alcoholism led to 'neurosis-like behaviour'. Dent really said alcoholism was a disease like diabetes, and one doesn't treat a disease by talking. Dent was a very persuasive personality, a great friend of alcoholics. I think most of us agreed with Dr. Hobson at that time, when he said that Dent without apomorphine would be a much better therapist than apomorphine without Dent—but Dent was upset when being told about this.

BJA: *How often did the S.S.A. meet?*

MG: The meetings were quite regular, every three months, and the attendance was roughly about fifty people (including many interested non-professionals), and always too a bit of a social gathering with coffee and biscuits. There were often very good lectures, which were then usually written up in the Journal together with a discussion, and the discussions were sometimes more interesting than the lectures. But the meetings were certainly dominated by Dent and by the apomorphine approach.

BJA: *What about the European connection at that time? Were you travelling a lot?*

MG: Having come to England in '39 and then having been sent as an 'enemy alien' to Australia (three months on the water either way and sea-sick most of the time) and having learnt after the war what had happened on the Continent, I didn't want to travel any more. I didn't leave this country again until I got engaged in 1960—my wife is a Hungarian who then lived in Vienna. I thought I had finished with the Continent or probably that the Continent had finished with me. But then I met Dr Hans Rotter in Vienna who told me of the conferences of the International Council on Alcoholism and soon afterwards I went to the Stockholm International Conference in 1960, and there I greatly enjoyed meeting the European experts—with well-known 'references' coming to life. I found these conferences very stimulating but I must say that what really seemed to count with me had previously come out of Jellinek's researches and from the *Quarterly Journal of Studies on Alcohol*. The American work seemed more relevant to the British situation than the Continental ideas; and the mid-European countries seemed then stuck with their mainly organic-oriented therapeutic notions. T. P. Rees was a member of various W.H.O. committees and he passed along a number of excellent World Health Organization reports, which obviously reflected Jellinek's thinking. Having said that, from the early 1960s onwards, I gained a lot from frequently mixing with people from other countries and they obviously faced the same difficulties in their countries which we had over here.

BJA: *Did you know Jellinek?*

MG: I didn't know him very well but I always admired him, as I still do although I no longer agree 100 per cent with what he said. I first met him when he visited Warlingham about 1954 (as incidentally did Marty Mann). Jellinek came into our treatment group and he got on very well with the patients; he came back one or two years later and I think that was written up by the patients in their magazine. I seem to remember that Jellinek said something to the effect that he was quite impressed with the therapeutic community and with the psychotherapeutic group, but he felt perhaps that we were not doing enough about the organic approach though we used antabuse and non-addictive drugs. I met him once or twice later and he invited me to contribute to his projected encyclopaedia on alcoholism (which I did, enlisting the help of Cecil Heath for the British statistics), but Jellinek died before the Encyclopaedia was finished. I was very impressed by him. He had a very broad vision, he seemed to know everything about alcoholism that was going on in all countries in the world. He was a very stimulating character and (perhaps similar to Freud) he was always putting forth lots of hypotheses. But what he said in 1960 he would necessarily have been saying in 1983.

BJA: *Were you yourself involved in any of the W.H.O. Expert Committees?*

MG: Yes, in 1965 and 1966, the Committees which put forward the idea of a 'combined approach' to alcohol and drug problems. The idea was not necessarily to treat alcoholics and drug takers in the same group, but to recognize that basically alcohol is a drug like other drugs. Some of the Americans felt that so much heartache and headache had gone into persuading society to regard alcoholics as people in need of help, and that the image might become contaminated by bracketing alcoholics along with 'dope fiends'. David Pittman was against the idea, so I asked him (about 1967) to write an article for the *British Journal of Addiction,* which he called 'The Rush to Combine'.

BJA: *In 1962, D. L. Davies published his paper on normal drinking among former alcohol addicts. What did you make of that paper, and what do you make of it now?*

MG: Well, I have to be careful not to talk from hindsight. I always thought that it was *theoretically* possible but not *practically* likely to return to normal drinking, and that's still my position. By that time—after my marriage—I started also to practise in Harley Street where I met middle-class alcoholics who were usually convinced that they could drink in moderation. Previously if alcoholics had come to me and said they wanted to drink in moderation, I probably would have said I can't help you, though I wish you good luck. But from 1962 on I had begun to make a kind of gentleman's agreement with that type of patient. I said to them, well, whatever I believe or don't believe, there are very reliable research workers who say that it is possible for you to achieve that goal. Try your own way if you want, but if you don't succeed give another method a chance. Some of these patients could indeed hold to social drinking for a little while; and I had also told them, look, if you want to do it that way then try to sip your drinks and don't gulp, try to stick to beer rather than spirits, drink with your spouse and above all don't drink when depressed.

One certainly did see people who could control their drinking for a short period, and I began to see it in terms of a variable threshold-range—if people by hook or by crook could keep to the right side of that threshold-range, they might get away with drinking. The debate raises the difficulty of trying to keep a fair position between two extremes—between, on the one hand, those people who say it is quite impossible, and certain sociologists and psychologists who now claim that 'normal drinking' could almost become the rule. My present position is that I believe that in theory every alcoholic could drink normally if the going remained good in three areas—in the area of the individual's personality, in the area of work and the environment, and in the area of the 'agent' (the drinking rules the individual is employing). For instance, as far as the individual is concerned, this might mean drinking only when cheerful and contented and not taking drink as a medication for one's nerves. In relation to the environment, it could mean drinking in the company of the spouse or of moderate drinkers only; and the drinking rules might be sipping wine or beer rather than gulping spirits. If the going remained good in all those areas, that person might go on drinking in a controlled way for ever, but unfortunately the wife does sometimes nag, unfortunately one does sometimes have to listen to boring lectures, unfortunately England doesn't win all the cricket and soccer matches, and unfortunately it does sometimes rain in this country, and one's boss does not always recognize what a wonderful person one is. And given that reality-situation, while in theory I don't see any reason why it should not be *possible* to return to 'normal' drinking, because of the unlikelihood in reality of the perpetual fortunate constellation in the three areas, I believe that what in theory is possible, in practice is not all that likely. I have been looking around for these elusive controlled alcoholics now for twenty years at least, I keep in touch with many ex-patients, and I would have thought sooner or later I should have met one of these cases, but I haven't seen one. Critics then say, perhaps rightly, that this is the result of a self-fulfilling prophecy: and although (initially) I do not tell such patients at the first interview that I don't believe in alcoholics' 'normal' drinking, they may perhaps still know or suspect my scepticism. Critics might also say the results of a systematic behavioural approach aimed at normal drinking would be different from the results gained from my approach (although such a view would not be confirmed by Pendery *et al.'s* recent follow-up of the Sobells' patients). I think one has to keep an open mind about it.

BJA: *Did you and Davies know each other at the time his paper came out? Did you and he ever discuss things together, or was it two separate worlds divided by the Thames?*

MG: Yes, we did know each other, he was at my wedding, and that was two years before he published that paper. As to the Thames, I think you are right. Since I left Warlingham in 1958, visiting the Maudsley and crossing the Thames has always been a bit of a—South Pole expedition. I don't think Davies and I ever discussed the issue privately, but we debated it for example on a platform in Ireland where the hefty, stocky chairman was sitting between the two of us because he seemed afraid that we would come to blows. This discussion was written up at length in an Irish newspaper. But in practice, I don't think in actual clinical practice we were all that much far away from each other as it seemed when the debate was reported.. Initially of course Davies did not say 'Come all you alcoholics I offer you an eternal paradise where you can all drink in a controlled way till the end of your days.' He only said it seemed possible but not to be recommended. It was only later that he gradually moved his position a bit or a lot further— possibly prodded along in the main by psychological and sociological fellow travellers.

BJA: *When did you start to get interested in drug problems?*

MG: One of the first things I learnt about drug problems was that many alcoholics feel that if you give them one tablet, four tablets would do them four times as well. From 1953 onwards we were seeing quite a few barbiturate and amphetamine addicts at Warlingham, mainly middle-aged female patients. We also had an occasional narcotic addict, mainly doctors, several years before the new wave of young addicts came along in the early 1960s. In 1967 Roger Tredgold and I opened an out-patient addiction centre at University College Hospital, and this was a year before the new

N.H.S. Clinics opened—there was one earlier centre at Westminster Hospital. By then I was at St Bernard's (I had moved there in 1958), and because nobody knew where to send these young addicts and as St. Bernard's had a large alcoholism unit with 60 to 70 beds and we were already taking some barbiturate and amphetamine users, we were sent these young addicts from about 1961 onwards. We put them together with the alcoholics, and they did fit in, despite all the differences in personality, age, social and economic circumstances, pharmacological agents. But after a while we began to have separate group sessions for the young narcotic addicts on the one hand, and on the other hand for the alcoholics and some more middle-aged sedative and amphetamine users though keeping them in the same ward. That started in about 1962, and the aim was to get them off narcotics completely within about a week and then start group therapy. The U.C.H. O.P. centre was started five years later.

BJA: *Did you give evidence to either of the Brain Committees?*

MG: No, but I had of course by that time written quite a bit about drug problems. I was present at the quite memorable discussion (about 1961) when Lord Brain talked at the Society of Addiction about his first Report. I'm sure it was not Lord Brain's fault, but it was a whitewash committee.

All, or rather the few, of use who were then treating narcotic addicts knew that not everything in the garden was lovely. The Committee said they hadn't found any evidence of any doctor prescribing in an unethical way. And everyone of us knew that this was not so. There were one or two world famous prescribers; Francis Camps was so indignant about the indiscriminate overprescribing that he once seriously intended to test the matter in court, but he was told that if he was bringing addicts as witnesses, the court would throw their evidence out. It was well-known that there was overprescribing going on; but this first Brain Committee said nothing needed to be done. There was at that S.S.A. discussion a Mr. Benjamin, a pharmacist working in the West End, who asked the Committee members 'how is it you only have found so few cocaine takers? I can give you many more from my own pharmacy'. Their answer was 'Why if you knew that, didn't you tell us before?' And there was at least one official in the Home Office who probably knew more about the drug situation than any of us but he felt he was not at liberty to talk.

Immediately after, as you know, they convened a second committee which changed most of what they had originally said. In between the publication of the First and the Second Brain Report, Peter Chapple, Tom Bewley and one or two others, formed an unofficial committee. Those of us who were involved in treating addicts went along to these meetings as did some of the over-prescribing doctors. It was called, I think, the London Committee for Addiction. Chapple was a moving force. Most of us were very adverse to prescribe what we thought were killer drugs. But in the end when we were asked to man the new addiction centres, the arguments were that if we didn't prescribe, the black-market would take over. The aim was to take the prescribing of narcotics out of the hands of private and general practitioners and put it into the hands of the N.H.S. doctors at specially licensed clinics. Whilst one hated doing what one was doing, one would participate, as it seemed the lesser evil. But it's quite wrong to say (as people do nowadays) that we thought at the time this was the *treatment* for drug addiction. It was just a kind of first aid and one hoped, partly naively, but partly to give one's own conscience a kind of alibi, that the new centres would not be just prescribing units, that they would have sufficient multi-disciplinary staff and sufficient time to establish relationships with addicts and motivate at least some of them to give up drugs.

I remember that I felt guilty whatever I did at that time. When I prescribed the stuff I felt guilty prescribing killing drugs. And if I didn't prescribe to someone who came alone and said 'I really need it, I've got severe withdrawal symptoms and you only give me so little', well then again I felt bad. Nevertheless, compared with the sometimes scandalous over-prescribing that had been going on before 1968, I still feel that at that time the Clinics were justified and for a time did quite well. The criticism that was later always levelled that we were only dealing with a small segment of the addicts was again something of which we were fully aware; at St.Bernard's we of course always also admitted and treated addicts to non-narcotics.

BJA: *At that time you were favouring the possibility of compulsory treatment for addicts?*

MG: Yes, though for certain addicts only under certain circumstances, and I still think compulsion has a role, provided that one has got a decent treatment centre. If one sees people who are undoubtedly doing a lot of harm to themselves and to others, then for all of us to stand by and say 'These people are free agents, this is a liberal country and one objects to compulsion in any shape or form', that is an easy cop-out. It comes back to what we were saying about compulsory treatment of alcoholism. An alcoholic or a drug taker with severe dependence is not a free agent, and it is quite wrong to say that motivation cannot be induced in at least some of these patients.

BJA: *You've been a witness to everything that has gone on in this country in relation to drug and alcohol problems over a span of thirty years, and an active participant in nearly everything that has happened. Have we made any progress?*

MG: There is often criticism today that the medical profession by-and-large doesn't care about these problems and that so little is done, with the supposition that much of our organized response has gone wrong. But each of us is interested in our particular field, and there are hundreds of dedicated people who feel passionately the same as we do about other medical needs and other social needs. There are higher-ups who have to work out the balance between our respective demands. Taking such problems into consideration, I don't see that many other countries respond much better to alcohol and drug problems than does Britain. Of course, one cannot be satisfied and there's a lot of room for improvement, but it hasn't gone all that badly. I think doctors have begun to wake up, or as Dent once put it, to 'catch up'. I think alcoholics certainly now get a better hearing—perhaps one should now also try to understand the plight of the families of addicts who often suffer as much as the drinker or drug taker.

BJA: *I have one last question. What were the roots of your compassion? You bothered to get interest in people who were discarded by the medical profession. You bothered to listen when many people wouldn't listen. You concerned yourself with young drug addicts, you sat around in Wormwood Scrubs Prison. I am wondering whether you understand, as much as any of us can ever understand such things, the origin and motivations of your involvement?*

MG: Of course I don't recognize myself in all these things you say. But may I first briefly take up your Wormwood Scrubs remark? The addicts' therapeutic community in Wormwood Scrubs Prison—the 'Annexe'—has now been going on for a decade or so, and I think (as do its patients, ex-patients, staff and former staff) it is a great shame that hardly anything about it has ever come to the notice of anyone. Certainly in all the group meetings which I have attended over the years in and outside hospitals I have hardly ever come across such honest, searching and critical confrontations among patients, with—at the same time—an obvious underlying caring attitude for each other, as among these prisoner-patients with their double handicaps of often serious personality disorder and addiction. We all feel strongly that similar experiments—setting up therapeutic communities within certain prisons (followed up, if at all possible, by special half-way houses), should be tried elsewhere.

But as to your main question, I don't know whether I have got the real answer. Once I began to know alcoholics I developed a high respect for them as individuals. When I got married some years later we had about twenty recovered alcoholics at our wedding. It is quite difficult to come back from nowhere in the face of an ostracizing, non-understanding society. Very often they are good, even great personalities. The nearest I can come to answering your question, and I don't know how deep this goes, is that most of us pride ourselves that we care for the underdog. Coming from Germany as a refugee and having seen what happened in that country to a minority left in the lurch and forgotten by everybody—but whatever it was in 1952, it must have been in me before, and I think I always tended to side with losers. If I see a soccer game I always want the underdog to win. I think I felt guilty that I had completely misjudged the first alcoholics I met before 1952 when I had just said 'drink less', or some great statements such as that. I felt I had done them wrong and society, everyone

Interview with Max Glatt

else, was doing them wrong too. Here were people who suffered and deserved help and none of us were doing anything for them. Perhaps I felt it was somebody's, I don't know, responsibility to open his mouth, even, or perhaps because, it was with a German accent and a Jewish refugee mentality and background.

15

Interview with Bing Spear

HENRY BRYAN ("BING") SPEAR, b. 1928. ISO and BSc from Exeter. After National Service in RAF (1949–51) entered Civil Service. Appointed Inspector, Home Office Drugs Branch in 1952, Deputy Chief Inspector in 1965 and Chief Inspector in 1977: retired 1986. Publications include review and comments on evolution and working of British drug policies.

BJA: *Why don't we start at the beginning when you first went to the Home Office Drugs Branch? When was that?*

BS: I came into it in February 1952, having completed my National Service in the previous December. It was actually through the R.A.F.—they gave me notice of the job. None of those I asked knew what an Inspector the Dangerous Drugs Branch did. So I came up, had the interview—and got the job which was only a temporary appointment at that time. We had an Assistant Secretary who was administratively in charge, but the Chief Inspector Frank Thornton had been there since before the first Dangerous Drugs Act [of 1920]. He came across, as I understand it, from the Board of Trade when they were dealing with licensing in the First World War. There was Frank Thornton as the Chief Inspector, Len Dyke, his Deputy and three Inspectors, who were Mac (Robert McBride from Northern Ireland), Jeff (Charles Jeffery) and I was the Junior; there were only five people to do what was then necessary. I didn't really have much idea what it was all about until I had been there some time.

BJA: *What was it like then?*

BS: Well, it was interesting. I've always had an interest in police and legal matters, and also my mother always wanted me to be a doctor; I would never have made a doctor, and I'd never have made a policeman, but this job brought me in contact with both sides, so really I had the best of all worlds, and as a boy from Cornwall, coming up to the great big city and Whitehall, it was all quite exciting. The job itself was interesting, because you worked on your own to a large extent once you were competent to go out and you got involved in a variety of things. The main excitement in those days, of course, was provided by doctor addicts. The first Friday I was there, this doctor, a pethidine addict, came in and I remember being allowed to sit in on the interview. Jeff [C. Jeffery] gave him a bit of a wigging. It was the first time I'd ever come across drug addicts and doctors. The bread-and-butter work was very largely inspecting pharmaceutical firms. It was a matter of keeping companies and the people who handled the drugs legitimately—I wouldn't say in check—but seeing whether they observed their license conditions and so on—that there were no leakages.

BJA: *Who were the different Chief Inspectors?*

BS: Thornton was in charge during the war, and he remained Chief Inspector until he retired in 1956. He was succeeded by Len Dyke who had come across from the Yard. He had been a detective sergeant; in fact he was, I believe, one of the first, if not the first, specialist Metropolitan Police Drug Squad Officers. He was a very interesting character because he spanned that period just before the war when there was a little upper-crust heroin circle which he and Thornton knew quite well. Len Dyke was made up to Chief Inspector in 1956, Jeffery was made Deputy over McBride, who was actually senior in service, so McBride resigned. I went from fifth to third in a fairly short space of time. Then, when Len Dyke went in 1965, Jeffery took over as Chief Inspector, and I took over from him in 1977.

BJA: *Many of you stayed there for a long time. Is that unusual for a Civil Service department?*

BS: When I came in we were recruited directly by the Home Office in what was known as a departmental post and we had no secondary avenue of promotion into the main Civil Service. We recruited from outside till the late 1960's when it was suggested that we might do better for recruiting if we came into the mainstream of the Civil Service. Since then our Inspectors have come from other parts of the Home Office.

BJA: Do you think continuity was important?

BS: I do. Quite frankly, I have never regarded myself as a Civil Servant in the sense where you are quite content to do one job for 3 or 4 years and then another for the next 3 or 4 years. I see the Civil Service now as being to much concerned with administration and presentation and less with actual problems. I know that sounds a bit critical, but you get an awful lot of high fliers who, quite frankly, don't really get involved. Some years ago, one of these characters said that the trouble with the Drugs Inspectorate was that they were too involved with the people. Whatever the subject of the paper which comes into their in-tray, they will deal with it efficiently, very efficiently; they have very good minds and their drafting is superb, but 'administration' is the name of their game. I don't think solving problems is of great concern to them. It is more important that the administration should be correct. Not that I am claiming we had a sense of mission or anything, but at least we could occasionally see we were achieving something, for example, with addict doctors.

BJA: Something that cropped up in many books and articles was that "Bing Spear knew all the addicts by name".

BS: That was a bit of an exaggeration. I think if you go back long enough, back to the days before the drug problem really took off, in the sixties, it was reasonable then to remember most of the names because you only had a fairly small number and I was particularly interested in the heroin problem. If things were slow in the office I'd say "I'll put my coat on and go to Boots and John Bell and Croyden (the chemists) for the afternoon".

I'd look through the books and pick up three or four new names of addicts who'd just surfaced with doctors. I had that sort of close contact, so I was picking them up regularly and the names stuck.

BJA: *And sometimes reasonably close contact with addicts themselves.*

BS: Yes indeed, and that has gone on. I still get letters from addicts now. They've always believed the myth about 'being registered', and the idea that the Home Office can tell a doctor to take them on and crack the whip over the doctor to make him prescribe. For some reason, they felt I was the one in particular who could do that. They'd phone me, I'd make a few non-committal responses down the phone, the addict would have got it off his chest, and everybody was happy. I haven't done anything for him, but he's unburdened himself to somebody and he thinks somebody's listened to him. The reason I've maintained a link with addicts is, I've always believed that if you're trying to deal with a problem, you've got to know what that problem's about and the only people who can really tell you are the clients.

BJA: *Were you unusual in going out and going round the West End and getting to know people, or was that a general way of working in the Branch?*

BS: I think Frank Thornton and Len Dyke certainly did in the pre-war period—but that was largely because Len Dyke in those days was a policeman—they had contact with the pre-war addicts. But no, I think it was largely a special interest of mine. I could see the problem. But that's a bit conceited; I couldn't see the problem developing to the extent that it has today, but I could see the number of heroin addicts going up. Shortly after, if you recall, we had the fiasco about heroin—the proposal to ban it in 1955.

BJA: *This was to try to bring Britain into line with other countries and ban heroin from medical practice.*

BS: Yes, it wasn't because of any problems in this country or, I think, any initiative here. It was simply that we were playing our part internationally.

BJA: *It brought forward quite a reaction from the medical profession?*

BS: Well, it was certainly interesting, although I was not directly involved. What happened was that, in good Civil Service fashion, the various bodies that had to be consulted, were consulted. No objections were raised—you have to wonder how seriously the proposal was considered because one of the people on the then Government's advisory committee subsequently signed a letter with his colleagues from his teaching hospital protesting vehemently against the ban, and yet he'd been a party to allowing the Government to go ahead. So, in fairness to the Departments, they went ahead on a green light given by the people they had to consult. Maybe there's a lesson there for the Advisory Council on the Misuse of Drugs, you know, letting things go through on the nod. When it was realized what would happen, all hell broke loose; I think quite rightly, because I've never felt that barring legitimately produced heroin is going to have an impact on the illicit traffic. It was, of course, rather different in the 1920's and 1930's when a lot of legitimately made heroin went into the black market.

BJA: *In the fifties you have evidence of an increase in the use of heroin. You have some doctors prescribing heroin and then the first Brain Committee was established in 1958.[1] Why was it established?*

BS: I think there were to main reasons; there may have been others. One was, of course, that you had had Rolleston a long time ago. I think there was a feeling that Rolleston ought to be looked at again, although there was no pressure for it; and the other thing, of course, was that since Rolleston you had the introduction after the war of the synthetics—pethidine, methadone and all the others.

BJA: *Were you involved? Did you give evidence.*

BS: No.

BJA: *I get the impression that junior people, yourself included, could see things happening and these views weren't accepted by your superiors?*

BS: Yes. Whether they were accepted or not, it's very difficult to say. I know that Johnnie Walker recognized that there was a problem. He was the Assistant Secretary at the time, but he had gone by the time Brain was set up. I'm not quite sure who made the running, how far it was the administrators who went ahead. I would often say to Len Dyke 'three more', when I came back from Boots at Piccadilly, with details of three new heroin addicts. I think he took every new addict as a personal defeat. And, of course, as good Civil Servants, we all know that if you leave a problem long enough, it will often solve itself. So, perhaps there was a feeling that you deny the existence of a problem. I wrote a report on heroin in 1955, well in advance of the first Brain Committee. I got into a bit of trouble because I drew attention to the increasing heroin problem and suggested that we should go back to Rolleston Tribunals which were then in abeyance. I got a rap over the knuckles for my pains because that was 'not on' at that time.

Rolleston was an important milestone,[2] they foresaw the problems, they were dealing with a totally different problem to the one we had in the fifties. By allowing, or by saying that doctors could prescribe, they had the foresight also to provide the machinery to police it [the Tribunals]. Now, if we had had that machinery in the early fifties—I'm not saying that we wouldn't have the problem today because there are so many other factors that apply—but we could not nail those doctors who were being exploited, apart from those whose motives were perhaps slightly different.

Certainly, we produced case-histories for the Brain Report. I think Jeff probably did most of the typical addict cases, most of which I think were therapeutic.

BJA: *Those cases showed that some people in some circumstances could lead fairly ordinary lives as long as they were getting their drugs.*

BS: Yes, that's right. I would argue that today for some heroin addicts. They are a minority but that's one of the things that I'm interested in at the moment. Even knowing the way that Brain was going to report, I put in a couple of supplementary reports showing the numbers still going up, but it didn't do anything. I had great delight in going with Benny Benjamin to the famous meeting of the Society for the Study of Addiction at which Lord Brain pre-viewed his report. Benny Benjamin was the pharmacist at John Bell and Croyden, a very shrewd and knowledgeable character. Lord Brain had quoted statistics (I forget the figures). Benny Benjamin made his famous remark, he got up at the end of the talk and said he was interested in Lord Brain's report and in particular the figures, because of the 20 cocaine addicts that Lord Brain quoted, he was personally dispensing for 40, or something to that effect. It brought the house down. We had a chat outside with one of the Committee subsequently, who said "We were never told this".

BJA: *Was Isabella, Lady Frankau prescribing then?*

BS: No. She didn't come on the scene until about 1958; she'd not been involved before. In fact, her reason for starting, as I've always understood it, was that a perfectly responsible lady practitioner, who had one or two addicts and who had some contact with Lady F on other sorts of cases, said to her one day "Why don't you try your hand with an addict?" Up to then Lady Frankau had dealt with alcoholics and some of the other problems of the upper classes, and so she took on one of the well-known addicts of the fifties: in fact, this addict is still around, and used to send me a Christmas card each year. She could and would tell lovely stories about Lady Frankau.

BJA: *Some addicts in Britain used heroin and cocaine together. How did that start?*

BS: Lady Frankau. She started it with her Canadian addicts, the idea being that a little bit of cocaine would give them a little bit of energy and they could work. You could then also bargain with them that, by giving them a little bit of cocaine, they would accept a cut in their heroin. Cocaine was seen as not so much a problem for withdrawal and cutting down. The net result, of course, was the heroin dose never came down and the cocaine went up! That's where it started because, of course, cocaine was virtually dead until then.

BJA: *Am I right that she made a lecture tour of Canada at some time and that soon after there was an influx of Canadians addicts?*

BS: I know she certainly went out there, but in fairness to her, I think that has been misrepresented. I have never blamed or attributed to Lady Frankau the reason for the influx of Canadians. I can remember the first Canadian—met him—but obviously he didn't like us and he went back. This was in 1956 or 1957 I think; I'd need to look that up. Then, in the Christmas of 1957 another chap came over. He had difficulty over the Christmas period finding a doctor, and he didn't go straight to Lady Frankau because in '57 she was not really involved. He came over and eventually settled with a doctor. Then about a couple of months later two more came over and there followed a gradual procession. One of them, in fact, wrote back and said "This is addicts' seventh heaven" and it's not surprising as they had never had legitimate heroin prescribed to them. A former RCMP officer who was then Liaison Officer at the High Commission over there—Bill Kelly—predicted that we would get only about a hundred. And he was right; it was of that order. Several of them went back on their own initiative, a few we managed to export, a few died, one or two are still here, and one or two of them are off. But certainly, after she'd been over, there was a lot of publicity given in Canada to these stable addicts and several of them figured in articles by Canadian journalists, which all helped to encourage the flow. But it was over by about 1964.

BJA: *In 1964 the Brain Committee was reconvened.*[3] *How did that come about?*

BS: Because of a report we put in; we drew attention to the increasing number of heroin addicts. It was largely Lady Frankau we were concerned about, but the report covered all the prescribers. We collected details of as many heroin pre-

Interview with Bing Spear 235

scriptions as we could trace, both NHS and private. That's where all the figures in the second Brain Report come from—the six kilos prescribed by one doctor over the year and the individual large prescriptions for a thousand tablets of heroin, etc. Les Ackroyd helped a lot on it but I did most of the legwork, and wrote it up. It went up through our channels to our administrators and then up the chain and obviously there had to be consultations with the Ministry of Health. I doubt whether it would have gone to Ministers. I can't recall. Certainly what was decided, probably at CMO [Chief Medical Officer] level, was to ask Lord Brain if he would undertake a further enquiry. Those were only the scripts we picked up. I've photographs of the famous prescription for 1,000 tablets of heroin and 252 grains of cocaine. This was a report of the deteriorating situation and our inability to do anything about the liberal prescribing. Peter Beedle by that time was our Assistant Secretary. A nice man. I went to every meeting of the Committee. We didn't see ourselves as having any wonderful solution to the problem. All we were really saying was "Look, let us get at this excessive prescribing" because so much of it was ridiculous, as the examples quoted in the Brain Report prove. But they went their own way and they came up with the recommendations we all know. I'm sure we in the Inspectorate would have been content with a return to the Rolleston Tribunals or some system whereby if you had a doctor whose prescribing was clearly stupid, something could be done about it. You must remember this was well before the General Medical Council had a welcome change of attitude about what they now call 'non bona fide prescribing'. We had no grand vision of a massive treatment organization or anything like that.

BJA: *Who were the people who influenced the second Brain Committee in wanting to develop a new treatment system?*

BS: Thomas Bewley and Phil Connell gave evidence and I suspect the then Consultant Adviser to the CMO, who I think was Dr. A. B. Monro, had his say. A lot of this no doubt went on behind the scenes but certainly I wasn't privy to any of those discussions. The only meeting that I was privy to was later on about the implementation of the recommendations. There was a meeting at the Home Office with Ministry of Health colleagues who explained how they proposed to implement the Brain recommendations. When they said that there would be no heroin prescribing—it would be only methadone, I don't know who was first, Jeff or me, but more or less with one voice we said "In which case, gentlemen, this conversation is entirely academic. You won't have any addicts coming to clinics". They went away and had a rethink. I believe it was after this that one of their doctors went to see John Owens at All Saints Hospital, Birmingham, where his approach seemed to be containing the heroin outbreak there. I think it was Jeff who suggested such a visit might be of value. So I suppose we could be said to have had a little say.

BJA: *You are recorded several years later in Arnold Trebach's book[4] as saying that you would have liked general practitioners to be more involved, but having a limited number of patients.*

BS: Yes. because I can think of one or two doctors (general practitioners) who have done very good work with addicts, having one or two patients with whom they've been able to establish good relationships. It's all very well for psychiatrists now to assume responsibility and to make all the running—they were conspicuous by their absence in the sixties. Most of the people who are prominent now weren't on the heroin scene then, with the exception of Tom Bewley and Jim Willis and one or two others. You had Peter Chapple making the running, but Peter fell foul of the bureaucracy and I suspect the medical establishment who aren't too keen on doctors having a high media profile. He had a number of ideas and he got into a bit of trouble for trying to set up a prototype centre before the 'official' treatment centres came into existence, at St. John's at Battersea, just up from Clapham Junction station. It was mainly Peter's enthusiasm which led to us having a small group which used to meet, usually at Tooting Bec. This was before treatment centres were set up, before Brain reported in fact. There was Tom Bewley, Jim Willis, Geoffrey Gray, Peter Chapple—I can't think of all the others—and we just used to meet about once a month and talk about what was happening because there were the few people who were involved. The general practitioners who were involved then have been badly treated by the press, both lay and medical and as a consequence by those whose knowledge of the pre-Brain II period is limited to press reports, and those professionals who themselves chose not to get involved but were nevertheless free with their criticism. I think of dear old Doctor Hawes in Fitzroy Square—he used to say "I'm not here to treat addicts. I can offer emergency treatment, first aid, and I can arrange for them to go into hospital" and he would take them on for a fortnight, make arrangements for them to go to one of the Epsom mental hospitals, where they would probably kick up a stink and get booted out, back to Doctor Hawes and he was left holding the baby. Psychiatrists didn't want them because they were unruly in the wards and that was it and, of course, as the Brain Report shows, drug addiction was not a mental disorder within the meaning of the Mental Health Act. Therefore, any doctor who showed the slightest sympathy quickly became inundated and that led to control problems and mistakes, and naturally criticisms could then be levelled at them. You could criticize the medical profession in those days for its apathy, rather than the six doctors who were much maligned in the Brain Report. That was a travesty--to talk about 'the naughty six'. At the end of the evidence given by Lady Frankau, Lord Brain looked down at the table over his glasses to where we were sitting and said "Well, gentlemen, I think your problem can be summed up in two words—Lady Frankau". And that was basically it.

[The second report of the Brain Committee was published in 1965.]

Brain didn't provide a very detailed blueprint. I have felt always that the period between publication and implementation of the recommendations was when we really lost it. Because you had a hiatus: nobody knew what was happening; more doctors were getting involved like John Petro who, after he was stopped from prescribing opiates, made the bridge, as Ken Leech has pointed out, between the amphetamine users, causing the methedrine problem which you had at that time. Unfortunately for the planners, before the first treatment centre was ready to take patients, Lady Frankau was taken ill and she eventually died. When she was ill, Dr Petro suddenly appeared. Now the only connection I know of was that he had a brother who practiced in South Kensington and occasionally he (the brother) would write a weekend prescription when Lady Frankau was away at her country address. But John was not in practice with his brother, so I understood. Whether it's folklore or not, the story I heard was that he meet up in the West End with a couple of Lady Frankau's Canadians and that was where the contact was established. When she went sick, he came around offering to help out and then he built up his own addiction practice. It was in that period too in 1966 in September, when you got evidence of Chinese heroin for the first time. I'm not saying that it wouldn't have come, but I can remember talking to an addict outside Boots and he said "The Chinese got stuff; they smoke it; can't be heroin, can it?"! As I've always understood it, the bridge was established then between some of our addicts and the Chinese in some of the gambling clubs in Wardour Street.

BJA: *The Home Office had kept records on known addicts from the mid-thirties, mainly from inspection of pharmacists' registers. In 1968 it is formalized under the Dangerous Drugs Act. What was the purpose of notification?*

BS: We've got to put the blame if critics of the present system wish to allocate blame, and responsibility with the Brain Committee. The Brain Committee proposed notification as a means of epidemiological assessment and to help control. I think you've got to remember you were going to give responsibility for dealing with addicts to a section of the medical profession which had not been involved before. They were not going to be tainted or in any way run the risk of being criticized as 'the naughty six' had been, so they wanted a system which would protect them. As far as I recall we in the Home Office certainly didn't propose it because, quite frankly, the system that we had operating at that time was perfectly adequate. You'll never know the total addict population and I don't think that anybody ever pretends the 'addict statistics' figures mean that. To give you an idea of what was happening, we used before 1968 to have informal notification from the GPs who prescribed. Coming back to my periodic visits to Boots, I'd come back with a name, I'd ring up the doctor and with no problem at all, I'd get the information I needed. Often doctors would ring up, Lady Frankau in particular, "I've got so-and-so, three more for you". We also had the prisons covered through Home Office arrangements, so there was no need from our point of view to have notifications. What you've got to remember, in those days the black market was entirely diversion from legitimate prescriptions plus the odd theft from pharmacists, etc.

BJA: *Why did the notification system end up in the Home Office? Why not the Department of Health?*

BS: It was linked with the prescribing side of the control which was with the Home Office, and had been since the 1920's, and I think you would have had to move the whole lot over because the police were doing, and still do, the retail pharmacy end of it, so you'd have to change all that. I don't know that it was really seriously considered at that time.

BJA: *From that time notification must have become quite a major part of the work of the Home Office Drugs Branch.*

BS: In the early days, yes, because notification came in before we had the staff to deal with it. I remember Les Ackroyd, Ted Waters and I used to spend hours and hours helping process notifications before we had the staff and it all became a great big bureaucratic exercise and I am inclined to think it is now.

BJA: *There's often confusion about the uses to which the notification system is put. Who has or had access to it?*

BS: If you go back, first of all, to when the proposal was going through Parliament, it was made clear that the police had a responsibility for inspecting pharmacy records and it was accepted, with some misgivings and reluctance, that the information could be passed to the police to enable them to carry out that task. Now people would say "Once the police have got it, you've got no guarantee that they won't use it for other purposes". Frankly, I honestly haven't had too many worries on that score because, let's face it, the notification information, the name and address which is what most critics object to, is already on the prescription and therefore in the pharmacy records to which the police have access. But we decided some years ago that, as the problem changed away from prescriptions to an illicit market, there was no point in passing names to the police because they weren't going to see them in pharmacy registers. So we haven't passed details to them for some time. Police officers ringing up would *not* get information from the Index now. I know there has recently been a comment that people have been able to get information. I suppose, technically, if you say that you should only give it to a doctor, and the doctor's secretary or a clinic nurse rings up and gets it, that is a breach; I think it's a technical breach, but if you have been in day-to-day touch with the clinic staff anyway, I wouldn't regard it as a serious breach. I know the Index staff are scrupulous in observing confidentiality and certainly many are the letters I have written to lawyers who write saying "I am acting for Mr. So-and-so or Mrs. So-and-so, who is suing for divorce from his wife/her husband who, we understand, is a registered addict". I reply "There is no registration of drug addicts in the United Kingdom. I'm sorry we can't help you" and we wouldn't give information. I accept entirely the fear that addicts have that information could be used for other purposes. I would argue that, in the present circumstances, with a largely illicit scene, the name of the addict is not important. We could get the epidemiological information which is really its main purpose now, by other means, for instance by initials, half a postcode, date of birth, which would meet the confidentiality aspect. Notification no longer really fulfills the purpose which the Brain Committee envisaged.

BJA: *A lot of people think that you can become a 'registered addict'.*

BS: That will always guarantee a reaction from me. We all know what people mean by 'registered'; it suggests that addicts have a formal status and therefore they have an entitlement to a regular supply of drugs—they haven't at all. We keep trying to explain that, under the law, addicts are patients and they are entitled to such treatment as the doctor is prepared to give them, and the Home Office has no power to tell a doctor to prescribe or tell him not to.

BJA: *The Home Office Drugs Branch has had a benign involvement with researchers, writers, doctors and many others. How did that happen, because the tendency in the Home Office has often been to remain distance from the public?*

BS: I think we've always worked on the principle that, if we expect people to help us, and people in the categories you mention, can help in many ways, we've got to help them. You don't get information without giving a little bit in return. Similarly with addicts, because a man is doing something which we might disapprove of, there's no reason why we don't talk to him. It would probably be different if I was a police officer, where he might be doing something illegal that I would have to do something about, but I was not in that position; I was not there to make judgements, but he can help me and perhaps I can help him, not maybe directly, but knowing what his problems are, eventually maybe I can pass that onto somebody and ultimately have some benefit, and I've always worked that way. Anybody who is in this business is someone I'm prepared to talk to, and our lads have worked on the same principle. Without wishing to be bigheaded, that is why the Inspectorate has always been reasonably in touch with what is going on. After I became more office-bound, I could always rely on our Inspectors to keep me in touch and they have often surprised me with their range of contacts and analyses of the scene. I've also always worked on the principle that you don't necessarily have to have authority over somebody before you can talk to them. I can ask a doctor any question. He doesn't have to answer me; although there are some questions he has to answer; it is only if I try to pretend to him that he has to answer questions which he doesn't have to answer that I'm exceeding my powers.

If I use the word 'lucky'—it's perhaps a strange word to use about such a serious problem—but I have been very lucky in having had for 34 years, a job which has never made me think "God, I've got to get up and go to the office". I have had the unique opportunity of seeing British drug problem developing. It wasn't there when I joined: it's there now, so you can draw your own conclusions from that! It's been a fascinating opportunity. In the same way, the Inspectorate did a lot of things in the sixties that are now being done by a lot of other people. There was nobody else to do them. The DHSS has now got a commitment which it didn't have, the Police have got a commitment which they didn't have. We, the Inspectorate, ran the first conference for drugs squad officers back in the sixties and these were the pioneer officers who were the poor relations in most of their police forces. They were fighting against the tide. Drugs were not seen as a police problem by some senior officers until major criminals became involved. These pioneer drug squad officers looked to us for encouragement and support and we relied very heavily on them to tell us what was happening. In that sense, we've been very much in the centre of things. We were unique in that we were the only people who were seeing what was happening. Again that sounds a bit conceited, but we had information from the police, we had information from Customs, and we had our contacts with the doctors; we had our contacts with the street agencies and people like Ken Leech and APA [Association for the Prevention of Addiction] which, I think, was the first street agency dealing with addicts. We had our finger on what was happening and we could tell people. We were there, we had the information. It wasn't in our job description then to monitor the drug scene, but I'm glad to say the valuable role the Inspectorate can play, if that doesn't sound arrogant, is now recognized.

BJA: The Home Office hosts a regular meeting of consultants which many people look on as an inner group which is able to impose certain professional practices. Is that how it's worked?

BS: It may well have worked that way in the sense that the London consultants have been a clique and obviously have adopted certain policies which have had an effect well beyond London. It came into existence very largely simply for geographical convenience. If you go back to the sixties, when the clinics came in first, the DHSS used to host a meeting of treatment centre consultants; they came from all round the country with DHSS officials and a couple of Home Office officials. They stopped after a while. I think it was felt there wasn't an awful lot of point—after all to some people Brain II had solved the heroin problem. Then the London consultants started their own informal meetings; they would take it in turns to host them. They very kindly allowed me to go along and have my twopenny-worth, and then occasionally we would hold a meeting at the Home Office; it was convenient because it was central and we were able to offer parking facilities. Now, perhaps, it's unfortunate that it has been seen to be run by the Home Office, but DHSS are also involved—going back even before Dorothy Black's time and indeed, Ted Hillier for a while took the Minutes (one of the DHSS officials). From our point of view, we gained, because instead of going round and seeing 12 consultants, we had 12 in one place and we could hear their views. It's a very economical way of getting information. We've made it perfectly clear it is *their* meeting; they run it and we are there by invitation.

BJA: *What about relationships with Ministers?*

BS: Without making a party political point, I have to say that this is the first Government that has responded to 'the drug problem'. We should have had more political and therefore Ministerial involvement many years ago, but there wasn't. This is the first positive response. Once it took off politically, the momentum just carried on. I think the main thing was the realization that there was something that needed doing. I think it was probably the Wirral in Liverpool that really triggered it off because that's where the heroin problem first hit the headlines, and people like Joan Keogh made sure it did. There was a lot of concern there. Then there was that debate in the Lords in which Lord Ennals (I think it was) quoted a *Guardian* leader which had said that people would start taking this seriously when the sharp elbows of the articulate middle-class are felt in Ministerial ribs, or something like that. I think public concern began to express itself and it was a response to that. That's how the thing works.

BJA: *And are they on the right lines?*

BS: Let me answer it in this way. The first thing that had to be done was to create the machinery that we should have had 20 years ago. We're talking about the police—the enforcement community getting their act together which they now have. As I've said, it wasn't very long ago that senior police officers were saying "Drugs are a social problem—nothing to do with us". Not very long ago. I can remember officers coming back from Operation Julie—I can remember one who, when he got back to his police force, was told "Oh, you've come back; now you can do some real police work". That attitude's not long ago. Treatment facilities are still inadequate. Education—well, that really has only just got going in the last few years, hasn't it? Before, there was very little being done. Where is the real original thinking being done? I know you're now going to ask me about the Advisory Council on the Misuse of Drugs.

BJA: *Go on.*

BS: To me, the Advisory Council has been a disappointment. If you look at what the Act says—to advise Ministers on such matters as the Ministers refer to it, or to bring to Ministers' attention such matters as the Council feels should be brought to notice. It seems to me that the Advisory Council have fallen into a defensive passive role rather too easily and instead of being the body that brings matters to attention, they are quite happy to be fed things. Certainly this was very much the case in its early days. I'm not denigrating what they've done as there have been some good reports, but it doesn't seem to me that they fulfill the function that they might. The high expectations which, for example, drug squad officers had, have not been fulfilled—these officers used to tell us of problems for us to advise the Council that something could be done. If I can be *very* cynical—it has been said that the main purpose of the Advisory Council was to provide a repository for difficult issues, a sort of 'pending' 'too difficult' tray. That is a device beloved by Whitehall which of course provides the secretariat.

With the benefit of hindsight, I think the Advisory Council might well benefit from being serviced independently and not by Home Office or DHSS officials, whose efficiency and competence I am not criticizing. But it's not in a bureaucratic nature to rock the boat. You need an awkward Secretary; you can think of Secretaries of national bodies who really are thorns in the sides of government departments. I think that's what the Advisory Council should be. But in fact, it isn't. It is there largely to respond to what is put before it. I think it would benefit from being smaller and do more work by co-opting instead of having everybody in Christendom with a representative on it—a smaller body could be more dynamic. I also now think it wrong that the Chairman has always been a doctor and, moreover, a member of the medical establishment. It perpetuates the still widely held but erroneous belief that drug abuse is primarily a medical problem. It doesn't mean that an establishment man is necessarily the wrong person but you could use somebody who's outside. The difficulty is in finding the people for it. As I said, I think it's been a disappointment; the Council should chivvy Ministers, and you want a few more awkward members to ask penetrating questions. Oh, it's easy for me; probably I wouldn't say this if I was there because some of these would fall to me to answer.

BJA: *Your views on treatments policies have been quite at variance with the practice which has developed in recent years. You wrote a letter to* The Lancet[5] *recently, supporting a more flexible approach to prescribing.*

BS: I was brought up on Rolleston. Few people in the country have ever read Rolleston from cover to cover. There's a lot of wisdom in it although it was before its time and it dealt with a different problem. They weren't the fools people made them out to be. They were a fairly wise old bunch and they did provide safeguards. It seems to me that there will be addicts, and I've met enough in the last 30-odd years, who are not causing anybody any problems, and only cause problems when you interfere with their way of life. Now we may make a judgement on whether they should follow that way of life, but it seems to me that if they are under the care of a doctor and they're not causing any trouble to him or anybody else or the rest of society, why the hell should we upset them? The idea that we can offer a take-it-or-leave-it treatment ignores the fact that there are now alternatives, and I must confess I get a little irritated by those doctors who are quite unconcerned about the effect their actions may have on the overall drug scene. How often, for example, do you hear of doctors who tell difficult patients that they had better go back to the black market until they are prepared to accept the doctor's conditions for treatment, or while they are waiting to be taken on for treatment? The point I try to make in that letter is that nobody is saying 'You must have heroin indefinitely'. Brain didn't say that; Rolleston didn't say that. All we're saying is some people aren't ready or able to come off when a doctor says they should. Let us hold them until such times as you can motivate them. Use all your medical, nursing, social skills to motivate them to come off.

The medical profession had a lot of stick in the sixties and I think they have gone from one extreme to the other. They had so much stick that they are not going to put their heads above the parapet to be shot at again. I'm not saying that the kids in Bermondsey or the Wirral or Possil in Glasgow should be given a prescription. Rolleston was talking about the losers, and people who could be shown to be capable of leading fairly normal lives whilst still taking drugs. There is a medical practice not too far from here, where I sat in on a clinic not long ago; I met several addicts there (some of them I'd known before) who were working and stable, and still taking drugs. This is not a green light for prescribing. It is an amber light for prescribing in certain circumstances. We've gone from no traffic lights in the days of Lady Frankau, to a red light since the end of the 1970's when the clinics said 'Stop'. Another thing I'm probably arguing for is flexibility. Let us have a number of approaches; that's as far as I go. It's not going to work for cocaine; nobody's advocating giving cocaine. That is a different sort of problem. For opiates, you have physical dependence to contend with more than you have with cocaine, and prescribing is merely one of a number of options. I think my concern is that we have just thrown everything out. We've just gone down one road. You once used the word 'psychiatrize'—that's a good word—I say the psychiatrists hijacked it, which is much the same thing. All we're saying is "Right, your [the psychiatrists'] option is one,

Interview with Bing Spear 247

but there are a number of others; please consider them and please, please, general practitioners come back in".

BJA: *Who or what has been the biggest influence on your way of thinking?*

BS: When I came in first, *I* saw things in black and white terms. I think I was influenced as we all were, by the prevailing orthodoxy from America. I can remember reading some of Harry Anslinger's comments about 'that terrible stuff, Indian hemp', and all the terrible things that that did to people. When you realize what has been handed down over the years isn't quite black and white or even accurate, you begin to question a lot of other things. I would now like to think that I see things in more realistic terms,what is and what is not achievable and I hope I can keep things in perspective. If you talk about realistic terms, I think this comes down to the question of the future. There was a conference in Vienna recently. The reports I've seen in the press highlight one of the problems. They were talking there about international co-operation for hammering the trafficker, which is a nice political objective. Fine. But, according to the reports I've seen, the Latin-American countries are apparently dragging their feet. Now, that says an awful lot about the likelihood of getting international agreement about stamping out the drug menace, about fighting drug wars. That's the reality of it.

This comes back to several of the things that we've been talking about. Where is the new thinking about the drug problem? We are getting, *ad nauseum,* the old business of locking up the trafficker which, as we've seen, is guaranteed to get the party faithful jumping. I think I've got to preface what I say, because anybody who questions current thinking and policies is immediately branded as 'soft on drugs'. I am not soft on drugs, I am not liberal or permissive. In fact, on many things I would probably be to the right of Ghengis Khan, so let's get that in perspective. But let us be realistic about it. Drugs have been around a long time; they will always be around. We are fighting to stamp it out, 'we're going to lock up the trafficker'—fine.

'We've got to reduce the availability; we've got to deal with the criminal'. But has anybody really looked at the relative roles of the customer and the trafficker? The trafficker is being branded as the villain of the piece but isn't the man who's got the demand for drugs as much a villain? Would traffickers continue to operate if there was little demand? That's the end you've got to tackle. What did Al Capone do when prohibition was repealed?

The sooner we cast off the shackles of American thinking, the better; this country and Europe should start to have a new approach to the drug problem.

I would end up by saying that I think it's about time we started putting some of the best brains in this country to thinking about a response to the drug problem rather than merely respond to public concern about the problem.

We are relying too heavily on the forces of law and order to solve this problem for us. They are doing a very good job, but they are only part of the solution. We've got to get at the demand. Is it entirely coincidence that you've got drug problems in some of the inner cities? With some of the problems that they've got? You don't have to be a Militant to think that. A couple of years before I left, Don McIntosh and I drove on to one of those estates in Glasgow. We looked at each other and we said, "God, if we lived here, we'd turn on".

References

1. Interdepartmental Committee on Drug Addiction (1961) *Report* (London, HMSO).
2. Departmental Committee on Morphine and Heroin Addiction (1926) *Report* (London, HMSO).
3. Interdepartmental Committee on Drug Addiction (1965) *Report* (London, HMSO).
4. Trebach, A. (1982) *The Heroin Solution* (London, Yale University Press).
5. Spear, H. B. (1987) Management of drug addicts, Letter, *Lancet,* p. 1322.

16

Interview with Benno Pollak

BENNO POLLAK, *b. 1912, Czechoslovakia. Failed to complete medical qualification in Berlin and then Prague because of world events. Went to France in 1938 and subsequently served in Czech and British armies before qualifying in Medicine at Leeds in 1949 (MRCS, LRCP). Retired from general practice in 1989. Previously also Clinical Tutor, in Department of General Practice, St. Thomas's Hospital, London, and Clinical Assistant (now Emeritus), Maudsley Hospital, and tutor on AEC's Summer Schools.*

BJA: *For the last 30 years you have worked as a family doctor in South London. Can you tell me something about the locality?*

BP: It has about a 50:50 ethnic division between the black and white population. The area is now 'going up' and Yuppies are moving in who can't afford living on the other side of the river.

BJA: *When did you first get interested in drinking problems?*

BP: My wife and I took over this practice in 1958, and later, in about 1964 the Addiction Research Unit were carrying out a GP survey and they wanted to know how many alcoholics general practitioners thought they had on their practice lists. I was visited by a charming lady called Celia Hensman and she asked me questions. I reviewed the 5,000 patients who were by that time on my list, and I was frightfully embarrassed because I could only think of three of four who had drinking problems. Shortly afterwards we decided that the practice would have a coding system for about 80 different pathologies; I included drinking problems on this list. That was in the mid-sixties and from then on, I developed a list of diagnostic clues for drinking problems. Within 10 years or so, I moved from only knowing of three of four heavy drinkers to having identified 200 cases in a practice population totalling about 9,300.

BJA: *What did you do for those patients when you had detected the problem?*

BP: I thought I should treat then within the practice context, although it was a do-it-yourself scheme. My theoretical knowledge about alcohol was small. General practitioners have to be do-it-yourself agents because everything in their working life changes roughly every 5 years so they are always having to learn different attitudes and techniques. For instance, 30 years ago psychiatric matters were rarely aired; one would have felt much too embarassed to discuss intimate matters with patients, one would have expected the patients to be startled if asked "How's your psychological life?" or "How's your sexual life?" Eventually, one got used to these perspectives and here the greatest influence on general practice was a psychiatrist called Michael Balint from the Tavistock. He was a psycho-analyst who took a special interest in general practitioners. He organized groups of six to eight GP's who would bring their cases to him for discussion. He wrote a book about this approach which made a tremendous impression on me—*The Doctor, His Patient and The Illness.*[1] I learnt that one could, in fact, ask patients the most delicate questions provided one did not talk in an embarassed fashion. Patients were only too willing to give one floods of personal information. Another thing which came out of Balint's teaching was that the doctor could be used 'as a drug' in the sense that the treatment can be the doctor. That means we have to be caring and able to relate. We must be able to cope with the undifferentiated and undefined in medicine.

BJA: *What for you was the personal reward in working with patients who had drinking problems?*

BP: You see I have this phlegmatic temperament, so often I was just hanging on to patients, not judging the situations, and people came back, they began to listen to me and we talked with each other. That was the way—holding on and hammering away in a gentle manner. And that showed results—sometimes dramatic results. So, my personal reward was I felt that at times one was really helping patients whose lives were in danger. But who can say, as a doctor, that one really saves lives?

BJA: How many minutes would you be able to give to a patient? We are always told that general practice is so cramped for time that 3 minutes to 6 minutes is quite a long consultation.

BP: That is quite true, and it is a dilemma of general practice. I realized it would take time, so I saw these patients when necessary, for longer, outside surgery (coffee) hours. Once I became intrigued by alcohol problems, I thought these patients were just as deserving as any others with difficult illnesses. After all, looking after chronic and relapsing conditions is all part of a GP's daily life, so why should alcoholics be treated any differently?

BJA: Did you use any formal screening methods?

BP: Yes, I used screening methods. When we started our coding system we decided that we would look for people who had certain clues or key indicators. These were: physical, psychological, social or based on information from the family. For instance, there was a large number of family members who once they knew that the practice showed some interest in the subject, came forward to tell me about drinking problems in their family. The disadvantage of using relatives is that you often can't get further because the wife or the mother tells you immediately that under no circumstances must it be disclosed that they have spoken to you about the problem. I designed a questionnaire for people whom I thought had drinking clues and identified a profile. I operated various schemes over the years. If it was a new patient, I suggested that he or she should come for a special 'check-up'. Patients adore having 'check-ups'. At first, I brought up the question of their family life, social life, food habits, hobbies, and introduced the issue of drinking within this context. With hindsight, this was probably unnecessary camouflage. Nowadays I think, patients are quite willing to answer straightforward questions on drinking without wrapping it up.

BJA: *Did you ever have patients who told you to get lost and it was none of your business?*

BP: No. Interestingly, that never happened. Recently, I have been screening 200 patients who were consecutive consultations in my surgery. These 5-minute consultations, which are quite different to those longer screening interviews that I mentioned before, offer about a minute or two during which I am able to ask some questions on drinking. And I can't say that any of these 200 patients were offended by this questionnaire. Some asked me why I was asking them and I said it was a research study and was on a topic in which I was interested. I don't think that these patients were in any way put out by these enquiries.

BJA: *What sorts of problems were you as a general practitioner picking up? Were you picking up gross pathologies or was it a matter of people drinking a little bit too much?*

BP: When I started in the field, I was mesmerized by people who had very characteristic and extreme problems of drinking, so I concentrated on those types of presentation. Later, when I became more sophisticated in dealing with drinking problems, I was able to pick up a patient who was not necessarily dependent on alcohol but who had alcohol-related disabilities and drank too much, or who presented with illnesses which gave a hint of drinking. For instance, I carried out a study of gastrectomized patients in our practice. There were 50 of these patients on my list. I was originally interested in looking for biochemical changes and the haemotological and vitamin problems that may arise. Interviewing these people, I found that 17 of these 50 had, in fact, contracted their ulcers whilst drinking too much and it was amongst these 17 (a third of the group) that most of the continuing troubles from the gastrectomy were rampant. Nobody had told them to change their drinking habits and adjust the drinking to a new situation. They went backwards and forwards to the hospital.

The surgeons even undertook further surgery in order to improve their results, but all to no avail because no-one had woken up to the significance of the drinking.

BJA: At some points you get involved with what is known as Rathcoole House in Clapham, part of the Alcoholism Recovery Project. Can you tell us about that venture?

BP: Rathcoole House was the first hostel in the U.K. solely for Skid Row or vagrant alcoholics and it was funded initially by the Carnegie Trust. A committee was formed which included Stella, the Dowager Marchioness of Reading, Lord Stonham who was a Minister at the Home Office, together with various other people of goodwill. I was invited to join this group as a medical adviser. I was keen to gain from the experience. In May 1966 Rathcoole was opened and it was staffed by an extraordinary team—the warden was Tim Cook, a barrister who had moved to being a probation officer before taking on this wardenship. Dr Gethin Morgan also helped us—he was then a psychiatric registrar, but is now Professor of Psychiatry in Bristol. We experimented with what to do for vagrant alcoholics and didn't, at the beginning, have much real idea how they and we would cope. We had an excellent way of entertaining the first group of residents by having supper with them twice a week and asking such people as Lord Soper and Lord Longford along to meet them. They had individual sessions with the psychiatrist and with the GP. We published the first results in 1968.[2] In the first year we had about 38 people passing through the hostel; only a third of them lasted 6 months or longer. We found that we were over-treating them by offering them sleeping drugs, by giving them intensive psychiatric support and so on. We needed a simpler approach. We went through various crisis situations—at the first Christmas my wife and I decided to bring a Christmas cake to the 10 residents, only to find that the whole group had flown the nest. One of them had received a large sum from his family for Christmas and he took all his friends down to drink at Waterloo Station. The poor warden had to take out the van and collect them, whilst we shyly had to take our cake back. Life went up and down. Gradually, we changed our techniques, our approaches, we introduced AA into the meeting and we tried to make the hostel residents more responsible for themselves. Long discussions were held over whether residents should have house keys, and the role that residents should play in admission of new members. These were helpful and interesting new changes supporting the scheme. I published in 1970[3] medical results on 3 years at Rathcoole, dealing with the physical states of 83 residents. The fascinating thing was that the majority of them enjoyed good physical health—apart from broken ribs in 22% and old TB in probably 10%, but nothing much which was directly related to the drinking problems. There were possibly two or three who had liver disease. I believe that they never drank long enough to get cirrhosis. Our Skid Row drinkers would be floating between Waterloo Station and the parks for about 3 weeks and then land themselves in prison for 1 or 2 months—there was this rotating door. Eventually they had, by the age of 40 years, possibly 50–60 convictions for drunkenness. It was those enforced periods of sobriety which protected their health.

BJA: You then got involved with Dr. D. L. Davies and with his initiative in setting up a Summer School and the Alcohol Education Centre.

BP: Well, I met Davies at the Maudsley Hospital and often lunched with him and other doctors. He had reached some fame by his study and 'return to normal drinking'. He was an interesting man in various ways. He was a general psychiatrist, a Dean here, a man of enormous learning, intelligence and culture who took an interest in drink problems and put the Maudsley's interests in this subject on the map. But he was only interested in middle- and upper-class alcoholics. He told me frankly that he was not happy with Skid Row alcoholics; he thought that he could not relate to them. His first Summer School in Brighton opened in 1970. I was a student there for the first year, but after that I became a tutor to the School until the '80s. I was also on the Alcohol Education Centre, as an executive member.

BJA: What were those Summer Schools like?

BP: I thought they were the most exciting and dynamic venture which could have happened in the development of studies on alcoholism. It was an excellent idea to mix people from different professional lives into six or eight multidisciplinary groups. There were roughly 100 people attending each year and they came from many different backgrounds. There were doctors, probation officers, nurses, hostel staff, psychologists and so on. In the morning, lectures were given by experts covering a wide range of topics. Then we separated into groups to discuss both the lecture and relevant subjects. Some members of each group had prepared, beforehand, extracts from important papers of the world literature so in this way one collected an enormous amount of information. I thought it was a tragedy that the Summer Schools ceased to operate. The demise of the Alcohol Education Centre was, of course, also a terrible loss.

BJA: *You then had another development in your professional involvements: you became a doctor who worked on a sessional basis in the Maudsley's Alcoholism Treatment Service. What are the difficulties and the possibilities when a GP comes and works on drinking problems with a hospital-based team?*

BP: I started at the Maudsley about 1972 and I was, of course, marching into a new world—a world of academia, of hospital practice and team work. I suddenly found myself confronted with the fact that I could spend an hour, or an hour-and-a-half, with a patient. I was also expected to join in weekly seminars where I was exposed to multidisciplinary thinking, and input from the Addiction Research Unit. All this whilst at the same time doing practical clinical work. At the beginning I was curious how patients would take to me or how I would take to this situation. Possibly I had the advantage that one is forced as a family doctor to establish a relationship with a patient very quickly. That stood me in good stead. I had a way of talking to patients which came easily to me and probably had advantages over young registrars in that I was older. In some ways, I was probably more skilled in speaking to people and getting them to explore their social life, quite apart from the psychological and medical problems with which they presented. I felt ambitious that my patients should get just as good treatment from me as a non-psychiatrist, as they got from my psychiatrist colleagues with whom I shared the clinic work. I could then transplant some of what I learnt into my own practice work. I possibly became a better doctor through these fairly sophisticated and ambitious conditions under which one operates at the Maudsley.

BJA: *Was it difficult working in these two different modes—sitting in a hospital outpatient room with an hour-and-a-half for your patient, then going back to your South London practice where you were seeing people in a consultation lasting perhaps just 5 minutes?*

BP: Yes, initially, it was, but later on it did not seem difficult. I enjoyed being away from my practice and looking at practice problems from the outside. One can get a burnt-out feeling in either situation. By mixing the two experiences, one counteracted the other.

BJA: *But you were also, of course, mixing two different types of colleagues together. Did you, with a kindly outsider's view looking at hospital colleagues, think that they were in some ways too distanced from real life?*

BP: Well, I felt there was a mutual curiosity but, yes, I agree, I sometimes thought they had little knowledge of life 'for real' and general practice in particular. But I got on very well with all of the registrars whom I met and who are now Old Boys of the Maudsley Hospital, like Terry Spratley. I worked a lot with him and I gave some advice on his research—the Maudsley Alcoholism Pilot Project.[4] He and his colleagues were funded by DHSS to make proposals on how alcohol problems, could be managed in the community and I took part in interviewing general practitioners in the Camberwell area. I was very interested to read that Betsy Thom in 1986[5] visited a similar group of GP's in this area and, 10 years later found that the problems which were apparent in 1975 were exactly the same. I also worked with Robin Murray, the present Dean of the Institute, when he was a registrar and later he sent his research assistants to sit in with me on my hospital consultations to learn something about drinking problems.

BJA: *How much have you been engaged in professional teaching? What are the problems of teaching in this area?*

BP: I have been teaching mostly in two areas. I was involved early in the academic development of teaching in general practice at St Thomas's Hospital, and our practice has been a teaching practice to St Thomas's and takes students on a continuous basis. They come to us for 4- to 6-week placements. I have always liked teaching and now, of course, I am interested that medical students are beginning to ask me "How is it that when we come to you we hear all about drinking and you have so many drinkers; whereas the students who go to other teaching practices hardly hear anything about alcoholism?" The other area was that as I became more knowledgeable about alcohol, I tried to transmit my interest to the Royal College of General Practitioners. I gave lectures on this topic all over England. And, of course, the Summer School teaching which we have already spoken about.

BJA: Have you generally found medical students receptive or resistant to teaching on drinking problems?

BP: I find medical students are very interested in this topic and in being taught to look out for the clues. This was quite the opposite to my experience with doctors. With qualified doctors discussions and lectures can be very tough going at times. Meetings, unless a free dinner is thrown in, can be poorly attended. It is most important to include alcoholism in *all* undergraduate curricula.

BJA: You have referred to the fascination of alcohol problems in medical practice. What is this fascination?

BP: One is dealing with *undifferentiated* medicine where symptoms are presented in an absolutely enormous variety of disguises. The diagnosis is often hidden away, yet alcohol can affect every system of the body. Then, by dealing with patients with chronic illness, one probably develops a special intensity in the caring relationship and that applies to drinkers just as much as to people who suffer from, for instance, chronic bronchitis, or TB. One learns that one has to sell oneself as a therapist. The quality of care depends very much on the therapist. It's important for the therapist to analyse what he or she says; how he should talk to this man or this woman; how can he produce empathy; what should be avoided? This sort of searching and looking at people as a whole—psychologically and biologically—that is the fascination if one is curious about life and the meaning of life. What interested me for example, about Skid Row alcoholics is that one is unable to relate their way of life with anything one has personally experienced. How they managed to let life go by yet they have survived. And then, how they can change so dramatically for the better under the influence of very simple procedures such as changing their social milieu in a hostel or breaking their social isolation?

BJA: *You've travelled quite a bit and have, for instance, visited centres in the U.S.A. I wonder what you made of that.*

BP: That was in 1971. My wife had a research fellowship to the States to study child development, and I asked for study leave myself to see their alcohol treatment centres. We travelled quite widely. I went from San Diego right over to Rutgers, where we had lunch with Mark Keller and Selden Bacon. It was a very new world. The Americans have a major drinking problem which they attacked in a typically dynamic and systematic fashion. In every state you came to you found there was a Coordinator who was a Government official and who could direct you to all the alcoholism treatment centres. I was with Milton Gross in New York and I visited Downstate Hospital, where he and Benjamin Kissin had a very interesting unit. Later, as you know, he contributed to developing the distinction between alcohol-related problems and the dependence syndrome.

BJA: *Was the exchange of ideas at all two-way?*

BP: Not always! In general, Americans are bursting to talk about their own work rather than question their visitors. This applied especially to the experts on alcohol. I also visited university departments of General Practice. Here America was far behind British developments; and very few universities had an academic department of general practice and they were interested in what was going on in British teaching centres.

BJA: *You've also been in Israel.*

BP: Yes, in 1985. I visited come centres in Jerusalem and Tel Aviv. They were just then beginning to admit that they had drinking problems. The government was reluctant to fund alcoholism treatment services and the work had to be on a shoestring. Their approaches are probably, however, similar to the kind of package which you would see in most other Western countries. I visited one centre outside Tel Aviv and what struck me there was that the justified claim that Jews have a strongly family sense was being used therapeutically. The treatment was based on making the family a dynamic part of the therapeutic process. For instance, no man was allowed to come into these ATUs unless the wife gave her agreement that she would spend weekends there and take part in group therapy. She would sign a contract that she would stay with her husband for a year or two whilst he was under treatment. Their research studies were not at that time very well developed, and workers in this field are perhaps handicapped by lack of professional recognition.

BJA: Is the level of drinking problems in your view changing in Israel?

BP: The people I talked to convinced me that the problem is rising. Autopsies are rarely performed but are compulsory in road accidents. Few post-mortem findings are therefore available so it was interesting to note a significantly high alcohol content in subjects who had died in car accidents. The amount of wine imbibed on the sabbath could not make anybody drunk. It's also very poor quality because it's kosher wine. Studies clearly show that if Jews become less orthodox, they can drink just as heavily as anybody else.

BJA: Do you find that moving around the country, talking to other GP's, your contacts with the Royal College of General Practitioners, do you ever hear that what is really happening is that your colleagues bow nicely and say "What a splendid thing you've taken this interest in drinking problems"—and this while what they are really thinking is, "What an odd-ball you are Dr. Pollak, taking this strange minority interest with these unsatisfactory people; congratulations, but not for us". And nothing changes. What's your view?

BP: Well, you hit the nail on the head! This is in fact a feeling I am often having. My medical friends are very complimentary about the work I am doing; so are my partners, but quite honestly, they think I am slightly mad to waste my time on a subject which is hopeless, doesn't bring any rewards and doesn't change anything practical in life. That's the sort of feeling one has to live with, that one is an outsider and in the minority. Now, if you carry on for long enough you gradually get used to these reactions. It is something that irritates one from time to time, but there it is. To work in this field one has to have a special philosophy of life and a certain type of temperament.

BJA: *What kind of temperament?*

BP: Phlegmatic and not looking for quick results. You have to think "Well, it may look hopeless, but I am not going to think about that". Like Scarlett O'Hara says in *Gone with the Wind*, "I will think about this tomorrow". I probably learnt this from my political experience, when I was exposed to living for a long time of my life under the shadow of Hitler and thinking "Well, I can't really do anything; I just have to stay alive. I must not look for a dramatic solution". Afterwards, in the Army, I did not end up as a major-general. . . .

BJA: *When did you leave Hitler's Germany?*

BP: Well, I left Germany in 1933; but I retreated to Prague where my family originally came from. I had to start my medical studies there all over again. Then I was in the last student year when Hitler marched into Czechoslovakia and Jews were not allowed to continue their final year studies. So I spent 12 years in the wilderness, seven of which were in the British Army. I volunteered for the Second Front, but ended up in the Himalayas, near Mount Everest. This had the advantage that I never heard a shot fired! At the age of 33 years, I returned to my medical training; I was forced to repeat my second M.B. which meant that I had to learn anatomy and physiology all over again followed by another clinical course. But I enjoyed being in a British medical school because I had far superior teaching than you can get in central Europe. If you qualify in Vienna or Prague you have no practical idea about anything, whilst the sort of practical way of learning in English medical schools was a great asset.

BJA: *It's interesting that you speak of your temperament, of this patience, this dealing with adversity, this not being overwhelmed with too high expectations. Do you remember reading a Journal Interview[6] with Max Glatt? Did you feel any echoes with Max, who also left Germany and went on to take a major and distinguished interest in drinking problems?*

BP: Yes, well I asked Max Glatt why he went into alcoholism—he could have gone into any part of medicine really, general or psychiatry. He said it possibly had something to do with being a refugee, when, as a young doctor, he had to fight for his existence, that he must have developed a sympathy for the underdog. He could understand the underdog probably better than somebody who had a smooth upbringing and none of the political explosions to which he was exposed. Well, I didn't quite think that applied to me.

BJA: *If you were giving advice today to a young man or young woman entering medicine and beginning to take an interest in drinking problems, what would be your advice to them? How should they equip themselves for this interest?*

BP: First of all, it must be part of every medical student's curriculum; part of the medicine they will practice because no matter in which branch they work they will come across alcohol-related problems. Then, society has so many prejudices and fixed ideas, especially about alcoholics, they will need to free themselves of these. The importance of good history taking cannot be exaggerated and the ability to ask people straightforward questions will have to be learned. The doctor has to see the patient in a holistic way against that individual's social background because each patient may require a slightly different approach. Analysing a drinking problem with a patient is therapeutic in itself, so the young doctor needs to understand how to involve a patient in his own treatment. Probably the most important advice one can give is to suggest there's nothing like knowing a lot to increase one's effectiveness! How to be knowledgeable about alcohol and it's abuse; how to inspire confidence without being over optimistic; and how to deal with physical and psychological dependence.

Those are the skills which that young doctor has to demonstrate if he is to have a sophisticated toolbox at his fingertips.

BJA: *Do you believe that all, or the majority, of drinking problems could be dealt with in general practice? What residual place, if any, is left for the hospital or do you think that the hospital's role has been vastly overplayed?*

BP: Yes, I believe the hospital role has been overplayed. The crucial issue remains—whose alcohol consumption are we trying to reduce? There are in the population 1–2 million people whose hazardous alcohol consumption may slide into serious alcohol disorders. They are never seen in specialized units, nor could hospitals ever be expected to cope with these numbers. But, of course, at present there is this dreadful tendency amongst all generalists to think they cannot do anything—or they don't want to do anything—and wash their hands of these patients by sending them to hospital or ATUs or even AA. So long as this attitude prevails, nothing will change. Should, however, a more favourable climate gain ground, community care is a more realistic proposition for preventive and therapeutic management of most patients. But there will always be the need of specialist hospitals for complicated and difficult cases and research.

BJA: *Supposing someone came along to see you tomorrow and you find that his or her liver is marginally enlarged and the biochemistry just a little abnormal, how would you as a GP proceed?*

BP: Well, the GP has the great advantage now that he or she can investigate the situation physically with great finesse. I wish I had enjoyed that 20 years ago. Nowadays I can write a form out and send the patient for a liver or brain scan directly. I can send the patient to the laboratory for important investigations. I can get in touch (with permission) with the family and I will then have a much clearer idea how to define what the problem is. The other advantage I have is that the patient is stuck with me, because I am his doctor and his family's doctor, and he will have to come back to see me again about something which may or may not be unrelated to his drinking problem. Something has, however, been left from that initial discussion of ours—because once the patient and I have talked about the harm of his drinking he will have analysed his situation and even if he does not realize it he is less sure of his behaviour.

BJA: *Are you someone who will go for a confrontation?*

BP: I go for a 'softly-softly' approach and I don't think it pays at all to frighten a patient. I think if you scare your patient you are losing the battle either immediately or later. One knows from experience that a dramatic confrontation may in fact be the worst thing one can do. I would try a gradual build up. For example: "you know there is this liver showing . . . we don't really know if they mean anything definite, but there may be a . . .". Then I can say "I think if you just leave off drinking for a week and we repeat these tests again and we then will discuss what would be the right thing to do". In this sort of gradual way—a philosophical gradualism—you may get very much further than with a confrontation. I have played confrontation and I have lost, and I think it's a bad habit.

BJA: *Have you ever tried confrontation with your colleagues, who won't take a blind bit of notice or do you go softly-softly with them too?*

BP: I am coming back to the same song. You never know how much you may influence your colleagues, so I like to talk about my experience and convey what I've learnt rather than lecture. Creep forward, in a subtle way, to influence people. I think that's the best method.

BJA: *Have you any worries about the growing official emphasis on the primary health care response to drinking problems?*

BP: I want to bring up questions like: Is there any risk that we are getting mesmerized with the general practice dimensions? Many recent British reports have been emphasizing this perspective, and the whole field has shifted towards primary care. Once the implications of these recommendations have all been followed, what are we really going to do then? Nobody has ever got beyond theoretical points and developed any convincing practical ideas that will work. For instance, who runs the primary health care team? How will it relate to the hospital? How indeed will it relate to the community? These are the major questions which have to be thought through. However, the puzzle of how you make the community dimension work is still a favourite hobby-horse of mine. It is, of course, something that exists already for instance in midwifery. The professor of midwifery at St. Thomas's comes to our ante-natal clinics and conducts part of the clinic with the doctor who is running it. The advantage that has for the functioning of the clinic and the quality of the services is unbelieveable. The GP learns a lot from the specialist; the patient has an immediate familiarity with this obstetrician when she goes into hospital and perhaps the specialist even learns something from the community. I think this is the kind of model we should think about in the field of alcohol.

BJA: *Can you just tell me something else. You've talked about all these aspects of alcohol, but we haven't talked at all about drugs. Can they be separated? Are you seeing the same issues involved in your practice?*

BP: I'm afraid I neglect drug addicts. I am so involved with alcoholics. I do treat a certain amount of people with drug problems, but I feel they are different. It's a different age group. . . . I think it has different psychological and physical associations and it's not necessarily easy for the same doctor to develop the same skills in this area. I do not think that I am personally equally successful with people who are drug addicts.

BJA: *You recently endowed the Benno Pollak Lecture at the Institute of Psychiatry. What was your purpose in doing that?*

BP: I think alcohol addiction is something of the cinderella of psychiatry and I wanted to boost it's low profile. I think alcohol is such an enormously wide but confusing field, there has been such an avalanche of research in every sector that it would be heartening to have lectures which would give some cohesion and this problem has to be led academically. Looking back at the first lecture[7] we have been very lucky. I, too, felt well rewarded by reading Sir George Godber's remarks "That the first Benno

Pollak lecture was the best, short, dispassionate appraisal of the use of alcohol" and . . . "The most significant contribution to the literature of health promotion this decade".[8]

References

1. Balint, M. (1964) *The Doctor, his Patient and The Illness* (London, Pitman Medical).
2. Cook, T., Morgan, H. G. & Pollack, B. (1968) The Rathcoole experienced: first year at a hostel for vagrant alcoholics, *British Medical Journal*, 1, pp. 240–242.
3. Pollak, B. (1970) The role of the general practitioners in support of an alcoholic rehabilitation hostel, *British Journal of Addiction*, 65, pp. 19–24.
4. Cartwright, A. K. J., Shaw, S. J. & Spratley, T. A. (1975) *Designing a Comprehensive Community Response to Problems of Alcohol Abuse*, Report to the Department of Health & Social Security (London, Mauldsley Alcohol Pilot Project).
5. Thom, B. & Tellez, C. (1986) A difficult business: detecting and managing alcohol problems in general practice, *British Journal of Addiction*, 81, pp. 405–418.
6. Journal Interview (1983) Conversation with Max Glatt—Journal Interview 4, *British Journal of Addiction*, 78, pp. 231–243.
7. Kendell, R. E. (1987) Drinking sensibly, *British Journal of Addiction*, 82 pp. 1279–1288.
8. Godber, G. (1987) The most significant contribution to the literature of health promotion this decade, *British Journal of Addiction*, 82, pp. 1292–1293.

17

Interview with Philip Connell

PHILIP CONNELL, b. 1921. Medical training St. Bartholomew's Hospital and psychiatric training at Maudsley: MD, FRCP, FRCPsych, DPM. From 1963–86. Consultant Psychiatrist at Bethlem Royal Hospital and Maudsley Hospital in charge of Drug Dependence Clinical Research and Treatment Unit. Chairman of Advisory Council on the Misuse of Drugs 1982–86, and service to numerous Government departments and voluntary organisations in UK. Work for WHO, Council of Europe, and ICAA. In 1986 awarded CBE.

BJA: In what year did you qualify in medicine?

PC: In 1950, at the age of 30. In 1953 I joined the Maudsley, and in 1956 gained the Academic Diploma in Psychological Medicine (Academic DPM), the academic specialist qualification in psychiatry of those days. I wrote a dissertation for the DPM on amphetamine addiction, and carried out work on amphetamine psychosis as the thesis for the MD London University. At the time I took the MD one had to complete a clinical examination and later present a thesis. I had met a number of cases of amphetamine addiction where there was no psychosis, so I took those out separately and analysed them for the DPM. This work was never published but is available as an Academic DPM Dissertation in the libraries of the Institute of Psychiatry and the University of London.

BJA: What led you into an interest in amphetamines?

PC: I came to the Maudsley (the Post Graduate Medical School in Psychiatry of the University of London) without a Membership (MRCP) or other higher qualification (such as MD., PhD., MSc., etc.). Students at the Maudsley were not appointed as senior registrars (senior residents) just on the basis of the Academic DPM. Although the Academic DPM would have secured appointment as a consultant in psychiatry anywhere else, one could not achieve a continued education or experience at the Maudsley at a more senior level without a higher qualifications. At that time there were very few undergraduate academic departments in teaching hospitals. So when I joined the Maudsley in July 1953, I knew that I had to obtain an MD or other higher qualification if I wanted to keep in the higher realms of academic and teaching practice. I started thinking of a subject for a thesis, having obtained part 1 of the MD (London University). I spent quite a lot of time looking at the realms of occupation therapy until I gave that topic up as being far too imprecise and with few aspects which could be measured and form the basis of a thesis. It was then that D. L. Davies, indirectly, put an idea in my way. One of the first cases I saw when I was on his unit was a patient who was rushing around the fields after having sniffed and ingested methedrine inhalers. This man had a florid psychosis. So I decided this was interesting and I talked around in the coffee room like we always did and where we learnt an awful lot. I then managed to collect a few more cases, which had similar but not identical features. I thought, well, I can collect cases in a time-honoured way, but it would be awfully nice if I had some objective measure to know when these patients were taking the drug and when they weren't. So I looked through the literature and found an approach suitable. I then took the idea (which I wrote up as a project) to Aubrey Lewis.

BJA: And his advice was what?

PC: His advice was that he thought that all drug psychoses would show a toxic confusional state, and that one wouldn't find anything specific about amphetamines: perhaps one ought to concentrate on examining for organic brain damage by the use of psychological tests. Such as the Block Design Rotation Test. So I went away and thought about his advice and decided that I'd persevere with my research.

BJA: When you saw Davies's patient was it generally known around the Maudsley that amphetamines could produce a psychosis?

PC: Oh no, it wasn't known at all. These patients were likely to be diagnosed as schizophrenics.

BJA: So when this one man raced around the fields in a psychotic state after taking amphetamine inhalers, what was the common explanation at that time?

PC: The common psychiatric explanation was that such a patient had an acute schizophrenic illness. In the Observation Wards where I located quite a number of other cases, they were all called schizophrenics and were sent to mental hospitals: I went round the mental hospitals and picked them up. Famous psychiatrists such as Erwin Stengel were all diagnosing schizophrenia. However, Eliot Slater, when he reviewed the monograph, made it clear that he thought that these patients must have had toxic confusional states. The role of amphetamine, if indeed it was even considered, was thought to be possibly one of lighting up a pre-existing schizophrenic psychosis.

BJA: How many cases did you collect altogether?

PC: I think it was 42.

BJA: Was it difficult to find them?

PC: It wasn't easy. One had to go by contact with colleagues in other hospitals. They began to know that I was interested in this possible association and would sometimes get in touch with me.

BJA: When you completed that monograph, it must have been quite a heady moment for a young man?

PC: I was very excited because everything seemed to work out. The biochemistry eventually worked out after I had tried one method over some months which was not reproducible. The new techniques of paper partition chromatography were being developed, so we had another way of determining the presence of drugs, such as amphetamines, though it remained necessary to determine that the 'amphetamine spot' was not due to interfering substances. One could observe all sorts of grades of psychotic experience from the development of paranoid ideas without florid psychosis through to a very florid psychosis. And furthermore there seemed to be a dose relationship. A lot of these subjects were dunking amphetamine inhalers in coffee: I had one patient who was taking two inhalers in that way, and not becoming psychotic, but when he took three or more he had a psychotic illness. The main thing to remember about this condition is that it doesn't have to be a florid psychosis: the patient does not have to be climbing on the roof of buildings and throwing tiles at imaginary gangs below. The disturbance can be much more like a chronic schizophrenic illness and much less florid. Certainly most of these cases were diagnosed as schizophrenics although there was some doubt being expressed after, say, the third admission and when patients seemed to recover each time rather quickly from their illness. I didn't know anybody else at that time who was interested in this issue. Some years later, I met a Scandinavian professor who was collecting cases with a view to writing them up but he acknowledged that I got in first, and this professor had not contemplated using biochemical methods. The thing that thrilled me most of all was the ability to bring pure science into the art and practice of medicine by the use of objective laboratory methods [1]. I could say look, this person is not on amphetamines, and if he's got a psychosis when he's not on amphetamines, we'll have to think again.

BJA: Were you aware that there had been an earlier report on cocaine psychosis, and that cocaine psychosis closely mimicked what you were describing as amphetamine psychosis?

PC: I was not fully aware at the time. Whilst I did read cocaine references and remember a few case reports and was interested in the symptomatology which included haptic hallucinations, I do not recall coming across any series of cases or specific studies which would have formed the basis of worthwhile comparisons with the much more extensive material I was collecting.

BJA: Your book was published as a Maudsley Monograph [2]. What exactly is the status and intention of that series?

PC: It is a series of monographs published now by Oxford University Press on behalf of the Institute of Psychiatry, dealing with topics which otherwise would probably not have been thought likely to be likely to achieve commercial publication. It was, I think, a great honour at the early stage in my career to have a book published in that way. You don't get any royalties, it's just honour and glory.

BJA: How was the book received? Did people recognize its importance?

PC: The reviews were all very favourable. Some criticisms were made—one was that there was no index, which was simply due to the fact that the administration felt it would increase the cost of production. But the book didn't I think achieve more than reviews in professional journals; it didn't create a stir within the profession as a whole. When subsequently I spoke around the world on amphetamine psychosis and addiction, and tried to alert people to the dangers, the message fell on stony ground. People didn't listen. It was some 5 or more years after publication (nine years after I had started the study), that the profession as a whole became worried about amphetamines in the early 1960s with the purple heart problem. In fact I was asked in 1966 to give a lecture to the American Medical Association as a person who knew about amphetamines. And people in the academic units there whom I visited, said no, we don't have a problem even though there was an American Congressional Committee looking into the problem of amphetamines at that time, nearly 10 years after the monograph.

BJA: People sometimes talk of the special intellectual atmosphere of the Maudsley at that time. Do you see that as exaggerated?

PC: No, I think I owe a great deal to the Maudsley—the journal clubs, the discipline of attendance at meetings, everything was much tighter than today. You weren't in a situation where you could have much time off to think. You followed all the arrangements, you turned up at Monday conferences, you turned up at journal clubs. Journal clubs were very helpful, and a good discipline too. To be asked to talk on a subject about which you knew nothing, preparing it for two weeks by looking through the literature, was extremely demanding. To hear at conferences and seminars experts from many other fields, this was intensely rewarding. When we got together and talked, we weren't talking about girlfriends, we were talking about the work we were doing. I did a Journal club on phenylketonuria, galactosaemia, and the Fanconi Syndrome which was mainly based on Bickel's work in which the new paper chromatographic technique was central. It would be wrong to say that I was encouraged to do research at the Maudsley. It would be more correct to say that the setup was such that if you had an interest you could pursue it. I went to Professor MacIlwain and Dick Rodnight and got permission to work in their labs. They were very happy for me to do so, and they would help me if I wanted help, but they wouldn't take any part in the directing or the supervising of the work. The stage was obviously very wide open to allowing people to follow their interests. These days I think it would be much more difficult to get laboratory facilities and use of expensive equipment without any really major administrative application.

BJA: You worked on D. L. Davies's firm. He was of course an historical figure in alcohol studies. What was going on in alcoholism treatment on Davies's firm?

PC: There wasn't a separate alcoholism unit as far as I remember, he just had a few alcoholics in his general beds. He was busy exploring the use of antabuse. Davies was a great man for encouraging people to think and he was very knowledgeable. He didn't suffer fools and he certainly didn't suffer slackers. He hadn't quite accepted the full implications of the multidisciplinary approach. He was still the consultant with registrars who talked as doctor to doctor, and who occasionally had a social worker in on the discussion. Of course there were nothing like so many registrars in those days as now and one felt very privileged to be at the Maudsley. I had gone to Will Sargent to get his advice because I worked for Raymond Daley (the son of Sir Alan Daley chairman of the Board of Governors of the Maudsley) at St. Stephens

Hospital doing a house job and I said I was interested in psychiatry. He said, see Will Sargent. Sargent said for God's sake don't go to the Maudsley, because he and the Maudsley were not getting on at that time. We chatted about psychiatry and the importance of knowing the physical aspects and he said what type of psychiatry do you think you might eventually want to enter. And I said I was very interested in children. Oh, in that case you must go to the Maudsley, he said.

BJA: You've spoken about your two strands of professional interests—drugs, and child and adolescent psychiatry. Did they at all come together?

PC: Yes. Perhaps before I answer that question I ought to say that I've always been determined to do a little adult psychiatry at the same time. But going back to your question, I think the relationship between these two strands of activity has been very important. A high proportion of the sort of addicts one meets within the hospital framework are pretty immature, impulsive, hedonistic people. Such patients often seem to have the kind of behavioural pattern of an adolescent who hasn't resolved his adolescent problems. Certainly in teaching I've always tried to point out the similarities between working in the child psychiatry field and working with young drug addicts. I worked with Peter Scott when I was at the Maudsley and was his senior registrar, and, my adult work has continued, usually just one day a week in the health service and later in private practice. More recently I've done an increasing amount of court work. In the Family Division and the custody of children, but also on the psychological aspects of accidents.

BJA: What brought you back to the Maudsley in 1963?

PC: I always hoped that I might get back to the Maudsley because I thought that this was an atmosphere in which I could thrive and to which I might be able to contribute. I came back to a child and adolescent psychiatry post. I ran the boys' adolescent unit and I had young children's beds in the children's department. I was also the director of the Brixton Child Guidance clinic. Later I had the honour of being the first chairman of the child and adolescent

Psychiatry Section of the *newly* constituted Royal College of Psychiatrists and some time later a Vice President.

BJA: *Then slowly drugs, the second stream of your professional life, got under way again?*

PC: That was rather serendipitous. After I had been back at the Maudsley about 6 months, I thought to myself, I really am not keen on dragging adolescents out of school and their fathers from work, for me to investigate and treat their psychological problems during the day-time. If they were fit to be at school why should I take them away, and if the fathers were going to lose money by coming up to the hospital, why should one add to the tensions within the family by causing loss of wages? So I opened evening clinics for adolescents. That was about 1964. And of course this was at about the beginning of the purple heart (Drinamyl, an amphetamine—barbiturate mixture) scene [3]. Young kids were coming up to Soho and staying there the whole weekend, and taking purple hearts to keep them awake. Parents were getting worried and some of these young people were sent to my adolescent clinic. People were looking for someone who knew both about adolescents and amphetamines. So that's how my drug interests were brought back into the fore. To cut a long story short, my evening clinic became almost entirely drug problems and then not just amphetamines, but other drugs including heroin, methaqualone, barbiturates, methedrine, etc. Then it seemed a good idea after the publication of the second Brain committee report [4] that the Maudsley should make a contribution to meeting this problem and consider providing clinical and academic facilities.

BJA: *So in 1968 you opened the Drug Dependence Clinical Research and Treatment unit at the Bethlem?*

PC: Yes the reason for that name, which is long and complex, was that it described the function of the unit [5]. Having accepted this description it gave a basis for research staffing, etc. to be funnelled to the unit and under my direction, rather than things having to go through the Institute of Psychiatry, which I later learned to my cost was interested in furthering its own research and service interests rather than trying to make a contribution to a very complex and unrewarding field. I set up the unit to provide clinical services and to promote research and teaching into all aspects which were practicable.

BJA: *And then soon afterwards you began to move beyond being a clinician towards heavy involvement in committees and policy. Did you always feel that was one of your destinies?*

PC: It's another strand of my personality, I suppose. Ever since I went into medicine I have been interested in organisation. As the Chairman of the Junior Common Room I was the first person at St. Stephens Hospital in 1951 ever to be invited to attend the beginning of medical committee meetings to discuss matters of interest to the junior common room. As a student at the Maudsley, I was elected chairman of the Junior Common Room and, an unheard of possibility, I brought about a monthly meeting between the Chairman and Secretary of the Junior Common Room and the Professor of Psychiatry, the Dean, and the House Governor, to discuss issues of concern. When I returned to the Maudsley as a Consultant in 1963 I soon found myself in administrative and committee areas since I was appointed Secretary to the Medical Committee in 1964 and then Vice Chairman and Chairman. I was also asked to take over from Brian Ackner the Chairmanship of the Project Planning Group which was planning to build a new hospital. I found myself tremendously interested in the hospital and the Institute as a whole and I enjoyed that very much, so I suppose this was the origin of my interest in chairmanships. I like to feel that people who have something to say are allowed to say it, without fear or favour and not bullied. Within that sort of framework and with a good chairman you get the maximum benefit out of what is available. I also learnt a lot about medical politics which was of great help to me. But as far as the international work is concerned, this has arisen entirely because I was interested in travelling around and talking about amphetamine psychosis and what was happening Great Britain, the purple heart scene and so on. So I travelled the world, and the next thing was that I was asked to sit on WHO committees and be rapporteur and do this that and the other. It was a natural development which was not planned.

276 Addictions

BJA: *You gave evidence to the second Brain committee [4]. Do you remember the actual occasion?*

PC: Oh yes, you just came in and answered questions and talked for about twenty minutes or so. There was no written evidence from me. The next person after me was Lady Frankau who was prescribing large amounts of heroin and cocaine (pure British made and not black market) to addicts.

BJA: *And you were a member of the Wayne committee which preceeded the current Advisory Council on Misuse of Drugs?*

PC: Yes. It was an extremely hardworking group of people trying to face this new and awful fact of drug addiction in young people. There were working groups which presented reports on rehabilitation, LSD, amphetamines, barbiturates and so on. Aubrey Lewis did the review on cannabis. The number of known heroin addicts was about 1300.

BJA: *You were a member of the Wootton committee [6], the Wayne committee's group on cannabis. How do you remember Barbara Wootton?*

PC: Oh with great admiration. You can tell how distinguished a person she was by the fact that the report is known as the Wootton Report. Very few committees adopt the name of the chairman unless that person is very exceptional. She was an impeccable chairman; she never dictated any of her own views. One knew that she had certain views, but she never pushed them. She was supportive, stimulating, sometimes a bit irascible, and she did a very good job. It was a great shame that the Wootton report was so vandalised in the House of Commons debates. The now Lord Hailsham, I think it was, as reported in Hansard, critisised the report seemingly as though he had not read it, and accused it of wanting to legalise cannabis. Well, the Wootton report made it quite clear that it did not wish cannabis to be legalised at that time. The debate in the House of Lords was much more balanced and helpful.

BJA: *How is a report of that sort actually written? Is it put together by the civil servants?*

Interview with Philip Connell 277

PC: Yes, the secretary of the committee is the civil servant who writes the report, but he draws upon members of the committee for help in drafting. So a report's success depends to quite a large extent upon the willingness of members of the committee to help in the drafting. It would be invidious to draw attention to reports which weren't very good, but this consideration may sometimes be the key. I have helped a lot in the drafting of some reports but primarily it is the responsibility of the civil servants and Committee agrees the report: after discussion and modification.

BJA: *Let's turn next to the Advisory Council on Misuse of Drugs. You became Chairman of that group in 1982 and held that post through to 1988.*

PC: The ACMD is a statutory body set up under the Misuse of Drugs Act 1971. It has the responsibility to advise ministers on any matters relating to drug misuse. Ministers have to consult it on any matter relating to the control or decontrol of drugs already under the act. So it has a tremendously wide remit, and that's its strength. How I got on to it is a different matter. I was Advisor twice to the Department of Health and Social Security on drug addiction. So I was moving in those circles and I was co-opted onto the Treatment and Rehabilitation group of the Advisory Council. The ACMD up to that time had been rather a low-profile body with reports not yet published after 6 or 7 years of work. For some reason or other, they decided to co-opt me on to the last stages of the Treatment and Rehabilitation report [7], and I did a lot of work on it because it needed a lot of drafting and a lot of historical accuracy put into it. I also had some contact with the Home Office civil servants, because as a member of the Board of Management of the International Council on Alcohol and Addictions I attended meetings of the United Nations Narcotics Commission. So they knew me quite well and of course I was also Chairman of ISDD (the Institute for Study of Drug Dependence). But when I was asked to take over the Chairmanship of ACMD I was extremely surprised because one believed, on historical precedence that they never appointed a Chairman that actually knew anything about the field clinically. All the previous Chairman of ACMD and the Wayne committee had expertise in other than clinical aspects and had not dealt with drug abusers in terms of their diagnosis, treatment or management.

BJA: *Do you remember your first meeting as Chairman?*

PC: I remember at the first meeting, I was terrified of all these people sitting round the room. I remember saying that my assessment of the ACMD was that is was time that it should pull its socks up, and start to respond not just to long-term problems, but to medium and short-term problems. Also I remember saying that I was very distressed to see leaks in the press about what was going on in the Council, and as far as I was concerned this was unacceptable: this was a confidential body, advising ministers. So I pitched myself in at the deep end, and it has been one of the most rewarding experiences of my life. I may be wrong, but I felt that from a body which was a lot of individuals saying a few things with no real corporate spirit, it developed into a group with a dynamic. So many people gave so much of their time to doing things which were for the public good. It's developed into what I would say is a going concern. I don't want to critisise previous chairman and politics comes into this. I know very well however, that when the ACMD was set up, it was expected to be a rather quiet body not causing too much trouble: historically the Wayne committee had done all the work and at that moment there wasn't a lot more to be done. When I took over the time seemed right for action.

BJA: *Is there a disadvantage in the Chairman of such a committee himself being too much of an old hand in the field?*

PC: I think that being chairman when you know quite a bit about the field is difficult. You are bound to have your own views. I thought right from the beginning that's the one thing I must not do, ever, was to indicate to Council or working groups what my own ideas were. The advantage of being somebody who knows a bit about the field is that if a debate is taking place you can spot the areas which are not being discussed so that you have the opportunity to say "now, what about so and so", we haven't talked about that, and if you know something about what is happening in the field you can also perhaps introduce the arguments to balance the debate. Actually, I think it makes it much harder work being chairman if you know something about the subject, but it is very rewarding that way. I also think that my international work has been helpful to the Departments, one has known what is going on in the world. I was also appointed Chairman of the Guidelines on Good Practice working committee of the DHSS and in fact prepared a first draft of the report [8]. This group had the disadvantage of changes of departmental secretarial staff and Dr. Dorothy Black did heroic work in bringing things together to meet the six months deadline within which the report was to be completed.

BJA: Does Britain have the organisational basis to make policy to deal with an evolving drug problem?

PC: That's a very difficult question. I don't know whether I can give you a mature answer. I'm still too recently involved in the organisations which we have here. My hunch is that it's a very good thing to have a body like the ACMD which is independent of government. But any advisory body must recognise that an advisory body's advice is not always followed and also that the advice may be wrong. I'll give you an example. The ACMD advised (after the problem with Diconal) that all opioid drugs should be put under the strictest prescribing control so that only specially licensed doctors could give these drugs to addicts in the treatment of addiction. The government, on the advice I presume of the DHSS, said, well we'll delay putting the whole lot under strict control, because the prediction that if you control only diconal GPs and others will then use some other drugs in the same way, may be wrong. In the event, they were right to sit on the fence. There are also instances where advice may be technically correct but not politically sound. I would hate the main source of advice to be from a government body which was following political lines. So to answer your question, I think the system of an independent body like the ACMD is good, but we are very very amateurish in the way we tackle the problems of providing services and guaranteeing the right kind of research. It's far too haphazard. I do think there is a need for some sort of central organisation which is also in some way independent of government and which can look more deeply at some of these problems. I don't know enough about the organisation of NIDA and the American structure but I think one should avoid mammoth organisations. On the other hand, I believe there is a need in this country for some sort of central organisation for research and to develop training. Something which can co-ordinate and plan for the total endeavour over a wide variety of professions. This is where we are amateurish. What we do in this country is say, look, we've got a first-class consultant, he must help but by the time that first-class consultant has had three requests, he's overloaded and has no more time to do anything else. And then when they can't get hold of a first-class person, they use somebody who really isn't first-rate and develop all sorts of ad hoc things. Occasional ad hoc development is one thing, but to have that as the main approach is another matter.

BJA: *The ACMD does have its own research staff?*

PC: It has no research staff, and it has no executive functions. Its operation is based upon working groups and support from the secretariat to get together the meetings and arrange for people to attend to give evidence. The Advisory Council is under-resourced. Take the secretary for instance. The secretary has to work very hard. And if the Advisory Council has got a lot of projects on, he's going to be away probably a fortnight in February at the United Nations' Narcotics Commission. He's going to be away at Pompidou Group meetings. He's going to be away at WHO and at discussions of the Council of Europe. It takes some time to learn about the drugs field, and they change these people around rather frequently. So we muddle along and I think this is not as satisfactory as it might be. The problem is well known in the Departments and to ministers, but ministers have of course to face demands for extra resources from so many areas. I have drawn this problem to the notice of Ministers from time to time in no uncertain terms.

BJA: *Let's talk about another organisation which you know well, the Society for the Study of Addiction. You were for a time its President.*

PC: Yes, after Francis Camps died, I was President of the SSA for 4 or 5 years. My presidency was a labour of love. I was determined to do what I could to keep the society going. At that stage it had no money. More psychiatrists and general practitioners and others were interested in the drug and alcohol field but fewer people were coming to the Society's meetings, and if you ask a well-known speaker to come and lecture and you've got only 20 people in the room, it's not long before Royal Colleges, etc., were including this field in their academic meetings. I helped reorganise the constitution so that the SSA became more democratic and I drew up a document comparing the roles of the ISDD, the SSA, and the Medical Council on Alcoholism.

BJA: *Were you in favour of merger?*

PC: I was not in favour of merger. I'm in favour of these organisations being in the same building. I think each has important things going on. The ISDD has to be a body which sticks to its remit of being a completely unbiased organisation with a library and information resource unit with a certain amount of research from its own research unit. This Institute with its computerised data base and its Thesaurus is sought after world wide. The Medical on Alcoholism is a body which has an ethos and a remit of a different kind and the SSA also has a different purpose. The Society for the Study of Addiction has, however, developed very much in the last few years, partly as a result of a generous bequest from a previous member, and the efforts of D. L. Davies and then of Malcolm Lader who has grasped the opportunity to raise the academic level of activities.

BJA: *If you hadn't been a doctor, what career would you have followed?*

PC: I don't know. I was a secretary before I went into medicine having had a difficult time with asthma during the war. During the war I helped a voluntary organisation in the field of parent-teacher associations and child welfare. I taught myself touch typing and I have never regretted this (my writing is abysmal). I wanted to go into medicine about a year before I actually started but knew this was impossible, but I inherited £3,000. I managed to be accepted at Bart's, even though I hadn't got Higher School

Certificate, and I started in 1945 when all the earnest and hardworking people came out of the armed services and joined medical schools.

BJA: How did you manage to avoid getting a Higher School Certificate, the "A" level examination of those days?

PC: The answer to that is very simply that I didn't have a good academic career at school, what with all my asthma and other problems. I left school in 1939 at 18 years of age. If I hadn't inherited money I would either have had to try and get an educational grant to enter medical school, or I would have gone on in some sort of secretarial business field. But it's interesting, that £3,000 took me through a six-year training. I was left with a small amount when I qualified. These days a medical training costs many, many thousands of pounds.

BJA: I'm going to ask you about giving heroin to drug addict patients. Specially to some of the BJA's American readers, it may come as a surprise to be reminded that the respectable doctor who is the subject of this interview has in the course of his career prescribed heroin to many addict patients. Today what do you feel about that approach?

PC: Well this approach is something that developed in this country historically [9]. With the Dangerous Drug Act 1965, the power of doctors to prescribe heroin to addicts was restricted (it used to be available to any qualified medical practitioner on the Medical Register), and only doctors with a licence could prescribe heroin. So within the hospital service, clinics which were set up took over from GPs those patients to whom heroin had been prescribed on the basis that these clinics were going to continue the treatment that the GPs had been giving, at least at the beginning of the clinical contact. And of course heroin had been prescribed by doctors to addicts over many years, and sometimes heroin and cocaine together. Huge quantities. One of my patients when first coming to the clinic at the Maudsley had been prescribed 25 grains of heroin (1500 mg) and 25 grains of cocaine a day. Which is a massive amount. Now the reason for the clinics going on with the prescribing was very simple. If you can keep these patients happy with the same regimen of the drug then you theoretically prevent the development of the black market—at that time there wasn't a black market except for diverted, home-produced (by pharmaceutical companies) pure therapeutic heroin. The other part of the rationale was that if you have these patients in your clinic and the law has said that you're the only person who can prescribe for them, and you force them into a method of treatment which is not to their liking, then this may not be very useful. After that, one can discuss the fact that having prescribed drugs which a person injects intravenously carries dangers, but you have to say then, well, what happens if you don't prescribe? Do you want them to be getting other drugs and still injecting intraveneously or would you rather they were keeping with you? At this stage we didn't know how these patients would behave, whether they would keep with the system or look for drugs elsewhere. We've learnt that the hard way. So not very many people now like to prescribe heroin.

BJA: *So one of the problems in your clinical experience was that if you give heroin to people in the hope that they will restrict their use to what you give them, they have a nasty habit of still buying other drugs on the side?*

PC: That's right, and as time went on it was quite clear that this was a likely outcome. There was a revulsion to giving heroin, and the methadone experts were promoting the idea of methadone as being safer.

BJA: *Did you have this revulsion, did you yourself dislike prescribing heroin?*

PC: I certainly disliked prescribing heroin. In fact I would go so far as to say that in my view there are probably only a very small proportion of very chaotic and disturbed addicts for whom it is justified to prescribe this drug, and I think the sad thing is that we still don't know which they are.

BJA: *In your experience can some people lead normal lives, while being prescribed high dosage heroin?*

PC: Yes, recognising of course, that what is a normal life means different things for different people. But when you see patients who are working and well dressed and they come to see you regularly on time, and there are no policemen after them and so on, they seem to be living a normal life.

BJA: *What dose were the patients you were talking about receiving?*

PC: The maximum dose was 25 grains of heroin. We started off prescribing the dose that the GP had prescribed to that patient and my registrar at the time said, look, this is ridiculous, 25 grains, he can't be taking 25 grains, what will happen if we give 25 grains, he'll die. I said what will happen if you give him five grains, he may go into acute withdrawal, what's the answer? So we talked it over and I knew what the answer was, of course, to have the patient in for a day, supervise the drug he's taking and make sure he takes it, and see what happens. If he wasn't taking 25 grains he would certainly have his bluff called. In the event, he took his 25 grains without batting an eyelid. We did, of course, have resuscitation measure available.

BJA: *So in 1969 there would have been some hundreds of addicts at London clinics receiving a steady supply of heroin for intravenous injection. Some people would see that as a recipe for chaos, albeit historically forgivable. Others would argue that we should in the era of HIV infection move in that kind of direction again. What did we learn from that earlier experiment?*

PC: Well we never did the crucial experiment which would have been to give heroin to half and give none to the rest, and force their withdrawal. We do know that now with all the black market heroin and cocaine coming into the country the time to attempt effective rationing through the clinics is over, out of our hands. So I think that today is a very different setting. Most people are anxious not to prescribe intravenous drugs, most people are anxious that patients who are receiving drugs in whatever form are not taking drugs from other sources. But the 60 million dollar question is whether the life of somebody who is not given any drugs at a clinic and who is therefore thrown back on to criminal resourses, is better or worse off than if they are given some drugs at a clinic. Here personal bias has come in and we've all got our biases. There are some doctors in this country who would regard themselves as "user friendly", which is a phrase which is coming into fashion. This can mean that if you give the addict everything he or she wants, he will live a better life and not be so much trouble to society. If I had my time again and there was a big heroin or cocaine black market around, I would take the same view as I did on amphetamines, which was, when there was so much amphetamine around, don't use the hospital to give drugs to the addicts. So today I would be less inclined to prescribe on a long-term basis than I was before. Having said that, you can't be rigid. One must recognise there are exceptions and do one's best to define who the exceptions are. And that's the crux of it. But if one does prescribe, it is important that it is under strict management surveillance.

BJA: Are you saying to people today "I was there, I saw it happen before and I think that heroin prescribing is not a good recipe, please do not forget that lesson," or are you saying "I was there, and I think the question is still open?"

PC: I was there, don't forget history. But I'm also saying times have changed, and it may be that with a different kind of control approach some experiments under very careful scrutiny might be justified in special cases to determine whether or not prescribing is sometimes a valuable approach.

BJA: Prescribing of intravenous heroin?

PC: Yes. But the last thing that I would recommend anybody should do is to say, right, all you have to do is give heroin, give all the drugs you want to an addict, and everything will be fine. That would indeed, in my view, be a recipe for catastrophe. But an important and vital new dimension has crept in. That is the problem of AIDS and HIV positivity. This will and has meant that there must be a new scrutiny of prescribing practices in relation to the prevention of AIDS. I am proud to think that as Chairman of ACMD I pioneered the setting up of the Working Groups which have studied this problem and whose reports receive great respect [10, 11]. It was a privilege to attend the groups and contribute to the meetings whilst not giving any personal views.

BJA: *Why do you think that the stability of the British drug problem broke down again in the late '70s, and why did notifications again show this rapid escalation? Was it as some American critics have suggested, because we abandoned heroin prescribing, and made the supplies so tight as to invite a new black market? Do you think that is a valid historical analysis? Again, you were an eye-witness.*

PC: I was there [12], but I don't think I knew enough about what was actually going on. You see, it's similar to the question of the amphetamines. Why did amphetamines spread so rapidly in the 1960s? That was a sociological phenomenon. There were various complicated reasons including the international attitude towards drugs and psychedelic experiences that built up a pressure within the community to experiment.

BJA: *What about the American-British connection?*

PC: Well I think this rich cousinly connection is a bit one-sided. The Americans are far more interested in us, than the generality of people in this field in Britain are interested in the Americans. We have this "British system" label which is a misnomer anyway. People like myself and those who are really wanting to think things out rather than just get on with the clinical work have always been interested in what the Americans do.

BJA: *It's always valuable in these interviews to catch up some views on contemporaries. When you first got involved in WHO, was Dale Cameron running the drugs program?*

PC: Yes, and I met him first at a London conference where I gave a paper on adolescent drug use, and I also met him when I gave a lecture at the American Medical Association in 1965, and I had seen him at St. Elizabeth's Hospital. Then he asked me to participate in an Expert Committee of the World Health Organisation and that was a very interesting experience because we were really getting down to the bedrock of trying to define what dependence was, or on another occasion trying to define the essentials of prevention. Cameron was an extremely able administrator and a very cautious one too. I remember the first meeting he had with all of us going on until one o'clock at night. Then I was asked to go to the next Expert Committee and I rang up Dale and said I don't know who you are going to have as rapporteur, but do you think it wise for me to bring my typewriter with me? And he said, well I don't know who we are going to have as rapporteur but bring your typewriter with you. In the event, I was the rapporteur and was in charge of putting it all together. Dale's perspective was very much American and a basic science perspective. Nathan Eddy was also a regular contributor at this time and he had his finger on the pulse of all the good laboratory research. Of course we had to recognise that the vast majority of research in this field emanated from America. If you were to look round now and say, let's find 20 people of high distinction in the pharmacology of heroin, you'd have a job to find them in Europe, wouldn't you? But since then, the move at WHO has been much more toward the developing world.

BJA: *Were you ever tempted to move more full time to international work?*

PC: When Dale Cameron retired, I was invited to set up a division of mental health at the World Health Organisation. It was very tempting, but there were several reasons why I didn't accept this challenge. The first reason was that they would not at the Joint Hospital (The Bethlem Royal Hospital and The Maudsley Hospital), say that when you've done your 5 years or so at WHO you can come back to run your unit. That was in great contrast to what would be done in America where they would think it an honour that somebody was going over to help WHO and would be happy to have him back. I would therefore have been throwing up my clinical teaching and clinical work for good, with no road back. Secondly, although it was a challenge, I didn't fancy spending interminable time travelling around the world with the red carpet put out and all those Expert Committees and so on. That was an aspect of life that I didn't feel was so much to my liking, forever. Thirdly, I did not fancy a position in which I could not speak my own mind and had to keep to a corporate view. Finally there were family reasons against it. But these are the sort of issues that you have to think about when going to WHO. You have a very important status and a good deal of power, but what happens later is the question.

BJA: Can you explain this. There you were, a man still in his 30s, and you had produced this amphetamine research and got a taste for clinical investigation. Why didn't you enter an academic psychiatric life?

PC: Well it didn't happen. I was informed by Aubrey Lewis that I would get a good job in a mental hospital. I was never offered an academic job and if I had been at that time, the pay was a good deal less and I was married with two children and older than most people at this stage of my career. I didn't want to work in a mental hospital and I also had a tremendous interest in child psychiatry. So I went up in 1957 to Newcastle upon Tyne to start up Child and Adolescent Psychiatry in that city [13]. So I've had two specialist fields of interest during all my consultant life, which is something that you probably couldn't do these days. So I went up to Newcastle to work with Martin Roth, and that was very rewarding. I was the First Consultant Child Psychiatrist in the Health Service up there and worked closely with Donald Court (now Sir Donald) and other paediatricians. They wanted you to know the answers, since factual knowledge in child psychiatry was limited at that time. In Newcastle building up a service, administration, and committee work were time-consuming. But all through my career I have been interested in research and have approached my work and teaching with academic aspects in mind.

BJA: When Christopher Wren was asked about his monument, he hinted that the answer was to look at St. Pauls Cathedral (si monumentum requeris, circumspice). You are rather young to start talking about a monument. But looking back on some years in this field, what mostly do you want people to see as Connell's mark?

PC: I've spent many years of my life being a facilitator. My role on the Expert Committees have helped I hope various groups and committees to come I think, to a more balanced consensus than if I hadn't been there. If I am sitting in on a meeting, if it goes off at a tangent, or the atmosphere starts getting rather aggressive, I feel that I have the ability to draw people together. I regard my work as often having been concerned with facilitating optimum developments. That's a very diffuse role. I suppose the only thing I shall be remembered for is Amphetamine Psychosis. Which I am told on one survey is the second most widely quoted work in the field of clinical pharmacology.

BJA: *What is the greatest sense of unfinished business?*

PC: My life has been very much like a leaf in a storm. Doors have opened and I've been blown in and done the job as best I could, and then people say come and do this next job. I've not been single-minded. Probably one of my weaknesses is that I like to be wanted and to help. To have been given the opportunities to do all these things is phenomenal, but one had to pay a price. If you are one of the few people perhaps of some academic status, available at a time of national and international need, then that will divert you from a single-minded plan. I would also say that the Drug Dependence Clinical Research and Treatment Unit was probably one of my most happy and successful productions: it took a lot of hard work getting the money and welding the staff together. I was also responsible for helping to get the whole of the drug clinic system started in London, having to go to meetings and persuade hospitals to set up outpatient clinics that no-one would contemplate unless they were given central money. But my main satisfaction is that I have tried to provoke young psychiatrists, both in this field and in child psychiatry, to think and have tried to indicate some lines of research which might be pursued. Many of the contributions, for instance, of the Drug Dependence Clinic Research and Treatment Unit derive from discussion in which I put up ideas which were followed up though my name does not appear on the list of authors.

Again, one has spent a lot of time trying to assist in research design and a lot of time assessing papers for possible inclusion in such journals as the *British Journal of Psychiatry,* the *British Journal of Addiction,* the *British Medical Journal,* the *Lancet,* etc. But also, I have been concerned to help junior doctors to achieve the kind of career they wished and were suited for. But one does not get feedback from such efforts so whether or not I succeeded remains to be seen.

Then, for the last 9 years I have, as a member of the General Medical Council, been very concerned as Preliminary Screener for Health in looking after (administratively) sick doctors most of whom have alcohol- and/or drug-related problems. With all these interests and the demands related to them I could not have been a Professor, though I have had a number of invitations to be so.

References

1. Connell, C. (1957) Amphetamine in the urine of mental hospital patients. *Biomedical Journal,* 65, pp. 1, 7.
2. Connell, P. H. (1958) *Amphetamine Psychosis.* Maudsley Monograph No. 5 (London: Oxford University Press).
3. Connell (1964) Amphetamine misuse: the present position with regard to misuse of amphetamine barbiturate mixtures. *British Journal of Addiction,* 60, pp. 9–27.
4. Interdepartmental Committee on Drug Addiction (1965) Second Report. (London: HMSO) (Second Brain Report).
5. Connell, P. H. (1968) The Drug Dependence Clinical Research and Treatment Unit: *Bethlem Maudsley Gazette,* 9, pp. 4–8.
6. Advisory Committee on Drug Dependence (1968) Cannabis. (London: HMSO) (Wootton Report).
7. Advisory Council on the Misuse of Drugs (1982) Treatment and Rehabilitation. London: HMSO.
8. Department of Health and Social Security (1984) Guidelines of Good Clinical Practice in the Treatment of Drug Misuse. London: DHSS.
9. Connell, P. H. (1969) Drug Dependence in Great Britain—a Challenge to the Practice of Medicine. pp 291–299 in H. Steinberg ed. Scientific Basis of Drug Dependence. London: Churchill.
10. Advisory Council on the Misuse of Drugs (1988) AIDS and Drug Misuse. P. 1 (London: HMSO).
11. Advisory Council on the Misuse of Drugs (1989) AIDS and Drug Misuse. P. 2 (London: HMSO).
12. Connell, P. H. (1986) "I need heroin". Thirty years' experience of drug dependence and of the medical challenges at local, national, international and political level. Dent Memorial Lecture. *British Journal of Addiction,* 81, pp. 461–472.
13. Connell, P. H. (1961) *Newcastle Medical Journal* 26, pp. 271–280.

18

Discussion. Two Separate Plays: The Evolution of Britain's Alcohol and Drug Policies

Griffith Edwards

The five subjects in this group of interviews have, in different ways, each made outstanding contributions. The debt owed to them for their labours in this field should be gratefully and warmly acknowledged. Under the heading which follows, the attempt will be made to scan these transcripts and see what ideas can be gleaned as to the actual substance of "personal influence"—a checklist of strategies and stratagems for advance and manufacture of change. The chapter will then go on to consider what these interviews reveal about the background play of British alcohol and drug policies over important decades.

What Makes Influence?

Several of these interviews speak to the significance of professional training as a vital ingredient in any mix of strategies which aim to bring about improvement in a country's responses to alcohol and drug problems. Long before the Americans invented the phrase "career teacher", David Davies was teaching on drinking problems and influencing young psychiatrists toward an interest in this topic. The roll-call of Davies's registrars (residents) who later made significant contributions in this area demonstrates that this one strategically placed teacher succeeded in training and inspiring a whole cadre of young professionals who were to be leaders in the addictions for the next generation. He was not only a clinical teacher but he was instrumental in pointing his registrars toward research opportunities. The multidisciplinary British Summer School which he initiated and ran with Marcus Grant was also very influential. The lesson would seem to be that if a country can get outstanding and committed teachers in place, and specially if it can be ensured that, as with Davies, one or two of these teachers wield the influence which comes from being Dean of a medical school, it will have put in place a strategy which is likely to have large, multiplicative, and long-term pay-offs.

To give this emphasis to Davies's impact as teacher is not to discount the contributions made under that heading by several other of the people interviewed. Philip Connell's and Max Glatt's contributions to hospital-based teaching deserve acknowledgement, as does Benno Pollak's influence on medical student teaching in a general practice setting.

Turning to another type of strategy which can be detected as a thread within these interviews, the Warlingham Park Alcoholism Treatment Unit provides a classic example of how the timely establishment of an innovative clinical centre can function as a beacon, giver of hope, and practical instrument of change. It should never be forgotten that a particular clinic or hospital which by its nature will only treat a limited number of patients, nonetheless may carry a message and influence entirely disproportionate to the immediate day's clinical work done. Those who beat a path to Max Glatt's Warlingham doorstep included not only Jellinek and Marty Mann, but, in a metaphorical sense, the British Medical Association, the Magistrates' Association, and in due time the Ministry of Health itself. Benno Pollak makes brief mention of Rathcoole House, and, as the first British hostel (half-way house) dealing specifically with the problems of the alcoholic offender, that voluntary initiative provides a further example of an action experiment as impetus for change. The consequences stemming from the setting up by Philip Connell of the Drug Dependence Unit at the Bethlem should also be noted under this heading.

If the influence of teachers and of pioneering treatment or rehabilitation centers are two of the major themes of influence to be drawn out from these interviews, there are certainly many other themes and variations latent in these stories. The influence

The Evolution of Britain's Alcohol and Drug Policies

of the particular scientific paper or monograph or the totality of a published output is an obvious vehicle of influence. The reports written for governments, contributions to WHO's debates, the committee steered in a productive direction, a lecture endowed, all provide further instances of how change is manufactured. Most fundamental, but present only between the lines, is, of course, that essential but ultimately mysterious instrument of change—the unique and personal influence of each person as person himself. Bing Spear, with his personal and humane interpretation of his role as civil servant, exemplifies exactly that kind of influence.

Policies and Movements

Let's now move on from this scanning of how the individual actors influenced the scenes through which they moved and turn our attention to the nature of the plays in which they were involved. At that level there appear over these years to have been two shows in town with rather minimal exchange of cast. One play dealt with the evolution of British drug policies, while the parallel production dealt with British alcohol policies. Max Glatt was probably the only one of the five people interviewed who put in a significant appearance in both theatres.

Turning firstly to drug policies, the interviews with Bing Spear and with Philip Connell will undoubtedly stand as key statements to which scholars interested in the relevant historical developments will have to return time and again. They are chronicles of our time, partly in the *genre* of the documentary film, but partly also *cinema verité*. Who would have expected that the soliloquy of the Chief Inspector of the Home Office Drugs Branch on driving through the streets of Glasgow would have been the words "God, if we lived here, we'd turn on"? Given that the Home Office has often been viewed as the government department representing the interests of "control" and which was outplayed by the benign "addict as sick person" perspective of the Rolleston committee in 1926, it is fascinating to find the following passage in Spear's interview—he is talking here about the setting up of the National Health Service drug clinics following the second Brain Report of 1965:

> There was a meeting at the Home Office with Ministry of Health colleagues who explained how they proposed to implement the Brain recommendations. When they said that there would be no heroin prescribing—it would be only methadone . . . more or less with one voice we said, "In which case, gentlemen, this conversation is entirely academic. You won't have any addicts coming to clinics." They went away and had a rethink.

Spear is perhaps referring in this passage to one of the more crucially significant Whitehall meetings in the history of British drug policies and certainly to one of the most neatly paradoxical instances of role reversal ever likely to be revealed by the workings of government.

The accounts of the last 30 or so years as given by Connell and Spear usefully supplement each other, but at times also reflect interestingly different viewpoints. Between them they throw light on the significance of committee reports and workings behind the scenes which bear on how the drug clinics came to be established. Of particular relevance to contemporary debate are the views of these witnesses on how the move away from heroin prescribing came about, the consequences of that development, and the possible future for more flexible prescribing.

Glatt, Davies, and Pollak can then be seen as throwing an equally strong light on the genesis of British alcohol policies. Sub-themes which can be identified in this group of interviews include the way in which the National Health Service was moved toward taking on a formal commitment for alcoholism treatment. Here it is particularly interesting to find Davies giving committee support for the Ministry's decision to take Warlingham as a model for service development but at the same time viewing such a strategy as a political device rather than as a scientifically determined move. For Davies, specialised units were a stepping stone, a necessary evil, a short-term response which should in due time work itself out of a job. There was also a creative tension between these two experts in the positions they took on the "return to normal drinking" question. In terms of developments in national alcohol policy Benno Pollak's general practice perspective foreshadowed the change in Departmental thinking which later led away from the initial heavy emphasis on hospital care and towards a greater stress on G.P. and primary health care involvement. A careful reading of what Pollak has to say might be seen not only as pointing toward the present growing edge of policies in this area, but also growing pains. Pollak does not fudge the fact that despite his enthusiasm for working with problem drinkers in a family practice setting, many of his colleagues who congratulate him will still see his interests as rather odd. He is in fact insisting that change cannot be brought about by platitude but only by finding answers that are feasible in real life conditions:

> Many recent British reports have been emphasising this perspective. . . . Nobody has ever got beyond theoretical points and developed any convincing practical ideas that will work.

National Case-Study and International Context

Earlier in this chapter it was suggested that an attempt to identify the nature of "influence" as revealed in these interviews could perhaps in some ways be of generalisable interest and carry significance for those concerned with the advancement of practice and policies in other settings. That suggestion should be modestly tempered by awareness that different countries are indeed very different, but the influence of, for instance, the teacher, or the catalytic impact of the innovative service or treatment centre, are probably the types of strategy which translate into almost any national setting.

What do these witnesses tell us about the international contacts that were affecting British policy development over these decades? Max Glatt refers to his pleasure in re-entering post-war continental professional circles through the aegis of I.C.A.A. Although he puts rather more emphasis on the American influences, he was always informed on European developments and under his editorship the *British Journal of Addiction* became strongly international in outlook. As Dean of the Institute of Psychiatry, Davies retained a commitment to supporting professional training in developing countries and made many personal visits. Glatt and Connell were both involved with WHO. Davies, Pollak, Glatt, and Connell all made visits to the U.S.A. Thus in general there can be no doubt that in this professional field and over this period British leaders tended to be interacting with colleagues in other countries in diverse and fruitful ways. On the negative side there is the reproach from Philip Connell. When asked about the American-British connection he answered:

> Well I think this rich cousinly connection is a bit one-sided. The Americans are far more interested in us than the generality of people in this field in Britain are interested in the Americans.

There are thus in these interviews same pointers toward the influence of country on country—a question which might elsewhere (and with a "larger sample") repay closer analysis. Indeed, the fascination of these particular five interviews, as with the other material in this book, is that the more one reads into them the more extensive the questions they generate.

IV

CANADA: THE ADDICTION RESEARCH FOUNDATION

19

Interview with David Archibald

H. DAVID ARCHIBALD, b. 1919. Graduated MSW from University of Toronto, DSc (Honorary) from Acadia University, Nova Scotia. Founded and, from 1950–76, was executive director of, the Addiction Research Foundation of Ontario. Chairman, Co-operative Commission on Alcoholism 1970–73. President ICAA 1981–83. Jellinek Award 1986. Chairman, Canadian Center on Substance Abuse 1988–89. Extensive international work including WHO. Recipient of the Order of Canada 1989.

BJA: *Perhaps we could begin by talking about how you first became interested in the problems of addiction?*

HDA: It goes back to the late 1940s. Initially my interest was one of puzzlement. During the war I saw a number of my colleagues obviously using alcohol differently from the rest of the fellows. I was curious and so when I came back to the University I begin to look at this phenomenon in more detail.

My enquiries led me to Alcoholics Anonymous. This was just beginning to get a foothold in Canada and a group of seven people used to meet in a Toronto restaurant. I knew one of these persons. He was a clergyman and he introduced me to the others. They welcomed my curiosity and were very generous to me. They asked me to attend some of their open meetings and so on. It was quite a fascinating experience for me, partly because it was the first time I'd seen a self help group in action. Also, of course, this was the only game in town as far as alcoholism treatment was concerned.

So I did some research on Alcoholics Anonymous and wrote a few term papers and then after graduation I was appointed as, among other things, lecturer at the University of Toronto. I used to have to lecture on social problems, and one of the major problems I dealt with was alcoholism. I had to give two hour lectures, so I used to take one hour and for the second I'd bring in a member of A.A. This was fantastic from the point of view of the students. They'd sit there with their eyes wide open.

Now, apart from lecturing at the University of Toronto, I was also with the then National Committee for Mental Hygiene which is now called the Mental Health Association. That's where I first met a fellow by the name of Jack Seeley who subsequently came to ARF as Director of Research. Then in 1948 the Yale University group wrote to the Mental Hygiene group and said there were a couple of scholarships to their summer school and would they recommend somebody. Seeley was at that point one of the executive officers of the MHA and so he sat down with a couple of colleagues to discuss who they could send on the scholarship and they suddenly thought (to quote Seeley) 'why not send Archibald, he's been making some noises abut this business so he's our man.' So I went to the Yale University summer school on alcohol studies on this fellowship. This is where I first met Dr. E. M. Jellinek. He later had an important influence on the Foundation. Well, I came back from Yale and continued lecturing at the university and the chap that I mentioned previously, the United Church minister, who was a member of A.A., heard about this and he used to come up and sit in the back row at my lectures. This clergyman happened to know a fellow by the name of Major John Foote, a very well known member of the Provincial legislature. He'd won the Victoria Cross at Dieppe. One day John Foote made a speech in the Legislature in which he said that if he had his way he'd do away with the large, impersonal drinking establishments around the province and he'd introduce the English pub as a community or family institution. This, he felt, would be a major factor in resolving the problem of alcoholism. What he did not realize of course was that the English pub is very much a part English culture and if we were going to introduce English pubs, we'd have to bring over the Englishmen as well. But anyway, the Premier, Leslie Frost, in his wisdom said 'Alright John I'm going to appoint you

Vice Chairman of the Liquor Control Board—so go down there and see what you can do about it.' Well, immediately John Foote called our mutual friend the clergyman and said 'what have I got to do now?' This clergyman said 'this fellow I know by the name of Archibald is up there, he's lecturing at the University, why don't you call him in?' So he did and I started as Director of Research at the Liquor Control Board. The objective was to decide what kind of organization and program to develop rather than to carry out specific research projects.

BJA: *What sort of things were you saying at the time? Were you talking about the disease of alcoholism?*

HDA: I was talking about alcoholism as a major disease or illness of the contemporary society. I was pointing out that alcoholics were obviously sick and that because the province was raising enormous sums of money from the sale of alcoholic beverages, we had a responsibility to provide treatment services. I was also emphasizing the need to start doing some basic research to try to find out what the problem was really all about.

BJA: *At that time were you, or was anyone else talking about availability as a factor?*

HDA: No, as a matter of fact we (or I should say I) was caught up with disease concept. This was consistent with the general philosophy at that time which said that it really didn't matter how much alcohol was around, alcoholism was really found in the psyche of the individual. Alcohol was not seen as the cause of alcoholism. I don't think I went so far as to say that, but that was the general concept.

BJA: *Was this in any sense a reaction against the prohibitionist ideas?*

HDA: Yes, this was part of the great attraction of the disease concept of alcoholism. It was an enormously valuable public educational statement because it shifted alcoholism from a simple moralistic notion to a health issue. It was only later on that the data began to emerge that indicated the importance of the availability of alcohol and per capita consumption as important factors in determining the prevalence of alcoholism and alcohol-related health damage.

BJA: *What other factors influenced the Premier and the Legislature to take an interest in alcoholism?*

HDA: Certainly the temperance organizations were strong at the time and they were quite influential politically. Also, there was A.A. which was becoming quite well known and clearly demonstrating that alcoholism was not something that was confined to skid row. In fact, a number of prominent figures in the province became known as recovered alcoholics and those also became an important influence.

There was also another important political factor. Two years previously, in 1946, government had announced without due process or discussion, that there would be cocktail lounges in five cities in Ontario. This became highly controversial given the temperance climate of the day. Another factor was the beginning, the very beginning of some scientific studies, at Yale University. I must say, however, that one of the key factors that led to the ultimate decision to create this Foundation was the fact that Leslie Frost (the Premier of the day) was considerably influenced by his wife who was an active member of the temperance movement.

BJA: *So your first discussions with the Liquor Control Board concerned the need for treatment?*

HDA: About the need for treatment, yes. But from the start I emphasized also the need for research. I was personally very interested in research. I'd been influenced very much by Harry Cassidy, the Dean of the School of Social Work. He'd done some substantial policy studies across the country so I was really interested in research related to public policy.

From the start I applied the same principle that I apply today. That is, if you are going to prescribe policies for a community or a country, then you must diagnose the nature of their problems first. The diagnostic process is, by my definition, research.

BJA: *How did this talk about research go across? Did others share your views?*

HDA: I don't think we went into it that deeply actually, because certainly there was no hesitation in incorporating research into the title and objectives of the organization at all. It made sense.

Alcoholics Anonymous members didn't care about research of course. What they wanted really was some place to put their potential members for four or five days to get them dried out so they could begin to work with them through A.A. That's really what they wanted. In fact, the first sizeable grant the Liquor Control Board gave was establish a hospital run by A.A. people. It was a bit of a disaster and we had to bail out.

BJA: *What happened?*

HDA: Well they had an open door policy for A.A. and I had insisted on this, but it got to the point when people in varying degrees of sobriety would be pounding on the door in the middle of the night wanting to get in or to admit persons they were trying to do twelfth step work with. It was pretty chaotic.

This was before the Foundation itself was established as a legal entity but the hospital was funded on the condition that it be incorporated into the Foundation when it came into being.

BJA: *Were you involved in actually drafting the legislation to establish the Foundation?*

HDA: Yes, as a consultant to the Government I recommended that the Legislation of the Cancer Research Foundation be used as a model, and simply substituted the word alcoholism for cancer. This was not brilliant drafting on my part at all, but it was a good piece of legislation and it's stood with us well to this day. The basic principle was that the Foundation had to be separate from government. It had to have it's own independent board of directors. It had to be out of the civil service. It had to have freedom to study and publish. As we used to say, the Foundation had to be 'of the Health Department', but not 'in' it and 'of' the University, but not 'in' it. So the Foundation was established and I was asked, by Premier Leslie Frost, to take charge.

One of the first things I did was to spend two weeks consulting with Dr. E. M. (Bunky) Jellinek. He had impressed me enormously when I met him at Yale. He was a tremendous person—a real scholar and a scientist of the old school. He had dedicated his life to seeking answers to fundamental questions in a wide range of areas. Did you know that he made original contributions to the knowledge of such different subjects as schizophrenia and plant pathologies? He also spoke 13 languages. He well deserves the memorial of the Jellinek Memorial Fund that we established following his death.

I spent two weeks with Jellinek at Texas Christian University where he had moved from Yale University. This was shortly before he went to the World Health Organization. We talked about the tremendous opportunities that were here in Ontario and about the sort of major objectives and programs that should be built into the Foundation and what kinds of problems we should begin to research. For about the first eight years our major research efforts were inspired by hypotheses that Jellinek had suggested to us. He became a member of staff in later years, but in the earlier days he was our primary consultant—a very outstanding fellow.

BJA: *How would you assess the overall impact of the Foundation?*

HDA: That's awfully difficult. Certainly the Foundation has brought Ontario a tremendous amount of credit from all over the world. This is not credit you can easily identify, but I'm sure you feel yourself the profound influence the Foundation has had in our field. In the earlier days we had a very significant influence. All of the provinces of Canada adapted in some form or the other the model of the Foundation. We also had a profound impact in the United States. We were earlier in the field than most places in the U.S. There was only one other Commission operating at that time. That was in Connecticut. It was developed by the Yale group. And so we had a profound impact there as well. You wouldn't get many of the contemporary workers in the U.S. admitting that, but it's certainly true historically.

As for the impact of the Foundation on social policies, that's a really hard one. Ontario is not enamoured with some of the policies that we have recommended as a consequence of our research. As is true for many Canadian endeavours, we are better known and better appreciated outside of Canada.

Our work has certainly made a major impact on research into

the incidence and prevalence of alcoholism the world over. It was Ledermann of France who started us thinking of the direct relationship between the availability of alcohol, per capita consumption and alcohol-related health problems. When Wolf Schmidt and Jan de Lint examined Ledermann's data and started working on it, then the subsequent research turned the whole field around.

It has had an impact on policy making in a number of places, too. We're not the only ones who should take credit, but I think that policy making in Scandinavian countries, in Poland, in other European Countries, and even in some Canadian provinces have been influenced by the work of the Foundation. One day it will have an impact in Ontario as well. Alcohol related health and social damage is simply too great to ignore for very long.

BJA: Do you think that had it not been for the Foundation, Ontario would have developed more liberal alcohol policies?

HDA: Yes. I can't speak for more recent years, but certainly for a substantial period of time, we kept the moral conscience of the politicians on edge because we were very clearly pointing out the extent and nature of the alcohol problem and the responsibility of government to attempt to contain the damage.

BJA: Did you have personal connections with politicians?

HDA: Yes. I used to meet with the Minister of Health regularly. I still hear from him from time to time. He's the person who got us our headquarters building. He was Minister of Health for ten years, so the communication was very real and very easy.

BJA: That seems to be something that's been lost, or at least changed?

HDA: It's changed a lot. In part it's the growth and the strength of the bureaucracy I guess. Now it really is a different situation.

The conscience of the legislature used to be much more strongly felt by the government. And it was a strong conscience about, not only alcoholism, but about the general welfare of people. Currently, the pendulum is swinging in a conservative direction, and when it swings in that direction things get tough. Programs for people tend to suffer.

BJA: *You talk as though the politicians that you were involved with were really concerned with the 'moral fibre' of the community.*

HDA: Well of course, so was everyone. I mentioned the fact that the temperance organizations were strong. The churches were strong too. As a matter of fact I think the Foundation at one time made a negative contribution because I think we were responsible, in part, for the weakening of the temperance organizations. I don't wish to establish a complete cause and effect relationship here. But we established a policy early in our history that we would not accept financial support from the alcoholic beverage industry on one hand or the temperance organizations on the other hand. We had to be independent of any of the vested interests. Our strength and our purpose was research; we had to maintain scientific integrity. It had to be. Consequently the people of Canada used the Foundation as the basic reference point for information. This I think, in part, weakened the force of the temperance movement whose major modus operandi was oratorical. They were believed to be biased. However, some of the statements they made are now remarkably similar to statements that are being said today, based on contemporary research findings.

BJA: *The Foundation was originally concerned only with Alcoholism. When did its interest in other substances emerge?*

HDA: Well, from the outset we were interested in all psycho-active substances. For example we would not exclude from treatment persons who presented with multiple drug problems. Use of alcohol and barbituates was rather common. And then, as one started to look at the problem physiologically and psychologically, it didn't make sense to single out alcohol from other chemical substances. We were interested in comparing drug effects from the beginning. Then heroin began to emerge on the scene. The government became somewhat concerned about it. I remember discussing this with the Minister of Health and he was wondering what to do about it so I suggested we take an interest and that our legislation be amended accordingly. The Minister thought this to be a great idea, so our legislation was amended and our responsibilities greatly increased.

BJA: *There was a paper by David Pittman called* The Rush to Combine *where he said 'what's all this about, why are these fellows in alcohol research getting involved in this drug business—We shouldn't do it.' In other words, we should try to keep them separate.*

HDA: David Pittman's paper became an issue, but the issue of combining research on alcohol and drugs was never a problem here. Shortly after that there was a large conference in Washington. I gave a paper there, together with Harold Kalant. Max Glatt came over from England to present a paper on working with both alcohol and drug dependent patients from the clinical perspective. And before that of course we had had this meeting at WHO and recommended that it was logical to examine both alcohol and other drugs within the same broad context. This doesn't necessarily mean combining the treatment, which is how a lot of people tend to think about it. But anyway, it was never a major issue here at the Foundation. Our interests in both alcohol and other drugs grew naturally and I think in a very healthy way. I think it's just a waste of time and resources to build two enormous establishments as they have in the United States—NIAAA and NIDA, but that's quite another story! As a result of the interest in drugs, the Foundation did expand much too rapidly during the 70s. We were forced to, literally forced to. We were the only game in town, we had the flexibility that enabled us to move fairly rapidly and the government poured financial resources into the Foundation. The Government of Ontario made the Foundation responsible for virtually everything that was developed in our field in response to the drug panic of the late 60s and early 70s. Consequently, the Foundation was forced to expand its operations beyond what would be considered to be reasonable under normal conditions. Fortunately we decided that many of the new programmes would be financed by grants-in-aid (project money) rather than through our core operational budget. This policy enabled the Foundation to maintain a reasonable degree of stability during a very difficult period. The grants-in-aid program provided support for a large number of 'crisis intervention centres' designed to provide some kind of treatment for persons experiencing 'bad trips' as a result of the widespread use of relatively impure illegal drugs. Because impure drugs were being consumed indiscriminately, and in large quantities, by young people throughout the country, we decided to develop the first laboratory in Canada for analysis of 'street drugs' for content. We found that approximately 50 percent of the drugs analysed contained many impurities. Incidently, the Foundation's current President, Dr. Joan Marshamn, developed our first 'street drugs' analysis laboratory. Canadian legislation did not permit the possession of drugs by 'non-physicians' for laboratory analysis at that time; however, our first concern was for the health of young Canadians. Later, legislation was passed by the Government of Canada to legalize the street drug analysis work. Following this development we provided training in drug analysis techniques for laboratory workers in government labs so that the responsibility was spread to other institutions.

The fact that the Foundation survived, reasonably intact, this very difficult period is, in my opinion, a tribute to the core strength of the organization. As hockey coaches say, the secret is 'strength down the middle.' The strength of the organization lies in the core staff. If I ever made a good decision, it was the early decision to establish a policy whereby the Foundation would provide career opportunities for scientists. I'm not sure that I sat down and thought out the long range implications of this policy, but it was a simple fact of the matter that at that time, if we wanted quality staff and we had to compete with the universities. What special inducement could we offer? Obviously careers in research. So that's what we did. And that enabled us to obtain the Kalants, Popham, Schmidt and many others who have made a career of scientific research without the need to search constantly for grants-in-aid. That policy probably contributed more than anything else to the development of the reputation of the organization internationally. We could have developed the best clinical program known to man, but I doubt that we would have made any major impact beyond Ontario.

BJA: Perhaps now we could talk a bit about your international interests and connections? When did these begin?

HDA: Well it really started, I guess, as a consequence of the influence that Jellinek had on me. Jellinek was such an international person. He saw the problem from so many different dimensions, geographic, cultural, historical. It became obvious that if we were going to try to examine the problem of alcoholism in our part of the world, we must be able to compare our experiences with other countries and to learn from these countries. And so, almost from the outset, we developed international contacts. Also by this time Jellinek was with the World Health Organization in Geneva and I automatically started thinking internationally. Our involvement with the alcohol and road traffic area also led us into international comparisons. In 1951 the first International Conference on Alcohol and Road Traffic was held in Sweden. I went to that and met a lot of leaders in that specialty area. Jellinek was there and so was Dr. Leonard Goldberg, one of the Swedish experts. While there, I suggested that the next meeting be held in Toronto. So in 1953 we had the 2nd International Conference on Alcohol and Road Traffic in Canada. As our Foundation grew in size and reputation, Jellinek used to recommend that International scholars should come here. Through the World Health Organization, he had a system of international fellowships and we started to receive visitors from many other countries. Each one brought with them their own experiences in their own country and we learned a great deal from them.

BJA: *What about the connections with the Third World?*

HDA: Well that really developed much later although from the start people from developing countries used to come to the Foundation. But my third world connections are due more to my involvement with the World Health Organization than with the Foundation *per se.* The Foundation has never really financed, from its own budget, any work in third world countries much to the surprise of some people who sometimes make accusations without bothering to find out the truth. That work has been done either through the World Health Organization and financed by the United Nations, by the Canadian International Development Agency or by the Government of Canada. My first major experience in a developing country was in Thailand in 1975, a long time after the start of the Foundation.

BJA: *Now that you've introduced the topic of Thailand, could you tell us how you approach your work there?*

HDA: My approach in Thailand was very much the same as when I was asked to get the Foundation going in Ontario. When WHO asked me to go to Thailand, it really was as a one man commission. When I found myself flying by helicopter and dropped down into a jungle village, I had to ask myself 'What on Earth can I do to help these people?' Two things became very clear. One was that anything worthwhile was going to have to be developed in Thailand and in the remote tribal villages, not dreamed up in Geneva. I was profoundly influenced by what I believed to be Canada's great mistake with respect to our native populations. Programs for the native populations used to be drafted in Toronto or Ottawa "for the good of your soul and by God you'd better believe it!" So when I became exposed to the hill tribe population in North Thailand and witnessed their isolation, I was convinced that whatever was going to be done had to be developed within the villages—with full participation by the tribal peoples.

The second major consideration was that I had to find people in Thailand who were capable and on whom we could rely. As was the case when setting up this Foundation the key was to find good people and provide them with support. I knew what I was looking for and I knew the kind of persons we had to have. So after searching around Thailand and principally around Bangkok and Chulalongkorn University, I finally came across an institution known as the Health Research Institute. The staff of that Institute had done quite a bit of work with the World Health Organization in family planning, so they were interested in community development programs. Fortunately, they were considering turning their attention to other major health problems in their country—such as drug dependence. They had never been up in the Northern opium producing villages, so we discussed, at some length, the possibility of undertaking work in that region of their country. They agreed to undertake the project provided financial support could be provided by the United Nations.

In some ways they were the last people you would expect to become involved in work in the remote hill tribes villages. Dr. Charas Suwanwela is probably the leading neurosurgeon in Southeast Asia and Dr. Vichai Poshyachinda is a specialist in nuclear medicine. They are both brilliant men. But they went up into the villages, became deeply committed, and were able to develop really good working and personal relationships with the hill tribe peoples. The villagers respected and accepted them. So that's been the key. The one thing I did in Thailand was to sow the idea of how to develop a program, find the people to do the work, and get them the necessary financial support. They've done all the rest themselves. So I'm very proud of my colleagues in Thailand.

I came back to Geneva, got the whole thing set out in a written workplan which was subsequently agreed to by the Royal Thai government, by the United Nations partners ILO and WHO, and then obtained financial support from the United Nations Fund for Drug Abuse Control. An interesting experience with international bureaucracies! Then I went back and worked with my Thai colleagues to develop a detailed work plan and so the programme got started. When I returned to Canada I met with the staff of the Canadian International Development Agency and discussed the possibility of Canada taking some direct responsibility for the basic development work in Thailand. They really didn't want to do any work in what they called the drug field, because they had seen this primarily as a matter for law enforcement officials. But when they realized that we were really dealing with a basic health development programme and that drugs were really just the symptom, they showed interest. And now they've provided support for the last three years and they've just agreed to support for a further 4 years.

BJA: Did anyone ever say to you 'Hey Mr Canada what are you doing here in our country?'

HDA: Not really, because right from the outset I was so thoroughly convinced that the program had to be developed by the local people—not by a Canadian or any other foreigner. At one time WHO's policy had been to send a foreign person in to direct their projects in developing countries. But many of the foreign 'directors' caused considerable local resentment, which greatly inhibited programme development. I'm not sure why WHO followed that policy, but anyway it has since been reversed. The key is to find the right people in the developing country and help them to develop their own program for their own country.

312   Addictions

BJA: One other area I'd like to tap into and that's your work now as president of the International Council on Alcohol and Addictions. Could you briefly describe the goals of the organization and what you as President have been trying to do?

HDA: The major function of the International Council is education and training. Education being defined as information transfer, and training being skill transfer of specific skills. But let me go back a little. ICAA has had along history. As a matter of fact we're having the centennial congress in Calgary in 1985. It grew out of the temperance organizations in Europe, principally those in Scandinavia. I first became involved when Dr. Jellinek recommended that I attend some of their meetings. Then the Director, Archer Tongue, asked me to serve on one of their committees. And about that time the Council was concerned about whether or not they should extend their functions to include drugs as well as alcohol. I pushed them fairly hard to take an interest in drugs. I had no license or right to, I was just involved in one of the committees, but I'd always seen the organization as important because of its international character. But, organizationally, and financially, like every volunteer international organization in the service field, they were having a difficult time. You know when they'd run short of financial support for some of their work, the director, Archer Tongue would decrease his salary—which wasn't very large in the first place. Also, there was no provision in the organization for any pension or security for the staff. Archer and his wife Eva had been completely and totally dedicated and I think have made very significant contributions the world over. When they asked me to accept the Presidency I had some reservations, but nonetheless I finally accepted because I believed there was a tremendous amount that could be done in our field and if I could help a little, so much the better. So the first thing to do obviously was to try to get some reasonably secure financial support. That's coming now. A very generous donor provided a million dollar loan which when invested over a period of years will provide a capital fund for the organization. This capital fund will in turn be invested and the interest used to provide core budget support for the work of the International Council. The original capital loan was from a great friend and benefactor of our field, Brinkley Smithers. This kind of financial support illustrates the deep commitment of Dr. Smithers, not only to our field, but also to the work of the staff and officers of the International Council.

The next major objective was to 'institutionlize' the organization. Now we have a strong international board of directors representing all regions of the world. It is not a 'rubber stamp' board! When we come together as a board of directors, nobody's fooling. The responsibility of the members of the board is very clear. They are the body responsible for charting the major policies and priorities of the organization, for monitoring progress, and for developing the financial support.

One of the special things that we're now able to do is to develop training problems in Developing Countries. The objective is to train trainers so that the country can then move to self sufficiency. The first 3-year programme was developed in Nigeria with financial support from the Canadian International Development Agency and the United Nations Fund for Drug Abuse Control. Programmes are now being planned for Zambia, Kenya and South East Asia.

The Board of Directors of ICAA, together with our Executive Staff have decided that within the limits of our financial and human resources, training programs in Developing Countries would have top priority. This is the kind of thing that ICAA can do really well!

BJA: Just one general question before we finish. One gets the sense that whatever you decide to do you would turn it into a success. Are there any other issues other than addiction that you would like to have a crack at?

HDA: Yes. There are so many problems facing the people of the world today—and many that I could be deeply interested in if time and resources would permit—development of basic health programs in Developing Countries, development of programs for world peace, for better understanding and appreciation of the richness of so many cultures, are just a few.

Whatever talent I have is probably more in the field of development than elsewhere—getting things going, seeing and grasping opportunities to develop programmes for the betterment of the human conditions in the world today is what excites me. A very trite statement indeed—but true!

BJA: *Do you find the addictions business itself exciting?*

HDA: Yes. Take a look at it from a professional's point of view. Look at the number of professions that are directly involved: sociologists, clinical people, basic scientists, biologists, pharmacologists, economists, legal experts. To me they are a tremendously fascinating group and working together, each in his or her own way can do marvellous things. Also look at the countries that are involved. What other field encompasses so much geographically and culturally and professionally? In our field we are working with a cross section of the world and its people.

20

Interview with Harold Kalant

HAROLD KALANT, b. 1923. Medical education, University of Toronto (MD, BSc, PhD). Professor of Pharmacology, University of Toronto from 1964, member of Addiction Research Foundation's research staff from 1959. Served on various national and international committees and contributed to work of WHO and ICAA. Awards include Jellinek Prize 1972, and Nathan B. Eddy Memorial Award 1986.

BJA: Harold, before you entered medical school, I believe you started out in a 4 year honor science course at the University of Toronto. Did that imply that you were aiming at a research rather than a clinical career from the beginning?

KALANT: Yes and no. Since I was a child I had wanted to study medicine, and always thought of doing medical research. But the practical reason for going into science first was that my family didn't have enough money to pay the fees for medical school, and I won a scholarship to science, so that's how it happened.

BJA: There are those who consider that medical school is not the best route to a career in medical research. That view may be right or wrong, but since there is a strong clinical emphasis in medical training, did the experience affect your initial orientation towards research in any way?

KALANT: Temporarily it did. I think it's true that medical school doesn't really prepare you for research. One of my graduate students, a particularly brilliant biophysicist who studied medicine after having completed his scientific training, became so enamored of clinical practice that he dropped out of research and is now a general practitioner. I guess something like that happened to me. I loved the clinical work, and after finishing medical school I started to specialize in internal medicine. Getting back into research was almost by accident.

BJA: *I believe that shortly after graduation, you went to Chile and worked in a hospital there. Why Chile?*

KALANT: That's easy. While I was working at the Banting Institute, during the basic science year that was then part of the total 5 year preparation for internal medicine, I met Oriana Josseau who had come from Chile to work with Charles Best. We got married, but she had to go back to Chile for at least a couple of years. The professor of physiology with whom she worked there, arranged with the professor of medicine at the University of Chile to give me a clinical fellowship. I worked in Clinical medicine there, but did a bit of clinical research as well in the area of liver disease.

BJA: *When you returned to the University of Toronto, you began work toward a Ph.D., did you not?*

KALANT: Yes. At that point I was still planning to stay in clinical medicine, but we came back to Toronto half way through the year. I needed one more year of residency before I could write the FRCP exams, and the professor of medicine suggested that I go back to the lab for 6 months until there was a suitable opening on the ward. At that time the professor of pathological chemistry, with whom I had spent my basic science year previously, suggested that I take a Master's degree. That would not really provide a very thorough scientific training, so I asked him whether he would be willing to have me stay on for a Ph.D., and he agreed. My intention was to return to clinical research afterwards, but I never did get back to the clinic.

BJA: *You eventually went to Cambridge, did you not?*

KALANT: Yes, that was after completing the Ph.D. Oriana had completed hers in Physiology and mine was in Pathological Chemistry. We were looking for a place where we could both do post-doctoral work. Cambridge offered the best opportunity.

BJA: *What was the nature of the experience there, and did it affect your aims in any way?*

KALANT: Not permanently. I spent my post-doctoral period there in Biochemistry, and the project that I was working on gave me some interest in cancer research, but that didn't prove to be a permanent career interest.

BJA: *Why not? Some say that cancer research is the epitome of medical research—that is, a matter of basic biological science.*

KALANT: I wouldn't say that. Cell biology, which is a prominent part of cancer research, is basic science. But cancer research actually spans a whole range of topics from molecular biology to the most applied clinical work, just as the field of addiction research does. In that sense, cancer research is no more nor less attractive scientifically than addiction research.

BJA: *How did you happen to join the staff of the Department of Pharmacology at the University of Toronto? Did that follow the experience at Cambridge?*

KALANT: Not immediately. I came back originally to a position in Biochemistry at the Defense Research Medical Laboratories (DRML) north of Toronto. The Director of DRML was the late Edward A. Sellers who, after I had been there for 3 years, accepted an invitation to the University of Toronto as professor of pharmacology. He offered me a position in Pharmacology at the University. At the same time, the Addiction Research Foundation offered me a position to set up a biological research program in alcohol actions and alcoholism. The two invitations came at the same time. I was attracted to both, and asked the University and the Foundation if they would consider setting up a joint appointment. They did, and that's been the arrangement since 1959.

BJA: *Did you engage in any work relevant to the addiction field when you were with the Defense Research Board?*

KALANT: Not specifically on addiction, but on a topic that contributed to my eventual entry into the alcohol research field. While I was working on my Ph.D., I supplemented my scholarship by doing clinical work at the Bell Clinic for alcoholism on evenings and weekends. I had known Gordon Bell as a student, and when he offered me a position as an attending physician at his clinic, I was delighted to accept. As a result of this experience, when I eventually went to DRML, the Air Force people asked me to look into the question of finding a biochemical marker for the post-drinking hangover, that would enable them to determine whether a pilot was fit to fly or not, the day after drinking. Dr. J. K. W. Ferguson (who developed Temposil®) was a consultant to the Air Force, and he was also on the Professional Advisory Board of the Addiction Research Foundation, as was Gordon Bell. When the Foundation looked for someone to set up a biological research program, both Dr. Ferguson and Dr. Bell recommended me and that was how it came about.

BJA: Once you were really committed to a career in alcohol and drug research (and I guess in the early days it was principally alcohol), did you have any expectations about the nature of the problem that you were going to do research on, which later proved unrealistic? For example, did you think that there was a better chance of achieving a major breakthrough than, say, in the cancer field?

KALANT: I didn't think there was a better chance, but I didn't feel that the chances were any worse. What was attractive about the alcohol field was that there was really very little systematic research being done on it at that time; it was almost virgin territory. It was attractive to be able to define the problems in terms of what you felt you could investigate profitably. The cancer research field had been far more extensively worked over by then. Consequently, you had to become a super-specialist in one or other aspect from the start. In contrast, in 1959 when I began alcohol work one could legitimately range rather widely: you could be a bit of a tinkerer, a jack-of-all-trades, and it was attractive to be able to tackle questions over a wide range of subject matter.

BJA: Even cancer has proved to have its sociological components. For example, the principal cause of lung cancer is smoking, and that's a human behaviour. On the other hand, I think we could agree that the social component is much more prominent in the case of alcoholism. For example, the most widely used definitions of alcoholism are essentially sociological. Given that you were trained in the more fundamental aspects of biology, did this characteristic of the field affect your research aims?

KALANT: At the beginning it probably made me very modest in my aspirations. I knew nothing about sociology, and almost nothing about psychology, and I felt that with my preparation I would have to stick to those aspects of the subject that concerned strictly physiological and biochemical mechanisms of action, and the production of organic damage. At the beginning I decided to concentrate on metabolic aspects of alcohol action in the liver and to stay away from behaviour and from the central nervous system. But one of the very gratifying aspects of being in this field has been that I felt gradually more and more confident in tackling broader aspects of the subject.

BJA: *Am I correct that much of your time in the first few years was devoted to critical reviews of theories based on unsatisfactory evidence? In other words, you found, did you not, that you had to get rid of an awful lot of chaff before you could get down to new experimental work?*

KALANT: Yes, but that was part of the process of self-education that I had to go through to find my footing in the field. In picking problems that I wanted to investigate, I had to read extensively about them first, and much of the literature proved to be of rather poor quality, and very patchy. In many areas, people tended to pass off pet speculations in lieu of actual research, so that my early reviews were really just part of the preparation for defining the areas that I wanted to work in.

BJA: *What were some of the ways that your views were affected by the multidisciplinary environment of the Addiction Research Foundation?*

KALANT: There is no question in my mind that my research path was very markedly affected by the context of the Foundation. It really was almost an ideal environment to work in for someone who wanted to become educated about alcoholism. There were strongly motivated people in all of the relevant disciplines. They had entered the alcohol research field at a time when it was not the most attractive or the most highly regarded field academically, so that all of them must have been truly dedicated. When I started, the group at the Foundation included Bob Popham in anthropology, Wolf Schmidt in epidemiology, Bob Gibbins, Muriel Vogel-Sprott and Reg Smart in experimental psychology, and Jack Seeley in sociology. The group was small, and was housed in a small building with small offices that practically opened into each other, so that it was impossible not to talk across disciplinary lines nearly every day. This was for me immensely beneficial and exciting intellectually. It was a chance to see my area of work in the context of the whole complex field and inevitably reshaped my thinking.

Then, as an outgrowth of these contacts, Bob Gibbins and I later began to collaborate actively in the laboratory, he as a psychologist and I as a pharmacologist. Together with one of our early graduate students, Eugene LeBlanc, we had the temerity—perhaps that's the right word for it—to step into the then murky waters of behavioural pharamacology. I probably would not have had the stimulus to do so if I had been working exclusively in the university pharmacology department. It has meant that over the years it has been possible to broaden the questions, to look at alcohol consumption and its consequences in terms not only of the pharmacological but also of the behavioural and environmental factors that influence it. To me that has been the most gratifying aspect of the evolution of our work in this field.

BJA: The psychologists you mentioned used to say that one vehicle was as good as another to study human behaviour. Evidently, they didn't think of themselves as being in an applied field, but as contributing to general psychological knowledge. Was that true for you? Do you think it was a good way to contribute to basic scientific knowledge?

KALANT: Alcohol and drug dependence research is a perfectly good way of contributing to basic scientific knowledge. I have always been a great admirer of Louis Pasteur who, in seeking to answer practical questions, was able to discover some very important fundamental principles in microbiology. That feeling has been strengthened by my clinical experience. I see research as being defined methodologically, not by the applications to which the knowledge is put. One can do excellent basic research on an applied problem and one can do rather hum-drum research on a very basic problem. It really depends on the definition of the question and on the imagination and the skill with which the questions are answered. In alcoholism, one can do research on very basic issues. For example, if you want to study how alcohol acts on the cell membrane, that is just as basic a biological question as discovering how glucose is metabolized or how DNA is transcribed. Whether the discoveries are of importance to basic science or not really depends on the questions you ask.

BJA: *But isn't the ideal for you a combination of the two?*

KALANT: Yes. The greatest satisfaction for me comes from discovering something of basic significance that also leads to a clinically useful application.

BJA: *Would you give some examples of such work, from your group over the years?*

KALANT: I think that perhaps the most striking example is the work that Yedy Israel began when he was a graduate student, that our group continued after he became a staff member, and that he and Hector Orrego have advanced brilliantly since they became an independent unit. When Yedy started his Ph.D. program in my lab, he began to work on the effect of alcohol on the $(Na^+ + K^+)$-ATPase, the enzyme which is responsible for the transport of Na^+ and K^+ across the cell membrane. In the course of the work we found that alcohol initially inhibited the enzyme, but that chronic alcohol consumption led to a compensatory increase in its activity which resulted in an increase in oxygen consumption.

In the case of the liver, this meant that the oxygen requirements in the liver go up substantially when it is metabolizing alcohol chronically, while the oxygen supply is limited. Therefore the parts of the liver at the distal end of the blood flow along the sinusoids become subject to the risk of damage caused by insufficient oxygen. In the case of alcoholics, this risk is enhanced by the fact that they are often heavy smokers, that alcohol itself impairs oxygen uptake in the lung, and that if the liver cells become swollen because of fat accumulation they impinge on the blood flow in the sinusoids. All of these factors contribute to a decrease in the availability of oxygen while at the same time the need increases. Therefore, the liver suffers hypoxic damage.

Yedy Israel realized that this was in many ways similar to the metabolic situation in the liver of hyperthyroid patients, and came up with the idea of using the antithyroid drug propylthiouracil, or PTU, to treat the alcoholic liver. Hector Orrego, Yedy, I, and other members of our group did a first clinical study in which we found that PTU actually doubled the speed of recovery from alcoholic hepatitis. Then Hector and Yedy subsequently did a large-scale study involving a minimum 2-year follow-up, which has recently been published in the *New England Journal of Medicine*. In that study, patients suffering from alcoholic hepatitis and cirrhosis were treated with PTU for as long as their symptoms and laboratory and clinical signs indicated a need for it. The results of this study, in my view, represent a major breakthrough. It's the first treatment which has apparently resulted in a substantial improvement in the survival rate of cirrhotic patients. To me, that's a very exciting clinical outgrowth of what began as a very fundamental problem in the biochemistry of alcohol metabolism.

BJA: *Am I correct to think that the basic work you mentioned at the outset of the example was also related to another line of fundamental research with a potentially practical outcome?*

KALANT: Yes. The ATPase work was initially conceived as part of a biochemical investigation of mechanisms of alcohol tolerance, and I think it is true that among the major contributions of our group has been the redefinition of the concept of tolerance. Tolerance was originally seen by pharmacologists as a purely physiological homeostatic response to the presence of alcohol in the brain, and one looked for physiological or biochemical changes that might constitute the basis of this adaptive response. Psychologists, on the other hand, were more inclined to think of tolerance as a learning process which enabled the person to compensate for the impairment produced by alcohol; without learning, they said, there was no tolerance.

Bob Gibbins, Eugene LeBlanc and I re-examined these concepts and it became clear that it was impossible to differentiate between them. What had formerly been thought of as purely physiological tolerance was directly modifiable by learning. When the subject had to perform a test repeatedly while under the influence of alcohol, the tolerance was acquired more rapidly than if the alcohol was consumed under conditions of no behavioural demand. Subsequently others found that classical Pavlovian conditioning of environmental cues, from the environment in which a drug was received habitually, could also trigger the appearance of tolerance as a conditional response. A. D. Lê, Jatinder Khanna, and other members of our group showed that this applied also for alcohol. When we examined this in depth we found that the amount of alcohol the subject received, the frequency with which it was received, the environment in which it was received, the on-going behaviours that had to be carried out under the influence of alcohol, all modified the development of tolerance, but we could not differentiate the end state. In other words, there don't appear to be different kinds of tolerance, but rather, different and very important modifying factors which can determine how quickly and how markedly the tolerance develops, how long it lasts, whether it applies only to the test in which it was originally measured or transfers to other tests, and whether it is transferred to other drugs with actions similar to those of alcohol. All of these things became greatly clarified, I think, by the work of our own group and by the work of many other groups that later became attracted to this field.

I think this area of tolerance research is now at a stage in which one can begin to visualize possible clinical applications. For example, if the environment in which the alcohol is received plays an important part in the development of tolerance, and if tolerance increases the tendency to drink more (because it gives you the chance to get the rewarding effects of alcohol at a lower cost to yourself, since you've become tolerant to the punishing effects), then alcoholism treatment programs might aim to decondition the cues from the environment in which the person has habitually drunk. In any event, I would expect that, in the not-too-distant future, individual treatment will be modified—and hopefully rendered more effective—through taking into account these changes in our understanding of the nature of tolerance.

BJA: *Do you think this concept of tolerance applies equally well to the opiates and other addictive drugs?*

KALANT: Oh yes. The separation of alcohol research from other drug research is no longer justifiable scientifically. The basic principles of motivation for drug use, the search for reinforcement mechanisms that cause individuals to want to repeat the drug ingestion, the factors that determine tolerance, the relationship between tolerance and withdrawal reactions, the relationship of these to exaggeration of the drive for taking more drug, all of these things are common across drugs. Moreover, with the growing recognition of cross-tolerance between alcohol and opiates, benzodiazepines, and other psychotropic drugs, it's becoming clear that you cannot reasonably compartmentalize research in the field. It's also obvious from clinical experience that people who stop using heroin when they are treated with methadone maintenance or other techniques often increase their drinking to the point where a latent alcohol problem becomes an overt alcohol problem.

BJA: *I guess the pioneer work on the relationship between increased tolerance and physical dependence as, in effect, opposite sides of the same coin was done by the Lexington group. But has your research contributed anything further to our understanding of this relationship?*

KALANT: I think perhaps we have contributed something in terms of possible cellular mechanisms, but so have many other investigators, and I should point out that the concept is not yet universally accepted. There are still very good researchers who believe that they can show tolerance independently of physical dependence and vice versa. I think this is probably a methodological problem. One of the difficulties is that people have tended to measure physical dependence (i.e. withdrawal reactions) with different methods than they have used for measuring tolerance, and on the whole they have used much more sensitive measures for tolerance than they have for physical dependence. Thus the ability to show a one-to-one correspondence has perhaps been limited by inappropriate choice of techniques. The majority of investigators do believe that tolerance and physical dependence are two sides of the same coin, and I think we've made a contribution to that concept, but so have a great many others.

BJA: It seems to me that the tolerance research greatly clarifies the role in the addictive response of the ingestion of large quantities of a drug, especially alcohol, at a particular point in time, the mechanism underlying a bender, if you like. But that leaves at least one very big question: what triggers a bout of heavy consumption in the first place? Does any of your research bear on this issue?

KALANT: Yes, that's really the latest major line of research that our group has taken up. Some years ago I began to feel that we were putting too much emphasis on consequences of heavy drinking without really tackling the question of why heavy drinking arose, and there was not a great deal of work on that in relation to alcohol. There had been a lot of work on the nature of the reinforcement of self-administration of other drugs such as the opiates and the central stimulants because there was an excellent model available for the purpose. This was the intravenous self-administration model developed by the Michigan group that could be used with rats, cats, dogs and monkeys. With this model it was possible to study the efficacy of a drug in initiating and maintaining its own self-administration. Then, by pharmacological or anatomical manipulations in the brain, one could define the nerve pathways involved in the production of the rewarding effect that caused the animal to acquire and firmly establish a pattern of drug self-administration. However, in the case of alcohol this model didn't work very well. Animals would drink alcohol if given a choice between a weak alcohol solution and water. They would drink even more of a solution of alcohol sweetened with sugar or saccharin. But they spread out their drinking over time in such a way that they seldom became intoxicated, and it was very difficult to prove that alcohol really had reinforcing effects in laboratory animals.

BJA: Would you say, then, that neither your group nor any other has developed a successful animal model of alcoholism yet?

KALANT: Yes. Mardones in Chile, the Alko group in Finland, and T. K. Li in the U.S.A. have made great advances in developing rat models of genetic factors affecting the level of voluntary consumption of alcohol, but these are still far from being complete models of alcoholism in humans. I think our group has improved some of the previous models, but I don't feel that we yet have anything that we can point to with conviction as an animal model of the whole complex process of alcoholism. I think that it is essential to develop such a model, not only as a means to further our understanding of the causes of alcoholism, but for immediate practical reasons as well. There are many laboratories, both in the pharamaceutical industry and in universities and research institutes, in which a search is going on constantly for drugs that would be useful in the treatment of alcoholism by decreasing the desire to drink, decreasing the reward obtained by drinking, or increasing the punishing effects of drinking. The trouble is that the drugs screened in these programs are come upon by hit-and-miss methods. For example, someone may find, in the course of using a drug for another purpose such as the treatment of depression, that the patient appears to show some reduction in drinking. Then an attempt is made to test the usefulness of the drug, both in humans and experimental animals, in reducing alcohol intake. There have not been great successes so far, and I think the reason is that these efforts lack a sound rationale. As long as one simply screens drug after drug without a good theoretical basis for predicting that it will diminish specifically the reward initiated by alcohol, the research is not likely to have an important practical pay-off. If, on the other hand we had an animal model from which we could learn something about the neurological basis of the reward system in the brain, then we would be able to target drug development much more specifically towards that action of alcohol.

BJA: As you look back on your experience in this field over the years, do you think you would go into it again if you were just starting out now?

KALANT: That's hard to answer because the conditions have changed so markedly from the time when I began. In 1959, as I said, I had the very rewarding experience of working closely with a group of colleagues who were intellectually stimulating, exciting, who opened for me doors to fields that I had known nothing about. One of the most rewarding aspects of working in this field has been the opportunity to integrate my own area of knowledge with that of people in other quite different areas. I'm not sure whether it is still as possible to do that. The growth of the Foundation, for one thing, and the tremendous growth of research in the whole field of alcoholism, means that there is a huge task in just keeping up with the literature in one's own little area of specialty. Therefore, one of the more attractive features of the field, when we started in it, is no longer there.

BJA: *You have said that you are interested in applied research and applications if they can be found. But have you found it difficult to cope with external pressure to produce practical results rapidly?*

KALANT: I can't really say that there has been, within the Foundation, any obvious pressure from outside to make us do that. By inclination I would like to see our work have practical applications, but certainly the Foundation has always accepted the idea that theoretical research is a long-term investment which ultimately yields practical applications and doesn't need to justify itself by producing those practical applications tomorrow or next year. Some years ago I did a little calculation which completely satisfied me on that question. After the first study with PTU, when we found that the average stay in hospital for patients admitted with alcoholic hepatitis could be cut in half by PTU treatment, I looked up the number of hospitalizations for alcoholic liver disease in Ontario each year, the mean duration of stay for each, and the average cost per day of hospital care. On the basis of those figures, I calculated that the savings produced by this treatment in the course of 2 years would more than repay the entire research investment of the Foundation from its establishment to that point. So I feel that if one can make a single such important practical advance in the course of one's career, that amply justifies all the resources expended in basic research, and we don't need to feel any qualms of conscience about using taxpayers' money for such work. I think that it does pay for itself in the long term, and any good research institution and any intelligent government should recognize that, and shouldn't be looking for a constant flow of practical applications. They come in their own good time.

BJA: *What have you seen to be your role in communicating the results of research to relevant non-researchers—clinicians, educators, legislators, or the general public? Do you feel that the researcher has a responsibility in this regard?*

KALANT: Yes, I think the researcher does have a responsibility for making sure that scientific knowledge reaches its potential users in forms which are accessible to them.

BJA: *Can one rely on professional educators to do that, or do you think the researcher himself has to be involved?*

KALANT: I think the researcher has to be involved in some way, although not necessarily as the final communicator. It may be that the researcher is best used in speaking to the communicator who in turn speaks to the final audience, but that's an individual matter. Some researchers are also excellent communicators to the public, and if they can do it and enjoy doing it, then I think they should, because they will probably be more successful in communicating their concepts and information than an intermediary will. On the other hand, if they feel uncomfortable, if they are rather shy about talking to the public, if they don't know how to free themselves from jargon, then it's better for a skilled communicator to do the transmission for them. But the scientist does have an obligation to make sure that, one way or another, the information reaches the people whom it is ultimately likely to benefit.

BJA: *Apart from that purely educational function, that is, communicating information, do you think the researcher is ever justified in taking the position of an advocate? Should he push for a change in policy, a particular practical application, or a change in legislation when his research appears to justify such action?*

KALANT: That is an important philosophical question that I doubt will ever be agreed on by the whole scientific community. Oriana and I dealt with it at some length in our book *Drugs, Society and Personal Choice*. We feel quite strongly that the role of the scientist as an educator, and the role of an individual scientist as an advocate, should be clearly separated. In the case of alcoholism, for example, sociological and economic research have revealed quite clearly that legislation, attitudes, enforcement of laws, the economic consequences of taxation policy, and so on, have important influences on the consumption of alcohol. At the same time, recent research shows that alcohol can have not only harmful effects, but also beneficial ones. For example, there is fairly strong evidence now that moderate or light consumption of alcohol confers some net protection against morbidity or mortality from certain causes, primarily cardiovascular disease. Should the scientist therefore press for policies that *decrease* or *increase* the probability of drinking? You might argue that non-drinkers theoretically ought to be encouraged to drink small amounts, while heavy drinkers ought to be encouraged to drink smaller amounts but not to stop drinking altogether.

My feeling is that scientists really should not be pressing for specific policies of that kind, *in their role as scientists.* As citizens, yes; every citizen in a democracy ought to be contributing towards the formulation of policy by at least making his or her views known, through the vote, or through letters to the editor, or pressure on Members of Parliament, or other democratic means. The scientist's role is to help inform his or her fellow citizens about what is likely to happen if this or that policy is adopted, or what the consequences of this or that behaviour are likely to be. On the other hand, to decide whether the behaviour is good or bad is not a scientific question but a value judgment. The scientist, as a citizen, has just as much right as any other citizen to press for the adoption of what he considers to be good and the elimination of what he considers to be bad. But scientific knowledge *per se* doesn't make one's concepts of good or bad any more valid than the concepts of good or bad held by other citizens. Therefore I feel that it's dangerous for the scientist to become an advocate when he purports to do it in his role as scientist. It risks making him adopt potentially non-scientific attitudes towards the work itself, and on the other hand it attempts to give to his value decisions a scientific aura which value decisions don't intrinsically have.

BJA: *If I understand you correctly, you're saying that the scientist as an individual may push a particular point of view, and if he chooses to be consistent with the philosophy that you're enunciating, he would then make it quite clear that he speaks as a private citizen. Do you think that's a realistic view? Is it possible for the well-known*

Dr. Kalant to appear on television or before reporters and say "Look, forget that I'm Doctor Kalant, call me Mister. I am now going to give you my personal views, and remember that they have nothing to do with my role as a scientist"? Won't the journalist, even if you don't, remind everybody that you are a scientist, the implication being that because of your expertise you know better what's bad and what's good, and what's right and what's wrong, than other people?

KALANT: I think the easiest illustration to use in answering that question comes from the area of nuclear weapons. Any nuclear physicist who worked on the Manhattan project or subsequent developments from it could probably agree with other nuclear physicists what the force of a blast generated by a particular bomb is likely to be, what the shock waves are likely to do to buildings of a certain strength or structure, what the number of deaths or injuries in a population of a given size and density would likely be from a nuclear blast of a given kind, but whether they are good or bad depends on ideology. The person who says 'better dead than red' will say "yes, development of nuclear weapons is a good thing because it gives us the ultimate defence against a political system that we don't want". The person who says "no political system is worth wiping out mankind" would hold that nuclear weapons are bad because they make it all too possible to achieve a destruction that will make subsequent evolution of human society impossible. Neither of those points of view is based essentially on science. The knowledge derived from science is used to make predictions, but whether the predicted consequences are held to be good or bad depends on ideology, not on science, and every other citizen *given the same factual knowledge* is equally entitled to make an individual decision, on the basis of his or her own values, as to whether the consequences are good or bad.

In the same way, if we come back to the field of alcohol or drug research, we can predict on the basis of scientific knowledge that certain policies will achieve certain results. Whether those results are good or bad depends on our ideology. Banning access to alcohol, for example, would diminish the death rate from alcohol-related diseases. In spite of what people have said about the failure of Prohibition, it's clear that the death rate from alcohol-related diseases did fall during Prohibition, even though there were other social consequences that most people consider undesirable. Whether the reduction in morbidity and mortality outweighs the evils of organized crime, police corruption, and restriction on individual freedom—in other words, whether the overall effect is good or bad—depends on your balance of values. That is why I feel that the scientist should clearly dissociate his personal value structure from his gathering, interpretation and communication of knowledge.

Now you asked, is it possible? I think that it is possible if you learn regularly to separate the two, that when you speak as a scientist your role ends with the communication of facts, the explanation of them in terms that the audience can understand, and your demonstration of how they can be used to predict certain consequences. But when the time comes to say whether those consequences are desirable or undesirable, I think it is then the scientist's responsibility to say "From this point on I am talking as plain Joe Smith rather than Prof. Joseph Smith, I am expressing my own personal views. You may differ in your personal values, but here are mine and here is what I think." Then the listener is free to accept or reject Joe Smith's values on the basis of his own value judgments.

BJA: *You've been a researcher in this field for nearly 30 years. What are the most significant changes in the field over these 30 years from your perspective?*

KALANT: The field has changed in a number of rather obvious ways. Certainly it occupies a much higher profile, both publicly and scientifically, than it did when we started in it. There has also been a change in the concept of alcoholism. The Jellinek disease concept of alcoholism had been enunciated just about the time I started working with the Foundation, and I think it was interpreted very literally at the beginning. People tended to think of alcoholism as a disease in the same sense as pneumonia or cancer or diabetes are diseases. Since then, there has been an evolution toward a more sophisticated interpretation. Alcoholism is now seen as a disorder of behaviour, rather than a metabolic disease caused by something which obligatorily makes the person drink. This is reflected also in the evolution of research on treatment methods, which is more geared towards changing behaviour than looking for a magic pill.

There has also been a change in the sense that there is a vastly greater research effort devoted to alcoholism now than there was 30 years ago. I think this has had a negative effect in some ways. Undoubtedly it has generated a much greater flow of information about alcohol and all of its actions and consequences, and about the nature of alcoholism. But, as I said before, it has also tended to make it more difficult for people working in the field to retain a global concept of the behaviour and its consequences, and has created too much of a tendency to atomize research into tiny subproblems. On the other hand, sociological or social research in its broadest sense has greatly clarified our understanding by making it clear that alcohol drinking is a normal human behaviour and that heavy drinking is a variant of that behaviour. It has helped to focus our attention on those aspects of the subject that deal with the transition from a normal to an excessive behaviour: on the social and individual controls that normally keep drinking within healthy bounds, and on the factors which remove those controls and push towards unhealthy levels. I think the evolution of the disease concept has been very important, because it has largely eliminated the rather simplistic picture of alcoholism as either a moral disorder or a purely medical disease.

BJA: *Do you think we are any closer to effective treatment or prevention now than we were when you first came into the field? In some respects, doesn't it seem at times that we are farther away?*

KALANT: I don't think we are any farther away because what may have been effective treatment and prevention 30 years ago depended upon the fact that our society was relatively more homogeneous than now, and had more universal acceptance of its social values. Society has changed, and therefore the approaches that will be necessary for effective treatment and prevention are also changing, and we're more likely to identify those if we have a better fundamental understanding of the process on both biological and social levels.

BJA: *What do you feel might be some of the obstacles to further progress in the field? For example, there is more concern about the ethics of human experimentation than there appeared to be 30 years ago.*

KALANT: Yes, that's unquestionably true. One outgrowth of the Nuremberg trials was a growing general acceptance, and personally I think a well justified acceptance, of the need to respect the human rights and dignity of people who take part, whether voluntarily or involuntarily, in experiments or clinical treatments of one kind or another. An analogous view is now widely held in the case of experimental animals: one mustn't use unnecessarily cruel or scientifically unjustifiable procedures, and even some that are scientifically justifiable cannot be used for ethical reasons. There is no doubt that all of the ethical aspects of both clinical and laboratory research do make certain types of investigation more difficult, but I think that if the questions are well defined it is still possible to do good research, even within the limits imposed by ethical considerations.

Another obstacle is the increasing bureaucratization of research. When far more people are doing research and competing for relatively limited funds, and having to go through scientific screening processes which are done by one's peers within a specific discipline, it becomes harder and harder to be wide-ranging in one's formulation of a problem. It is also harder to be truly innovative, because applications for funds have to be seen as feasible, practical and consistent with existing knowledge, and this tends to foster orthodoxy and conformity. Thus there may be a pressure *against* truly innovative research. But it is possible to have new ideas and to test them experimentally if one is conscious enough of the need to explain, in a convincing enough way to one's peers, the reason for doing something differently.

One other obstacle is also a consequence of the large growth in research in this field, namely, the problem of keeping up with the literature. When one had to read perhaps half a dozen journals to be in touch with most of what was going on in the field, it was possible; when you would have to read hundreds of journals, as now, it becomes close to impossible. I think that takes away some of the satisfaction, and also some of the opportunity for doing research that truly bridges disciplinary approaches.

BJA: *A considerable obstacle, in the early years at least, was that in order to conduct clinical studies one usually had to have the cooperation of persons convinced that they already knew the correct way to treat alcoholism or drug addiction: persons who may have been physicians, social workers or what have you, but who definitely were not scientists either by training, or more importantly, by inclination. Therefore it was really difficult to prosecute this kind of study. Do you think this situation has improved at all? Are there more scientist clinicians?*

KALANT: Yes, I think there has been a definite improvement in that sense. This is illustrated not only by the Clinical Institute here in the Addiction Research Foundation but also by a number of excellent groups, throughout the world, of clinicians who treat patients but who at the same time have a scientific background and are able to put their treatment research on a thoroughly sound scientific basis. I think the Addiction Research Unit at the Institute of Psychiatry in London, Avram Goldstein's group in California, the intramural research groups of NIDA and NIAAA, and many others in the U.S. and elsewhere provide examples of excellent clinical researchers who combine scientific rigour with first-rate clinical practice.

BJA: *Do you think it likely that this field of research will remain a specialty area or is it likely to be absorbed into older established fields?*

KALANT: I don't think it will be absorbed, because scientific research works essentially on a cross-indexing or matrix basis. There are traditional disciplines which provide skills, methods, and to some extent concepts, and then there are problem areas. For example, one uses biochemistry, molecular biology, or physical chemistry, which are disciplines, to answer questions in cancer research, in cardiovascular research, in addiction research, and so on. You can use any discipline you wish in the study of addiction, it doesn't compete with the disciplines, it uses them. And in turn the study of addiction contributes to the knowledge in those disciplines. Therefore I don't think there is ever likely to be a risk that a specific problem area will be absorbed into a classical discipline. They are two different axes for approaching the same research questions.

BJA: *Perhaps a slightly different way of approaching the same question would be to ask, do you think specialist foundations such as the Addiction Research Foundation are likely to continue or is the field, at least in its research aspect, likely to be turned over to the universities?*

KALANT: I think both will happen. Both have happened up to now and they are likely to continue. The university-based researcher does not have the same incentive or the same motivation to continue a sustained interest in a particular applied field. For example, someone in a department of Biochemistry may study, let's say, the action of a particular neurotransmitter on the biochemistry of cell membranes, in relation to the action of alcohol and other drugs. But then he may find something about a particular enzyme or receptor or second-messenger system which catches his fancy, and he pursues that, no longer specifically in relation to alcohol but to some other agent which may manipulate the system in a way which gives him more information about its workings. On the other hand, in a specialized institution such as the Addiction Research Foundation, or the National Cancer Institute, there is always a mission orientation that says "You can ask basic questions, please do, but always ask them in relation to the specific problems that justify our existence as a special institution". Such specialized institutions are more likely to maintain a continuing effort directed towards a particular broad social or medical problem, but they depend upon advances in the basic disciplines to provide them with many of the tools and concepts. The two approaches are complementary, and therefore I think they are both likely to continue.

21

Interview with Wolf Schmidt

WOLF SCHMIDT, b. 1923, Czechoslovakia. Doctorate of Jurisprudence, University of Graz, Austria 1950; MA in Social Science, University of Toronto 1956; subsequent study of epidemiology. Staff member Addiction Research Foundation, Toronto 1951–86; Associate Director of Research, Social Studies. Previous Consultancies including WHO and National Academy of Science, Washington. Editorial position, Journal of Public Health Policy. *Jellinek Prize 1981.*

BJA: What led you to Canada?

WS: In the post war period I was a displaced person and had no country. I had lived in Czechoslovakia all my life but after the war I was not able to do that. In 1946 I had no homeland and that made it difficult. I thought about where to settle again. One is more likely to go abroad than to try to go back home when there have been such difficulties and I came to Canada.

BJA: What was the nature of your background?

WS: I received my university education in Austria and in Canada. I got my early training in law in Austria from the University of Graz. In Canada I had training in Social Work, Biometrics and Public Health from the University of Toronto.

BJA: How did you get into the alcohol field?

WS: The ARF made some grant money available for people who did theses in the alcohol field. That was in 1956. Part of Bob

Gibbin's thesis was about how gains in abstinence in treated alcoholics related to 'social reconnection'—that is reestablishing families, jobs, etc. It might be called rehabilitation now. I did a follow-up of a segment of the ARF patients he studied. He was interested only in gains in abstinence. However, I asked what were the determinants of this gain; was it only treatment or other characteristics as well? I found that gains were unrelated to what treatment the person got, but closely related to their social characteristics. I concluded that patients bring their own success in treatment with them. The ARF asked me to stay on and I did. I became a full time researcher in 1956.

BJA: What led you to the particular theme of your work in the alcohol field?

WS: It was clear to me that work had to be related to alcohol consumption and damage. These are two areas that delineate key interests in the field. The questions were what consumption patterns produce damage and what determines these consumption patterns? What is the magnitude and nature of the damage resulting from consumption? The first influence was the atmosphere of enquiry that prevailed when I first joined ARF. There were many talented people at ARF (Bob Popham, Jack Seeley, Dave Archibald, Jellinek, and the Kalants). I spent my first years in a kind of apprenticeship to them. They were very generous with ideas. There wasn't any territoriality or competitiveness. I can't say how these influences dictated my interests but these early contacts were very important in allowing me to develop my own interests.

BJA: How did you manage to stay on course?

WS: To stay on a research theme at ARF was not that complicated. I was fortunate that usually one piece of research contained the next question. It fed on itself and the next question was usually obvious from the last piece of research. The people responsible for the research, H. D. Archibald, J. Seeley, R. Popham and others allowed me to pursue the research lines as I wished. I felt protected. There existed an atmosphere that allowed researchers freedom and finances to pursue their work. That seems to have largely disappeared now in the ARF as it has in other research organizations around the world.

BJA: *What has the work established?*

WS: I can't talk just about myself here—many people contributed to the work and what it achieved. Over the years many things were produced by the original ARF group but others contributed as well. The areas investigated included the epidemiology of liver disease which I have described in detail. A description of the effect of heavy alcohol use on longevity has been made. How drinking relates to the various causes of death has been described. We have also been able to show the separate effects of drinking and smoking on the mortality from cancer in heavy drinkers. An empirical test of Ledermann's theory of the distribution of alcohol consumption has been made. The implications for prevention of this work have been outlined and presented to governments; how availability effects consumption and problems has been described. In fact, we first proposed that Government control measures on availability should be used to prevent alcohol problems. My most recent line of research shows the effect of specific doses of alcohol on longevity in mice. It introduces into the alcohol field a method of enquiry which may be called experimental epidemiology. The results of that study are quite interesting. They depart somewhat from expectation but it will be necessary to have the work repeated to be sure of the results.

BJA: *What is the relationship between research and the political process—as you see it?*

WS: We might ask does research affect the political process or vice-versa? Both are happening at the same time. The relationships between research and politics become problematic when the political process dominates the research. This happens when research monies are made available for politically chosen areas of study. In my own career in the 1950s and 1960s the relationship between the researcher and the political process was very distant. The amounts of money given for research were modest and there were few strings on them. Financial accountability was not so important as it is today. There was a cordial relationship between researchers and politicians. However, when researchers made increasing demands for funds and when alcohol and drug problems became prominent, difficulties arose. Solutions to these problems were demanded by both politicians and the public. Under these circumstances the political process dominated research. It even influenced the selection of research questions. For example, at ARF research on detoxification centres and skid row alcoholism was politically inspired. The same was true of some studies of illicit drug use. Much of the research undertaken was not the outcome of theoretical thinking but was research due to political and public pressure. It wasn't necessarily bad for ARF or the field but the work under such circumstances is not always optimal. Probably the ARF can't avoid responding to public and political pressures. If we don't respond who would? Research organizations such as ours must respond. Of course, governments are not always perfect. We need a balance between responding to government and following important scientific questions. Working out the tradeoffs is never easy.

BJA: *How have you carried the research message to the political arena—what are the delicacies and difficulties?*

WS: Initially we had opportunities to talk directly to government ministers especially the Ministry of Health. We could make presentations to them in person. By that method we could establish political contacts and convey as much detail on research as we wanted. In addition, we produced position statements to government on how to prevent alcohol problems and what the costs and benefits would be. We were successful in bringing our research to government. However we were not successful in getting them to accept the recommendations. Our recommendations, for example, around increasing prices and decreasing the availability of alcohol were not politically acceptable. Also, there was, lately, a rapid turnover of Ministers of Health. It takes many presentations and personal contacts to convey a complex message to ministers in government. By the time a minister reached enough understanding of our message he was often moved to another ministry. We have had that experience several times and it was very frustrating.

BJA: *What have been the resistances from government and liquor interests in accepting the message?*

ws: The resistance from government was not so much in accepting the message but in acting upon it. The Ministry of Health made our position their position. They carried the philosophy for a long time but had no program of action. The ministry in government responsible for selling alcohol and for the administration of the Liquor Control Act was opposed to the philosophy. Also, government became aware that the media were entirely opposed to any form of control in the alcohol field. They reported in a very biased way any effort by government or citizens to use any alcohol control. They saw it as a puritan control on morality with no place in contemporary society. It came as a surprise to us to realize how determined the media were on these issues. We were also surprised at how ruthless the liquor industry could be when controls on sales were discussed as a health measure.

BJA: *What future directions should be taken in this work?*

ws: Usually, if one knows the answer to that question the direction has already been taken. We are in the period when availability and alcohol controls are exhausted as a research topic. Things may be underway that are new but I don't see where the future in this research lies. With respect to applying this body of knowledge much still needs to be done. It is a matter of education, and persuasion to bring about a broad acceptance of the message that controls on availability are important. Such things must be used intensively for a very long time until there is general agreement to accept the approach.

BJA: *What are the problems with the quality of the data and data gathering necessary to pursue the work?*

ws: The problem with data is to realize how good or bad they are and to have a sense of what problems exist with particular types of data. With data on price, consumption and health consequences careful use is of the utmost importance. Indiscriminate use may create havoc. But great familiarity with such data leads to knowledge of how to use them. Corrections may have to be introduced.

Some data must be rejected altogether. For example, admission data for alcohol and drug problems and criminal statistics are very problematic. On the other hand consumption data, especially those from countries with a monopoly sales system are usually very good, even excellent. With vital statistics it is possible to refine them through adjustments and standardizations to obtain information that is entirely usable. The best approach is to begin with not trusting such data at all. Through various steps we give the data a chance to convince the investigators of the opposite. This is a laborious, tedious, process. The time required to do it is not reflected in the report. Unfortunately most investigators don't bother with such refinements but use the data just as they are.

BJA: *What is your overall view of the current ARF and its history?*

WS: The ARF has succeeded in bringing along a new generation of scientists, who are well-trained and very capable. At least for the life of this generation the scientific future of ARF is secure. There is, currently, a shift in ARF from the international arena to more regional preoccupations. It is difficult for me to judge whether this is a desirable shift. I am not sure whether it is due to government pressure or an internal pressure. My own bias is to think that the ARF's successful past was intimately linked to the world scene in our field. The ARF gained much from the interchange with colleagues around the world. I hope that the current reorientation does not preclude international collaborative work.

BJA: *How are research and researchers best organized?*

WS: Research and researchers do very well in relatively small groups. If researchers are part of very large organizations they must have an independent role and be protected from the various intrusions for which big organizations are known. Within these small groups a loose structure which maximizes informal communication is ideal. In my experience regular meetings become necessary when this informal network begins to fail. A very important productive period for research in ARF was when people like Popham, Seeley, Schmidt, the Kalants, Smart, Israel and de Lint worked together closely. It was marked by a total absence of meetings. There was an intense almost daily exchange among these scientists. Research managers should aim to create that type of atmosphere. It is necessary for productive research settings in my experience. I fear that ARF is growing a little away from that sort of research setting towards more bureaucracy. But this may be unavoidable in the current political atmosphere.

BJA: What are your recollections of early people in the field? Jellinek, Seeley, Ledermann for instance?

ws: I had the opportunity to know these people quite intimately. They came to this field after many years of having been successful scientists in other fields. They were established scientists who applied their experience to a new set of questions. All three had great charm but would, in today's terminology be considered hopeless managers. For example, Jellinek's style of work was to show up only occasionally in his office, and be totally indifferent to issues of budget. He would not understand accountability as it is required today. He simply looked at the research product—either he liked it or he didn't like it. If he didn't like the research output of a person for any length of time he had no use for the person. Seeley's view of looking after a research unit was to "hire the right person and let nature take its course". This implied that he thought of hiring as the key, most important aspect in research management. He felt that an error in hiring could not be corrected. On the other hand, he believed that the right person would do the right things if given the opportunity to do so. Ledermann was a loner. To researchers with such inclinations an organization will simply have to give total freedom—in other words stand back so as to not disturb their productive force. It was a very rewarding aspect of my work that I have known these people well. I realized within a week of my acquaintance with them that they were extraordinarily gifted people. I took every opportunity to learn from them. They made this very easy because all three were most generous in conveying their ideas, plans and understanding to me. For that I have always been grateful.

22

Discussion. What Made the ARF?

Reginald G. Smart

It is a pleasure to reflect upon the three interviews with people from the Addiction Research Foundation. The interviews with H. D. Archibald, H. Kalant, and W. Schmidt cover a period of early growth and development of the ARF and the addiction field in general. They create an opportunity to examine both the history of ARF and the whole addiction field. I see myself as a younger contemporary and a colleague of all three people and a person whose major professional satisfactions were derived from ARF and from working with them. To some extent, the successes and problems of the ARF and the three outstanding figures interviewed are intertwined with my own. Naturally, it is difficult for me to be objective about many facts and opinions expressed in the interviews. Rather than examining each interview individually, I prefer some general observations on how personal influences and setting affects the scientific study of addiction, especially in Canada. Another interest I have is in how science in Canada has affected policy and action in addictions treatment and prevention. All three interviews have something valuable to say about these issues.

The Early Days in Addictions Research

Many of us, including the three interviewees, were fortunate to come into the addictions (really alcoholism) field at an early stage.

The views expressed in this chapter are those of the author and do not necessarily reflect those of the Addiction Research Foundation.

In the late 1940s and early 1950s, the alcoholism field was largely undeveloped. For that reason, there were opportunities in Canada to create knowledge, careers, and reputations unequalled ever before. Dave Archibald received money and political support to start a research foundation in a province which traditionally had almost no research interest in mental health or social problems. In addition, he was able to develop a semi-independent or "arms length" relationship with the government. This, too, is an arrangement which was rarely followed in the past or after his success in getting it. Most government spending in health and social problems is by the large ministries or in agencies closely controlled by them. Probably, the arms length relationship gave ARF the freedom and flexibility to pursue addictions research in an indifferent climate. Given the anomaly that ARF represented, it is likely that Dave Archibald's personality, style, and approach were major factors, although the political will was also important. We might ask if Dave Archibald had been interested in schizophrenia or depression, might we have had no ARF but an SRF or DRF (Schizophrenia or Depression Research Foundation)?

Scientists such as Wolf Schmidt and Harold Kalant (and myself) benefited greatly from coming into the field at an early stage. Wolf Schmidt got some ARF grant money "for people who wanted to do theses in the alcohol field". ARF has not done that sort of thing for many years. Harold Kalant states that "it (alcohol research) was almost virgin territory". Both Wolf and Harold were able to develop their research interests almost unfettered by bureaucracy, political demands, or the need to account too closely for their efforts. Funds were readily available for almost any research project, and research assistants could easily be found. Scientists entering the alcoholism field in the 1950s found favourable funding and political situations which may never be repeated. Those situations are perhaps analogous to the field of HIV-AIDS research a few years ago. There were interesting problems, the political will to do something about them, and ample resources which could easily be found. However, Wolf Schmidt is right when he says that the freedom to do your own thing in research has disappeared from ARF and most other research places too.

During the 1950s there were very few research groups working on alcoholism, and hence there were few people from whom ARF people could learn much. Dave Archibald has made reference to E. M. Jellinek and the Scandinavian research groups. Many Scandinavians such as Kettil Bruun, Leonard Goldberg, Pekka Kuusi, and others gave ARF scientists good advice. For some time in the 1950s, there was a Canadian-Scandinavian domination of the research field. However, since the founding of NIAAA and NIDA and their large grant programs, American influences have become predominant. Most of the journals in the field now are American, and most "addiction" scientists must now be American, although I do not have a good estimate of the numbers.

Different Approaches to Research Funding

It is interesting that the American approach to research funding is very different than the ideal proposed by the three interviewees. Both Schmidt and Kalant emphasize the freedom to develop their own interests and rail against the increasing bureaucratization of research. Archibald states that one of his best decisions was to create career opportunities for scientists and allow them to do their work largely without grants-in-aid of research. ARF scientists have always preferred this system, and it exists there in modified form today. However, the vast increase in NIAAA and NIDA supported research is done in a totally different way. There are very few stable, long-term career positions, and most American scientists compete for grants lasting a few years at most. Despite the U.S. grant system, some scientists do stay in the field for a long time, and many are able to get successive large grants to support their research. It is also clear that many of the important developments in research have come out of the NIAAA and NIDA grants system. A number of winners of the Jellinek prize for excellence in alcoholism research are Americans, and hence the system must be a productive one.

This all raises the issue about what system for doing research is best—large block grants to research institutes to use in ways they see best or a random grant arrangement where any scientists who wish can apply. The emphasis in the first or ARF model is in choosing the right person to begin. If a poor personnel choice is made, then the research institute has a weak career scientist. If a good choice is made, the institute has a committed scientist who will spend a large part of their productive life in research on addictions. The problems with the grant-in-aid system are well explained by Harold Kalant who points out that it makes it harder to be truly innovative and fosters orthodoxy. However, the grants system assures that only good and relevant research is undertaken and that certain standards of science and ethics are maintained. It allows governments to change their priorities quickly by increasing or decreasing the total amount of grant money for a given area.

My contention is that we do not really know whether there is a "best" system for organizing addictions research. We are not sure how many important findings per scientist have been obtained from each system nor whether we could even agree on what was an "important finding". It may be that the system must fit the time and the culture. Certainly, a large grants-in-aid system would not have been successful in Ontario in the 1950s. The field was too unpopular and underfunded to attract much sustained interest from university-based researchers. I also believe that the politicians in Ontario placed a special trust in Dave Archibald, and a self-selected group of researchers in different centres could not have generated the same trust that the major research problems were being addressed.

The Influence of ARF

All three interviewees have spoken of the large research contribution of ARF. Much of this came because the early ARF managers in research, especially John Seeley and Robert Popham, were adept at hiring. Dave Archibald's decision to provide research careers rather than short-term funding was also important. Other decisions not described were also important. One decision was to closely associate ARF with universities and academic models and to keep some distance from all other alcohol movements, e.g., the Temperance Movement, Alcoholics Anonymous, and National Councils on Alcoholism. In fact, a national council on alcoholism has never developed in Canada, and we are one of the few developed countries without one. These decisions helped to reinforce ARF scientists' independence in choosing research questions. Perhaps they do not seem very radical decisions in 1989, but they were in the early 1950s.

The interviews remind me, too, of the problems ARF has had in making research relevant to the interests of politicians and the general public. Most people are not much interested in research or theoretical advances; only in what ameliorates the alcohol or drug problem of the day. It may be easier to develop an international reputation for research than a local or provincial one for excellence in prevention or treatment. As Dave Archibald says, "we [ARF] are better known and better appreciated outside of Canada". Probably ARF has not been able to develop a local reputation as strongly as it should. For one thing, we are not always sure how to do prevention and treatment yet, but research is something that we know a great deal about. Harold Kalant is unable to agree that we are any closer to effective prevention and treatment than we were 30 years ago. This has meant that ARF is sometimes (not always) seen as an elitist organization more interested in research per se, rather than solving the problems people have with alcohol and drugs.

In the beginning, we could claim that our research had just started and that it was too early to expect results. However, after 30 years have elapsed and we have not solved the major treatment and prevention problems; politicians and the general public have the right to question whether they should still support us. My own contention is that both treatment and prevention for addictions are much better than 30 years ago, although this is not the place to argue the details. Of course, much remains to be done on research in both prevention and treatment.

Probably we at ARF and in research generally do not pay enough attention to the broad application of our research findings. Harold Kalant mentions the important work on PTU and the findings that its use can reduce the average hospital stay of cirrhotics by 50%. Harold has calculated that the potential savings in terms of hospital care costs for 2 years could more than repay the government's investment in ARF research. Unfortunately, PTU has not been made widely available for the treatment of liver cirrhosis. Only those few cirrhotics involved in the clinical trials have had it, and there is no major thrust to make PTU available to all physicians. Problems seem to exist with side effects and also more clinical trials may be necessary. It could be that making PTU or its derivatives available for cirrhosis treatment requires a new sort of worker—a biomedical research applications specialist.[1] They would take existing biomedical research findings and make them known to those who could use them in treatment or prevention.

The Role of Scientists in Policy Analysis

The interviews also point out the differences in opinions about what the role of scientists is in promoting government policies. Harold Kalant feels that scientists should not advocate particular policies "as scientists" but only as private citizens. Rather, the scientists should make people aware of what the consequences are of adopting various policies. It may be possible for biomedical people to take this position, but social scientists at ARF often could not. We were constantly asked for our opinion on the best policies or practices to adopt on alcohol and drug controls. Wolf Schmidt describes his role in this very well. Some of the most recent policy interests in Ontario have dealt with drinking age laws, on premise consumption regulation, and alcohol advertising. Often we do not have enough research evidence to be certain what the outcomes of different policies could be. We, therefore, make an educated or scientifically sophisticated guess. To have no opinion at all or to often say "the results are not all in yet—we cannot be sure" is to reinforce the opinion that politicians have that alcohol researchers are not much help and irrelevant to policy issues. ARF has often issued "Best Advice" documents on various policy issues. These are documents which review the literature on current policy problems (e.g. whether to sell beer and wine in grocery stores) make calculations about the probable results of various policies and recommend government action of a certain type (e.g. keep alcoholic beverages out of grocery stores).

Wolf Schmidt makes it clear that ARF social scientists often made presentations to the Ontario Cabinet on alcohol policy. These presentations advocated controls on alcohol availability by way of age restrictions, less alcohol advertising, shorter hours of sale, etc. and a consistent, health-based approach to alcohol pricing. They generally argued what had become known as the Ledermann theory or the Single Distribution concept. There can be no doubt that Canadian governments want and expect alcohol scientists to suggest ways of preventing alcohol problems, and to state which ones they think are the best.

Despite many presentations, Ontario did not adopt the premise that alcohol problems vary with per capita consumption and that they should be controlled by decreased availability and increased prices for alcohol. Of course, the reason for that is not that the research findings are disputed; there is little real dispute about the facts. However, Wolf Schmidt reminds us that scientific findings are but one part of the arguments for and against that politicians hear on any issue. If prices for alcohol are increased, the government fears the loss of taxes through reduced sales, farmers see fewer opportunities to sell their fruit and grain, and hotel owners complain of decreased business or a disruption in the tourist trade. Alcohol researchers, at least in Canada, are but one small voice scarcely heard amongst the many eager to influence alcohol policy. It is very unlikely that scientists will get a chance to overstate their case, even if they wanted to do so in the way Harold Kalant seems to fear. Important unanswered questions for scientists exist on how to present their results to get the best hearing from politicians. Does the presentation depend upon the status and prestige of the presenter or the institution or on the number and quality of competing view points? What can alcohol researchers do in the face of evidence or opinion than what they are proposing (e.g. higher prices) for health reasons makes bad economic sense? How can we assert the long-term public health gains of our policies and deny or compensate for short-term economic losses for some people?

In Conclusion

What overall impression do the interviews leave about these early builders of the ARF, and how they were motivated to do their particular work? All, of course, wanted to solve alcohol problems at a practical level and to provide scientific answers to interesting questions. All three interviewees see their early development as influenced greatly by particular colleagues who happened to be available at just the right time. Many of those colleagues worked in other fields. They also emphasize that local circumstances and the socio-cultural context influenced their work. Moreover, there is more than a hint that all three see themselves as lucky in their choice of career and in the people they met at an early stage. Often luck is no more than being in the right place at the right time, but the lucky have to be clever enough to see the time and take good advantage of it. Dave Archibald, Wolf Schmidt, and Harold Kalant were well able to turn their luck to advantage. That they were able to do so has benefited ARF and the addictions field immensely.

Note

1. Dr. Yedy Israel has been one of the first, in ARF at least, to describe the need for such people.

V

THE WIDE WORLD

23

Interview with James Ch'ien, Hong Kong

JAMES CH'IEN, b. 1922. Educated Tokyo (Psychology), Chung Chi College (Theology and Social Work), Denver (Social Work), Harvard School of Public Health: DSc, MPH, MSW. From 1963 to present worked with Society for the Aid and Rehabilitation of Drug Addicts, Hong Kong: currently Superintendent of Social Service for SARDA. Extensive international work for WHO, UNESCO, ILO etc. In 1986 awarded MBE.

BJA: *Before we get on to discussing your own work with SARDA (Society for the Aid and Rehabilitation of Drug Addicts), let me first ask you to sketch out briefly something of the history of the drug problem in Hong Kong.*

JC: The problem in Hong Kong has always been closely linked with the opium smoking tradition in China. Hong Kong was ceded to Britain as a colony as a result of the Opium War of 1839–1841. There was already a limited demand for poppy juice among the gentry and herb doctors in China when the East India Company accelerated the shipment of Indian opium to balance the trade between Britain and China, but the increased availability of opium created more demand and spread its smoking among all classes of people. Hong Kong quickly became the entry port for the West's trade with China. Opium was one of the many commodities marketed and stored in Hong Kong and it consistently provided a substantial part of the Hong Kong government's revenue until the 1930s. Before the Second World War, the government of Hong Kong had a monopoly of opium distribution and licences were given to opium dealers to sell to registered customers. After the first Shanghai Opium Convention of 1909, the Hong Kong authorities tried gradually to arrest the opium addiction by reducing the annual supply to the licensed opium dens, but in reality this led only to an increased supply through black market sources. Yet prior to the Second War, the opium smoking habit was largely confined to male adults and very few teenagers were involved. When Japan occupied Hong Kong during 1941–1945, the military government saw that opium was an effective instrument in controlling the population and in helping the occupation authorities to secure the services of Chines collaborators. The Japanese gave the opium distribution privilege to a secret society, the Sun Hop Wei, also known as 'the triad', and this, for the first time, married the opium problem with organised crime.

In 1946, the Colonial Government abolished the monopoly and prohibited further distribution, trafficking and smoking of opium. Unfortunately at that time no attention was paid to the socio-cultural environment in which opium smoking functioned as a medium of social intercourse and recreation. Nor was any attention paid to the treatment of thousands or tens of thousands of opium smokers already living in Hong Kong. The prohibition was settled by the stroke of a pen.

BJA: *And what was the impact of these new measures?*

JC: Overnight the opium smokers who had been addicted for 20–30 years found there was no more legal source of supply and they turned to the black market for smuggled opium. What made the situation worse was the introduction of heroin during the later stage of World War Two. In fact, Korean agents working for the Japanese military authorities and intelligence service introduced heroin to Northern China, Shanghai and then Hong Kong. Chinese chemists coming to Hong Kong from Shanghai started to convert opium into morphine and then morphine into heroin. So here was an alternative drug for the opium smokers in Hong Kong. Opium smoking yields a pungent aroma which is carried blocks away in the city. Heroin smoking yields no odour of any kind and is easy to conceal. If you add heroin powder to your cigarette you can smoke it openly in a restaurant and nobody would know what you are doing. So heroin quickly supplanted opium as the mode of drug abuse. But an individual's tolerance of narcotics built up much more quickly on heroin than opium. With opium you can maintain a plateau of consumption for a number of years, but with heroin, tolerance builds up and the addict spends more and more of his income on heroin. Consequently that creates personal, family and social problems.

BJA: What impact was there from the influx of people from China during the Civil War? Did that change the drug using population, or did it build up new supply lines?

JC: Starting from 1948, a large number of refugees started to come into Hong Kong to escape the Civil War raging in China at that time. The Peoples Republic of China was established in 1950 and in the next few years large numbers of refugees flocked to Hong Kong, which included thousands of opium smokers from different parts of China. Many of the refugees brought substantial amounts of gold or cash with them, but were unable to adjust to the urban industrialised society of Hong Kong. Heroin became a means of escape from their frustrations, whether they had smoked opium or not in China.

BJA: What then was the official pattern of response at that time in the early '50s to the heroin problem in Hong Kong?

JC: At that time, the government and the community viewed narcotic addiction purely as a law enforcement problem. Some of the addicts resorted, of course, to crime to support their habit. It was only in the late '50s, that the prison authorities of Hong Kong realised that the great majority of prisoners in our prisons were drug addicts. Organised treatment thus began within a correctional institution.

BJA: What kind of treatment was given?

JC: Well, it was a kind of liberal approach from the penal point of view, in that addicts were committed to an open prison where the inmates spent a lot of time working outdoors and got good food, and plenty of exercise. If a man was caught in simple possession of dangerous drugs, he was committed to the Tai Lam Centre for eight months to a year or so, and the individual usually gained 15–20 lb. weight during this time. Counselling services were provided by aftercare workers.

BJA: But this was only attacking a small proportion of the problem. What happened next?

JC: Yes. In those days a drug addict who required treatment, who really wanted to give up the habit, had to surrender himself with a package or two of black market heroin to the police, because according to Hong Kong law, being addicted to narcotics was not a crime but being in possession was. So the individual confessed that he was an addict, in possession of dangerous drugs, and asked to be committed by the Court to the compulsory treatment programme. Physically he benefited from the programme, but socially he incurred a prison record and submitted himself to a social stigma which existed against drug addicts, especially heroin users. So in 1960 a number of community leaders, including physicians, lawyers, business men and industrialists, decided to form a voluntary society called the Society for the Aid and Rehabilitation of Drug Addicts.

This was to provide voluntary treatment opportunities for drug addicts, a chance of rehabilitation without incurring a prison sentence or stigma. And about the same time the government felt a pilot centre for voluntary patients should be established in one of our mental hospitals, the Castle Peak Mental Hospital. A ward with 60 beds was provided for detoxification and preliminary rehabilitation. As soon as this ward was opened in 1961, thousands of drug addicts came forward. The demand for voluntary treatment apparently far exceeded the limited supply.

And that stimulated the founders of SARDA to take more active action in fund raising and in finding a suitable place to build a new treatment centre. This took two years. The Shek Kwu Chau Rehabilitation Centre was opened on an island in mid-1963. Since a pilot centre already existed at Castle Peak for detoxification, SARDA started out, not with detox, but with rehabilitation and aftercare. Being the first social worker employed by SARDA, I planned our aftercare services from the very beginning. In a way, we were fortunate not to start aftercare as an after thought, but gradually build up a comprehensive system of rehabilitation and community care with continued social rehabilitation in the community.

BJA: *Tell me then, what would happen to me if I went as a voluntary patient tomorrow?*

JC: Since 1965 SARDA has established a comprehensive programme that covers pre-admission services, detoxification treatment, rehabilitation and after-care. If you come to SARDA as a voluntary patient, you are registered and you are given a physical examination which includes X-ray and all kinds of lab tests. An intake worker would visit you at home to confirm the address which you give is correct, to check on the family background and to analyze any family problem which may influence their motivation for treatment and rehabilitation. Any difficulties that the individual may encounter after treatment and rehabilitation upon coming home are analyzed and dealt with. It is important to know whether there is a supportive and accepting wife or parents, or whether the family would be rejecting even after the individual's treatment. The registered individual is then offered methadone as an outpatient but not as long term maintenance. We use methadone with outpatients as the means of stabilisation before institutional treatment. We have 500 beds on Shek Kwu Chau for men and 30 beds in a smaller women's centre in Wan Chai, for female voluntary patients. Often there is a waiting list and while waiting for admission for detoxification, the individual is offered methadone. For the last three years he is also offered acupuncture treatment as an option to make counselling possible, to reduce his anxiety and to prepare him for institutional care. This interim period may last for two or three days, or two or three months. A small minority of heroin addicts are detoxified on an outpatient basis and go straight to aftercare. The majority would go into our Island treatment centre for detoxification from heroin and/or methadone. They are then assigned to one of 18 Houses (therapeutic communities), each of which is a separate unit for group living, working, recreation and group counselling. These activities all take place on the Island of Shek Kwu Chau which is easily kept free of illicit drugs. The Island has 200 acres of land and we pay the government 1 dollar per annum for its exclusive use. Through organized use of voluntary patient power, we have developed the Island into a garden with our own farms, workshops and factories. So the Island itself is a large therapeutic community within which there are individual houses, each of which is operated according to the therapeutic community concept in North America.

BJA: *But I am sure they don't run with the same underlying philosophy as New York?*

JC: There are similarities and differences. All therapeutic communities are a drug-free milieu where one enjoys good fellowship and mutual support, but the difference lies in the cultural traditions. Chinese culture always stresses harmony and cooperation. Few of our residents would feel free to attack a fellow resident openly in a small group discussion situation. Although we did try to encourage them to confront each other with any faulty defence mechanism or rationalized pretenses, the American type of attack therapy is impractical in a Chinese cultural setting. We do encourage inter-house competition, healthy, wholesome competition in sports and work and in environmental beautification. That creates a healthy atmosphere for doing one's best, contributing one's talent and ability for the good of one's new reference group.

BJA: *These residential communities, do they have names?*

JC: Yes, each house has a name which represents the traditional Chinese cultural values. For example, Yan House symbolized humanity, Yee–righteousness, Lai–fortitude, Chi–wisdom, Shun–faith etc. All the 18 houses contribute to the physical and aesthetic development of the Island Centre like that. If you come to visit our centre you will feel that it is not a hospital but a sort of museum, with a lot of cultural artefacts, traditional Chinese art objects painted or created by our patients who are encouraged to give free expression to their artistic talents. It is also like a library, because Confucius sayings and the quotations of Chinese sages and philosophers are inscribed on the walls all over the Island.

Interview with James Ch'ien, Hong Kong

BJA: *The crucial question must be, what happens when these people get back into Hong Kong? How do you manage that problem?*

JC: That's very true. In the early years, we found, in spite of the intensity of professional aftercare rendered, the great majority of aftercare clients relapsed to drug use. They relapsed if they encountered difficulties or stressful situations, or they would relapse to celebrate some happy event. The better the aftercare service we provided, the more social dependence that was created. In the beginning, our aftercare, as in most social service programmes, was problem oriented. The client presented a housing problem and our aftercare worker would try to arrange low cost housing and the relocation of his family from a slum area to a new housing project. Yet the more problems we solved for our clients, the more dependency on the agency was created inadvertently.

BJA: *How did you get over this problem of social dependency on the agency?*

JC: In 1967 we had a dozen or so ex-patients who had completed their 3-year aftercare programme and whose cases were supposed to be closed. They came to see me saying that they really had no confidence in themselves. They knew individual casework service was to be cut off, and there was no longer to be a helping hand to lean on. They asked me to extend their aftercare service. But instead, I said 'Why don't you form a self-help group and I will use my own time to give you advice. Although case workers are no longer available to give you counselling, you are now experienced with a new life style; you have learnt your way around without the chemical crutch, and I am sure you can benefit from social interdependence, even when complete independence is premature or impossible'. So they took my advice and formed a club, in some ways similar to Alcohol Anonymous, except that cooperation with professional staff is encouraged. And this small nucleus grew naturally with more people who were completing their aftercare joining the group subsequently. A year later, there was a membership of nearly 100 people who decided to register a separate and independent society and they adopted the name of 'Alumni Association of SARDA'. They viewed themselves as graduates of an educational programme. They have been growing steadily year after year.

BJA: What is its size now?

JC: Two years ago the Alumni celebrated their 10th anniversary, and there were about 1,300 members located in six district chapters. Its organization was decentralized because the membership was getting too large to be in one club or one big association.

BJA: Do the professional staff, at the end of the rehabilitation period, encourage people to join the Alumni Association, or is it very much left to each person?

JC: In fact, involvement with the Association begins even before discharge. The representatives of the district chapters visit SARDA's treatment centre weekly and participate in peer group counselling and encourage patients to join the Association as probationary members. Only after six months of drug-free and crime-free living in the open community can a person qualify as a voting member. Then at the end of one year of drug-free, crime-free and productive life, the member is given a bronze badge bearing the insignia of AA, and he becomes eligible to be elected as an officer in the local chapter. After two years, he is given a silver badge and now he can qualify to be a director, to sit on the board of the central association. And after three years, he gets a golden badge; and after five years, he gets an 18K gold badge. In the beginning, SARDA subsidized the operation of the Alumni Association, but now they depend on their own effort and receive some help from the Community Chest in Hong Kong. But they also raise funds for the Chest and donate blood to the Red Cross; so it is a kind of a reciprocal altruism which the Association has promoted.

BJA: Does the Alumni Association just give mutual support, or does it also help with rehabilitation, in employment, housing and things like that?

JC: The district chapters of the Association are divided according to SARDA's aftercare districts so, at each of our aftercare centres, there co-exists a district chapter of the Alumni Association. All the new discharges can receive professional social service on the one hand, and on the other, enjoy the mutual support and recreational activities provided by the district chapter. In the neighbourhood where the individual lives, he is encouraged to obtain community acceptance by serving the community. Our ex-patients offer voluntary manpower in cleaning up the streets, cleaning up housing projects, transplanting trees and flowers from our Island to beautify their own neighbourhoods, thereby gaining friendship and good neighbourliness. They also participate in crime prevention and in drug abuse prevention activities. In the beginning, the community did not trust ex-addicts and I had difficulties in arranging employment for our ex-patients. But now the Association receives notices or telephone calls from prospective employers saying: 'I need ten workers in my plastic factory; can you provide them?' It is very gratifying to see that the once mutual rejection has turned into mutual acceptance, and I think that's an unique outcome which we have achieved.

24

Interview with Kettil Bruun, Finland

Kettil Edmund Bruun, b. 1924, d. 1985. *Undergraduate and postgraduate training in sociology, University of Helsinki: PhD. Actuary, Statistical Office of Helsinki, 1949–54; Secretary and Research Director, Finnish Foundation for Alcohol Studies 1955–80; Professor of Alcohol Studies, Stockholm 1981–84; researcher, Social Research Institute of Alcohol Studies 1985. Work for WHO. Jellinek Prize 1971.*

BJA: When did you first come to work in alcohol research?

KB: In 1955, and with a background in journalism and history, and after working as Editor of the Monthly Statistical Bulletin of the city of Helsinki.

BJA: Were studies already going on about the effects of changes in alcohol controls?

KB: The first programme of the Finnish Foundation for Alcohol Studies was in progress. Pekka Kuusi who was in charge of the control and sales department of the Monopoly was working on his dissertation, an experimental study concerning alcohol sales in rural Finland. The classic study comparing the effects of beer and brandy was also in process. So I was in a way happy to come to a working situation where, let's say, the results were guaranteed without my contribution. I came in as Secretary of the Foundation, elected by the university professors of that autonomous body. But I was formally an employee of the State Alcohol Monopoly and functioned as head of what later was named the Social Research Institute of Alcohol Studies. This was (and is still) an odd arrangement, which however in practice has functioned well. All parties were from the very beginning clear that my loyalties were with research and not with the Monopoly.

BJA: *And you had no contact with alcohol research before that?*

KB: Not much. I had only reviewed two books. One was Pekka Kuusi's handbook 'Liquor Question' and the other was Sakari Sariola's 'Drinking Patterns in Finnish Lapland'. In my review of the Lapland study I had some dispute with the author about the statistics. This meant that I was wrongly perceived as a statistical expert for a very long time in the Monopoly and its research department. In addition I had done a small interview study about youth for the Statistical Bulletin and there we had included a number of alcohol questions.

BJA: *And what was your first study when you joined the Foundation?*

KB: I involved myself with a very modest project—the Monopoly was experimenting with various variations in the buyer surveillance system. In Finland at that time you had a purchase permit which gave you the right to buy alcoholic beverages from one particular shop. All purchases were marked in the permit. Now there were doubts about the system and in the city of Tampere the system was changed so that the permit still was needed but the purchases were not marked. We studied the effects of this change by following buying habits, interviewing buyers with alcohol problems etc. [1]

BJA: *Was the study you've just described seen as constituting a new tradition in Finnish research?*

KB: This tiny piece was typical at that time. Disagreement in the public debate and among experts gave impetus to work out experiments in order to use research results for decision making.

BJA: *What was the position of alcohol research in Finland?*

KB: The big advantage was that alcohol research started rather early and it was in a way the first specialised research centre in any area to be founded. A lot of people perceived the alcohol research unit as an attractive place to work. The 1950s saw the real start of alcohol research in Finland. The key to success lay in the fact that from the beginning they were able to attract very good people. A lot of the outstanding social science research at that time was on alcohol studies because it provided one of the few opportunities. The expansion of positions in the universities came only much later.

BJA: *In terms of the international context, the evaluation of control changes that were done by yourself and others were very early compared with other countries. Where did the ideas come from?*

KB: A curious combination of influences. In the first place I think there was a strong Natural Science orientation within the Foundation. Due to the interdisciplinary thinking the social scientists became influenced by the experimental approach presented by, for instance Martti Kaila who was a psyhiatrist but still very much experimentally orientated. Secondly Pekka Kussi was very much impressed by Stuart Chapin's 'Experimental Sociology' which was one of the important books referred to in his dissertation. There was a very optimistic view about the impact of 'experimental' studies in sociology. At the Sociological World Congress in the late fifties we said something like, 'From now on no big change in alcohol control policies will occur in Finland without their being guided by preceding researches.' Certainly it was a very naive and optimistic view. But 'experimental' studies of this sort had a very important place in the Foundation for about 15 years.

BJA: *Your dissertation* on small group drinking was in fact an experimental study.*

KB: Yes, and although I am not now as optimistic about the impact of this approach, there is something here that we have lost. There is still I think a place for experimental studies in sociology.

BJA: *Then in the late fifties you did some travelling?*

---

*Bruun, K. (1959). Drinking Behaviour in Small Groups. The Finnish Foundation for Alcohol Studies, Helsinki.

KB: To Yale and to the ARF in Toronto, yes. I was in a very fortunate position because as I said the research programme had started and had its momentum and no one pressed me to immediately get on with research. I had practically 2 years at my disposal in which to read without engaging myself in much research. I visited the First Summer Institute which Jellinek ran in Geneva, and then I spent half a year at the Yale Center in New Haven.

BJA: *What were your impressions when you first ran into the international alcohol scene?*

KB: I was most impressed by Jellinek. He lectured several times at the Institute. I visited Jellinek in his hotel room in Geneva which he had transformed into a library and in fact spent half a day with him talking and talking. We both in a way had the same job of creating some sort of research programme and I discussed this problem with him. He had visited Finland earlier and felt that we were serious about developing research. I have only vague memories of the exact discussion but from this moment I became an admirer of Jellinek, although not an uncritical one.

BJA: *At the Yale Centre did you find a different tradition of research from that you had been used to in Finland?*

KB: Chuck Snyder, Chandler Washburne, Peter Park and Earl Rubington were there at the third floor at Hillhouse Avenue. Seldon Bacon too, of course, but he was running the thing so he wasn't so much in the daily discussions. I had considerable difficulties with the language and was rather handicapped. What was new to me was primarily the anthropological approach. Snyder had made his study about Jewish drinking. Rubington was making observational studies on alcoholics and worked in a very different way than I was used to—for me up till then it had been hard data statistics and experiments.

BJA: *Jack Seeley, when he was at the Addiction Research Foundation, published in about 1960 an article on price, alcohol consumption, cirrhosis and their interrelation. Was that seen as important at the time?*

KB: Seeley did a number of things that were important but I don't think he was able to communicate his ideas internationally. He was a knowledgeable person and he also had a lot of ideas about research organisation and the ethics of research which I only came to see as important much later on.

BJA: *Let's now go back to the progress of your own research. The Northern Youth Study* was published in 1963, which means it must have been under way some time before.*

KB: We started in 1959. In fact it was completed very quickly. This was one of the few studies I have ever been forced to do, in the sense that the newborn Nordic Council for Alcohol Research just made the decision and I was more or less ordered to run the study. It took me quite a long time before I recovered from this frustration. But when we really got going and had formed a team with one researcher from each country the situation changed. What was very interesting was confronting the methodological issues. There was so much diversity in national traditions about how an interview study should be carried out that it took some time to sort things out. I went to all four capitals and conducted pilot interviews. It was a remarkable experience to do these interviews in Copenhagen. In all the other cities you just rang the doorbell and said something about alcohol and youth and it was obvious to all why you were studying this topic. Not so in Denmark. In Denmark it was impossible to explain. How could one study such a silly thing as drinking? In Denmark the youngsters were asked to come to the interview place, and they even had to get paid.

BJA: *Turning to another issue, when did you first become involved in international narcotics policy?*

KB: I was a member of the Finnish State Committee on narcotics and during the cannabis discussions they often referred to the 'international obligations'. Then I went as an observer in 1972 to

---

*Bruun, K. and Hauge, R. (1963). Drinking Habits Among Northern Youth. Finnish Foundation for Alcohol Studies, Helsinki.

the UN Narcotic Commission and for the first time experienced its machinery, I became very curious about what they did behind the scenes. I met Dick Blum there and we both had the same feelings. Over a glass of whisky we discussed the original idea of studying the international control community. Dick was instrumental in forming the original study group and financial support. The Scandinavians had a somewhat different idea about the project but independent subgroups were formed for specific tasks. It resulted in a monograph, 'Gentlemen's Club' [2]. The job would never have been done without Dick Blum's original contributions.

BJA: One of the things that repeatedly comes up in your works is the issue of bureaucratic secrecy—in the 'Gentlemen's Club,' over the medicines question in Scandinavia, and so on.

KB: Yes, I have been a little bit paranoic! One of the few conflicts I have had with the Monopoly was concerning the right to publish a study which was originally based not on our own material but on the material owned by the Monopoly. However, the view of the researcher's was accepted. Such conflicts are necessary in order to clarify basic norms.

BJA: You in fact led a small project on secrecy in government in the Nordic countries?

KB: Not really. I initiated work on this topic, we formed a group which in a book tried to formulate some sort of policy against too much secrecy about the rights of the individual to publish. We took a number of examples from various fields, and the starting point was the pharmaceutical industry and its very special position in regard to secrecy. We discussed the police, and also a lot of environmental questions. The impetus came from a Nordic study on psychotropics control [3]. Secrecy issues were touched upon in Appendix 2 to that book. You see, the manuscript to the book was sent to a few people and came into the hands of the head of the medical board in Denmark, and he was quite furious. He wrote a letter to various authorities and the Nordic Council for Drug Research.

BJA: Which had funded the study?

KB: Not funded but supported. He asked the Council how it could support such an unscientific study and so on. So afterwards I published his letter and a similar letter from the former head of the Finnish medical board. These letters illustrate how central administration may resist studies on its own activities. I published these letters in order to analyze the arguments. The interesting thing is that such documents are seldom published.

BJA: The reviews of the book don't mention the Appendix?

KB: No, and even in scientific discussions about pharmaceutical controls people are likely to avoid questions of the relation between industry and government. This is a persistent problem—important delicate issues remain hidden. If struggles for data are themselves secret you will never get a clear idea about what are the rights of the researcher. Of course sometimes the researcher goes too far, no question. But norms cannot be developed in secrecy.

BJA: One of the studies that you've taken part in is known sometimes as the purple book, the 'Alcohol Control Policies in Public Health Perspective' [4]. The project which gave rise to that book was started, I think, in 1973, under the auspices of the European Office of WHO. Where do you see that project as coming from?

KB: I was a member of the committee which developed and followed the WHO mental health programme in the European Office in Copenhagen and there I proposed a study in this vein. In the beginning there was a lot of hesitation but Dr. May (Mental Health Advisor at Euro) became interested. He encouraged me and I didn't wait for a formal agreement with WHO, I then just invited people to test their interest.

BJA: What did you hope to accomplish?

KB: I don't know exactly. I was certainly very vague. The background was that I had to rethink my ideas of alcohol control in the light of the Finnish experience in 1968/69 when controls had been suddenly relaxed with dramatic increase in consumption and harmful effects. My own liberal views on alcohol policies had received a blow. Then I was confronted in the European Office with international issues. I thought that I had to reconsider my position and that probably the best way to do it was to try to have a group which could develop a perspective beyond the specific situation in Finland. The situation was fortunate because many of the relevant questions had by then been focussed for research. The group which emerged from my invitation did a marvelous job. In a way I am surprised how smoothly our text was generated. A number of dialogues were gong on. Some of the discussions between the participants became much more sophisticated than I was able to follow. Often that sort of incomprehension is not too disadvantageous. Let's say that the operation was not so difficult because I didn't understand all the conflicts.

BJA: *You've worked in a number of fields in the last few years. Narcotic policy, alcohol controls, the medicines question. It is quite noticeable to an outsider that researchers at the Social Research Institute for Alcohol Studies in Helsinki have on their shelves books which go beyond alcohol—you all seem to see alcohol in a much broader context.*

KB: As I said earlier, this fortunate situation has to do with the early creation of the Institute as one of the few social research institutes in Finland. It became some sort of tradition that people were not only permitted but supposed to look more widely than the immediate alcohol question. A philosophy was developed that the alcohol researcher has the right to exist only if he is able to contribute to the general social science and social policy field. I am a little worried when there is a new type of researcher coming up, the professional alcohol researcher, which didn't exist in the middle of the sixties. But fortunately the Institute has this curious structure where there are permanent researchers with permanent positions who will be there for a life time, but at the same time there is mobility with the research contracts at the Foundation. This means that those who are permanent will be challenged by those who are working there temporarily. This contrasts with centres in the U.S.A. where there are no permanent positions. No one thought out the implications of the Finnish structure when it was started but it has advantages.

BJA: Let me ask you about the strategy of building research programme because you've had a lot of experience in that direction. It seems to me that one of your strategies has been to pick young people and try them out, and very rarely have you drawn in senior researchers who were already established in other fields. Is that a fair statement?

KB: I think so, yes. Earlier I think we did try to set up a research programme which tried to cover too much. We had the idea that we were looking at the whole field and covering everything. I think that was indeed naive. You have to make choices, you have to pick out something which is important either on theoretical grounds or because it has been neglected, but you don't need to say that this topic is so vastly important compared with everything else. I believe in a more modest view, but I don't think you should neglect thinking about what are the gaps in the research activities around the world. The history of research shows how easy it is to go into some sort of common stream and just do the same over and over again, even without the advantage of strict replication. The difficult question is how do you develop new research approaches. In a way you have to start from the assumption that we have forgotten something important and try to locate that.

BJA: If you identify an important issue then you have to look for someone who can do that work?

KB: For a new approach you can't take old senior researchers who have their views fixed. And from where do you get this idea that there is a gap? Of course, they may not first be able to formulate their ideas. But you should draw on young people and then try to help them formulate their ideas.

BJA: So that's one of the functions of the Foundation's Fellows who come on contracts?

KB: Yes, I think so because you can't just bank on the older and established scientists to innovate.

BJA: You've been now Professor in Sweden for 3 years and have in some ways moved into a very different academic environment and *different society, although you've been running research projects within that context. Was this a difficult adjustment?*

KB: I have had a very privileged position in Sweden. I was also clever enough to get the position and then get leave for half a year. During this time I had time to plan what to study in Sweden and I got a grant which was big enough to guarantee my independence from the Sociology Department. Although the Sociology Department has quite different views on research than myself, I have never been in any conflict with them. I have also had the pleasure to meet Gunnar Boalt who is Professor Emeritus and who was in the late fifties in the Nordic alcohol research council.

BJA: *How do you see your views as different from the Department of Sociology?*

KB: I don't think it is only a question of the Stockholm Department. Basically any Department is bound to a discipline, and I as alcohol researcher have no discipline. The inclination of a department is to limit the interpretation of alcohol issues to what a specific discipline can say.

BJA: *Is there a general point that areas like alcohol studies or drug studies are not well served by disciplinary boundaries?*

KB: I don't know about other universities but the Finnish ones have not been able to tackle interdisciplinary issues. In fact they have no administrative ways to deal with problems which cross disciplines. That is true also for Sweden. If you accept a problem orientation then you have to accept that there should be other types of units dealing with such issues than just university departments. In some countries a university department can be very flexible but in many universities that is impossible.

BJA: *But on the other hand in Finland you've ended up with the Foundation having three main sorts of alcohol studies—clinical research, social and policy research and then biological research, and these are organised very separately. Is that fair?*

KB: Yes and no. They are separate but the Foundation constitutes a body where all these approaches are represented.

BJA: *The research units are organised separate but there is an overall research policy that mediates or aggregates?*

KB: Yes, but not a very firm policy which is challenging the autonomy of the units. And secondly, the Biological Unit and the Social Research Institute are neither of them bound to one discipline.

BJA: *I know you are planning on or proposing to lead a project on the Finnish language within the Swedish school system. It seems to me that in your research there is a general theme of social commitment, not necessarily a political commitment but at least a social commitment. You want to be working on topics where you feel there is a good social point to be made.*

KB: The school issue is a burning and delicate question for the Finnish minority in Sweden. I think that I like to study this conflict and conflicts often mean an indication of involvement. In the scientific process you clarify people's positions and you get a clearer view of the ideas which are determining people's behaviour. You get a clearer idea about the power forces in society. Even if I personally were to be too paranoic in some of my conflicts I learn more about society.

References

1. Bruun, K. and Sääski, J. (1955). The effect of relaxed liquor sales control in Tampere. *Alkoholpolitik,* 18, 115–116.
2. Bruun, K., Pan, L. and Rexed, I. (1975). The Gentlemen's Club. International Control of Drugs and Alcohol. The University of Chicago Press. Chicago and London.
3. Bruun, K. (ed.)(1983). Controlling Psychotropic Drugs. The Nordic Experience. Croom Helm. London & Canberra.
4. Bruun, K., Edwards, G., Lumio, M., Mäkelä, K., Pan, L., Popham, R. E., Room, R., Schmidt, W., Skog O-J, Sulkunen, P. and Österberg, E. (1975). Alcohol Control Policies in Public Health Perspective. The Finnish Foundation for Alcohol Studies. Helsinki.

25

Interview with Michael Beaubrun, Trinidad

MICHAEL BEAUBRUN, b. 1924, Grenada. Medical Education, Edinburgh (MB) and postgraduate training in psychiatry Edinburgh and Maudsley, London (DPM, FRCPsych). First Professor of Psychiatry at University of West Indies, Jamaica (1964–74). From 74-present, psychiatrist in Trinidad. Foundation President of the Carribean Psychiatric Association, and (1971–75) President of the World Federation for Mental Health. Independent Senator, Trinidad and Tobago, 1976–81. Extensive consultancies including WHO.

BJA: *First perhaps you could tell us about the current background situation in Trinidad.*

MB: We are a Third World country where oil has been found and where the rise in OPEC oil prices in 1973 suddenly threw what was a poor agricultural country into the condition of a relatively oil-rich country. The result is that we have sudden economic development and industrialisation taking place to the point where the budget this year was in the region of 3,000 m. U.S. dollars, for a little island with only a million people. That works out at an average per capita income of U.S. $3,000 per annum which is very high for a small country. Now the accessibility of wealth is causing enormous escalation in alcohol consumption levels. *Per capita* consumption is in excess of 10 litres of absolute alcohol for those aged 15 and over and cirrhoisis of the liver rates bring us somewhere near 6th or 7th in the hemisphere, a region which has some very high wine producing countries like Chile and Martinique which, of course, have very high cirrhoisis rates. We are approximately comparable on these indices to Canada. So, a small and relatively poor country has suddenly become rich, and with these changes have come a sudden escalation in consumption and demand. I've demonstrated statistically that there is a close relationship between the relative price of rum and road traffic accidents, a correlation of $-.978$, an extraordinarily high correlation which permits one to predict the number of road accidents that are going to occur in a year, given that one knows the price of alcohol.

BJA: *Is this rise in consumption merely a result of increased availability?*

MB: Availability is the major factor but socio-cultural factors are also important. The picture is now of sudden industrialisation with the development of iron and steel and other industries, bringing cultural changes which are breaking up patterns of life. In addition to the economic factor of availability, which is still probably the major influence. So you have the situation of increased economic availability plus social-cultural changes. We have many different cultures, but we have a particularly high rate of alcoholism among the East Indian population. Forty per cent of the population of Trinidad is from India. There are roughly equal numbers of Afro West Indians who came from Africa as slaves and indentured labour that came from India. The rates of alcoholism amongst the Indian population are very much higher than among the African population.

BJA: *What treatment facilities are available in Trinidad?*

MB: There is really only one official treatment programme in Trinidad—the one started in 1956. It is housed in a building which stands apart in the grounds of the Mental hospital and it has 20 beds. The emphasis is on short-stay because we don't believe in prolonged stays in hospital, certainly not more than two to three weeks. The focus of treatment is on group therapy. When the treatment began, I used to do group aversion treatment which I think was very effective, but was later abandoned after I stopped running the programme and others took it over. I think they stopped using aversion therapy because Emetine is a toxic substance and people with, for example, cardiomyopothy, need screening, plus the fact that this treatment is very difficult to administer. We now believe that you can probably achieve as much by group persuasion and increased self-esteem, provided partly by the sight of successful recovered alcoholics, as well as general support, as by anything else. So the major programme is very much a traditional programme and based on group therapy and some Antabuse and relaxation techniques, plus a few other things. People have dabbled in psychodrama, for example, but that's not a major treatment yet. Of course, a major input is A.A. and good follow-up with A.A. But even though the treatment is fairly traditional, I think there are small things that make the difference between our programme and others. For example, the extent of the good relations between A.A. and the service is far better than in most other countries that I've seen. In one study we did, something like 90% of the patients thought that the treatment service helped them, and people regard the treatment centre as their own.

BJA: *Is A.A. the same as we know it in the U.K. or North America?*

MB: In the cities it is much the same but outside the towns it has adapted to the local culture in significant ways. In rural Trinidad, A.A. has become a family thing, not like in America. Whole families attend, they sing songs, they serve food, there is a festive atmosphere. We had a recent Anniversary meeting where children got up on the stage and sang songs of how nice life was now that father had stopped drinking and wives got up and sang songs made up specially for the occasion. A.A. is playing the function of an organization that not only provides a chemical-free life and companionship and support, but is actually doing more—it is changing attitudes to alcohol in the country as a whole. There are 115 groups of A.A. in Trinidad, roughly one group to every 10,000 inhabitants, roughly one A.A. member for every 240 people in Trinidad. A.A. has adapted very well in our country and has taken on the particular Trinidadian culture. Perhaps it has done this more so over there than in other countries because it has fallen upon good soil. A.A. began at the same time as the treatment programme in Trinidad, in 1956, and they had the same people running both programmes from the beginning, so there was no conflict and no competition. Moreover there is something in the Indian cultural climate, the group consultation or whatever, which means that this culture lends itself to this kind of family group coming together. The tradition of the Hindu Panchayat, a sort of group of elders who run the villages, may have provided a tradition of group consultation and collectivity. A.A. is culturally suited to the needs and that is why it does so well. I am not saying that A.A. is the only method, but it is the method to hand and it works very well. Perhaps maybe something else will come along, but for the moment, I've not found anything to persuade me to abandon A.A. There are though, people who do not need the total abstinence programme and who don't fit into A.A. and who may not be receiving the help they need. My private consultant practice sees a number of people who want a controlled drinking programme and they can try various approaches, but if they don't succeed, they must, accept abstinence. Of course, there are a range of fringe practitioners, cultural healers for example, pentecostal healers, faith healers of various kinds, who try to treat alcoholics, and I am surprised that they don't have more success. I would have thought that they should have a role and they might produce attitude change, but I suspect that they don't offer adequate follow-up, and follow-up and support is what the A.A. programme seems to do so well.

BJA: *Perhaps you could tell us how you got into this field?*

MB: I graduated from Edinburgh in 1949 which is where I began my psychiatry, but I completed it at the Maudsley. After I returned home, I set up these services in 1956. I first met A.A. in Edinburgh in about 1950. I was assisting Dr. David Clarke in some work on disulfiram and we looked around for alcoholics to try it on. We found a group of six alcoholics who said that they had achieved six months sobriety. We found that their secret had been A.A. that had come across from the United States and were so intrigued that we presented these patients to a case conference. We were thoroughly laughed at and were chided about the association with the Oxford group and they alleged overtones of homosexuality and all sorts of things. They said that if it were such a

Interview with Michael Beaubrun, Trinidad

good thing why didn't we have Psychopathics Anonymous for example? Well, we said 'All we know is that they are doing far better than anyone else has been able to do with them.' And I took that experience back to the West Indies in 1950. By that time I had started to read books about A.A. I could not start A.A. myself because I wasn't an alcoholic, but I started talking to alcoholics in groups in 1951 and introducing them to A.A. ideas. After a further period of study at the Maudsley I returned to the West Indies again in 1956 and it was then that A.A. was born.

BJA: *You also have the role of being a Senator in your Parliament. What have you been doing in this regard?*

MB: Well, I have been a Senator for the past 5 years in Trinidad and Tobago and, in fact, I've just come to the end of a 5-year term during which I have managed to encourage some recognition of the problem of alcoholism. I am proud of the fact that just this last week I got the Attorney General to answer forthright questions that I posed. I have achieved two things. I've got the Ministers of Health for the Commonwealth Caribbean to pass four resolutions on the basis of papers that I presented. Among other things, they have passed a resolution that a reduction in alcohol consumption should be adopted as a goal of health. All they can do is recommend that the individual governments adopt the strategies recommended, but no Government thus far has adopted strategies to reduce availability as a goal of health. Of course, alcohol is so much a part of our way of life in the Caribbean that it would be a mistake to attempt to reduce consumption by too drastic a programme of legal measures. What we recommend is that the relative price of alcohol be prevented from falling by indexing the price of alcohol to the rising cost of living, whilst we attempt to modify our drinking lifestyles by other measures, such as education. This was adopted as part of Resolution 26 on Alcoholism. The question I put to the Attorney General of Trinidad in the final stages of Parliament was 'Is the Government of Trinidad and Tobago planning to implement Resolution 26?' And he said consideration was being given to it. I also posed questions about advertising and the breathalyser.

BJA: *What is happening with the breathalyser?*

MB: Well, they asked me to recommend a level and I suggested it should not be lower than 80 mg.%. I don't believe there is much point in making it very low even though there is evidence that people will be adversely affected by much lower levels. But there is no point in proposing a very low level when it frightens the legislators—they think they are going to get caught themselves. In fact, I actually took a small Alcoholmeter into Parliament with me last December. At lunch break, the Attorney General and the Foreign Minister, had been out to lunch. They came back a bit later in the middle of my speech. I offered to demonstrate the Alcoholmeter right there and then in Parliament. They came forward and actually allowed me to breathalyse them. They were so pleased to find that neither of them would have been convicted of dangerous driving and that their breath levels were quite safe. The Attorney General said 'this is very good, we must get one of these at once'—a demonstration which obviously enhanced the prospects of the breathalyser being adopted.

BJA: *What are your views on liquor advertising?*

MB: I have been calling for restrictions on advertising and asking for warning labels. There are no guidelines on this. There is one particular campaign called 'Rum is Macho'—it is everywhere and shows alcohol as glamorous and sexy. We, the National Council have brought out our own poster showing a wrecked car which says 'Rum is Smasho' and underneath that the line 'and Whisky too'. We have another poster, our 'Anti-Macho' poster showing the male sex symbol made to droop by alcohol and above it is written the quotation from Shakespeare's Macbeth 'it provoketh the appetite and reduceth the performance'. The Minister of Health came out and told the T.V. to stop all advertising of alcohol and tobacco, but as he had no authority to do this the ads have continued.

BJA: *How are your own alcohol producers reacting to all this?*

MB: They are making small concessions. They give the National Council on Alcoholism donations and they are definitely moderating the tone of their advertising. It may be significant that the liquor producers themselves revised rum prices by 20 per cent after my speech in a Budget Debate. Of course, they are modifying their advertising voluntarily because they don't want to force harsh legislation.

BJA: *You are also President of the National Council on Alcoholism. How does that organization operate?*

MB: We are a Voluntary body. The Government gives us some subsidy and the rest of the money is raised from the private sector. We have a full-time paid Executive Director and, of course, voluntary helpers. We have offices in the North and the South, with three full-time staff members and they do a good job. We do a lot of programmes for schools. If you just send out people to talk to 6th formers at school and they are not very informed themselves and are not capable of fielding the questions and giving the appropriate information, they can do more harm than good. So along with enthusiastic A.A. members, you do need professional staff. In addition to education, the N.C.A. does many of the same things that N.C.A. does in the United Kingdom and the U.S.A., such as counselling. We also arrange events like Alcoholism Awareness Week, where we usually bring in guest speakers from abroad, have poster campaigns, banners, calypsos, plays put on. Alcoholism education is everywhere. The rest of the year we are doing the same thing, but on a smaller scale.

BJA: *It has been said that prohibition in the U.S. brought all the trappings of an illicit alcohol trade to the Caribbean. Is that true?*

MB: Yes this is true in the Bahamas especially. The Volstead Act made the Bahamas rich but brought them many problems. And just now we have a similar thing, with the spin-offs from the decriminalisation of marijuana in the United States. Cannabis has been decriminalised in many American States and they say there is no great harm, but it has in fact created problems in other countries, ours included. Nearby countries which have access to marijuana are now a major source of supply. You can't create a market by decriminalisation without providing any supply. So what happens is that immediately criminals move off-shore to where they think the police forces are less strong, or where they can be bribed, they begin to wreak hovoc in places like Columbia or Jamaica. Columbia exports 4 billion U.S. dollars worth of marijuana every year. Of course, marijuana is illegal, although it was legal up till 1925 in Trinidad and in Guyana even later. There used to be licenses to sell marijuana, but Mr. Aubrey Frazer, Head of the Law School at our University recently produced a Paper reviewing all the laws on cannabis over the entire region, and clearly demonstrated that the problems related to cannabis developed only after the drug was banned.

Some people are now advocating that places like Jamaica should legalise marijuana and openly benefit from the market created by decriminalization in the U.S., but this course has not been adopted and we have not recommended it because of other reasons. There are some hazards with cannabis use and we are not yet sure what the effects of a permissive liberal attitude to it would be at this stage of our development. However, we have recommended that there should be no harsh penalties for simple possession.

BJA: *Do you think that your experience in the West Indies may have relevance for other developing countries?*

MB: Only to a limited extent. Drug problems, including legitimized drugs like alcohol can only be understood in the socio-cultural context. For that reason there are few universal rules. Each culture must decide what are its problems and what measures are appropriate to solve them.

On the whole alcohol-related problems are probably best dealt with by a judicious mixture of control strategies and demand strategies. It seems to me that the control strategies like price manipulation and the regulation of production, marketing and sale are more effective measures than attempts to reduce demand by education and treatment. However, there are limits to the effectiveness of control and as we have seen excessive controls like prohibition may be counterproductive. In any case our major problem is influencing the public to do what needs to be done. We in the Caribbean are still probing for ways of minimising the damage due to the two drugs in most widespread use, alcohol and marijuana.

26

Interview with Jorge Mardones, Chile

JORGE MARDONES, b. 1908. MD University of Chile. Junior appointments in that university before becoming Professor of Biochemistry in 1932 and of Pharmacology in 1936; professor emeritus since 1975. Minister of Public Health and Social Welfare 1950–52. Founder member and first chairman of Latin American Association for the Study of Alcohol and Drug Dependence and involved in many learned societies. Work for WHO.

BJA: *I think that readers of this Journal might be interested to know the reasons why a pharmacologist like you, working at a university in the farthest corner of the world, has been focussing on biological aspects of alcoholism for more than 40 years. Could you tell us something about this?*

JM: To answer that question I better start at the beginning and tell you how I got going on this line of work. When I was still a medical student at the Universidad de Chile I took the first step in my academic career as an instructor in the Department of Physiological and Pathological Chemistry of Professor Eduardo Cruz-Coke, whom I consider my real master. Shortly after my M.D., I was elected Professor of Biochemistry and Nutrition in the Institute of Physical Education of the same University, but I continued to work in Cruz-Coke's laboratory. There I gradually shifted to experimental pharmacology, a subject in which I became 'professor extraordinario' (something similar to 'Privatdozent' in German universities) and afterwards full professor in the Faculty of Medicine.

BJA: *What at that time were the leading scientific ideas which influenced you?*

JM: Having a biochemical background and being orientated simultaneously to nutrition and pharmacology, I was deeply impressed by papers coming from the group of Curt P. Richter,[1-7] which appeared in the 1920s to early 40s. These authors reported that when laboratory rats were offered a free choice of pure nutrients in separate containers, they consumed a diet that was practically equivalent to that found experimentally as the best fitted to normal development and reproduction. I was specially interested in the finding that rats exhibit a specific appetite for ethanol—a substance that is at the same time a nutrient and a drug. In fact, rats recognize ethanol in water solution in concentrations as low as 2%. When offered free choice between distilled water and ethanol solutions from 2% to 5%, they preferred these solutions to water. It is also very important that Richter's group reported that rats are able to match the amount of single nutrients consumed to the pathologically altered requirements induced by, for instance, pancreatectomy, adrenalectomy or deprivation of vitamins of the B complex.

BJA: *If that was the scientific background, what influenced your immediate decision to start personal experimental work in this area?*

JM: I don't know exactly what influenced my decision to study this question experimentally. I was impressed by the clinical history of a friend who suffered from severe alcoholism and who consulted me about dermatological and neurological symptoms which appeared to be the consequence of vitamin deficiencies. This patient recovered with thiamin injections and oral administration of brewer's yeast, and at the same time his appetite for alcohol decreased in such a way that he easily remained abstinent for some months. Our first experiments were performed in a very modest laboratory at the Institute of Physical Education, where we received stimulating help from the Director, Joaquín Cabezas, who was an eminent educator trained in Sweden.

BJA: *So what was the initial line of experimentation?*

Interview with Jorge Mardones, Chile 387

JM: In order to explain our approach it's necessary to understand that at that time basic knowledge of biochemical processes and pathologies was less accurate than today. At the blackboard it was clear that the decarboxylation of pyruvate produces acetaldehyde, which is also the first product of the metabolic breakdown of ethanol. It was also known that this decarboxylation was blocked by thiamin deficiency, whilst this vitamin is not necessary for the formation of acetaldehyde from ethanol. The question naturally arose as to whether thiamin deprivation would induce an increase of ethanol consumption.

BJA: *That question led directly to the first experiment?*

JM: The experiments were rather easy to perform. Rats were fed on a diet which the only source of B vitamins was brewer's yeast autoclaved in an alkaline medium, and offered a free choice of 10% ethanol solution or distilled water. The result[8] was that these rats consumed significantly higher amounts of ethanol solution than the controls fed on a diet containing equivalent proportions of untreated yeast. When these experimental rats received a supplement of thiamin, the signs of its deprivation disappeared, but ethanol consumption did not decrease. In contradistinction, when they were shifted to the control diet, ethanol intake reverted to the basic level. This fact led us to think about a new factor present in untreated yeast.

BJA: *What happened about this factor?*

JM: Since we could not obtain active extracts from yeast or liver, we had to abandon this line after years of unfruitful work. We suspect that maybe Westerfeld & Lawrow[9] were right when they ascribed the increase of ethanol intake induced by thiamin deprivation to a compensation for the decrease in solid food intake that was also observed in that situation. This would explain why we only observed a decrease of ethanol intake when important amounts of supplement of dry yeast or dry liver were given.

BJA: *So that line of research appeared to be closed. In what direction did you go next?*

JM: Fortunately in the course of these experiments an important fact came to light. We observed wide interindividual variations in drinking behaviour among rats fed on a purified diet supplemented with the known vitamins. Some rats drank very low amounts of ethanol solution and others consumed daily more than 10 grams of ethanol per kg of body weight. We reported these findings[10] in a short paper in the *Boletin de la Sociedad de Biologia, Santiago, Chile,* a journal of rather local diffusion. At about the same time R. J. Williams and co-workers, who were working on biochemical individuality and its genetic origin reported on a similar observation. Williams took these facts as a basis for this theory on the genetic origin of alcoholism, from which it was deduced that this disease could be cured by the administration of vitamins.[11] Since this treatment did not work, the theory was disregarded. Williams would have been right if he had talked about genetic origins for the appetite for alcohol.

BJA: *Out of initial difficulties and disappointments, you made observations which led to a new line of research?*

JM: In 1948 we started on the artificial selection of Wistar rats through inbreeding males and females exhibiting equivalent voluntary consumption of ethanol under free choice conditions. In this way we obtained two strains, which we now denominate UChA (low ethanol consumer) and UChB (high ethanol consumer). The results of generation F_1 were consistent with the genetic transmission of the behavioural trait expressed in the amount of voluntary ethanol intake. We published a conclusive demonstration of this thesis in a short paper in the *Quarterly Journal of Studies on Alcohol* in 1953[12] in which we reported a highly significant hereditary coefficient in our rats of the first seven generations of inbreeding.

BJA: *Would you say that the results obtained remained isolated facts without general importance or did these findings have wider impact?*

JM: The genetic character of the appetite for alcohol was confirmed by McClearn & Rodgers[12] in mouse strains, and at the present time there are several strains of rats and mice exhibiting characteristic levels of voluntary ethanol consumption. These strains have been employed as useful tools in research concerning the mechanisms of appetite and satiety for alcohol. In fact, the search for characteristics which correlate with voluntary alcohol intake as well as the effect of drugs on alcohol consumption in each strain, are methods which allow some progress in understanding the relevant mechanism of appetite and satiety. As regards my own laboratory, we followed during many years a line of work looking for strain differences concerning metabolic pathways for different substrates, as well as examining the impact of alcohol on these processes.

BJA: *How did you develop this new line?*

JM: These studies were possible because Natividad Segovia—who collaborated in our experiments and continues to do until the present—was awarded a fellowship by the Williams-Waterman Fund of the Research Corporation, which enabled her to work for a year in the Nutrition Department of Harvard University under the direction of Professor Mark Hegsted. During her stay, she learned methods for studying the metabolism of substrates labelled with radioactive carbon. Coming back to Chile she received a grant from the Fund which allowed us to obtain the necessary equipment to continue her experiments here.

BJA: *Let's turn to another issue. E. M. Jellinek, a very important man in the field of alcoholism, wrote a book which became a classic called* The Disease Concept of Alcoholism[13] *which he dedicated to you 'in Friendship'. I see in your library copy that he also wrote "with particular gratitude to a man whose wisdom and knowledge has been a great stimulus for me, Bunky." Can you tell us something about the origin of this friendship?*

JM: In the early fifties we received a visit from Professor Jellinek—as you say, widely known for his important contributions to this field. He came here to assist our Public Health Service in studying the characteristics of the Chilean alcoholism problem in order to have a basis for prevention strategies. Thus started my friendship with him which lasted till he died. When he came to Chile, he was assistant to the Mental Health Department of the World Health Organisation in Geneva. At the time I was invited to join the Expert Panel for Addictive Drugs of WHO, a position in which I continue to serve today. In this capacity I attended two successive Expert Commitees on Alcohol and Alcoholism in 1953 and 1954, at which for the first time biochemists, pharmacologists and psychiatrists sat around the same table to discuss fundamental aspects of the problem of alcoholism. Jellinek was the promoter of these meetings. After the first meeting I was awarded a travel grant by WHO, that allowed me to enter in contact with several key persons in Europe. The itinerary for this trip was arranged by Jellinek. Undoubtedly this view of the problem at the human level enriched my mind in such a way that after the unfruitful work of searching for changes in the metabolism of nutriments correlated with alcohol appetite, we gradually changed the focus of our research.

BJA: *I know that the first public event honouring the memory of Professor Jellinek was a symposium held in Santiago de Chile. Would you like to tell us something about this symposium?*

JM: In August 1966, shortly after Jellinek's death we organized an International Symposium on Alcohol and Alcoholism in his memory. This was possible due to the local support given by the University of Chile and by our Public Health Service and we were also helped by important contributions from the World Health Organization, and specially its Regional Office for the Americas (PAHO). We had the honour of visits from experts on alcohol and alcoholism from all over the world, and that was the start of several friendships. The papers from this Symposium were published in English under the title *Alcohol and Alcoholism*, edited by Robert Popham of the Addiction Research Foundation in Toronto,[14] and in Spanish as a supplement of the *Archivos de Biologia y Medicina Experimentales,* edited by Anibal Varela and myself.[15]

BJA: *Going back to your research, you were telling us that you changed your approach to research on alcoholism. How would you describe this new approach?*

JM: In general scientific authors do not discuss the leading ideas of their experiments, because the emphasis of scientific papers is on facts rather than interpretations. I think that the aim of your question is to uncover something about the underlying ideas of our recent research. Let me try to answer very briefly. The specific appetite and satiety for alcohol exhibited by experimental animals implies the presence of a neurophysiological mechanism. At the present this mechanism is a 'black box'. Laboratory men are very fond of looking into black boxes. If the same mechanisms exist in human beings, alcoholism can be considered as a disturbance of these mechanisms, specially those involved with satiety. Experience teaches that no disturbance of a biological mechanism can be understood in such a way that allows rational actions to correct it, when the normal mechanism is not clearly known. Thus we decided that we have to contribute to opening that black box.

BJA: *Is there anything known about this black box?*

JM: Something is known. First, that alcohol appetite is related to that of calories, as Westerfeld & Lawrow demonstrated many years ago.[9] Second, that satiety for alcohol is also related to that of calories, as Marfaing-Jallat, Larue & Le Magnen demonstrated by reporting that rats submitted to lesions of the so called 'satiety center' in the ventromedial hypothalamus, increased the voluntary intake of alcohol, in such a way that these animals became obese by the extra calories provided by ethanol.[16] Third, it is clear that when rats drink ethanol solution they also ingest water and thus is is to be expected that the mechanisms of thirst and satiety for water may interfere with the ingestion of those solutions. Fourth, many facts are consistent with the idea that the acetaldehyde level in blood and/or in neurones is the trigger for the satiety mechanism for alcohol.

BJA: *And going on from those premises?*

JM: From these premises it is evident that in studies about appetite and satiety for ethanol, the simultaneous effects of any experimental condition in the consumptions of ethanol solution, water and solid food, must be registered. These experimental conditions can be established by electrolytical lesions or electric stimulation of single central nuclei or pathways, as well as through the administration of drugs known to stimulate or block specific central synapses. Our tools—perhaps because we are pharmacologists—are central acting drugs applied to rats of our two stains, in which the voluntary consumption of 10% ethanol solution, distilled water and solid food are measured. In the last 5 years we have reported on results of individual drugs, and we feel that we are close to postulating a tentative model for the mechanism of specific appetite and satiety for ethanol, founded on the results of other authors and of ourselves.

BJA: *It is well known that research work is more difficult in countries like yours than in more developed ones. What is your view on this matter?*

JM: Of course, experimental work is more difficult in the countries of the so called Third World, than in the developed ones. We progress at a rather slow rate, but with the necessary accuracy. I do not know why there is a generalized attitude of doubt concerning results reported in papers coming from Latin American laboratories. In order to overcome this situation, we need to be extremely certain about the accuracy and high significance of our results, before submitting a paper for publication. I feel that it is an advantage, because the worst thing a scientist can do is to pollute the scientific environment with data of poor value.

References

1. Richter, C. P. (1926) A study of the effect of moderate doses of alcohol on the growth and behavior of the rat, *Journal of experimental Zoology,* 44, pp. 397–418.
2. Richter, C. P. (1936) Increased salt appetite in adrenalectomized rats, *American Journal of Physiology,* 115, pp. 155–161.
3. Richter, C. P. & Eckert, J. F. (1937) Increased calcium appetite of parathyroidectomized rats, *Endocrinology,* 21, pp. 50–54.
4. Richter, C. P., Holt, L. E. & Barelare, B. Jr. (1938) Nutritional requirements for normal growth and reproduction in rats studied by the self-selection method, *American Journal of Physiology,* 122, pp. 734–744.
5. Richter, C. P., Holt, L.E. Jr., Barelare, J. Jr. & Hawkes, C. D. (1938) Changes in fat, carbohydrate and protein appetite in vitamin B deficiency, *American Journal of Physiology,* 124, pp. 596–602.

5. Richter, C. P., Holt, L.E. Jr., Barelare, J. Jr. & Hawkes, C. D. (1938) Changes in fat, carbohydrate and protein appetite in vitamin B deficiency, *American Journal of Physiology,* 124, pp. 596–602.
6. Richter, C. P. & Campbell, K. H. (1940) Alcohol taste thresholds and concentrations of solution preferred by rats, *Science,* 91, pp. 507–508.
7. Richter, C. P. & Schmidt, E. D. H. Jr. (1941) Increased fat and decreased carbohydrates appetite of pancreatectomized rats, *Endocrinology,* 28, pp. 179–192.
8. Mardones, J. & Onfray, E. (1942) Influencia de una substancia de la levadura (¿elemento del complejo vitamínico B?) sobre el consumo de alcohol en ratas en experimentos de autoselección, (Effect of a substance of yeast (element of B vitamin complex?) on alcohol intake by rats in self-selection experiments), *Revista Chilena de Higiene y Medicina Preventiva,* 4, pp. 293–297.
9. Westerfeld, W. W. & Lawrow, J. (1953) The effect of calorie restriction and thiamin deficiency on the voluntary consumption of alcohol by rats, *Quarterly Journal of Studies on Alcohol,* 14, pp. 378–384.
10. Mardones, J., Hederra, A. & Segovia, N. (1949) Fluctuación individual del consumo de alcohol en ratas carenciadas (Individual fluctuation of alcohol intake by rats fed on deficient diet) *Boletín de la Sociedad de Biología de Santiago de Chile,* 7, pp. 1–2 [In *Revista de Medicina y Alimentación,* Chile, 8]
11. Williams, R. J., Berry, L. J. & Beerstecher, E. Jr. (1949) Biochemical individuality: III Genetotrophic factors in the etiology of alcoholism, *Archives of Biochemistry,* 23, pp. 275–290.
12. Mardones, J., Segovia, N. & Hederra, A. (1953) Heredity of experimental alcohol preference in rats: II Coefficient of heredity, *Quarterly Journal of Studies on Alcohol,* 14, pp. 1–2.
13. McClearn, G. E. & Rodgers, D. A. (1959) Differences in alcohol preference among inbred strains of mice, *Quarterly Journal of Studies on Alcohol,* 20, pp. 691–695.
14. Jellinek, E. M. (1960) *The Disease Concept of Alcoholism* (Highland Park, N. J., Hillhouse).
15. Popham, R. E. (Ed.) (1970) *Alcohol and Alcoholism* (Toronto, Addiction Research Foundation).
16. Mardones, J. & Varela, A. (Eds) (1969) *Simposio Internacional sobre Alcohol y Alcoholismo, Archivos de Biología y Medicina Experimentales, Suplemento No. 3.*
17. Marfaing-Jallat, P., Larue, C. & Le Magnen, J. (1970) Alcohol intake in Hypothalamic hyperphagic rats, *Physiology and Behavior,* 5, pp. 345–351.

27

Interview with Jaroslav Skála, Czechoslovakia

JAROSLAV SKÁLA. *Obtained MD degree at Charles University, Prague; further studies in psychology and sociology. Has played central role in developing that country's treatment response to alcohol problems. Head of "Apolinar" alcohol treatment centre in Prague, 1948–1982. Expert Advisor to Czech Ministry of Health 1953–83. Director of Studies ICAA 1959–66 and Temporary Adviser to WHO 1966–76.*

BJA: *'Skála' and 'Apolinář' are almost synonymous in Czechoslovakia. First of all we should like to know what Skála had been before the Apolinar. You were born in Pilsen, in the town known for its production of Pilsner Urquell beer. Did you study in Prague?*

JS: I studied medicine at Charles University in Prague and at the same time I attended the Institute of Physical Training and Sports. After graduating from both of these faculties I read psychology and sociology at the university. In 1946 I started to work at the Psychiatric Clinic in Prague.

BJA: *What made you specialize in alcoholism?*

JS: One month after my coming to the clinic Professor Hořejší, chairman of the Czechoslovak Abstinent Union, was looking for a doctor to send to Brussels to the first postwar conference on alcoholism. He chose me. I went there and grasped the size of the problem. After my return I studied the alcoholism literature very thoroughly (including Jellinek, whom I did not meet personally until 1961) and decided to try out emetine therapy, which up to then had not been practised in our country.

BJA: So it was a coincidence, an external stimulus, a desire to enter an unmapped area? Later you surely asked yourself the question whether behind this conscious motivation there had not been a hidden reason of a more personal nature...

JS: Neither I nor anybody of my family had problems with alcohol dependence, if that is what you have in mind. I personally had been an alcohol consumer but a few years after the beginning of my work with alcoholics I myself started to abstain totally. I did have several experiences with drunkards in my childhood but I do not think they had any decisive influence on my orientation. A greater role was probably played by a certain feature of my character, manifested since my early youth—a tendency to help the weaker not by talking but by acting, energetically, rather directively, like a coach.

BJA: So you began applying emetine therapy...

JS: We started it with Dr Janda in 1947. We soon flooded the clinic with alcoholics. It was necessary to establish a separate department. At its birth stood another important realization. At that time, in the fifties, the biological therapy of alcoholism soon spread but the patients relapsed a lot. Psychotherapy was being neglected. It was necessary to work deeper and longer with the patients, even after the basic treatment. This gave rise to the sociotherapeutic club TROTTING (Czech abbreviation for 'Club of those Striving for Sobriety' KLUS) which is a few months older than the inpatient treatment in the Apolinář. It has been meeting ceaselessly every Thursday since 1948—tomorrow I chair its 1845th session.

BJA: Is it something in the style of AA?

JS: We were originally inspired by AA but the Club soon acquired its own specific features. I did not want to leave the patients by themselves—besides, the unified system of Czechoslovak health care would have to have a medical worker in charge of such an institution anyway—and so the Club became a platform for cooperation between patients and therapists. That ensured a certain continuity of work and prevented some dangers sometimes encountered in AA, several of whose groups disintegrated or were misled by psychopathic personalities. And then there is another specific trait—the Club meets on the premises of the alcoholism treatment centre, and its participants are the patients under treatment together with those who had gone through it. Thus already during the basic treatment we form a link between the patient and the Club, which can help in the post-treatment period.

BJA: *Were there any foreign models at the birth of the Apolinář any practical experience with similar therapeutic institutions, or theoretical models?*

JS: I had neither practical experience nor explicit theoretical models. I have a respect for theory but I have always been primarily a man of practice. I think that too much emphasis on theory and too great a link to a certain theoretical model sometimes creates *a priori* approaches and barriers, and somewhat hinders live creative work with patients. I am convinced that it is better to use theoretical knowledge mainly for 'tuning up' a system already working. I was pleased to find repeatedly that theoretical works confirmed what we had already practised before. The Apolinář had for instance many characteristics of a therapeutic community from its very beginning; M. Jones published his works in the second half of the fifties and I was able to get acquainted with them as late as the sixties. It was similar with social learning theory . . . our intuition was not bad.

BJA: *What is your attitude towards the other trends in psychotherapy?*

JS: In the Apolinář system there are many elements of behaviour therapy. I did not like psychoanalysis, though in 1948 in Switzerland I had the opportunity to hear the lectures of Anna Freud. Not until recent years did I somewhat revise my attitude to psychoanalysis; I studied with interest Kernberg, Kohut, Balint, the Blanks. I surely missed a lot and in some respects I did not give the patients their due during my neglect of the analytic approach.

BJA: *Your therapeutic system has its own specific features, some aspects of treatment can be regarded as European and world priorities. Is there anything you would like to add?*

JS: In 1951 our department set up the first 'sobering-up station' (detoxification centre) in the world run as a medical institution. I proposed this move as early as 1949. Acutely intoxicated persons are usually brought to the sobering-up station by the police but from the point of arrival they are solely in the hands of our medical staff. The medical staff are helped by the patients treated in the department and this work in the sobering-up station represents for them one of the psychologically very significant components of their treatment.

We discovered comparatively early the importance of the *length* of the treatment. The 3-week treatment which was—and often still is—common in the world, is in my opinion good for 'standing the patient on his legs'. However, on these legs he often walks only to the nearest pub. After this opening phase of the treatment, concentrated primarily on the basic physical rehabilitation, another couple of weeks must follow which are filled with a demanding therapeutic programme—community therapy, movement therapy, culture therapy, education therapy etc, ended by a 10-day daytime attendance. The basic voluntary treatment in our department takes 13 weeks, relapse treatment 4 to 6 months, compulsory treatment 4 to 11 months.

BJA: *Can you say something more about the Czechoslovak system of alcoholism care in the development of which you played a fundamental role? What precedes the treatment in your department, what follows?*

JS: The basic system was formed in the fifties. Now there are 30 inpatient therapeutic institutions in Czechoslovakia with a capacity of 1500 beds (Czechoslovakia has 15 million inhabitants). There is a network of more than 200 clinics providing outpatient services. With the help of these centres (especially when the outpatient type of care fails), the patient gets into the inpatient department from where he is later again referred to the outpatient centre care.

The Apolinář developed its own system of post-treatment therapy. In regular intervals the patients return to the inpatient department to undergo one-week revision treatment sometimes performed in the form of intensive therapeutic stays in the country. They take part in the work of the sociotherapeutic club. In this way the patients can and should, in the course of 10 years after the basic treatment, go through the post-treatment therapeutic programme in the time range equalling the length of the basic treatment.

From among our former patients we have gained a number of efficient co-workers helping mainly with the sociotherapeutic Club work. One of them is the already 20-years abstaining head of the biggest alcoholism treatment centre in Czechoslovakia which is situated in a beautiful castle in South Bohemia.

BJA: So the Apolinář kept growing . . .

JS: It did not, rather it differentiated and separated into specialized units. For years there were very few of us and even later our numbers did not increase much. I do not envy anybody who has many co-workers at his disposal. For that often leads to the situation where the pivot of the interaction is transferred to the team of the therapists, and the patients are thus deprived of the interaction.

Already in the first years we differentiated three types of treatment: voluntary treatment, compulsory treatment ordered by health authorities, and protective treatment ordered by the court. In 1958 was established a separate therapeutic institution for compulsory treatment and relapses (but the patients start and end their long-term treatment in the Apolinář). Twenty-five beds at the Research Institute of Penology, which came into being in 1967, were occupied by patients who had been sentenced for alcohol related crimes and who were undergoing their alcoholism treatment ordered by the court already during their prison sentence, mainly in the form of evening sessions of the group-psychotherapy type. In this work also some of our former patients participated as lay therapists who often waited at the prison gates for their charges after their release, and helped them with many social problems.

In 1971 a separate therapeutic institution was established for women, containing 32 beds. In 1967 there came into existence the Child, Youth and Family Centre, providing the necessary educative, advisory and psychiatric care for the patients' families. It organizes for instance summer holiday camps for the patients' children who are often physically deprived, holidays for entire families with family therapy done in community and group form; the Centre is regularly visited by school classes who come to listen to talks that are part of health promotion. In 1971 the Drug Dependence Centre was founded, which provides outpatient care and sends its patients to the inpatient department where they are treated together with alcohol-dependent persons.

BJA: *Thus differentiation, specialization, rather than increase of capacity. You evidently and personally wanted to spend your time not mainly managing your subordinates but in contact with your patients.*

JS: That is right. In addition, I did not have the professional and private spheres of my life strictly separated. After my divorce I was in the department practically day and night. I had a pleasant work apartment there. I saw the patients as early as 6 a.m. at the morning gymnastics and I ended the day reading the notes of often all 50 patients, handed in at 9 p.m. At my morning meeting with the staff or with the whole therapeutic community I was informed of what was going on. I also liked to participate in the work therapy with the patients in the garden of our department. I practically did not leave the patients, except for my trips abroad, the longest of which took 6 weeks.

BJA: *Could you say something more about these trips and about your international professional contacts?*

JS: At the beginning there was that conference in Brussels in 1946 and in 1956 I attended the World congress in Istanbul. In 1966 I became a member of the alcoholism advisory board of WHO. In the same year I was in Chile at the WHO conference dedicated to the memory of E. M. Jellinek, in 1968 in Washington, then in Britain, Norway, Yugoslavia . . . In 1970 I made by longest trip, lecturing in Australia, New Zealand, the U.S.A. and France.

I consider it a great honour to have been able to meet in person such pioneers in alcoholism work as Jellinek, Tongue, Mrs Moser of the WHO, D. Archibald (Canada), Fouquet (France), Glatt & Edwards (Britain), Krauwell (Holland), Strělčuk (U.S.S.R.), von Wartburg (Switzerland) and others. On my trips abroad I gathered information from various sources, but I also tried to offer experiences of my own.

BJA: So that you applied the system 'take and give' which you 'enforce in the patient's relation to the therapeutic institution,' also in international contacts. Are you also engaged in research work, has your system been a subject of research?

JS: I would mention three research studies that I consider the most significant. In 1976–1980 it was the research of Dr. Matějček and Dr. Kmošková 'Children of Alcoholic Fathers'. Their findings were confirmed by a later American study with which I became acquainted in Chicago in 1983. Further it was my own study 'Invalidity and Alcohol' which proved that it was primarily alcohol that was responsible for invaliding several thousand people in Czechoslovakia out of work in the course of 5 years. The most extensive research was conducted in the Apolinář, in the years 1971–80 (by the authors Kubička and Pintová), analysing in detail our entire therapeutic system from the point of view of the effectiveness of the treatment. It confirmed objectively the long-term therapeutic results we had stated before: 1 year after treatment in the department 45% abstained, after 3 years 35%, after 5 years 25% of all patients—but the results of patients who had *finished* the treatment (there were 72% of those) were always 10% better. It was also shown that the treatment of patients with satisfactory family conditions could be shortened by a few weeks without any harmful effects. I should like to mention that the research itself that was being done in the department had a positive influence on the patients—the patients treated at the time of the research (1971–80) turned out to be the most successful 'Apolinář generation' from the abstinence point of view.

BJA: I am certain you are engaged in alcoholism prevention in your country. Has this work of yours taken any special form?

JS: Ten years ago I offered the leader of the Linha Singers Chorus the script of a programme in which music alternated with the words of a doctor and discussion with the audience. In the course of 10 years we gave more than 250 performances of the programme and in this way I talked with more than 70 thousand young people. Now I cooperate in a similar form with the Baroque Jazz Quintet in an anti-smoking programme—all members of the group gradually gave up smoking and they go in for jogging; when performing in the country they organize football matches where they play the listeners—and usually win . . .

BJA: The lecturing and literary work obviously represents a significant part of your activities after your retirement in 1982, when you handed over the management of your department to Dr. Mareček, MD.

JS: I am finishing several books on alcoholism treatment problems, then the revised 4th edition of a popular booklet, and my part in the collective monograph on alcohol and drug dependence therapy. After handing in all the manuscripts I intend to start writing my memoirs.

However for the last 15 years an important part of my work has been the training of doctors and psychologists in psychotherapy. It has become a sort of my 'second career', to which I now devote the maximum of my time and endeavour. It is long-term training (basic training lasts 400–500 hours followed by supervision), work with groups, communities and clubs. Most of the participants are about 30 years old and so I regard this work as a rare opportunity for a fruitful intergenerational dialogue.

BJA: The last question—how do you feel on the eve of your seventieth birthday?

JS: I can honestly say that I feel less 'worn out' than I myself expected. I have invested much in my work, but on the other hand it has given me much in return. This I should like to emphasize for others, as well. You have already mentioned our principle 'take and give'. I have given a great deal to my work but I think I have gained much more from it for myself. That is why I not only want to continue it but I also feel obliged to do so.

28

Interview with Ignacy Wald, Poland

> IGNACY WALD, b. 1923. Medical training in Poland with subsequent postgraduate experience in Russia and the UK: MD, DSc. Head, Department of Genetics, Institute of Psychiatry and Neurology, Warsaw, and since 1977 Professor. Since 1975 Chairman, Polish Expert Advisory Group on Alcohol and since 1981 Head, Polish National Research Programmes on Prevention of Alcohol and Drug Problems. Work for WHO and ICAA.

BJA: Can you tell me something about your professional background?

IW: I'm a physician. I specialized as a neurologist and wrote my doctoral thesis in neurology, on aphasia in polyglots (people who speak many languages). Then I became interested in metabolic and genetic approaches. I worked with Lionel Penrose at the Galton Laboratory in London. Later I started a department of genetics in our Institute. In 1961 I became Director of Research at this Institute, and have continued in this position ever since.

BJA: Your initial training was in Poland?

IW: My undergraduate training, in British rather than American terms, was at Wroclaw University, and later in the medical academy in Wroclaw. I completed my doctoral studies in Moscow, at the Institute of Neurology which is part of the Academy of Medical Sciences in the U.S.S.R. I continued my studies in the metabolism of the nervous system at the Institute of Neurology in London, and in genetics at the Galton Laboratory. I then worked in neurology and on the genetic aspects of mental retardation. Then in the early '70s, while I was responsible for research in our Institute, I was asked to try and arrange support for alcohol research.

BJA: *Before that you had not been involved in alcohol research?*

IW: That's right. As a matter of fact I am a drinker and that was my only obvious link with alcohol! But in 1960 I wrote a casuistic paper on alcohol (Wald & Gadomska, 1961) and so had to read about it. Though I had some knowledge of the topic, I didn't work on it, nor at the time did I feel like working on it. It was a field that was over-populated with people who were active but not always competent. Everybody knew the questions were important, but they weren't interesting from a research or scientific point of view.

BJA: *The field was dominated by what you might call temperance interests?*

IW: A kind of temperance perspective influenced by people who were very active in the treatment position and who had created a set of rituals which were rather close to analysis.

BJA: *So where did the requests to you come from in the early '70s? Was it from the government?*

IW: Yes, the government considered drinking to be a health problem. So I tried to look into the matter, and very shortly afterwards they asked me to become the Chairman of the Government Advisory Board on Alcohol. The board served as an advisory body to the Government Commission on Alcohol. I refused, as I was interested in genetics and mental retardation, and I recommended somebody else. He was appointed for 3 years. At the end of this period the request to me was repeated. It was the type of invitation which you would call 'an offer you couldn't refuse'.

BJA: *So when did that happen?*

IW: 1975.

BJA: What kind of concerns really lay behind this awakening government interest?

IW: Drinking had become a big problem for the state. It was probably realized that there was a need for scientific knowledge. Without proper research on this subject there would be only myths. The members of the Commission held the rank of Deputy Minister.

BJA: That would be a sign that it was seen as an important issue?

IW: Yes, it was a sign that in 1972 there was a special government executive order to strengthen the struggle against drunkenness.

BJA: So when you agreed to become Chairman of the Advisory Board that came with the commitment from the government for some resources for research?

IW: No, support for research had come in the early '70s, in 1973, but only in terms of a very small sum which people could apply for from different institutions. We started to select some research directions and develop them. It was my feeling that the alcohol field, excluding some very important persons (some of whom were about to retire), was a very neglected field. It had no standing either within the universities or within the research institute. The task was that of creating an alcohol research community. When I became the Chairman of the Advisory Board, they asked me to prepare a report on alcohol. I refused to do it very quickly, and when we started, it took more than 2 years to prepare the report. We tried to bring a newer tune into these things. Mainly we didn't talk about fighting alcoholism, but we talked about alcohol policy. The name of the paper was: Report on Alcohol Policy. The approach to alcohol should be a kind of systems approach and not just a treatment or purely an oppressive approach. I should say that in going at this a great role should be assigned to the Purple Book (Brunn *et al.*, 1975) as a *catalogue natale.* Our approach went on the same lines.

BJA: You had contact at that point with Kettil Brunn?

IW: Yes, it was 1977, something like that. It was very important to talk to Kettil and to have this report.

BJA: Was your report on Alcohol Policy published?

IW: It was an official government report and only 100 copies were prepared. It came out in 1978 and I think that it played some role in changing the alcohol situation in Poland. You may know that this was the time in Poland when there was what might be called 'success propaganda'. The existence of any negative indications in terms of social pathology were simply suppressed, so the possibility of any publication on alcohol was very limited. But one of the results of our report was that much more started to be published about alcohol problems. Also in 1978 Poland organized an international congress and this was part of an effort to open up the agenda on alcohol. In 1980 we pressed the government to publish our report in a more public form. The first permit came for another 150 copies but the next year 15,000 copies were published at a trade union publishing house (Wald et al., 1981). In 1980/1981 the discussion of alcohol problems had become very big.

BJA: And I think I've read a comment by one of the Polish researchers that this was an issue over which Solidarity and the government could agree that the whole issue was serious.

IW: Yes. It has been my conviction, even today, that this is one issue on which national consensus could be reached.

BJA: We left the story of research with the small amount of money that came in 1973, I think. And as you said, some directions were developed in the Advisory Board.

IW: Well, the story was made much broader in 1979 and 1980 when the Polish National Anti-alcoholic Committee came to the President of the State with a request to organize an Institute of Alcohology in Poland, but Jabtoriski refused. He saw however the possibility of creating a research programme on alcohol, a research programme that would be at a high level in terms of prestige and money, a so-called principle research programme. Our Institute was charged with the task of preparing such a

Interview with Ignacy Wald, Poland

programme during 1980–81. It should have started in 1981, but, due to the protracted crisis, it was decided to start it not as a principle but as an interministerial programme. Then, because of some financial muddle the ministry decided to postpone the start of the programme. I had to write to a deputy Prime Minister. One deputy Prime Minister didn't respond. Then another did. We started with a very small amount of money—some 20 million zloty in 1 year in order to get 600 million zloty for a 5 year programme. This programme on alcohol related problems was the first interministerial programme that we started. Then we quickly realized that it should be on alcohol and drug-related problems because the late '70s was the period when there was a rapid rise in drug addiction, in opiate preparations. The number of people using simple technology for home grown and home prepared opiates was increasing. Opiates were often combined with alcohol. So, after a year, this led to our broadening the research remit.

BJA: Over many political and social questions Poland clearly sees divergent opinions but alcohol might be an area where there could be a national consensus. What kind of policy directions do you think Poles from different persuasions would be able to agree on?

IW: I think that formulation of the alcohol policy in relation to the law and on education. A new law was accepted by parliament in 1982 and was implemented in 1983. For the first time in Polish legislation there is an obligation on Polish administrative authorities to develop and support activities of voluntary organizations, and to support the activities of religious organizations in this field. There can be very conflicting ideas in Poland about many questions but in relation to alcohol, since it is a very dangerous factor, there is a kind of consensus in this society. Alcohol problems are treated be many people as the number one problem for society.

BJA: How much consensus would there be about supply restrictions?

IW: I would say that this question shows that it is a simplification to say that there is one government policy on this issue. There are conflicting interests. We witnessed this very clearly after the new law introduced some very clear-cut limitations and a separate government monopoly rather like Alko, the Finnish State alcohol monopoly. In a few months there was heavy pressure and lobbying from some economic circles, in order to change this law, and indeed it was changed. Now there is no separate government enterprise but co-operative dealers. Alcohol is only one among many of her food commodities which are being sold by this wholesale trade enterprise. The enterprise has no clear alcohol policy. Another example is that a year after the new law the limitations on hours of sale were also changed so that beer can be sold from the morning hours, and even vodka can be sold early in the day if you buy it with hard currency. The sales limits were to be determined every year by the council of ministers. But, from 1982, these limits were always over the quota. It is only this year that the sales were kept below the quota. So there are some lobbying groups within the government—because we have this socialist economy—who are interested in fulfilling their patriotic duty by increasing alcohol consumption!

BJA: *To what extent do other socialist countries pay attention to the Polish experiment?*

IW: Well, I think that the Polish situation is viewed closely by our friends and neighbours. Some experience of the Polish law was used in preparing the Soviet law. In Hungary there is growing interest in developing an alcohol policy. The model used nowadays of the government Commission on Alcohol is that the Chairman is a deputy prime minister. This is also the situation in Hungary where the deputy prime minister is responsible for alcohol. I think that it is very important that alcohol matters should usually be decided at a high level since these decisions must have bearing on many different economic and policy issues. Another thing is that it is only natural that a member of a commission who is a deputy minister really represents the interest of his ministry on the commission. This type of psychology is obvious and natural. But since there must properly be a broader perspective, a deputy prime minister should be the person on the commission.

BJA: *You've also been involved in wider international collaboration?*

IW: We started with ICAA and the organization of the Warsaw conference in 1978. We always felt that this type of international co-operation was important for our own development. We can learn from other people's experience. Then came the international study on alcohol control (Mäkelä *et al.*, 1981). We reached a very good working co-operation with researchers from other countries both in seeking common knowledge and in identifying differences. Then came the work with WHO in developing different aspects of alcohol policy. And recently we have joined the WHO Community Response work.

BJA: And there are psychiatric and neurological projects besides that alcohol and drug work which lie within your responsibility?

IW: Yes. I am involved also in managing a ministerial programme in psychiatry and neurological disorders. I am the chief neurologist in the country, so I am responsible for training neurologists, acting on a specialist board, developing services in neurology, and so on. This is indeed quite a responsibility. Then I am involved in genetic research, epidemiology and biological research. Our department is very active in this field. I am involved in work on mental retardation and with a psychiatric study of mental handicap in association with the International Association for the Scientific Study of Mental Deficiency.

BJA: One last question. Suppose you were not currently involved in alcohol studies and someone came to you and said "Well, this is an offer you can refuse, but we are giving you the possibility of money for the first time to expand research in the alcohol field on the basis of what you know now." How would you answer?

IW: This is a fascinating area of research. I could use my competence in my primary field of genetics and so on, but now I think I would respond to this pressure of policy needs. Notwithstanding how important genetic factors may be, the most crucial questions nowadays are environmental. Genetic training helps me to understand that in such complex interactions between genetics and environment, it is the environment aspect which is usually much more open to manipulation.

References

1. Bruun, K., Edwards, G., Lumio, M. *et al.* (1975) *Alcohol Control Policies in Public Health Perspective* (Forssa, Finnish Foundation for Alcohol Studies).
2. Mäkelä, K., Room, R., Single, E. *et al.* (1981) Alcohol, Society and the State 1. A comparative Study of Alcohol Control (Toronto, Addiction Research Foundation).
3. Wald, I. & Gadomska, B. (1961) O rzadkich postaciach encefalopatii alkoholowych (On the rare forms of the alcoholic encephalopathies in Polish), *Neurologia, Neurochirurgia i Psychiatria Polska,* 11, pp. 175–179.
4. Wald, I., Kulisiewicz, T., Morawski, J. & Boguslawski, A. (1981) Raport o problemach Polityki w Zakresie Alkoholu (Report on Alcohol Policy in Poland), Warszawa, Instytut Wydawniczy Zwiazkow Zawodowych (Trade Union Publishing House).

29

Interview with Pierre Fouquet, France

PIERRE D. FOUQUET, *b. 1913. Croix de Guerre and Chevalier of the Legion of Honour. Medical training and MD, Paris. Hospital practice 1942–48 and from 1948–1973 directed private clinic. Member of the Haute Comité, President and founder of the French Society on Alcoologie. Work for WHO. Publications on clinical and historical aspects of drinking problems.*

BJA: *How did your interest in psychiatry and then alcohol-problems develop?*

PF: As far as I remember I always wanted to do psychiatry. One of my earlier memories was while doing the baccalaureat in philosophy (as you know there is also the baccalaureat in science and in maths). At that time, 16 years old, I would say to myself that the cleverest people are those who can understand both the body and the mind. To possess both a knowledge of medicine and of the mind would be the true study of humanity. I remember writing to a now very old Journal, the *Annales Medico-Psychologiques* to ask for a sample. I can't remember much more about that as I think my enthusiasm for what I read waned. I did my medical training with some difficulty, working as a student supervisor in a college at the same time. At the end, in 1936, I re-found my initial direction and was an intern in the Psychiatric Hospitals of the Seine. When I finished I had reached the stage of Chef du Clinique. But I did not want to work in an asylum somewhere in the provinces. So I took a post in 1942 in a brand new service, Le Service de Prophylaxie Mentale, which meant for the first time we were going to do psychiatry outside the hospital. With two colleagues I set up a psychiatric service in the TB centres, which we called Consultations D'Hygiène Mentale. The TB physicians took a dim view of us. They put us in a corner behind the X-Ray equipment or somewhere—these strange people dealing with mad folk. But we were pioneers, we wanted to bring psychiatry out of the hospitals, pull down the asylums and so on. In 1946 I was sent for 6 months to the U.S.A. to see what American psychiatry was like and when I came back I felt it was too grim to just have an administrative job, organizing things and no contact with patients—it was a job with the Départment de la Seine. I hesitated a lot. The psychiatric hospitals did not interest me. But through a friend I was put in touch with a little private clinic with 13 beds for neurotics. Very rapidly I got interested in alcoholics. My previous training had been very bad. When I was a registrar attached to the Police Department's Service for the Insane, each Friday my chief presented a patient—some crazy chap brought in from the street for us to decide if he should be hospitalized. Naturally occasionally there were alcoholics. My chief would say: "okay, you, how many do you drink?"—"er, er"—"three litres?"—"er, er"—"Five litres?"—"Non, Monsieur le Commissaire".—"I am NOT the Commissaire".—"Right, Monsieur le Commissaire".—It was frightful.

At that time I knew a Doctor Le Coq who had found before the war that TB abscesses resistant to sulphonamides sometimes resolved in response to intravenous ethanol, and that patients who were alcoholics were helped out of their addiction at the same time. I had expressed interest in his work and he sent me some of my first referrals. I was surprised to find I was able to make good contact with these people they called alcoholics, with their reputation for being difficult, aggressive, untrustworthy, etc. So I began to look after alcoholics. At the time very few doctors did so. Most rejected or were afraid of the alcoholic. I felt alright treating them. I got in contact with the abstainers groups such as the Croix d'Or, Vie Libre who helped in aftercare and rehabilitation.

In 1951 I had the chance to go to the World Health Organization Conference in Copenhagan. WHO asked the Ministry if there was anyone who could attend. It was a revelation to me that there were people there who had a different perspective on alcoholism than the one we had been taught. Hearing Jellinek helped me realize there was a whole world of experiences that alcoholics had in common. My friend and teacher—Professor Henri Ey—my boss—had an influence on me in stimulating me to try to conceptualize, put some order into the confusion. But Henri Ey had an aversion to alcoholics—he had told me that "alcoholics don't exist—in my service there are none". Perhaps he meant that behind the symptom of alcohol there was always a neurosis, a psychosis or a perversion with alcohol just as an epiphenomenon. But there he was wrong, I think. We used to argue a lot!

I began to have a few successes and soon I had very many referrals. At that time in Paris there was no private practice in psychiatry—just the asylums. I stayed on various Commissions and in 1954 joined the Haut Comité d'Étude et d'Information sur l'Alcoolisme, at the time of its creation by Pierre Mendes France.

BJA: What was the story of Mendes France and the glass of milk?

PF: Mendes France was President du Conseil and a most interesting person. He often stood much above the usual level of politics, a remarkable man. He was profoundly convinced that it was necessary for the Government to do something about what he called—even although the expression is now obsolete—the fight against alcoholism. He had the idea of inviting certain top medical people, including Monsieur Debray who was a very eminent Professor of Paediatrics to form a Haut Comité with a base in the offices of the Prime Minister, well placed to advise Government. Mendes France was quite a figure. He had made an impact in French relations with the Tunisians and so on—a controversial man—he only stayed in power some 90 days. The day he wanted the creation of the Haut Comité voted in, he asked an attendant in the Parliament to put down a glass of milk in front of him at the Tribune as he began his speech about alcoholism. It was a sort of provocation!

BJA: How was it in those days at the Haut Comité with representatives of the alcohol production industry and doctors, working side by side?

PF: There were also representatives from the various ministries—health, education, justice, agriculture, transport, etc.—but very few doctors because there were none at the time with an interest in the subject. Debray himself, the Chairman, said that he knew nothing about alcoholism, but he had a great reputation having reformed the whole system of medical education in France and he regarded alcoholism as a scourge. For him the job of the Committee should be to inform the public, put research in motion and to suggest to Government legislation aimed at controlling the problem. It was not a particularly medical matter except for the research. Alcoholism had always been considered by doctors to be a social problem, not their problem. The pressure to sell alcoholic drinks seemed so overwhelming doctors felt that there was nothing to be done. Alcoholics were seen as difficult people, untrustworthy, twisted, so although it might be a medico-social problem, it was up to the Government to do something about it. And as for psychiatrists, they had no interest at all.

BJA: *Did Henry Ey's view of psychiatry as the 'pathologie de la liberté' have an application to your views of alcoholism at the time?*

PF: Henri was primarily a teacher. Before the war there was no formal teaching in psychiatry outside Paris where there was only his Chair. Psychiatry was not seen as important. Ey created his system of organo-dynamism based on the work of the neurologist Hughlings Jackson. He proposed a hierarchical ordering of psychic life—a balancing of positive and negative aspects.

BJA: *Did that influence your conceptions of alcoholism?*

PF: I was a special pupil of Ey. Perhaps I too have the fault of wanting to be too systematic. I like clinical work but I also like theory. I tried to give a definition of alcoholism[1] and as you know, later a definition of alcohology.[2]

BJA: *Did Jellinek visit you in France?*

PF: I met him prior to the Copenhagen conference in 1951 and he asked me if I would like to give a paper there. It was illuminating for me. Jellinek was a remarkable man, very intelligent. The conference was to be held at Copenhagen in homage to Jacobsen who had developed Antabuse in 1946. I was asked to lead a therapy section with Jules Massermann (known for his work on experimental models of neurosis in cats). I presented my classification of alcoholism and Jellinek seemed impressed.

BJA: *I believe Ledermann was not at that meeting?*

PF: No, Sulley Ledermann's involvement was different. He was one of those absolutely elite 'polytechnique' graduates, highly gifted young students. He could have gone into anything he wanted. Polytechnicians have an aura but can be out of touch with life. By the way he was a talented musician. He rather drifted into demography, and began examining mortality statistics comparing France and other European countries. He saw there was an excess male mortality in France which could only be explained it seemed by the enormous French alcohol consumption. I met him at a conference in Istanbul and we became close friends. His work was mathematical demography. It lacked definitions. He worked quite alone. He was astonished to learn about the human aspects of the problem as a clinician sees them. Sadly he died young in 1965 or 1966 of painful cancer. It was a privilege to have known him.

BJA: *You worked for the World Health Organization?*

PF: Archer and Eva Tongue of ICAA played an important role in Europe. At the conferences they organized, we realized that national differences existed. WHO included alcohol and drugs in their programmes—a frequently debated matter at the committees I went to where alcoholism was seen as a drug dependence like other drug dependencies.

BJA: *What was most important result for you of the WHO interest in alcohol?*

PF: At the time in France, as I have said, alcoholism was not taken seriously. There were a few young, crazy psychiatrists who took an interest. WHO funded research, published monographs, and helped a body of scientific work to emerge. This gave an air of respectability to the field. In particular this was thanks to Madame Joy Moser.

BJA: *Did you play a role in resuscitating your Comité National de Defense contre l'Alcoolisme?*

PF: Not really. The Comité National was founded over 100 years ago, partly as a result of the post mortem on the conduct of troops during the siege of Paris in 1870. The ravaging of the vineyards by a fungus in the 1850's and by phylloxera in the 1870's had contributed to a massive increase in the consumption of spirits. The Comité National was founded by among others, Louis Pasteur himself and Claude Bernard (the physiologist). Its great success was the prohibition of absinthe. By 1945 it was more or less defunct although since 1911 passers-by on the Boulevard St Germain had been offered the choice at its shop window of a pink sugary liver or a grey-green liver. Dr Perrin from Nantes in 1950 published a book *Alcoholism* which included a survey of the opinions of 1657 doctors. This helped to stimulate action and the re-awakening of the Comité National.

BJA: *Do you have a view on what might have been the important influences on consumption in France since the war and in particular its fall in recent years?*

PF: Well, after the war, the first railways to run were loaded with plonk and by 1950 we could see the problem was beginning once again. But there was a gradual awakening of interest in the subject and a willingness to take action. The discovery of disulfiram had given new hope to doctors and patients; there were the abstainers' and former drinkers' groups, the Croix d'Or, Croix Bleu, Vie Libre and later Alcoholics Anonymous; there was the law of 1954 allowing compulsory treatment of 'dangerous alcoholics'; there was the work of the Haut Comité; there was greater discussion among doctors—for example—the chief text for psychiatrists, the Encyclopdie Medico-Psychologique for the first time had a section (by me) on 'The Alcoholic Neuroses'; in 1960 there was the law on 'Sector Psychiatry' permitting expansion of psychiatry into the community; in 1970 under the influence of Dr. Le Go, chief Medical Advisor to the Railways (SNCF), a Government circular encouraged the setting up of centres for the prevention of alcoholism (the Centres d'Hygiène Alimentaire) and GP's and gastroenterologists began working in these centres (some psychiatrists woke up for the first time at that point and said, "Why GPs and gastroenterologists?"!). Another figure was Dr Haas, a gastroenterologist who transformed his Paris GI clinic into a Service d'Alcoologie.

BJA: But the expansion of treatment facilities surely could not account for the fall since the 1970's in national consumption?

PF: It's a mystery why since 1972 consumption, especially consumption of wine, has fallen and continues to fall. People say that the efforts of the Haut Comité and the abstainers groups have contributed. It is hard to demonstrate. Four or five years ago there was the start of the same phenomenon, fall in wine consumption, in Italy, God knows there has been little in the way of the fight against alcoholism there. The tastes of the French people have changed. Now for example, among young recruits to the Army, half are water-drinkers. Of the others, some drink beer and some wine. There was of course the rumour that the Army put bromide into the soldiers' plonk! There has been the shift to 'Saturday night drinking'; and also among the young the view that alcohol is a drug like any other and to take alcohol is foolish or unfashionable. We do not know the exact causes of these changes.

BJA: How important were the road safety campaigns?

PF: the Haut Comité was involved in education in schools, in the media, poster campaigns, etc. Perhaps that had an impact. At one time we had perhaps the worst record for road accidents in Europe after Austria. It was shown that 40% of accidents involved excessive drinking either of the driver or of the victim. We had precise data on that. Specific campaigns were conducted in factories, in the armed forces, on the roads. That all played a role probably.

BJA: Can we talk about the Société Française d'Alcoologie of which you were the founder and still are President.

PF: It has over 400 regular members: 60% are doctors and 40% are from other disciplines, including psychologists, administrators, lawyers, judges and others. For the tenth anniversary of the Society there will be an International Conference in December 1988 in Paris. In addition to the text book of Alcoologie[3] and our historical compilation, *Le Roman de l'Alcool*[4] [the story of alcohol] we are publishing soon a *Dictionnaire de L'Alcoologie*. As you see my work is now the work of an old man—books, committees, being President of this and President of that! Clinical work is tiring now, it takes a lot out of you. All individual therapy of alcoholics involves an intense empathy, you give out a lot. It is a very different attitude than that of the analyst, for example. I was analyzed, it helped me I think in modifying my attitudes to alcoholics. With alcoholics the therapist has to talk a lot, be warm, say what they themselves cannot say—that is one of the driving forces of therapy. And also I have been giving seminars to medical students and psychiatrists. It's different now than in 1958 when some colleagues and I for two years running planned a teaching day and absolutely nobody turned up! But in 1970, I did the same thing Under Professor Ey's sponsorship at the Psychiatric Hospital of St Anne and that was a huge success and now we even have a post-graduate diploma in Alcoologie!

Notes and References

1. Alcoolites, Alcooloses, Somalcooloses.
2. *Alcohology:* A discipline devoted to everything in the world which is connected with ethyl alcohol: its production, storage, distribution, consumption both normal and pathological, with the implications of this phenomenon, its causes and consequences, whether at the collective level—national and international, social, economic and legal, or at the level of the individual—spiritual, psychological and physical. This independent discipline borrows the knowledge, with which it works, from the principal human sciences, economic, legal and medical, finding its own laws by the impetus of its evolution.
3. Malka, R., Fouquet, P. & Vachonfrance, G.(1986) *Alcoologie* 2nd edn (Paris, Masson).
4. Fouquet, P. & De Borde, M. (1986) *Le Roman de l'Alcool* (Paris, Seghers).

30

Interview with Georges Péquignot, France

GEORGES PÉQUIGNOT, b. 1921. Received medical training in Paris: MD. From 1950–52 Chef de Clinique in the faculty of medicine. In 1953 moved to full-time research career and in 1973 was appointed Director of Research at INSERM (French national institute on health and medical research). Research interests focussing particularly on population drinking and alcohol problem incidence. Jellinek prize. Work for WHO.

BJA: *Dr. Péquignot, how did you get interested in alcohol-related problems?*

GP: I started my medical career as an internist at the Hôpital St. Antoine in Paris, in the Gastroenterology Unit of Professor Caroli. This is where I first became aware of the high frequency of liver cirrhosis. The prognosis of ascitic cirrhosis in those days was particularly poor. In fact, in the early fifties, the over-all survival rate after 5 years barely reached 5%. Even when better treatment became available in the sixties, the survival rate was still no higher than 20%—a figure actually lower than for many types of cancer. At that rate, prevention was likely to achieve much more, assuming, of course, that one would know the cause of the disease.

BJA: *Were you aware at the time that alcohol was responsible for the disease?*

GP: There is no clear-cut answer to your question. Among French clinicians there was a sort of common belief that alcohol was the main causal agent, but this was no more than the product of daily experience without scientific proof. At that time the prevailing ideas concerning alcohol and cirrhosis—particularly in the Anglo-Saxon world—were that alcoholics were at greater risk of cirrhosis, or, alternatively, that cirrhosis was a "nutritional" disease, alcohol bringing about the deficient nutritional status which would be the *primum movens* of the disease. This latter concept was partly based on the observation of cirrhosis at an early age in developing countries where under-nutrition was endemic. In this respect, however, we know already that the nutritional theory was unlikely to be true: during the last World War, our population underwent severe dietary restrictions and the rate of cirrhosis decreased dramatically. This we suspected as being due, in fact, to the unavailability of alcoholic beverages, but there was not yet sufficient evidence to convince the scientific community outside France. The alcohol producers continued to quote the opinion of our colleagues who denied that alcohol would be the cause of the disease. After the war, alcoholic beverages became available without restriction again and cirrhosis reappeared and spread very quickly. I have repeatedly pointed out this parallelism.

BJA: *How did you eventually "prove" that alcohol was a causative agent?*

GP: As I mentioned before, all French clinicians were already convinced of the causal relationship and they did not feel any need for further proof. To all of us, it was quite obvious that most cirrhotics, whether or not they were "alcoholics" were certainly very heavy drinkers. What was lacking, actually, was the epidemiologic confirmation that this was so. At that time, epidemiology was far from being so widely used in France as in England for investigating situations of the kind. So we therefore embarked on a case-control study simultaneously in Paris, Marseille and in Nantes, in an attempt to single out the respective responsibilities of alcohol and nutritional factors. In this first study we made two major mistakes. First, we took as 'cases' only those cirrhotics who had been labelled 'alcoholics' by the clinicians; secondly, we took as controls hospital patients matched for sex and age. As a result, we observed an enormous difference between cases and controls. There were no controls above the 160 g mark and no cases below the 80 g/day mark. We therefore came to the (wrong) conclusion that there was no risk below the 80 g. I am afraid that by writing this, we were supporting the concept that there was a threshold at 80 g/day—definitely a wrong conclusion which is unfortunately still widely quoted.

BJA: *What was actually wrong in this first case-control study?*

GP: Evidently our definition of 'cases' who were called 'alcoholics' based on ill-defined criteria. When we revised our cases, we found that sometimes they were called alcoholics when they had signs of dependency and sometimes simply because they drank more than what the clinician would himself consider to be normal—very often over the 80 g/day level thus excluding the cirrhotics of unknown origin who were drinking less (they were about 5% of all patients in Paris, not to mention another 15% who were labelled 'post-hepatitic' or 'hemochromatosis'). No wonder we found no cases at less than 80 g, as noted by Donald Reid.

The choice of hospital controls was another major mistake. Some of our colleagues also suggested that in our analysis we should have considered a more refined scale of alcohol consumption (D. Schwartz), instead of the 80-160 g limits, and also that we should express our results in terms of relative risks (S. Ledermann).

It is around that time that Professor Caroli and I attended a meeting of AA, after which Caroli, in one single sentence defined the basis of our future studies. He said "These people are *alcoholics;* they are different from our patients. Our patients are *drinkers".*

Having learnt from our previous mistakes, we planned a new case-control study in Ille et Vilaine. This time, we tried to interview all new patients with ascitic cirrhosis occurring in a well-defined population, without any selection other than the presence of ascites. We took as controls a representative sample of that same population. We also interviewed cases of delirium tremens and of oesophageal cancer—a disease in which the International Agency for Research on Cancer was interested, and participated in the planning and the analysis of the results.

BJA: *What were the major findings of the Ille et Vilaine study?*

GP: I think the most important finding was the concept of a dose-response relationship for both ascitic cirrhosis and for oesophageal cancer, and the probable absence of any appreciable threshold for these two diseases. For delirium tremens, things were not so clear. For cirrhosis and for oesophageal cancer, however, what matters is the amount of alcohol consumed, whether these drinkers are 'alcoholics' or not. I believe that these results marked a turning point in our thinking about the role of alcohol in these diseases.

BJA: *Dr. Péquignot, what are the main difficulties you encountered in your work?*

GP: The main difficulties I met in the beginning came from my own limited knowledge and understanding of epidemiological methods and reasoning. Next came the problems of finding funds to carry out studies which, by definition, were likely to stretch over several years. We had also to find and to train our dieticians/interviewers.

For several years we worked in the complete indifference of our colleagues: the Anglo-Saxons because they did not believe we were on the right track and the French who thought our research was superfluous. Needless to say, in France millions of people live directly or indirectly from the production or sale of wine and of other alcoholic beverages; they were not on our side—to say the least!

BJA: *Did you get support from national and international organizations?*

GP: Yes, indeed. We have in France a so-called 'Haut Comité d'Etudes et d'Informations sur l'Alcoolisme', which is a rather unusual kind of body within the structure of public health services. It was established in 1954 by the late P. Mendès-France who was Prime Minister at the time. He realized the danger of alcohol and he had the incredible political courage to create the 'Comité', regrouping research workers, clinicians, social workers and also political personalities; it was attached directly to the services of the Prime Minister and remained there until 1986. This group supported us right from the start and I would like to pay tribute to its first chairman, the late Professor R. Debré, who constantly supported us throughout the years.

The Institut National de la Santé et de la Recherche Medicale (INSERM) established a Unit of Nutrition to which I was attached and which I later headed, thus permitting the use of qualified personnel to carry out our studies.

When my friend Albert Tuyns and the International Agency for Research on Cancer (IARC) started to study oesophageal cancer in Ille et Vilaine, this Agency helped considerably, and this assistance was further expanded when the American National Institute for Alcoholism and Alcohol Abuse (NIAAA) showed interest in our work. They provided substantial support for many years to our group at a later stage; this is how we could repeat our study in Calvados and confirm our earlier results.

These various sources of support sometimes stopped their help after a while or for short periods of time, but they never stopped their assistance simultaneously. We have always been able to proceed without major financial shortage. In this respect, when I look at that period in retrospect, I think that we have been very fortunate.

BJA: *The Anglo-Saxon scientists have been somewhat reluctant to acknowledge the role of alcohol in cirrhosis. Why is that so, in your opinion?*

GP: I think it is a question of proportion. In Britain, in the U.S. and in Scandinavia, the population is relatively little alcoholized, i.e. in comparison with France, and among all cirrhotics, the proportion related to alcohol is probably much smaller than the 95% we have in France. In such a context, it is prudent to think of other causes first. In these countries, the role of alcohol is far from being so obvious as in France. There was also the fact that drinking heavily and being an alcoholic are concepts which were not always dissociated.

BJA: *Do you imply that the concept of 'alcoholism' is different in France from what it is in Britain?*

GP: If the concepts developed by Professor Kendell in a recent issue of the BJA reflect the views of all our British colleagues, then I would say that there is little difference in our concepts, if any at all. The difference is not between British and French, it is rather between psychiatrists and gastroenterologists. The former focus their attention on the alcohol-dependent state, while the latter consider the entire range of gastroenterological diseases. This difference in attitude exists in the U.K. and it also exists in France.

It is interesting to note that in most epidemiological studies carried out by U.S. alcohologists, the questionnaires aim at detecting symptoms of dependence (SAAST, MAST, CAGE are examples of this) which reflect mainly the psychiatrists' preoccupation. For us, the main information—perhaps the only one of importance—is how much alcohol does the person drink. The non-alcoholic drinker is at risk even if he is not dependent. To cover the wide field of alcohol-related pathology, there is a need for 'depsychiatrization'.

BJA: *What is the place of Ledermann in the views of the French?*

GP: Ledermann was a great man and the French scientific community did not notice it. He was the first to approach the problems of alcoholism without preconceived ideas, using statistical methods to analyse all the information available; he was also the first to formulate the relationship between overall alcohol availability and the related pathology. One may agree or disagree with his particular formula, which is still a subject for discussion, but the relationship does exist. He was the first to throw the ball. For a French alcohologist, it is painful to admit that Ledermann's work is better known outside than in his own country.

BJA: *Why do some drinkers get cirrhosis while others develop a cancer or delirium tremens?*

GP: There must be some combination of individual behaviour with some genetically determined component. The intake of alcohol is of importance. In Ille et Vilaine, the DT patients drank more than the cirrhotics, who in turn drank more than the oesophageal cancer patients; the ages were in the inverse order. In addition, there is an individual susceptibility. Dependence is in relation to the level of alcoholaemia, which depends not only on the consumption, but also on some liver enzymes. Besides the alcohol dehydrogenase, Lieber demonstrated the existence of a microsomal ethanol oxidizing system (MEOS) which is induced by chronic alcohol exposure. The induction of MEOS varies from one individual to another. Those who induce MEOS probably are at greater risk of developing liver disease, those who do not do so expose their liver to less risk, but are rather prone to cerebral damage.

BJA: In what direction, in your opinion, should alcohologic research proceed as from now?

GP: Three main lines of research should be developed.

(i) More attention should be given to health disorders that are not specifically caused by alcohol but are possibly favourized by alcohol: hypertension and other cardiovascular diseases, diabetes and obesity are obvious candidates.

(ii) Further studies on the metabolism of alcohol need to be undertaken in various categories of individuals—for example, heavy drinkers with and without gamma-glutamyl transferase (GGT) elevation.

(iii) More epidemiological population studies are needed to better define individual behaviour towards alcohol in various environments, using comparable methods, if possible.

31

Interview with Mustapha Soueif, Egypt

MUSTAPHA I. SOUEIF b. 1924. Undergraduate training in philosophy followed by graduate studies in psychology at University of Cairo (PhD); Postgraduate Diploma in Clinical Psychology, University of London. Academic positions held within University of Cairo since 1954; Professor, Department of Psychology. President (1970–71) Egyptian Psychological Association. Main research interests in drugs, clinical psychology, and creativity. Work for WHO and other international organisations.

BJA: *I understand that, back in the forties, you were a student of Philosophy. Later, you opted for Psychology. How did this change come about?*

SOUEIF: At the age of sixteen, I was given the Egyptian Ministry of Education Award for superior academic achievement. The award included, among other things, a decent collection of books. The one book which aroused my curiosity was Will Durant's *The Story of Philosophy*.[5] Within 2 weeks I had read it, and decided to study Philosophy. My 4 years of under-graduateship at the Department of Philosophy (Cairo University 1941–1945) were very happy. In addition to attending to my programmed studies, I wrote poetry and short stories and discovered classical music. What fascinated me about Philosophy was the perpetual quest for a comprehensive world outlook, combined with the attempt to generate and sharpen a critical attitude. Aesthetics gradually emerged as my favourite area. At that time Psychology was taught as a minor subject in the Department. A few months before graduation, on the occasion of presenting a term paper on experiments in parapsychology, I was invited to see the Professor of Psychology. We had a discussion on my plans for postgraduate studies. When I said that I was planning to specialize in aesthetics he took the trouble to persuade me to shift to psychology, assuring me that there was scope for the study of experimental aesthetics in Psychology.

I think that encounter was an important factor in prodding me to opt for Psychology.

BJA: Early in your youth, you wrote poetry and short stories. You stopped abruptly. Why? Is there a contradiction, in your opinion, between creative writing and scientific production?

SOUEIF: At a certain stage in my intellectual development, I was confronted with some conflict between my literary inclinations and my anticipated career in research. I was then about 19 or 20 years old. I felt I might not be able to excel in more than one area. At the same time I was frightened lest I should make the wrong choice. It was a real crisis, replete with all sorts of hesitations and worries. To cut a long story short, I ended by deciding that my productive activity should be devoted to research. To inoculate myself against relapse into anything like my prior uncertainty I made a big bonfire of all my previous literary production. And, of course, I have not had any relapse since. I still feel, however, that I carry remnants of that past, and they creep into my research activity occasionally.

For example, I feel I do have something like aesthetic pleasure in writing and reading. Roundedness of evidence and smoothness of transition from one argument to another are among my criteria in judging written material. I can also detect a faint concern with wording and phrasing, caring not only for the central or the most salient meaning of the word or expression but also for the most subtle shades and connotations. Sometimes I like to speculate on differences between various languages. For instance, we have a number of words in Arabic denoting different modes of consumption and others for various degrees of mind alteration under the influence of psychotropic substances. I always wonder if it would be possible to find corresponding terms in English.

I feel attracted to certain writers because of the elegance they show in handling their subjects. For example I have been impressed by E. A. Carlini's work[2,3] which he did on rats, giving them tetrahydrocannabinol and coming out with a differentiation between responses given by stressed and non-stressed rats. The former became aggressive, whereas the latter become docile. What I find attractive in this work is that, somehow, it transposes a perspective from human psychology to animal behaviour. One step further and this work would be reconciled with the idea of individual differences in human psychology and the need to address these differences as moderator variables.

And so on, and so forth. I can cite many such instances of remnants of my past literary or artistic interests.

BJA: *You started your work on cannabis in 1957. That is 30 years ago now. This continuation in itself is a remarkable achievement,*[4,13,15-17] *not only in a developing country like Egypt but also on an international level. What are the mechanisms that kept the momentum of your work? Were there obstacles and if so, how did you overcome them?*

SOUEIF: A number of mechanisms contributed to the continuation. First, there is what you may call the initial source of motivation: while I am involved in research, I am doing some sort of social service. This urge to do something socially useful by way of applying my scientific knowledge has, always, been a basic motive for me. A secondary motivating factor was the feedback I got because of my work, especially from the international scientific community. This feedback included a wide range of components, the most significant among which was acknowledgement.

Besides, there were minor additional drivers. For example, I realized quite early that the project could be instrumental in training my junior colleagues (who were, mostly, working for their Ph.D.s) in the acquisition of a number of research skills. I believe that in due time they, also, realized that their growing academic competence was generously nurtured by their accomplishments on the project.

BJA: *And besides these dynamic elements?*

SOUEIF: In addition to these important dynamic elements, there were some structural factors which I looked after in building up the team that has been carrying out the work. These are points of practical wisdom you acquire gradually. You have for instance to be very careful in selecting the personnel. They should be reasonably ambitious young people with a tinge of modesty or social shyness. Interest in research and achievement via research should be central to their ambitions. A serious mistake would be to invite peers to accept permanent membership in the team. At best they may be assigned the role of temporary advisors. This I learned through painful experience. I also learned that one should avoid adding new permanent members occasionally to the team. Such additions would probably be treated by the group as foreign bodies, and a whole chain of disruptive reactions might be triggered. An integrated team of researchers working together for a relatively long time on a project which dictates some kind of division of labour and entails the emergence of defined roles should be encouraged to develop a feeling of 'we', and establish their own boundaries.

BJA: *Obstacles?*

SOUEIF: Yes, I've been confronted with some obstacles. But they were mostly benign. Perhaps it was mere luck. Or possibly because I restrained myself from playing an active role increasing or enhancing such obstacles. Experience taught me that if I did my job well, and I did not boast about achievements people would tend to help. Gradually you build an atmosphere of friendliness combined with a good reputation inside and outside the academia. This enables you more to overcome hindrances and reduces the chances for new ones to emerge. Money was never an unsurmountable obstacle. On the one hand I never submitted fantastic proposals that would require huge budgets. On the other hand, the people at the National Centre for Social and Criminological Research under whose sponsorship I did almost all my drug research were keen on having my work going on. They felt that the whole thing was genuine and reliable. Therefore, we proceeded together smoothly; no cut-down, and no disappointments.

Outside the Centre bureaucratic obstacles could have been a threat. But that was taken care of in various ways. For example, in 1967 we planned to interview 939 men distributed all over Egyptian prisons, serving sentences for the abuse of hashish. An additional part of our plan was to interview about 950 comparable controls derived from the same prisons. This was quite a big job. What added to its complexity was the fact that we insisted on having the subjects interviewed and psychologically tested under the least threatening conditions to ensure authenticity of the data. This necessitated that we should have facilities in every prison which would enable us to administer the interviews and the objective psychological tests to each individual subject in complete privacy. At this point you can imagine the quality and the quantity of obstacles which could have been heaped against us. To overcome this 'potential danger' I made good use of a very privileged position I had at that time. Back in the early sixties I had been invited to give a few lectures in Social Psychology to high ranking police officers. The experience proved to be useful and pleasant to all parties. Friendly relationships grew between myself and a number of those men. When I started planning for the drug research project, I felt that I would not be confronted with problems concerning the required arrangements in the prisons. The Commander-in-Chief of the prison department at the Home Office, together with a big number of prison superintendents had all been reading social Psychology under me, at one time or other. I paid them visits in their offices and explained my plans. That was all I had to do. My assistants and I were granted an official permission by the Home Office to carry out our job the way we thought it should be done. We began our field work by mid-June 1967. Three months later we had already collected the data.[13]

BJA: You have been supervising and working on different lines of research, each for a long period of time, publishing widely on all of them. For your work in Creativity, Clinical Psychology and Personality different aspects of research got integrated with others. In drug research, however, the rule does not seem to hold. Some would ask why, for example, you did not carry out research on the relationship between cannabis taking and creativity? It is a very interesting subject and it seems to hold a promise.

SOUEIF: It is my contention that, when it comes to applied research, the investigator has to keep positively sensitized to a number of social requirements and constraints. He has to rearrange his research preferences or priorities according to what he or she feels to be of more social relevance. I have no doubt that the problem of the relationship between cannabis taking and creativity is an interesting one from an academic point of view. But my comment has always been, and still is, that that point can be studied later. For the time being, there are other questions which are of more concern to the people at large (and to the Board of Experts at the National Centre for Social and Criminological Research who sponsors and finances my work). For example, the question of whether there is a meaningful correlation between chronic cannabis consumption and social deterioration and/or decline of work capacities is of immediate concern to the society at large. In an attempt to provide an adequate and detailed reply to this question we chose our tools of research the way we did. These tools included, in addition to the standardized interview, a battery of objective psychological tests for the assessment of well defined psychological functions. Examine this battery closely and you will find that it measures abilities which are quite relevant to skilled labour, for instance speed of psychomotor performance, speed and accuracy of perception, time estimation, length estimation, concentration, etc. The same point sheds light on the reason why our initial interview included a big number of items which were directed toward exploring the interviewee's work capacities, plus the way he handled social duties and interpersonal relationships.

BJA: And integration of scientific interests?

SOUEIF: Well, here, I have two comments. *First*, the way I was introduced to the drug research area differs from the way I had moved on from creativity to social psychology, then to personality structure, and finally to clinical investigations. Drug research came to me from outside; I was requested by a certain social agency at a definite point in time, to invest my research skills in this field. But with the other areas I just found myself stepping into them one after the other through a process of natural growth.

Now, these are two different ways of transition. The latter, by definition, has 'built in' previous inclinations, usually embedded in newly emerging perspectives which include and, at the same time transcended the old ones. But the former does not necessarily imply anything like that.

However, I think I came to the field of drug research carrying with me some elements of my inclinations which were already developed in other areas. But these elements, I guess, are mainly methodological in nature, and are integrated within the drug field in a very subtle way. For instance the extreme care I explicitly paid to the selection and/or the construction of the tools of research; the way my colleagues and I went about developing our initial interview. We made a continuous effort for more than 2 years (from 1958 through 1960) experimenting with all sorts of words, phrases and sequences, administering them to scores of subjects, representing various age stages, educational levels and residential origins, until we felt satisfied with the version we decided to utilize in our main survey. This quite elaborate experiment did not appear in English, so the Western reader does not know anything about it, but it was published in a detailed Arabic Report in 1960,[4] comprising, among other things, five different forms of the interview. We were not happy with four of them for explicitly stated reasons and opted for the fifth. This early experiment uncovers a deeply rooted interest in technical as well as theoretical problems of methodology, which I can still detect in all my drug research writings published later. I do not see much of that stuff in the psychological literature on drug abuse. I think I brought it with me from previous areas of interest.

BJA: Most of your work was launched and you started publishing when the issues concerned were not in fashion in the scientific arena. This applies to cannabis research as well as creativity and response sets. The decisions to start such endeavours, were they deliberate and conscious? Was it a kind of challenge or was it just accidental?

SOUEIF: It had nothing to do with challenge or any deliberate effort to be conspicuous. For a research worker there are, at least, two main sources which suggest new ideas for research; either the literature or live experiences. What happened with me in the three instances you cited was that I began by running into the phenomena themselves. My interest in extreme response sets emerged (in 1951) while I was assessing attributes adolescents cared for when choosing their personal friends. I got a faint glimpse of some regularity in the response sets, irrespective of item content. Since I had no previous readings, not even mental readiness for addressing this kind of regularity, I could not understand what it meant, but I felt that it could imply something valuable. Therefore, I collected the data and kept it in my office. In 1955 I went to London to get some training for postdoctorate research at the Institute of Psychiatry. There, while I was looking through the literature hunting for some material on the MMPI, I came across Berg & Collier's paper on "Personality and group differences in extreme response sets."[1] It just clicked with me. I chatted with Professor Eysenck about the whole problem and he encouraged me to take a second look at my old material and get it properly analysed and reported on.[11]

Similarly, with creativity.[10] The whole thing started because I was interested in poetic creativity. It so happened that I was writing poetry and short stories when I was in my late teens. By the time I was 20 years old and about to graduate, I opted for scientific research in psychology. It just imposed itself on me, then, that poetic creativity would be the topic I would study. I took it seriously and began to search the literature but could not find anything with a well defined methodology. So, I had to depend on my gropings.

BJA: *And cannabis?*

SOUEIF: The same thing happened again in the area of cannabis consumption. I was approached by the people at the National Centre for Social and Criminological Research. I welcomed the contact, just because it meant a good opportunity for me to prove that my academic expertise could be socially useful. When I started to do the actual work (late in 1957) I discovered that the literature on the behavioural aspects of cannabis consumption was almost nonexistent. I therefore had to start from scratch.

In brief, what actually happened, was that through live experiences I got interested in understanding and explaining certain problems. When I began to take the first steps in the actual research I could not find anything helpful in the literature to provide me with some leverage. By that time I had become so committed that I never thought of backing out. I do not think that you can call this 'challenge'. It might be nearer to intolerance of intellectual frustration. In fact I feel that the emptiness I was confronted with acted as a disinhibitor of some daringness or adventurousness on my part. Moreover, I think there is something worth mentioning here, about the way investigators perceive problems. Some workers seem to be classifying perceived problems into researchable versus non-researchable ones. And by researchable questions, they mean (implicitly of course) those which have already been handled by previous workers. This premise should not, I think, be taken for granted.

BJA: *Your tendency to work for long periods of time (decades!) on the same issue is fascinating. Were there times you felt you were running out of steam? If so, what were the mechanisms that brought you back.*

SOUIEF: There is a big difference between working in the same field and researching the same issue. I do get involved in the same field for decades. But I do not keep concentrating on the same point for such long periods of time. Usually when one starts addressing a certain topic it begins to unfold, gradually, into various aspects. This process of unfolding, sometimes outgrows your efforts to get it under your control. So one of my early concerns was to identify and develop the skills required to cope with such a situation. Part of my strategy at present is that I first keep roaming around the new subjects I wish to study. I like to begin by getting the most complex idea about the forthcoming study; all sorts of expected correlations and implications. I do that by some reading; but, more important, by generating an active kind of receptivity, that is, receptivity which follows short periods of intensive speculation. It is a very complex process which I still find difficult to describe accurately. Anyway, it is only after I am through with this stage that I proceed to examine the parts, to go deep into one part after the other. So it may be that this kind of strategy immunizes me against premature boredom. I maintain some mental representation of the whole. That makes me feel, most of the time, that what I accomplish is only part of the whole which I intended to address. It seems that I am confronted here with something like a Zeigarnik effect, a sense of an unfinished task.

BJA: *From very early in your career, you have travelled a lot: guest researcher, visiting professor, attending international conferences and meetings, giving consultations and testimonies; in a sense you have become an internationally known figure. However, you have remained local, in the sense that you have continued to show the same strong interest in and give the same amount of effort to, local issues, such as establishing clinical psychology as an independent discipline in the Egyptian Health Service, establishing a department of psychology at Cairo University, overseeing the Institution of the First Academy of Arts in Egypt and so on.*

How did this come about? Do you suffer from any conflict between a national commitment and an international role?

SOUIEF: It is a long time now that I have been living with this double identify; on the one hand I feel a world-citizen, on the other I belong to Egypt. This complex 'consciousness' or oscillating began in the late fifties when I was carrying out my first piece of clinical research in Egypt (at Abbassia Psychiatric Hospital) while keeping an eye on getting it published abroad. This was the paper on 'Testing for organicity in Egyptian psychiatric patients'. It was accepted for publication in *Acta Psychologica* (in Amsterdam). That was the first step towards establishing my reference group, defined in this case as a group of international scientists who would judge the worth of my research on its objective merits. My international identity, however, was definitely promoted through my contact with the WHO in Geneva. In 1966 I was approached by the WHO people to prepare a paper for publication in the UN *Bulletin on Narcotics* reporting on our work on 'Hashish Consumption in Egypt' which has been under way since 1957. This I did, and the paper was published in 1967.[12] In 1970 I was invited to participate in a 'Scientific group' meeting to be held at WHO headquarters. The recognition my work received there was deeply gratifying.[18] In 1971 I was invited to be a member of the WHO Expert Committee on Drug Dependence. I felt greatly honoured. This event had two important consequences both reinforcing my international identity: Firstly, over the years, I have been requested to take part in numerous meetings convened either by the WHO or by other international bodies (e.g. ICAA, ARF in Toronto and so on) collaborating with WHO. Secondly, most of the drug research I have been conducting since (together with my Egyptian colleagues), was written in English and published abroad.

These events, however, with all their natural psychosocial implications, never conflicted with my local identity. The reason was quite simple, at lest the way I should understand it. I was recognized internationally, on the merits off the work I carried out locally and independently.

Hence, I always felt that my international career came as a reward to the way I played my role as a national scientist. And the end result that I am living with is a kind of conscious harmonious interplay between the two poles of my 'self'.

BJA: *Tell me about some of the people you have worked with.*

SOUEIF: I worked with eminent figures in academic psychology such as H. J. Eysenck, M. B. Shapiro, G. Jones, C. Franks, A. Yates and J. C. Brengelmann. In the field of drug dependence I worked with people like D. Cameron, H. Halbach, H. Isbell, P. Connell, G. Edwards, H. Kalant, G. Nahas, W. Paton, R. Smart, I. Bayer, T. L. Chrusciel, R. Schuster, H. Jones, A. Wikler, H. Brill, R. Jones and Archer and Eva Tongue. Those people were not only experts in the narrowly defined technical sense of the word, but also persons with genuine moral integrity.

The interaction among scientists, with various national backgrounds, participating in international meetings, has always been a fascinating subject to my mind. Not that I could find enough time to investigate it systematically. But I cannot help observing what goes on and speculating about it. I ran into all sorts of prejudices, and pretentions to mask the prejudices. The manifestations ranged all the way from patronizing, through undue reservedness to explicit unfriendly responses. I was never shocked; because when it comes to evaluating peoples' capabilities I am quite realistic; just short of becoming pessimistic. I knew, in advance, that people (scientists included) start by categorizing you. This is the a, b, c of 'person perception' research in social psychology. I knew that I was categorized, right from the beginning, as a 'scientist coming from the third world'. But as such, categorizing is no problem; because it can simply denote a fact.

The trouble comes next. There are tremendous individual differences among fellow researchers regarding the 'rigidity-flexibility' dimension of their initial categorizing response. Some can change, some cannot, and big numbers lie in between. I like to keep a vivid memory of relevant observations and speculations. For me they are part of the game. But more important is the fact that they serve as control data which would enable me to give due credit to people like Cameron, Halbach and the rest. Obviously, they could overcome one of the worst sources of human frailty.

BJA: And the Egyptian dimension?

SOUEIF: When I look closely into the national aspect of my career I do not find anything like patriotic chauvinism. I take it for granted that I live in Egypt. It is one of those postulates which one has to take into account when structuring the present or planning for the future. A number of implications are dictated by this postulate. For example, I have to be 'bilingual' if I care for international readership and acknowledgement. And bilingualism is not an easy job. You cannot reduce it to a pendular movement from Arabic to English and vice versa. Rather, you switch off a whole way of thinking, feeling and mode of expression; and tune yourself to a totally different wave length. At the start of your career you find that this exercise is really tough, and overloaded with frustrating moments. But you accept it the way it is, because you chose to have it this way. Gradually, you attain higher levels of relevant skills; your troubles decrease, yet they never disappear.

Another implication is that you have to accept a double load of responsibilities most of the time; I mean your local duties (the university, the private clinic, sharing in national meetings and writing in local periodicals) and international requests (usually meetings and writings). Sometimes you have to turn down a request from one side or the other. But you have to be very careful if you intend to play the two roles with optimum smoothness. It takes creative effort to find points of convergence between both, and it is, then, highly rewarding.

A third implication is that gradually your role is redefined for you. You are not more just a local scientist with international resonance. You are transformed into a culture-transmitter or a bridging factor. You are expected to behave as a medium for communication between two cultures. Whenever you cross the fence you should do something useful and interesting to the people on the other side. Of course what you carry with you should always be relevant to scientific endeavour. But it is sometimes peripheral. Yet it proves to be quite instrumental in promoting mutual understanding between investigators trying to transcend national and/or cultural barriers. This is all the more important when it comes to an area like research in drug abuse.

BJA: *Could you give us an overview of the scene of cannabis research as it is now from your perspective. What are the major issues that need to be addressed?*

SOUEIF: Research on the cannabis-behaviour relationship in man is my main concern. In this area what has already been published is really voluminous. Nevertheless, much more still needs to be done. By and large, the relevant literature is lopsided. There is an abundance of published material on the acute effects (and on psychosocial correlates) of cannabis use in young healthy males, who belong to upper or middle class families.

We need more work on the long term effects of the drug; real long-term or chronicity, where you have people with a history of continuously taking 'grass' for 15 or 20 years or even more. The Economic and Social Council of the United Nations, by its resolution 1984/22 on the cannabis problem, recommended that scientific research, especially long-term investigations into the effects of cannabis use on the human organism should be continued and accelerated.

The question of 'cannabis psychosis' still has the appearance of a riddle. One of the reasons for this regrettable state of affairs can be detected through the incidental type of published research which seems to be the rule rather than the exception in this area. Such investigations are, usually, characterized by being conducted on a small number of subjects, accidentally selected, while the clinical and demographic data are collected by tools of doubtful scientific value, within the context of a sloppy design. Large scale systematic studies, with more sound methodology are urgently needed on this subject.

More work is also required on females as users. S. Greenland and others[6] conducted a small scale survey on the effect of cannabis consumption on pregnant women. They reported more abnormal progress of labour among users than non-users. They also found that users' infants exhibit more meconium staining. Their findings were in line with previously reported results on animals and on human neonates who were found, in the case of mothers-users to demonstrate neurobehavioural and developmental differences compared with offspring to mothers-nonusers. But the researchers, themselves, admitted that the number of users involved in their study was small, hence there was a large margin for statistical error in the results.

This kind of work is worth replication by other investigators, in various other laboratories and on bigger numbers of pregnant women as well as women of child-bearing age.

BJA: *Is there a place for transcultural studies?*

SOUEIF: Well-designed, large-scale transcultural studies are, still, very much desired. These studies can be quite instrumental in sorting out what is caused by the chemistry of the drug and what is contingent on the user's life style. Eva and Archer Tongue of the ICAA once had plans to set up a group of national teams of researchers who would address this question in a systematic way. About mid-1977 they made some initial steps towards the execution of the project, after they had the blessings of WHO. A group of would-be participants were convened in Lausanne and the plan was thoroughly discussed. But the project was never actually started. Possibly, something can be learned from this experience to lend better leverage to a new study aimed at similar targets.

The subject of individual differences raises questions most of which are still awaiting answers. Examples of such differences are: age, intelligence, level of arousal, emotionality and extraversion/introversion. These should be brought, as moderator variables, into the designs of laboratory experiments as well as field studies. If they are treated this way and taken care of in the ensuing analyses they will then help integrating many existing conflicting results. They will make them more meaningfully inter-related within complex regularities.

BJA: Can one see different phases in society's response to cannabis?

SOUEIF: In 1986 Himmelstein[7] monitored two phases in the social history of cannabis use in the United States. The first stage lasted from 1965 to 1977, and witnessed what sometimes is labelled the embourgeoisement and partial normalization of such consumption. The second phase began around 1978 marking a marijuana backlash. Now Government officials reversed their stance on the drug, and hundreds of parents associations emerged to express concern about their children's drug practice attitude. This work of Himmelstein reminds me of, and indeed adds new dimension to a report published in the early seventies by the late W. McGlothlin[8] of California University (Los Angeles) in which he traced the socio-cultural factors which immediately preceded and encompassed the emergence of the cannabis culture among American white youth. In the same vein though with additional orientations, I published an article in the *UN Bulletin on Narcotics* in 1972[14] on the social psychology of hashish consumption in Egypt. The same topic needs to be addressed in other Western societies. We still need to understand more about cannabis consumption. It flared up in the West, around the mid-sixties, like an epidemic. Why and how? Psychologists and psychiatrists are, mostly, trained to view their research problems microscopically. With cannabis use, this is not enough. An additional macroscopic approach is needed.

Reg Smart and associates[9] carried out a well designed study on reasonably large samples of adults and students in Ontario, Canada. They examined the possible relationship between alcohol drinking related problems and smoking of cannabis. Using multivariate analysis they found that such problems were the best predictors of cannabis use in adults as well as young people. This work on predictors of drug use has far reaching implications and deserves replication in other settings and on various sectors of the population.

In brief, there are six or seven points which remain as serious loopholes in our knowledge concerning the cannabis-behaviour relationship. These are: chronicity, cannabis psychosis, the effects on females, the effects viewed trans-culturally, individual differences as moderator variables, the social history off the drug culture in various societies and the problem of predictors. The fact that there exists, already, some fragmented information on each of the mentioned topics means that what we really need, at present, is better organized knowledge. Such knowledge, I imagine, should be founded on a systematic approach, sound methodology and sufficiently sizeable samples.

BJA: You are now 63. You are no longer burdened with the administrative work of running a department. You have the opportunity to concentrate more on research, which you seem to be doing. What are your plans for the future? Are there any new directions which you are about to pursue?

SOUEIF: It is true; I have been relieved from a good deal of the administrative burden; but it is equally true that I have been charged with new responsibilities. When you reach this age colleagues would either tend to forget about you, or start to consider you as a member of the old guard. The role of the 'wise man' is bestowed upon you, and you are expected to give all sorts of advice through various committees and councils. At present, I am playing more and more of this role. And I accept it, wholeheartedly, as long as I can see that my efforts are sincerely requested and actually put to use. My plans for the future are in some respects definite, in others they are vague. For instance, I think I will keep on with the drug endeavours for a few years to come. And I intend to remain with the field-work so long as I can afford it. So, obviously, I shall go on conducting our series of large scale epidemiological studies until I bring it to a logical completion.

But there are other dreams which I would like to actualize, yet they are rather uncertain. Examples: I would like to write what may be called the story of my drug research; the events and circumstances which constituted the social, intellectual and international climate encompassing my research efforts. This would not be an autobiography. It would be the biography of the work itself. The main value of this kind of writing is that it uncovers some determinants (particularly social and international) which drive or even force a research worker to go about his work the way he does. Such determinants remain hidden most of the time; you suppress any remembrance of them when you come to write a journal article reporting on the research. And yet, it is exactly about these determinants that my students raise questions. Usually, I react with sympathy but I could never give a complete answer. I sincerely hope to get this material written in the near future, though I do not know when, or in what shape it will come out.

I have other dreams too, but these I entertain at a psychic level made to their measure: semiconcious, intermittent, yet quite persistent. These dreams you may call my secret ambitions: To arrive, eventually, at a theoretical structure that retintegrates, meaningfully, the neuropsychopharmacological and sociocultural pieces of information we already have. Such structure should give a balanced account for, and suggest testable hypotheses relevant to, drug abuse behaviour. Whether this I will be able to attain I am not sure. But, still, I hold fast to it, because it gives me a sense of orientation.

References

1. Berg, I. A. & Collier, J. S. (1953) Personality and group differences in extreme response sets, *Education and Psychological Measurement*, 13, pp. 164–169.
2. Carlini, E. A. & Masur, J. (1970) Development of fighting behavior in starved rats by chronic administration of (—)-Δ–trans-tetrahydrocannabinol and cannabis extracts, *Community and Behavioral Biology*, 5, pp. 57–61.
3. Carlini, E. A. (1974) Cannabis sativa and aggressive behavior in laboratory animals, *Archives of Investigative Medicine* (Mex.), 5 (Suppl. 1), pp. 161–172.
4. Committee for The Investigation of Hashish Consumption in Egypt (1960) *Hashish Consumption in Egypt: research in progress: report I: The interviewing schedule: construction reliability and validity.* Cairo: Publications of the National Centre for Social and Criminological Research, pp. 425 [In Arabic].
5. Durant, W. (1926) *The Story of Philosophy: The Lives and Opinions of the Greater Philosophers* (London, Ernest Benn).

6. Greenland, S., Richwald, G. A. & Honda, G. D. (1983) The effects of marijuana use during pregnancy. II. A study in a low-risk home-delivery population, *Drug and Alcohol Dependence*, 11, pp. 359–366.
7. Himmlestein, J. L. (1986) The continuing career of marijuana: backlash with limits, *Contemporary Drug Problems*, 13/1, pp. 1–21.
8. McGlothlin, W. H. (1973) Sociocultural factors in marijuana use in the United States. Paper presented at the IXth International Congress of Anthropological and Ethnological Sciences, Chicago, August–September 1973.
9. Smart, R. G. & Liban, C. B. (1980) Cannabis use and alcohol problems among adults and students, *Drugs and Alcohol Dependence*, 6, pp. 141–147.
10. Soueif, M. I. (1951) *The Psychology of Creativity: Especially in Writing Poetry* (Cairo, Dar-el-Maaref) [In Arabic].
11. Soueif, M. I. (1958) Extreme response sets as a measure of intolerance of ambiguity, *British Journal of Psychology*, 49/4, pp. 329–334.
12. Soueif, M. I. (1967) Hashish consumption in Egypt: with special reference to psychosocial aspects, *Bulletin on Narcotics*, 19/2, pp. 1–12.
13. Soueif, M. I. (1971) The use of cannabis in Egypt: a behavioural study, *Bulletin on Narcotics*, 23/4, pp. 17–28.
14. Soueif, M. I. (1972) The social psychology of cannabis consumption: myth, mystery and fact, *Bulletin on Narcotics*, 24/2, pp. 1–10.
15. Soueif, M. I. (1975) Chronic cannabis users: further analysis of objective test results. *Bulletin on Narcotics*, 27/4, pp. 1–26.
16. Soueif, M. I. (1976) Some determinants of psychological deficits associated with chronic cannabis consumption, *Bulletin on Narcotics*, 28/1, pp. 25–42.
17. Soueif, M. I. (1976) The differential association between chronic cannabism and impairment of psychological function: A theoretical framework. Paper presented at the International Institute on the Prevention and Treatment of Drug Dependence, Hamburg, 28 June–2 July 1976, pp. 106–118 (Lausanne, ICAA Publication).
18. WHO (1971) *The Use of Cannabis*, Technical Report No. 478 (Geneva, WHO).

32

Discussion. Intolerance of Intellectual Frustration

Marcus Grant

If you count them on the contents page, there are nine interviews in this section of the book. If you read them one after another, you could be forgiven for thinking that there are ten. The reason is that through virtually all of them there moves the shadowy figure of a man who has never been interviewed by the British Journal of Addiction but whose influence was clearly felt by all with whom he came into contact. That man was E.M. Jellinek, who was WHO's first consultant on alcoholism (and therefore, in a sense, the man in whose chair I now sit) and who knew, guided, influenced and changed scientists and scholars from around the world. In a sense, all these interviews are also cumulatively an interview with an absent giant.

More than any other section of the book, we become as readers silent witnesses to history in action, marvelling at the intricate webs of friendship, scholarship, and politics that bind together individuals and scientific movements so that they emerge as something which it is impossible not to recognize as a pattern. It is a pattern which provides the sociocultural context for understanding addiction. More than that, it is a pattern which demonstrates how sociocultural contexts are themselves part of a process of change, which is dynamic and moves as history does, sometimes subsuming the individual into the pattern, but sometimes allowing individual insights to illuminate the pattern in new and startling ways. Through these interviews, we can sense the urgency of the actions that make up the history. Nothing is obvious when it is happening.

Nor is there any facile consensus amongst these nine individuals about what are the priorities for action. On the one hand, Michael Beaubrun talks about "influencing the public to do what needs to be done" whilst Jorge Mardones tells us that "the worst thing a scientist can do is to pollute the scientific environment with data of poor value". The statements do not, of course, contradict each other, but they represent different perspectives on the relationship between individual scientists and the political events in which they may, either willingly or reluctantly, become involved. I wonder if the key to understanding the impetus for this interest (in understanding the complexities of psychoactive substance use and its attendant problems, including dependence) may not lie in Mustapha Soueif's rejection of the idea of commitment through challenge. "It might be nearer," he suggests, "to intolerance of intellectual frustration". Now there is a concept that spans the theoretical, the clinical, the scientific, and the political. There, if you like, is a mainspring to action; and it is one that Jellinek would certainly have recognized.

That there are individuals representative of the highest standards of scientific enquiry is apparent from the extent to which they question the field in which they are working and their own place in it. Ignacy Wald talks of it as "a field . . . overpopulated with people who were active but not always competent." Although he is describing a particular moment in history and a particular national situation, there are many who would not find it too difficult to echo these words in other times and other places. Mustapha Soueif suggests that the way to deal with this state of affairs is to search actively for "reasonably ambitious young people with a tinge of modesty" and to give them the opportunity to develop their skills under the guidance of a wise master.

Here again we are brought back to the sense in which Jellinek did just that for a whole generation of scientists who, if they are no longer quite so young, have at least retained, in the midst of their many successes, the tinge of modesty that enabled them to find their place in a global development. Although it is often the differences between cultures that are most vivid, it is their profound similarities which also provide fertile ground for international collaboration. In this, the scientists and scholars interviewed here have provided the medium for communication between countries, between disciplines and between the thinking and the doing.

For these are also active men, involved in the day to day compromises and showmanship of political life. That is why it is so fascinating to read about Michael Beaubrun breathalysing the Attorney General and the Foreign Minister on the floor of parliament when they returned from lunch. Or Pierre Fouquet describing the story of Mendes France and his famous glass of milk. At the same time, it also has its more problematic, even sinister side. When Kettil Bruun talks about the web of international secrecy surrounding some aspects of drug policy, it is difficult not to see long shadows cast across the patterns of sociocultural change. His is a plea for greater transparency in the linkages between science and politics, and greater accessibility to the data on which proposals for changes in policies purport to be based.

I have concentrated on the relationship between science and public policy because this is a subject which is particularly interesting to examine from a cross-national perspective. Another relationship which is equally interesting, and which also demonstrates the humanity of those interviewed in this section, is between science and the treatment system. Reading these interviews, one theme which emerges with intriguing frequency is that of the adaptation of the AA model to different sociocultural circumstances. James Ch'ien's therapeutic island of Shek Kwu Chau or Jaroslav Skála's sociotherapeutic TROTTING club are vivid examples of transformations which create something distinct but which acknowledge their origins. The influence of the AA philosophy (and the AA mythology) on treatment systems is something which has long merited close attention, and is currently pursuing this important agenda. The lesson is one of the flexibility of an approach and the clarity of a unifying vision. So there is no need to search for the one and only right solution, because the system already recognizes that the right solution is that there are many right solutions.

This too is a kind of transparency. So when George Péquignot describes the need for "de-psychiatrization" of treatment, he is not attacking one particular profession; rather, he is calling for an openness towards the range of options that are required for the system to give room to all those who could and should find a legitimate place there.

These are interviews with scientists from highly developed countries with rich research tradition and scientists from economically disadvantaged developing countries where every step into research has to be justified in terms of other urgent competing demands. They are interviews with scientists from many different countries with different preoccupations. What binds them together is the impulse towards integration that is apparent in everything they say. Integration does not mean that they all see alcohol and drug problems in the same way, or that they would agree on common solutions. What it means is that they share an impulse towards bringing together everything that is relevant. The laboratory research, the survey research, the clinical research, the policy research—all of these are presented not as isolated fragments, but as an effort toward integration. The integration is the pattern. As the absent Jellinek looks down at this consistent effort, he must be well satisfied that what he began when he was working for WHO is progressing along the lines he would have wished. I, for one, following modestly in his footsteps, am impressed by the sense of forward momentum that is so vividly demonstrated by these interviews with those who show us that it is not only possible but necessary to be simultaneously thinking and doing.

Index

Abstract Archive, 61
Acta Psychologica, 436
Addiction Research Foundation (Canada), 6, 34, 303, 317, 319
  Clinical Institute, 334
  current status, 342
  David Archibald at, 346
  development, 345–7
  drug and alcohol research, 307–8
  funding, 347–8
  Harold Kalant at, 319–20, 346
  impact, 304–5
  influence, 348–50
  local reputation, 349
  relationship with universities, 335
  research relevance, 348-9
  scientists in policy analysis, 350–1
  Wolf Schmidt at, 337–8, 346
Addiction Research Unit, Institute of Psychiatry (London), 334
Addicts, treatment of, 30–1
Adolescent clinics, 274
Advertising of alcohol, 129–30, 382
Advisory Council on Misuse of Drugs, 244–5
  Philip Connell as Chairman, 277–9
  staffing, 280
Advocacy, xvi
  and research, 328–9
Africa, attitudes to drinking problems, 16, 17
AIDS, 285
Alcohol
  appetite research, 391–2
  dependence syndrome, 13
  industry, 176, 414
  research and drugs, 307

Alcohol and Alcoholism, 390
Alcohol and Drug Problems Association (ADPA), 120
Alcohol and Drug Programmes of America, 40
Alcohol Education Centre, 254
Alcohol Explored, 68
Alcohol and the Jews, 134
Alcohol Problems, 182
Alcohol Problems: A Report to the Nation, 95
Alcohol Research Centre (Berkeley), 168, 169, 182
Alcohol and Traffic Safety, 166
Alcohol Treatment Units (Britain), 199
Alcoholaemia, 424
Alcoholics Anonymous, 40, 44
  in Canada, 299–300, 302, 303
  Croydon group formation, 208
  effectiveness, 151
  in France, 416
  Glatt's work with, 212
  model of sociocultural circumstances, 447
  National Council on Alcoholism influence, 64
  Rathcoole House, 253
  in Trinidad, 379–80, 381
Alcoholics and Vagrants Committee, 213
Alcoholism, 416
Alcoholism, Alcohol Abuse and Related Problems: Opportunities for Research, 98
Alcoholism Recovery Project, 253
Alcoholism and Social Stability, 89

449

Alcoholism Treatment Units, 215
Alcoholmeter, 382
Alko Group (Finland), 325, 407–8
Alumni Association of SARDA (Hong Kong), 362–3
American Council on Alcoholism, 131
American Drinking Practices, 166
Amphetamine addiction, 220, 267, 268, 269, 270
Anderson, Dr. Carl, 121
Anderson, Nels, 106, 107
Animal models of Alcoholism, 325–6
Annales Medico-Psychologiques, 411
Antabuse, 150–1, 197, 379, 415
Anti-Saloon League, 176
Anxiety, 154
Apolinář alcohol treatment centre (Prague), 395, 396
  growth, 399–400
  research, 401
  therapeutic system, 397–8
Apomorphine, 216
Archer, Loran, 168
Archibald, David, 95, 299–314, 338
  Addiction Research Foundation work, 346
  at Yale, 181
  reputation of Addiction Research Foundation, 349
Archibald, David—interview
  Addiction Research Foundation of Ontario, 303–5, 307–8
  biography, 299
  contact with politicians, 305
  international connections, 308–9
  International Council on Alcohol and Addictions, 312–13
  involvement in addiction work, 299–301
  Jellinek's influence, 308–9
  Liquor Control Board, 301, 302
  meeting with Jellinek, 300, 303, 304
  Thailand work, 309–11
  Third World connections, 309–11
  treatment policies, 302
  WHO fellowships, 309
  WHO work, 310–11
  Yale University Summer School, 300

Archivos de Biologia y Medicina Experimentales, 390
Arif, Awni
  accomplishments, 50
  influences, 52–3
  organizational context of work, 52
  personal life experiences, 51
Arif, Awni—interview, 25–35
  achievements, 29–30
  biography, 25
  cocaine and cannabis, 34–5
  drug problem, 32–3
  Iraq Health Ministry, 27
  in Libya, 28
  national responses, 33
  WHO appointments, 26–7, 28
  WHO training programmes, 31
Association for the Prevention of Addiction, 242
ATPase studies, 321–2
Australia, attitudes to drinking problems, 16
Authoritarian Personality, The, 160
Availability of alcohol, 77–8, 305
  Poland, 408

Baan, Dr. Pieter, 7–8
Bacon, Selden, xiv, 61
  alcohol control attitude, 183
  Director of Center of Alcohol Studies, 62
  political lobbying, 181
  proposed bill for federal commission on alcoholism, 122
  relationship with Straus, 86, 88
  research direction, 183
  scientist's role, 132
Bacon, Selden—interview, 67–79
  biography, 67
  Connecticut Prison study, 67–8
  contact with Howard, 68, 70–1
  contact with Jellinek, 68, 69–70
  move from Yale to Rutgers, 74–5
  publications, 74
  research directions, 75–6
  value of Center of Alcohol Studies, 72–3
Baghdad University, 25
Barbiturate addicts, 220
Beaubrun, Michael
  breathalysers, 447

Index 451

priorities for action, 446
Beaubrun, Michael—interview, 377–84
  advertising of liquor, 382
  alcohol producers, 382–3
  Alcoholics Anonymous, 379–80, 381
  at Maudsley, 380
  biography, 377
  breathalyser, 382
  developing countries, 384
  National Council on Alcoholism, 383
  political work, 381
  socio-cultural factors in Trinidad, 378
  treatment facilities in Trinidad, 378–9
  Trinidad situation, 377–8
Beedle, Peter, 235
Behaviour therapy, 397
Bell, Gordon, 318
Benjamin, Benny, 233
Berkeley University, 167
Bewley, Thomas, 222, 235, 236
Black Americans, 120
Black, Dr. Dorothy, 279
Black market for drugs, 283, 284
Block Design Rotation Test, 268–9
Blue Cross, 38
Blum, Dick, 370
Boletin de la Sociedad de Biologia, Santiago, Chile, 388
Boots the Chemist, 229, 232, 239
Brain Committee, 221–2, 231, 232, 234–6
  Connell's evidence, 276
  notification, 238
Brain, Lord, 221
Brain Report, 237, 293
British Journal of Addiction, xvi, 64, 114, 218, 289
  Glatt as editor, 295
British Journal of Psychiatry, 289
British Medical Association
  influence of Warlingham Park Alcoholism Treatment Unit, 292
  report (1961), 213, 214
British Medical Journal, 289
Bruun, Kettil, xiv
  at Yale, 181

  drug policy, 447
  Wald's contacts with, 405–6
Bruun, Kettil—interview, 365–75
  alcohol in broader context, 372
  at Yale Centre, 368
  biography, 365
  Finnish Foundation for Alcohol Studies, 366
  impressions of Jellinek, 368
  interdisciplinary studies, 374
  international narcotics policy, 369–70, 371–2
  international travel, 368
  Northern Youth Study, 369
  research in Finland, 365–7
  research strategy, 373, 375
  small group drinking, 367
  social commitment, 375
  Swedish appointment, 274
  WHO work, 371
Bulletin on Narcotics (UN), 436, 441

Cabezas, J., 386
Cahalan, Don, xvi, 99–100
  NIMH funding, 182
Cahalan, Don—interview, 163–77
  alcohol policy issues, 171
  alcohol studies, 165–7
  biography, 163
  drinking patterns, 176–7
  longitudinal studies, 175
  move to Berkeley, 167–9
  national surveys, 174–5
  NIAAA role, 170, 173
  public opinion research, 164–5
  research programs, 172–3
  retirement, 169–70
  social psychology training, 163–4
Cairo University, 427
California Prevention Demonstration Project, 168
Camberwell Council on Alcoholism, 202
Cameron, Dale, 10, 27, 28
  Connell's relationship with, 286–7
Camps, Francis, 221, 280
Canada
  drug addicts, 234
  influence on research, 347
Canadian International Development Agency, 309, 311, 313

452 Addictions

Cannabis, 34–5
  and creativity, 431–2
  current situation, 439–40
  response of society, 441–2
  Soueif's studies, 429, 431–2, 434–5
  see also marijuana
Carlini, E. A., 429
Carnegie Corporation, 59
Caroli, Professor, 419, 421
Carousel, 115
Casier, Henrietti, 135
Castle Peak Mental Hospital (Hong Kong), 358
Causes and Consequences of Alcohol Problems: An Agenda for Research 98
Center of Alcohol Studies, 62
  dislike by Yale staff, 85
  Haggard's role, 71
  move to Rutgers, 75
Centres d'Hygiène Alimentaire, 416
Chapple, Peter, 222, 236
Ch'ien, James—interview, 355–63
  Alumni Association of SARDA, 362–3
  biography, 355
  Hong Kong drug problem, 355–8
  relapse rate, 361
  SARDA work, 358–60
  self help and aftercare, 361
  therapeutic communities, 359–60
Ch'ien, James, therapeutic work, 447
Child, Youth and Family Centre (Czechoslovakia), 400
Chile, 389–90
China, Civil War, 357
Church influence in Canada, 306
Cirrhosis, 349–50, 419, 420, 424
Cisin, Ira, 157, 165, 167, 171–2, 180, 183
Clark, Walter, 165
Clarke, Dr. David, 380
Co-operative Commission on the Study of Alcoholism, 95
Cocaine, 233–4, 246
  production, 33–4
  psychosis, 270
Columbia University, 8, 25
Comité National de Defense contre l'Alcoolisme, 416

Community Response Project, 50, 51, 53
Community response to alcohol-related problems, 13–15, 49
Compulsory treatment for addiction, 223
Connecticut Commission on Alcoholism, 89
Connecticut Prison Association, 68
Connell, Philip, 235
  Drug Dependence Unit, 292
  drug policies, 294
  teaching, 292
  views on American relationship, 296
  WHO involvement, 295
Connell, Philip—interview, 267–90
  Advisory Council on Misuse of Drugs, 277–9, 280
  amphetamine psychosis work, 269–71
  at Maudsley, 267–9, 271–2
  biography, 267
  Brain Committee, 276
  committee and policy work, 275–9
  Drug Dependence unit at Bethlem, 274–5, 289
  heroin for drug addicts, 282-4
  invitation to WHO, 287–8
  member of General Medical Council, 290
  relationship with Dale Cameron, 286–7
  Wayne committee, 276
  Wootton committee, 276
  work with D. L. Davies, 268, 272
Cook, Tim, 253
Court, Donald, 288
Creativity, 431–2, 434
Croix Bleu, 416
Croix d'Or, 412, 416
Czechoslovak Abstinent Union, 395
Czechoslovakia, 395
  care for alcoholics, 398–9

Dangerous Drugs Act (1920), 227
Dangerous Drugs Act (1965), 282
Dangerous Drugs Act (1968), register of addicts, 238
Davies, D. L., xiv, 254
  disagreement with Pittman, 118

influence in teaching 291–2
international contacts, 295
normal drinking, 218
Philip Connell working with, 268, 272
summer schools, 292
support for Warlingham, 294
Davies, D. L.—interview, 189–205
  alcoholism work, 197–8
  appointment at Maudsley, 195–6
  biography, 189
  medical training, 194–5
  'Return to Normal Drinking' paper, 189, 191–93
  summer schools, 201–2
Davis, Allison, 106
de Lindt, Jan, 53, 305
  Mapother's influence, 199
Debré, Professor R., 423
Defense Research Medical Laboratories (Canada), 317, 318
Delerium tremens, 424
Demerath, Nicholas, 106, 111
Dent, John Yerbury, 216
Department of Applied Physiology (Yale), 87
Detoxification facilities in U.S.A., xvi
Developing countries, 10–11, 18
  health programmes, 17
  see also Third World research
Devils, Drugs and Doctors, 71
DHSS, 242–3
Diconal, 279
Dictionnaire de L'Alcoologie, 418
Dimas, George, 121
Disabilities, alcohol related, 12, 13
Disciplinary distribution of American research, 180–1
Disease concept of alcoholism, 43–4, 45, 53, 152, 161
  Canada, 301–2
  sociologists' views, 76–7
Disease Concept of Alcoholism, The, 6, 108
Disulfiram, 150–1, 380
  use in France, 416
Doctor addicts, 228
Doctor, His Patient and the Illness, The, 250
Drinamyl, 274

Drinking in College, 88, 91, 92, 108, 184
Drinking patterns, America, 176–7
Drinking Patterns in Finnish Lapland, 366
Drinking Patterns in the Ghetto, 120
Drug
  and alcohol research, 307
  clinics, 222
  control, 47, 48
  policies, 293
  problems and Britain's organisational basis, 279–80
  traffickers, 247–8
Drug addiction
  American-British connection, 286
  young people, 276
Drug Dependence Clinical Research and Treatment unit (Bethlem Hospital), 274–5, 289
Drug Dependence Unit, 10, 292
Drug Problems in the Socio-cultural Context, 30
Drug Scene in Great Britain: Journey Into Loneliness, 137
Drug Use and Misuse: cultural perspectives, 30
Drugs, Society and Personal Choice, 328
Durant, Will, 427
Dyke, Len, 227

Eddy, Nathan, 287
Edwards, Griffith, 10
  British study, 116
  follow-up of Davies's patients, 119
  inpatient and outpatient treatment, 151
Egypt
  cannabis studies, 429–35
  prison studies, 430–1
  Soueif's role, 438–9
Emetine therapy, 378, 396
Escape from Custody, 84, 99
Expert Committee on Problems Related to Alcohol Consumption (1979), 17, 49
Expert Committee on Services for the Prevention and Treatment of Dependence on Alcohol, 9

454 Addictions

Ey, Professor Henri, 413, 414
Eysenck, Professor H. J., 434, 437

Ferguson, Dr. J. K. W., 318
Filmore, Kaye, 175
Finnish Foundation for Alcohol Studies, 365, 366
  interdisciplinary studies, 374
Foote, Major John, 300–1
Fouquet, Pierre—interview, 411–18
  alcoholism work, 412–13
  biography, 411
  Haut Comité d'Étude et d'Information sur l'Alcoolisme 413–14
  meeting with Jellinek, 414–15
  Mendès-France glass of milk story, 413, 447
  psychiatry interests, 411–13
  therapy techniques, 418
  WHO work, 415
France
  alcohol consumption, 416–17
  attitudes to drinking problems, 16
  cirrhosis, 419–21
  concept of alcoholism, 423–4
  development of alcoholism treatment, 412–13
  road safety campaigns, 417
  treatment facilities, 416–17
Frankau, Lady Isabella, 233–4, 237, 238
Freud, Anna, 397
Friends Temperance Union, 42
Frost, Leslie, 300, 302, 303

Gachot, Dr. Henri, 39
Galton Laboratory (London), 403
Gardner, John, 95
Gastroenterology, 416–17, 419
General practice and drink problems, 262
General practitioners, Balint's influence, 250
Genetic origins of alcohol appetite, 388
Gentlemen's Club, 370
George Washington University, 165, 167
Gibbens, Trevor, 196
Gibbins, Bob, 320
Gildea, Dr. Edwin, 111–12

Gillespie, Duff, 138
Glatt, Max, xiv, 43, 137–8, 198
  international contacts, 295
  teaching, 292
  WHO involvement, 295
Glatt, Max—interview, 207–25
  Alcoholics Anonymous work, 212
  biography, 207
  compulsory treatment, 223
  Davies' normal drinking paper, 218, 220
  drug problems, 220–2
  education, 209
  function of units, 215
  inpatient treatment, 215
  international meetings, 216–17
  normal drinking, 218-20
  relationship with Jellinek, 217
  Warlingham Park Alcoholism Unit, 207–9
  WHO expert committees, 218
Goldberg, Dr. Leonard, 309
Goldstein, Avram, 334
Gomberg, Edith, 87, 180
Goodwin, Donald—interview, 143–54
  biography, 143
  Danish adoption studies, 147
  medical training, 143–4
  Oriental flushing phenomenon, 148–9
  writers and alcoholism, 149–50
Gouldner, Professor Alvin, 120
Government attitudes to drinking problems, 16, 17
Grant, Marcus, 292
Grant-in-aid funding, 348
Gray, Mr., 211
Greenland, S., 440
Group therapy, 199–200, 210
Guttmann, Eric 196, 197
Guze, Sam, 145, 147, 154, 180
  publications, 182

Habitual Drunkenness Offenders Working Party (Great Britain), 126
Hagan, Elliott (Representative), 121
Haggard, Howard, 60, 180
  Bacon's contact with, 68, 70–1
  multidisciplinary approach, 97

relationship with Jellinek, 71–2
Halbach, Professor, 27
Hallucinosis, alcoholic, 204
Handbook of Organizations for Research on Alcohol and Alcoholism Problems, 135
Harding, Dr., 11
Hargreaves, Dr., 4
Haut Comité d'Étude et d'Information sur l'Alcoolisme, 413–14, 422
Health
　programmes, 17
　warnings, 130
Health Association of Rochester and Monroe County, 109
Health Research Institute (Thailand), 310
Hegsted, Mark, 389
Hercod, Dr. Robert E., 38, 39
Heroin
　abuse, 25
　addicts, 232, 233
　administration to drug addicts, 282, 283–4, 286
　in Canada, 306
　Chinese, 238
　dosage for addicts, 284
　in Hong Kong, 356–7
　prescription of intravenous, 285
　problems, 229, 230–1
Hewlett, Augustus (Gus), 121
　proposed bill for federal commission on alcoholism, 122
Hills, Donald, 138
Himmelstein, J. L., 441
Historical aspects, xiv
HIV positive addicts, 285
Hobo, The, 106
Home Office
　consultants meetings, 242–3
　Drugs Branch, 241–2
　record of addicts 238–9
Homelessness, 127–8
Hong Kong
　development of treatment for addiction, 357–8
　drug problem, 355–8
Hopital St Antoine, 419
Hughes-Javits Alcoholism Act (USA: 1970), 128, 137

Hungary, 408
Hutt, Peter Barton, 121, 124

Institut National de la Santé et de la Recherche Medicale (INSERM), 423
Institute of Neurology (London), 403
Institute of Neurology (Moscow), 403
Institute for Study of Drug Dependence, 277
Internation Association for the Scientific Study of Mental Deficiency, 409
International Agency for Research on Cancer, 423
International Bibliography, 61
International Bureau Against Alcoholism, 37–8, 113
　international congresses, 139
International Congress on Alcoholism (Washington D.C.), 136–7
International Council on Alcohol and Addiction (I.C.A.A.), 7, 37–8, 312–13
　Polish involvement, 409
　role, 46–7
International Union Against Alcoholism, 39
Is Alcoholism Hereditary?, 154
Israel, drinking problems, 258–9
Israel, Yedy, 321, 322

Jackson, Joan, 180
Janda, Dr., 396
Javits, Jacob (Senator), 121
Jeffery, Charles (Jeff), 227, 228
Jellinek, E. M., 180
　Archibald meeting, 300, 303, 304
　at WHO 5–6
　Bacon's contact with 68, 69–70
　in Chile, 389–90
　death, 390
　Glatt's relationship, 217–18
　influence, 445
　influence on alcoholism thinking, 43
　influence on David Archibald, 308–9
　influence on Joy Moser, 51–2

Addictions

influence on Pittman, 108
Mardones' relationship with, 389–90
references to, xiv-xv
relationship with Haggard, 71–2
relationship with I.C.A.A., 40
relationship with Straus, 86–7
Schmidt's views on, 343
Summer School of Alcohol Studies, 61
visit to Maudsley, 199
work with Jolliffe, 59, 60
Jellinek Memorial Fund, 304
John Bell and Croyden, 229, 233
Johnson, Lyndon (President of USA), 95, 123
Jolliffe, Dr. Norman, 57–8
Journal of Studies on Alcohol, 119

Kaila, Martti, 367
Kalant, Harold, xvi
  at Addiction Research Foundation, 346
  hospital care costs, 349–50
Kalant, Harold—interview, 315–35
  Addiction Research Foundation work, 317, 319–20
  advocacy and research, 328–9
  animal models of alcoholism, 325–6
  biography, 315
  in Chile, 316
  education, 315–16
  ethics, 332–3
  human experimentation, 332–3
  scientist's role, 329–31
  Toronto University, 316, 317
Kalant, Oriana, 316, 328
Keep Busy, 82
Keller, Mark, 11, 87, 108, 183
  alcohol policy advocacy, 183
  editor of 28th International Congress on Alcoholism proceedings, 137
Keller, Mark—interview, 57–66
  biography, 57
  Center of Alcohol Studies, 62–3
  scientific study of alcoholism, 57–60
  social changes, 65–6
  social climate to alcohol research, 63–4
Kendell, Professor, 17, 201
Kendis, Dr Joseph, 112
Kedis, Joe, 114
Kennedy, John (President of USA), 123
Keogh, Joan, 243
Kessel, Professor, 201
Kmoškovà, Dr., 401
Knupfer, Genevieve, 165, 180
  NIMH funding, 182
  research, 184
Knupfer, Genevieve—interview, 155–61
  biography, 155
  drinking patterns studies, 157–9
  medical training, 156–7
  sociology training, 155–6
Kuusi, Pekka, 365, 366, 367

Laboratory of Applied Physiology (Yale), 68, 69
Lambo, Dr., 10, 11
Lancet, 289
Larue, C., 391
Lawrow, J., 387, 391
Lazarsfeld, Paul, 156
Le Coq, Dr., 412
Le Magnen, J., 391
Le Roman de L'Alcool, 418
Lebedev, Dr., 8
Ledermann, Sulley, 45, 50, 415, 421
  distribution of alcohol consumption, 129
  reputation in France, 424
  Schmidt's views on, 343
Ledermann theory, 351
Leech, Ken, 242
Lewis, Aubrey, 195, 196, 198, 199, 203
  Philip Connell working with, 268
Li, T. K., 325
Life story of patients, 211
Lin, Dr., 8
Ling, Dr., 28
Lipscomb, Wendell, 165
Liquor Control Act (Canada), 341
Liquor Control Board (Canada), 301, 302
Liquor Question, 366

Index 457

London Committee for Addiction, 222
Longitudinal studies, 119, 175

McBride, Robert (Mac), 227, 228
McCarthy, Raymond, 87, 108, 109, 180
McClearn, G. E., 388
McGothlin, W., 441
McIntosh, Don, 248
Magistrates' Association
  influence of Warlingham Park Alcoholism Treatment Unit, 292
  report (1961), 213
Malcolm Bliss Alcoholism Treatment and Research Center, 116
Malcolm Bliss Mental Health Center, 112
Maltbie, Chief Justice, 68
Mann, Marty, 64, 122, 139, 180
  NCA work, 131–2
  proposed bill for federal commission on alcoholism, 122
Mapother, 199
Mardones, Jorge, xv, 325
  priorities for action, 446
Mardones, Jorge—interview, 385–92
  animal studies, 388–9
  biography, 385
  relationship with Jellinek, 389–90
  Third World research, 392
  training, 385
  vitamin deficiency work, 386, 387
  WHO work, 390
Marfaing-Jallat, P., 391
Marijuana, 383–4
  legalization, 383–4
  see also cannabis,
Martin, Dr. Dennis, 208, 211
Matějček, Dr., 401
Maudsley Alcoholism Pilot Project, 256
Maudsley Hospital
  Alcoholism Treatment Service, 255
  Davies appointment, 195
  drug psychosis studies, 268–9
  intellectual atmosphere, 271–2
  Jellinek's visit, 199
  staff, 195, 196, 197
  training, 203–4
Mead, Margaret, 4
Medial Care for Seamen, 82
Mendès-France, P., 422
  glass of milk story, 413, 447
Menninger, Karl, 144
Mental Health Act (UK), 237
Mental Health Association (Canada), 300
Methadone, 236, 283
  use in Hong Kong, 359
Methedrine, 237
Mexico
  attitudes to drinking problems, 16
  WHO project, 15
Microsomal ethanol oxidizing system (MEOS), 425
Ministry of Health (UK), attitude to alcoholism, 214
Monro, Dr. A. B., 235
Moore, Frank, 83–5
Morgan, Dr. Gethin, 253
Moser, Joy, xv
  accomplishments, 49–50
  influences, 52–3
  Jellinek's influence, 51–2
  organizational context of work, 52
  personality, 51–2
  WHO publications, 415
Moser, Joy—interview, 3–22
  African report, 10–11
  biography, 3
  international work, 20–1
  seminar organization, 9–10
  Technical Discussions, 18–19
  WHO Mental Health Unit, 4–5, 11
  WHO projects, 12–15
  work with Baan, 7
  work with Jellinek, 5–6
Moss, Frank (Senator), 121
Mothers Against Drunk Driving, 176
Mulford, Hal, 171
Murray, Robin, 256
Myers, Edgar, 189, 190

Narcotic addicts, 220, 221
National Advisory Committee on Alcoholism (USA), 95
National Centre for Social and Criminological Research (Egypt), 430, 432

458   Addictions

National Committee for Mental Hygiene (Canada), 300
National Council on Alcoholism (Trinidad), 383
National Council on Alcoholism (USA), 63, 64, 122, 131
  Cahalan's views, 171–2
National Councils on Alcoholism, 40
National Health Service, alcoholism treatment, 294
National Institute on Alcohol Abuse and Alcoholism (NIAAA), 11–12, 95–6, 167, 423
  Cahalan's views, 170, 173
  formation, 182
  resources, 307
National Institute of Mental Health (USA), 94, 95
  federal funding for research, 182
National strategies, 19
New England Journal of Medicine, 322
New Zealand, attitudes to drinking problems, 16
NIDA resources, 307
Nordic Council for Alcohol Research, 369
Normal drinking, 117–18, 119, 218–20
North American Association of Alcoholism Programs (NAAAP), 40, 120–2
Northern Youth Study, 369
Notification of addicts, 238–9
  confidentiality, 240

Oesophageal cancer, 423
Operation Julie, 244
Opium,
  distribution, 355–6
  production in Thailand, 310–11
  smoking, 355, 356
Opium War (1839–41), 355
Oriental flushing phenomenon, 148–9
Orrego, Hector, 321, 322
Overprescribing, 221
Owens, John, 236

Papua New Guinea, 16
Park, Peter, 368

Penrose, Lionel, 403
Péquinot, Georges—interview, 419–25
  alcoholism concept, 423–4
  biography, 419
  cirrhosis work, 419–21
  Ille et Vilaine study, 421–2
  work at INSERM, 423
Péquinot, Georges, de-psychiatrization of treatment, 447
personal influences, xiv–xv
Petro, John, 237, 238
Phillipson, Brigadier, 214
Phylloxera, 416
Physical dependence, 324–5
Piaget, Jean, 4
Pinel House
  Alcoholic Unit, 211
  Neurosis Unit, 208, 211
Pittman, David J., xvi, 218
  alcohol control attitude, 183
  alcohol research and drugs, 307
  decriminalization of drunkenness, 181
  publications, 182
Pittman, David J.—interview, 105–40
  biography, 105
  British drug scene, 137–8
  career influences, 106–8
  collaboration with Tongue, 135–6
  disagreement with Davies, 118
  European visit, 113–14
  longitudinal studies, 118–19
  move to Washington University, 111
  NAAAP work, 120–2
  Pruitt-Igoe Project, 120
  relationship with Archer Tongue, 139–40
  Rochester study, 109
  St Louis Centre 112–13, 114–16, 117, 124–6
Plaut, Tom, 95
Poland
  government action on alcoholism, 404–5
  supply of alcohol 407–8
Polar Bear group, 204
Polish Expert Advisory Group on Alcohol, 403

Polish National Anti-alcoholic Committee, 406
Pollak, Benno
  colleagues' attitude, 295
  teaching, 292
Pollak, Benno—interview, 249-65
  academic teaching, 257
  American travel, 258
  biography, 249
  general practice and drink problems, 262
  in Germany, 260
  Israel visit, 258–9
  meeting Max Glatt, 261
  primary health care, 263–4
  Rathcoole House, 253–4
  relationship with D. L. Davies, 254
  screening methods for patients, 251–2
  summer schools, 254–5
  work at Maudsley Hospital, 255–6
Popham, Robert, 320, 338, 390
Poshyachinda, Dr. Vichai, 310–11
Prevention
  of alcohol related problems, 13–15
  programs, 100
Pricing, 45–6
Primary health care, 263–4
Primary Prevention of Alcohol Abuse and Alcoholism, 129
Prison and alcoholism, 68, 110, 122, 126, 127–8
Problem Drinkers, 166, 175
Problem Drinking among American Men, 166, 175
Prohibition, 57, 123
  effects of, 330–1
  repeal, 176
Pruitt-Igoe Project, 120
Psychiatric Annals, 99
Psychiatric Diagnosis, 154
Psychosis, drug-induced, 168, 269
Public drunkenness offenders, 122, 123, 124, 126
  California, 127
  hospital beds, 127
  Missouri, 127
Public health approach, 183
Purple Book, 405
Purple hearts, 274

Quakers, 41–2
Quarterly Journal of Studies on Alcohol, 60, 82, 217, 388
  Keller as editor, 87
Quenum, Dr., 10

Rainwater, Lee, 120
Rangoon (Burma), 30–1
Raskob, John, 176
Rathcoole House (Clapham), 253–4, 292
Rees, T. P., 208, 211
Register of addicts, 238
Reid, Donald, 421
Research
  addiction, 334
  and advocacy, 328–9
  Canadian-Scandinavian domination, 347
  clinicians in, 334
  communication of findings, 328
  disciplinary distribution of American, 180–1
  funding, 347–8
  growth, 181
  organization, 342–3
  Third World countries, 392
Research Council on Problems of Alcohol, 59
Research Institute of Penology, 399
Revolving Door, 108, 110
  implementation of recommendations, 125
revolving door alcoholics, 110
Richter, Curt P., 386
Road
  safety campaigns, 417
  traffic and alcohol, 309
Robine, Eli, 145
Robins, Lee, 182
Rochester University, 109
Rockefeller Foundation, 58
Rodgers, D.A., 388
Rolleston Tribunals, 231–2, 245, 293
Room, Robin, 100, 165, 167, 168, 169
Roosevelt, Franklin D., 176
Root, Laura Esther Marie, 114
Roth, Martin, 288
Rotter, Dr. Hans, 217
Rowntree Social Services Trust, 202

Rubington, Earl, 368
Russell Sage Foundation, 92

St Bernard's Hospital, 221, 222
St Louis Detoxification Center, 117, 124–5
  evaluation of effectiveness, 125–6
St Louis Globe-Democrat, 112
St Louis Psychiatry Department, 182
St Thomas's Hospital, 257
Sanderson R. A., 208
Sanker, Arthur, 208
Sargent, Will, 272–3
Sartorius, Dr. Norman, 11
Scandinavian influence on research, 347
Schizophrenia and drug psychosis, 269
Schmidt, Wolf, 45, 50, 53, 305, 320
  at Addiction Research Foundation, 346
Schmidt, Wolf—interview, 337–43
  Addiction Research Foundation work, 337–9, 342
  biography, 337
  Ministry of Health contacts, 340–1
  political involvement 339–41
  research organization, 342–3
  training, 337
Schulsinger, Dr. Fini, 147
Schwartz, D., 421
Scientific movements, xv–xvi
Scientists, role in policy analysis, 350–1
Scotland, WHO project, 15
Scott, Dennis, 208
Scott, Dr Donald, 204
Seeley, John (Jack), 180, 300, 320, 338
  Schmidt's views on, 343
Segovia, Natividad, 389
Self help and aftercare, 361
Service de Prophylaxie Mentale, 411
Shek Kwu Chau Rehabilitation Centre (Hong Kong), 358, 359–60, 447
Shepard, Marguerite, 112, 113
Single distribution theory of alcohol, 53, 351
Sisters of St Mary's, 125
Skála, Jaroslav—interview, 395–402

  biography, 395
  emetine therapy, 396
  international travel, 400–1
  prevention work, 402
  research studies, 401
  therapeutic system, 397–8
  training work, 402
Skid row, 107, 109
U.K. hostel, 253
Slater, Eliot, 269
Smart, Reg, 320, 441
Smith, Al, 176
Smithers, Brinkley, 312–13
Snyder, Charles (Chuck), 134, 368
Social medicine, 202–3
Social Research Institute for Alcohol Studies (Helsinki), 365, 372
Socially competent drinkers, 189
Société Française d'Alcoologie, 414–16
Society for the Aid and Rehabilitation of Drug Addicts (Hong Kong) 358–60
  aftercare, 358–9
Society, Culture and Drinking Patterns, 134–5
Society of Friends, 41
Society for the Study of Addiction, 216, 280–1
Soueif, Mustapha—interview, 427–43
  biography, 427
  cannabis work, 429, 431–2, 434–5
  creativity research, 434
  Egyptian responsibilities, 438–9
  international travel, 436–7
  literary aspirations, 427, 428
  philosophy studies, 427–8
  prison study, 430–1
  research publication, 433–4
  response sets research, 433–4
  transcultural studies, 440–1
  WHO work, 436
Spear, Bing
  drug policies, 293–4
  influence as civil servant, 293
Spear, Bing—interview, 227–48
  Advisory Council on the Misuse of Drugs, 244–5
  biography, 227
  Brain Committee, 231, 232, 234–6

Civil Service, 229
  contact with addicts, 230
  drug traffickers, 247–8
  general practitioners, 236
  heroin addicts, 232, 233
  Home Office Drugs Branch, 227–9, 241–2
  Lady Frankau's work, 237–8
  medical profession and drug addiction, 246
  Ministerial involvement, 243, 244
  notification, 238–40
Spratley, Terry, 256
Stella, Dowager Marchioness of Reading, 253
Stengel, Erwin, 269
Sterne, Muriel, 10
Stonham, Lord, 253
Story of Philosophy, The, 427
Straus, Robert, xv
  NIAAA formation, 181–2
  views on research, 183
Straus, Robert—interview, 81–101
  biography, 81
  college students drinking, 88
  Frank Moore study, 83–5, 93, 99
  Institute of Medicine, 98
  Italian-American study, 89–90
  move to Lexington, 94
  move to Syracuse, 91–2
  NIAAA formation, 95–6
  relationship with Bacon, 86, 88
  relationship with Haggard, 86
  relationship with Jellinek, 86–7
  relationship with Willard, 91
  work with Bacon, 81
  work with homeless men, 82–4
  Yale Plan Clinics, 89
Strickland, Donald, 130
Sun Hop Wei, 356
Suwanwela, Dr. Charas, 310–11
Swiss Institute for the Prevention of Alcoholism, 38

Tai Lam Centre, 358
TB Abscesses, 412
Technical Discussion on Alcohol Consumption and Alcohol Problems (1982), 49
Temperance movement, 38
  in Canada, 302, 306
  influence on research, 404
Temposil, 318
Therapeutic communities, 359–60
Third World
  research, 392
  see also developing countries
Thomas, George, 211
Thornton, Frank, 227, 228
Tolerance
  of alcohol, 322–3
  to addictive drugs, 324
Tongue, Archer, 7, 113, 415
  accomplishments, 50
  collaboration with Pittman, 135–6
  influences, 52–3
  international cooperation, 139
  organizational context of work, 52
  work with David Archibald, 312
Tongue, Archer—interview, 37–48
  biography, 37
  Eva (wife), 42
  I.C.A.A. appointment, 39–41, 42
  languages, 42
  Quaker influence, 41
  role of I.C.A.A., 46–7
Tongue, Eva, 42, 139–40, 415
Toronto University, 300, 316, 317
Treatment of patients, 115–16
Tredgold, Roger, 220
Trinidad
  breathalyser, 382
  wealth and alcohol consumption, 377-8
TROTTING club, 396–7, 447
Tuyns, Albert, 423

U.S.A.
  government moves on alcoholism, 123–4
  influence on alcoholism thinking, 43–4
  State programmes, 40
U.S.S.R., WHO travelling seminars on psychiatric services, 8
Ulett, Dr. George, 112, 113
Understanding America's Drinking Problems, 169–70
United Nations, 47, 48
United Nations Fund for Drug Abuse Control, 30, 313

462 Addictions

Varela, Anibal, 390
Veterans Administration Hospital (Syracuse) 92
Vie Libre, 412, 416
Vitamin deficiency, 386, 387
Vogel-Sprott, Muriel, 320
Volstead Act (USA), 383

Wald, Ignacy—interview, 403–9
  alcohol policy, 405, 406
  biography, 403
  neurology and other research, 409
  opiate study, 407
  Polish Expert Advisory Group on Alcohol, 405
  research programme, 406–7
  supply restriction, 407–8
  training, 403–4
  WHO work, 409
Wallack, Larry, 168
Walter, Grey, 4
Wan Chai (Hong Kong), 359
Warlingham Park Alcoholism Treatment Unit, 198, 199, 207–9, 212
  influence on clinical work, 292
Washburne, Chandler, 368
Washington University, 111, 145–6
Wayne committee, 276
Weber, Jim, 125
Weeks, Ken, 208
Westerfield, W. W., 387, 391
Whiteley, Stuart, 208
Willard, William R., 91
Williams, Lincoln, 198–9
Williams, Phyllis, 89
Williams, R. J., 388
Willis, Jim, 236
Winokur, George, 147
Wootton, Barbara, 276
Wootton committee, 276
World Congress of Friends (Oxford: 1952), 42
World Health Assembly (1982), Technical Discussions, 18–19

World Health Organization (WHO)
  Baan's employment, 7
  community projects, 15
  Community Response Work, 409
  Division of Mental Health, 49
  Drug Addiction Unit, 26
  drug and alcohol programmes, 20
  Drug Dependence Programme, 28
  fellowships, 309
  Glatt on expert committees, 218
  growth, 28–9
  Health for All by the Year 2000, 29
  influence on alcoholism thinking, 43
  Jellinek's employment, 5–6
  Jellinek's symposia, 40
  Joy Moser's work, 3–9
  long-term plans, 11–12
  Mardones work with, 390
  Mental Health Programme, 30
  Mental Health Unit, 4, 5, 7
  national responses to alcohol and drugs problems, 9
  NIAAA assistance, 12
  Pierre Fouquet's work, 415
  programmes, 9
  Rees on committees, 217
  seminars, 9–10
  Soueif's work, 436
  training programmes, 31
  women in, 21
Wormwood Scrubs Prison therapuetic community, 224
Writers and alcoholism, 149–50
Wroclaw University, 403

Yale Plan Clinics, 61, 89
Yale University, 181

Zambia
  attitudes to drinking problems, 16
  WHO project, 15